PAYBACK

PAYBACK

THE CONSPIRACY TO DESTROY MICHAEL MILKEN AND HIS FINANCIAL REVOLUTION

Daniel Fischel

HarperBusiness
A Division of HarperCollinsPublishers

A hardcover edition of this book was published in 1995 by HarperBusiness, a division of HarperCollins Publishers.

HarperCollins books may be purchased for educational, business, or sales promotional use. For information please write: Special Markets Department, HarperCollins Publishers, Inc., 10 East 53rd Street, New York, NY 10022.

First paperback edition published 1996.

Designed by Irving Perkins Associates

The Library of Congress has catalogued the hardcover edition as follows:

Fischel, Daniel R.
    Payback : the conspiracy to destroy Michael Milken and his financial
revolution / Daniel Fischel.
        p. cm.
    Includes index.
    ISBN 0-88730-757-4
    1. Milken, Michael. 2. Drexel Burnham Lambert Incorporated. 3. Junk
Bonds—United States. 4. Insider trading in securities—United States. I. Title.
HG4928.5.F57   1995
364.1'68—dc20   95-9154

ISBN 0-88730-804-X (pbk.)

96 97 98 99 00 ❖/RRD 10 9 8 7 6 5 4 3 2 1

For Phyllis, Joey, Matthew, and Sarah

We have innovated in a significant way, and while doing so, we have suffered "the penalty of leadership" that the Cadillac Motor Car Company talked about in its famous 1914 advertisement: "When a man's work becomes a standard for the whole world, it also becomes a target for the shafts of the envious few."

—FRED CARR (1985)

Contents

Preface

I have a unique background to write this book. As a teacher and author, I have spent my career studying the effects of tender offers, leveraged buyouts, high-yield bonds, insider trading, and many of the other practices that came under attack during the 1980s. My articles on these subjects have been cited repeatedly by courts of all levels including the United States Supreme Court.

I am also an insider to many of the events that are the subject matter of this book. In addition to my responsibilities as a professor at the University of Chicago, I have long been affiliated with an economic consulting firm, Lexecon Inc. Many of the central characters in the so-called Wall Street and savings and loan scandals during the 1980s—Michael Milken, Charles Keating, and David Paul—were clients of ours, and I worked on their cases firsthand. We were also involved in several of the other important cases of the 1980s, such as the prosecutions of James Sherwin and the Princeton/Newport defendants. All of these cases and many more are described in this book.

I also have considerable experience on the other side of the fence. Over the years, I have served as a consultant or advisor to the United States Department of Justice, the Federal Deposit Insurance Corporation, the Resolution Trust Corporation, the Office of Thrift Supervision, the United States Department of Labor, the Securities and Exchange Commission, and the Federal Trade Commission. I have been retained as an expert witness on behalf of the government on multiple occasions.

Finally, I even have personal experience with some of the abuses of the legal system that occurred so routinely during the 1980s. After our work for Charles Keating, we became enmeshed in several civil legal disputes, first as a defendant and then as plaintiffs. During part of our travails as a litigant, our lawyer was

Stephen Neal, the same lawyer who represented Charles Keating and David Paul in their criminal trials. I introduced Stephen Neal to Charles Keating.

The many existing books about the Wall Street and savings and loan scandals during the 1980s have been written by journalists. Relying heavily on interviews, anecdotes, and personalities, journalists writing about the period have all too often equated "speaking in hushed tones" or "refusal to make eye contact" with committing major crimes. My perspective in this book is different, and so are my sources.

Although I have spoken to many people, I have relied very little on interviews except as background. I have found that what people say is much less important in understanding what happened than objectively analyzing the actual accusations and evidence presented in particular cases, and the economic substance of the transactions involved. In my experience, for example, few understand what Michael Milken was charged with, what he pled guilty to, or what the evidence against him was. I try to provide that understanding for Milken and the other important cases during the 1980s.

Whenever possible, I have relied on the actual record in these cases as documented in trial and hearing transcripts, indictments and complaints, and supporting legal briefs and memoranda. I believe this actual record is a far more reliable source for reconstructing events than the self-serving statements and recollections of interested parties that have filled the existing books on the period. I have also relied heavily on the extensive economic literature on such subjects as corporate restructurings, the role of debt, insider trading, savings and loans, and the insurance industry. This economic literature has been completely ignored in the journalist-dominated accounts of the 1980s.

I owe thanks to many people. Andy Rosenfield and Dennis Carlton provided me with many insights and, just as important, with encouragement and support. Bill Landes and Judge Frank Easterbrook also gave me valuable suggestions. David Ross read much of the manuscript and gave me the benefit of his usual penetrating input. Parts of this book were presented to academic audiences at Harvard University and the University of Chicago, and the book benefited immeasurably from the feedback I received. My agent, Lynn Chu, was invaluable, sometimes acting more like a coauthor than an agent. I could not have written this book without research help I received from Lyle Roberts, Dan Hulme, Joe Morrow, Yashmyn Jackson, Jeff Cohen, and, especially, Greg Pelnar. Debbie Zimmermann's help in collecting materials was also critical to completing the manuscript, which Holly Scheurer cheerfully typed. I also want to mention David and Karen Sager, because it was during a conversation with them one night on the way to the opera that the decision to write this book was made.

Walter Blum, my teacher, friend, and distinguished colleague at the University of Chicago, deserves special mention. Walter died last year after living a long and full life. In my last conversation with him when we both knew the end was near, he made me promise I would send him draft chapters of the book for his comments. Even facing death, Walter had an intellectual curiosity and zest for life that is an inspiration to us all.

Finally, I want to give the biggest thanks of all to my family—Phyllis, Joey, Matt, and Sarah. I will never forget your patience, love, and support.

Introduction

Why have the 1980s been so uniformly condemned as the "decade of greed"? For that matter, what does this disparaging characterization even mean? The decade's many critics who pontificate against the evils of greed have seen no need to define the term. Dictionary definitions of *greed*—"inordinate desire for wealth" or "wanting more than one's proper share"—provide no help but merely restate the question. What is an "inordinate" desire for wealth, or the dividing line between one's "proper" and "improper share"? With no answers to these questions, how can we possibly know when an individual, let alone a whole country, is guilty of "greed"? And even if we could somehow identify "greedy" behavior, why should we care?

Why greed is always referred to as a vice, and never a virtue, is actually far from obvious. If the term is stripped of its pejorative connotations and defined instead as single-minded pursuit of one's economic self-interest, or even the pursuit of wealth, then greed has many defenders. In his classic description of the role of entrepreneurs and the "invisible hand," for example, Adam Smith described how self-interested economic behavior, no matter how seemingly shabby, is the cornerstone of society. "In spite of their natural selfishness and rapacity, though they mean only their own convenience, though the sole end which they propose from the labors of all the thousands they employ be the gratification of their own vain and insatiable desires . . . they are led by an 'invisible hand' . . . and without intending it, without knowing it, to advance the interest of society." Similarly, Alexis de Tocqueville, the nineteenth-century author who is still the most famous commentator on American society, wrote that entrepreneurship, including the pursuit of wealth, is fundamental to this nation's heritage and success. "[T]o clear, cultivate and transform

1

the huge uninhabited continent which is their domain," de Tocqueville wrote, "the Americans need the support of an energetic passion; that passion can only be the love of wealth. So no stigma attaches to the love of money in America, and provided it does not exceed the bounds imposed by public order, it is held in honor."

Smith's insight about the role of acquisitive economic behavior and the "invisible hand" proved prophetic in the 1980s when the Soviet Union and its Communist empire collapsed. Communist and socialist ideology have always equated capitalism and the pursuit of wealth with "greed" and moral depravity. In his classic book *The Road to Serfdom*, Nobel laureate Friedrich Hayek described this attack on entrepreneurship as "the deliberate disparagement of all activities involving economic risk" and the casting of moral opprobrium "on the gains which make risks worth taking but which only few can win." Thus workers in Communist countries are taught to "prefer the safe, salaried position to the risk of enterprise after they have heard from their earliest youth the former described as the superior, more unselfish and disinterested occupation." Hayek comments: "The younger generation of today has grown up in a world in which in school and press the spirit of commercial enterprise has been represented as disreputable and the making of profit as immoral, where to employ a hundred people is represented as exploitation but to command the same number as honorable."

Communist ideology also relies heavily on envy, the hatred of those who are successful and better their position. Communism teaches that envy is a virtue—just another name for "justice" and "equality." As Michael Novak commented in *Forbes*, there is even a joke in Communist countries about envy: "The Frenchman, given a last wish before being sentenced to death, wishes for a weekend in Paris with his mistress; the Englishman chooses to walk quietly with his setter in the countryside; the Russian wishes that his neighbor's barn will burn down."

These attitudes have persisted long after the official collapse of the Soviet Union. Russians have resisted the creation of a market economy, even after it was obvious their own system had failed. Harry Markowitz, another Nobel laureate, recounts a conversation with a Russian who explains why market-based reforms in the former Soviet Union are so difficult to implement:

"The basic problem is the Russian people's attitude toward profit," he explained. "If there are goods one place that are needed someplace else, and if someone makes a profit moving these goods from the one place to the other, he is considered greedy and evil. They do not ask 'what is it that will make these goods move from where they are to where they are needed?' "

Markowitz then describes how Mikhail Gorbachev, the Soviet leader who first attempted market-based reforms, soon abandoned them and instituted instead a crackdown on "greedy black marketeers":

In fact the Gorbachev reforms did not succeed. The Soviet economy crumbled despite its great and varied resources. The distribution system, in particular, performed abysmally. When economic collapse had proceeded far enough, Gorbachev took drastic action: He froze bank accounts, causing much distress among those who had managed to save anything.

The purpose of this harsh move was to frustrate those Gorbachev believed, or said he believed, were the true culprits: the black marketeers! Thus in Gorbachev's mind, or at least in his words to the Soviet people, the source of the Soviet ill was the greedy, evil people who seek to benefit from the misfortunes of others by moving goods from where they are to where they are needed, not out of altruism but out of avarice.

How ironic then, in the decade of capitalism's greatest triumph, that so many have mindlessly adopted the now discredited anti-capitalist rhetoric of failed economic systems in describing what happened in America as "the decade of greed."

In fact, Americans were not more selfish during the 1980s than before. Charitable contributions, an obvious measure of generosity, skyrocketed, rising in constant dollars from $77.5 billion in 1980 to $121 billion in 1989, a far greater percentage increase than in previous decades. As Richard McKenzie writes:

While critics imply that Americans were less compassionate during the past decade, none appear to have actually looked at the most relevant quantitative evidence—recent patterns of philanthropy in the United States. In fact, these patterns show that the 1980's cannot fairly be described as a "decade of greed." On the contrary, giving by individuals and corporations jumped dramatically, regardless of how gifts are measured. Indeed, giving in the 1980's was above the level that would have been predicted from the upward trend established in the previous twenty-five years.

Thomas Sowell makes the same point:

Despite those who equate free-market economics with "greed," the heyday of laissez-faire economics in the 19th century also saw an unprecedented outpouring of private philanthropy. Moreover, the "materialistic" Americans are unique in the many academic, medical and other institutions founded and sustained with private, voluntary contributions. These contributions accelerated to another all-time high during the 1980's, the "decade of greed," according to the political left.

But the facts are irrelevant. Antigreed rhetoric is not about truth or reality; its real purpose is to delegitimize and discredit the efforts and success of others. That's why Communist and socialist ideology have always denounced "speculators" and "profiteering." Individuals who exploit inefficiencies of a centrally planned economy by identifying market opportunities are threats to the state and need to be discredited. Antigreed rhetoric, capitalizing as it does on the envy of the masses toward those who are entrepreneurial and successful, fits the bill perfectly.

Greed bashing served the same delegitimization function for social critics in describing what happened in the United States during the 1980s. Consider, for example, the explanations given by left-wing intellectuals for the landslide presidential victories of Ronald Reagan. Arthur Schlesinger, a leader of this group and a confidant to Democratic presidents, describes the 1980s as the "me decade," when concern about "private interest and the pursuit of self" culminated in "the age of Reagan" and the "culture of narcissism." John Kenneth Galbraith, another guru of the left, agrees that Reagan's victories demonstrated "retreat and preoccupation with self-concern and private enrichment." Since Americans voted for the wrong candidate for president, in other words, it must have been because they are "greedy."

The attack on financiers and Wall Street "excesses" during the 1980s is a more virulent example of greed-bashing rhetoric to discredit and delegitimize the success of others. Financiers have long been described as "parasites" and "bloodsuckers" in popular culture. William Shakespeare's Shylock, the Jewish moneylender in *The Merchant of Venice* who with knife in hand relishes the opportunity to extract his pound of flesh from the body of the unfortunate borrower, is probably the best-known example, but there are many others. In Fyodor Dostoyevsky's *The Brothers Karamazov*, the character Grushenka was said to be a woman who "had a good head for business, was acquisitive, saving and careful, and by fair means or foul had succeeded, it was said, in amassing a little fortune." She did it by speculating in what are today known as junk bonds and was viewed then as being "no better than a Jew."

> It was known too that the young person had, especially of late, been given to what is called "speculation," and that she had shown marked abilities in the direction, so that many people began to say that she was no better than a Jew. It was not that she lent money on interest, but it was known, for instance, that she had for some time past, in partnership with old Karamazov, actually invested in the purchase of bad debts for a trifle, a tenth of their nominal value, and afterwards had made out of them ten times their value.

Not all descriptions of the financier are coupled with these anti-Semitic stereotypes. In the 1980s the symbol of the financier was Sherman McCoy, the bond trader and "master of the universe" from Tom Wolfe's *The Bonfire of the Vanities*. Wolfe perfectly captures the pervasive ignorance of what financiers actually do in the exchange between McCoy and his daughter, Campbell, in the presence of his mother, father, and wife, Judy, where McCoy unsuccessfully tries to explain the social importance of raising capital:

> "A bond is a way of loaning people money. Let's say you want to build a road, and it's not a little road but a big highway, like the highway we took up to Maine last summer. Or you want to build a big hospital. Well, that requires a lot of money, more money than you could ever get by just going to a bank. So what you do is, you issue what are called bonds."
>
> "You build roads and hospitals, Daddy? That's what you do?"
>
> Now both his father and his mother started laughing. He gave them openly reproachful looks, which only made them merrier. Judy was smiling with what appeared to be a sympathetic twinkle.
>
> "No, I don't actually build them, sweetheart. I handle the bonds, and the bonds are what make it possible—"
>
> "You help build them?"
>
> "Well, in a way."
>
> "Which ones?"
>
> "Which ones?"

"You said roads and hospitals."

"Well, not any one specifically."

"The road to Maine?"

Now both his father and mother were giggling the infuriating giggle of people who are trying their best not to laugh right in your face.

"No, not the—"

"I think you're in over your head, Sherman!" said his mother.

Eventually, Judy, Sherman's wife, describes the role of financiers as socially useless scavengers in terms that little Campbell can understand:

"Daddy doesn't build roads or hospitals, and he doesn't help build them, but he does handle the bonds for the people who raise the money."

"Bonds?"

"Yes. Just imagine that a bond is a slice of cake, and you didn't bake the cake, but every time you hand somebody a slice of the cake a tiny little bit comes off, like a little crumb, and you can keep that."

Judy was smiling, and so was Campbell, who seemed to realize that this was a joke, a kind of fairy tale based on what her daddy did.

"Little crumbs?" she said encouragingly.

"Yes," said Judy. "Or you have to imagine little crumbs, but a lot of little crumbs. If you pass around enough slices of cake, then pretty soon you have enough crumbs to make a gigantic cake."

Once financiers are perceived to be socially useless scavengers, it's just a short but critical additional step to label them criminals. With this step, financiers are totally delegitimized and there are no limits on what the state can do to them. Since by definition their success is due to criminal conduct, they are not entitled to keep what they have or continue their endeavors. They are not even entitled to their liberty. Criminalization is also popular with the public because it cloaks envy with self-respect. It is easier to believe that financiers' success is attributable to their corruption and venality rather than to their superior ability and willingness to take risks. That "speculation" was a crime in Communist Russia was clearly no accident. Even today, a draft criminal code in Russia still classifies "speculation" as a punishable offense, although no longer a crime that carries the death penalty.

With this background, the government's crackdown on financial markets during the 1980s can be better understood. The 1980s were years of tremendous innovation in financial markets and wealth creation. The much maligned wave of hostile takeovers, leveraged buyout transactions, recapitalizations, divestitures, et cetera dramatically increased the profitability and efficiency of corporate America. Many of these transactions were made possible by another innovation, high-yield bonds, which also provided a valuable financing alternative to new companies in growing industries. The investment banking firm of Drexel Burnham Lambert and its star employee, Michael Milken, were at the center of the financial innovations and corporate restructurings that dominated the decade.

But these innovations and corporate restructurings produced powerful dislocations. Old-line Wall Street investment banks were losers, as they ceded their previously dominant position to Drexel, which rose from nothing to become the most profitable investment bank in the country. The corporate establishment were also big losers. Many executives of Fortune 500 companies lost their jobs in corporate restructurings, and those who didn't were forced to downsize and streamline their operations.

Drexel and Milken upset the status quo and made phenomenal amounts of money in the process. The establishment losers in the marketplace, desperate for revenge and to restore their lost positions of dominance, turned to the government for help. There the losers found ambitious but unscrupulous prosecutors like Rudolph Giuliani, who were willing to help because they saw opportunities to further their own careers by capitalizing on the public's historic distrust and envy of financiers.

A series of sensational but ill-founded prosecutions followed, which ultimately led to the demise of Drexel, Milken, and others. To achieve these results, the government changed the rules in the middle of the game, radically expanded the scope of the criminal law to include harmless and even beneficial trading practices, and routinely engaged in questionable ethical practices as it pursued victory at any cost.

Throughout its reign of terror, the government enlisted popular support for its efforts by utilizing the same anticapitalist greed-bashing rhetoric used so successfully in Communist countries. The press (with some notable exceptions) aided in this effort by spreading the fundamental misimpression that financial markets during the 1980s were permeated by fraud and criminality. By delegitimizing the financial innovations of the 1980s, the government with the blessing of the press got carte blanche to do whatever it wanted. The resulting mob hysteria only encouraged the government to intensify the witch-hunt to stamp out "abuses" in financial markets, with the lives of many innocent people being destroyed in the process. Not since the time of McCarthyism in the 1950s has the government behaved so badly, and in many ways what occurred in the 1980s was even worse.

CHAPTER 1

The Restructuring of Corporate America

On December 1, 1988, the *Wall Street Journal* announced that the bidding for RJR Nabisco was over. Kohlberg Kravis Roberts & Company, better known as KKR, had won by offering $25 billion, or $107 per share. The leveraged buyout transaction, financed almost exclusively by debt, including billions of dollars in junk bonds, was the largest and most controversial in American history.

The size of the fees alone boggled the imagination. Lawyers, bankers, and other "advisors" received $1.2 billion in fees from this single transaction. Even the deposed Ross Johnson, RJR Nabisco's former chairman, one of the losers in the bidding contest, walked away with $53 million in severance pay and other compensation.

What was accomplished by the transaction, other than making everyone involved in it rich? RJR Nabisco in 1988 was the nineteenth-ranking company on the Fortune 500 list with sales approaching $20 billion. Its food and cigarette products, including Oreo cookies, Barnum's Animals crackers, and Winston cigarettes, were among the best known and heavily advertised in the nation. But few believed that the company could be run better now with management having as its highest priority the repayment of debt. At a time of widespread concern that America was ceding world economic dominance to the Japanese with their greater focus on long-term planning and investment, the transaction seemed to symbolize everything wrong with the deal-driven decade of the 1980s.

Robert Reich, then teaching at Harvard before later becoming secretary of labor under President Clinton, captured the negative public reaction to the transaction perfectly in an article published in the *New York Times* in early 1989. Titled "Leveraged Buyouts: America Pays the Price," the article criticizes the deals of the 1980s and particularly the buyout of RJR Nabisco. These deals created paper profits, Reich argued, but hurt American workers and competitiveness in the world. "America," Reich concluded, "has had enough. Even by the cynical standards of the 1980's, Wall Street is giving greed a bad name."

Time magazine made an even harsher assessment. In its December 5, 1988, cover story on the RJR Nabisco transaction, titled "The Game of Greed," *Time*, like Reich, claimed that the deals of the 1980s raised serious questions about "greed, debt and the well-being of American industry." The RJR Nabisco transaction was simply the largest of the many "fruitless paper-shuffling deals" of the 1980s. The reporter went so far as to see the buyout as a threat to American survival:

> The sums are so vast, and so apparently out of line with any fore-seeable benefits that the deal might bring to American industry, that they raise deep and disturbing doubts about the direction of U.S. business at a time when many firms lag badly in foreign competition. Seldom since the age of the 19th century robber barons has corporate behavior been so open to question. The battle for RJR Nabisco seems to have crossed an invisible line that separates reasonable conduct from anarchy.

Time's historical reference to the age of the robber barons struck a nerve. The bitter sallies against greed and the excesses of capitalism in the 1980s closely mirrored comparable attacks on J. P. Morgan, Andrew Carnegie, John D. Rockefeller, Jay Gould, and other prominent industrialists and financiers in the late nineteenth and early twentieth centuries. In fact, the leveraged buyout of RJR Nabisco itself had a close historical parallel—J. P. Morgan's 1901 debt-financed acquisition of eight steel companies to form U.S. Steel. That transaction, the largest acquisition in American history until the RJR Nabisco buyout, was also widely condemned at the time. Critics attacked the size of the deal and the role of the financiers on Wall Street who made it possible. Some even predicted that the transaction would lead to "socialism" and "rioting in the streets," just as *Time* predicted the RJR Nabisco buyout would lead to "anarchy."

The only problem with the historical parallel was that *Time* did not take it far enough. The age of the robber barons was also the time of the second industrial revolution, one of the great periods of economic growth in modern history. The critics of the robber barons focused superficially on the perceived excesses of the time but ignored their much more important legacy of building a nationwide system of railroads, power generation, and modernizing production, both industrial and agricultural. And the creation of U.S. Steel, far from leading to rioting in the streets, was ultimately viewed as one of J. P. Morgan's greatest accomplishments. U.S. Steel went on to become one of the most important and successful corporations in America for much of the twentieth century.

Time's criticism of the RJR Nabisco buyout and the other deals of the 1980s, like the outcry over the robber barons a century earlier, thus missed the significance of what was occurring. A deeper grasp of history might have suggested a different story, emphasizing how the 1980s, like the age of the robber barons, were completely misunderstood by contemporary observers. In fact, the decade's wave of restructuring transactions, including the RJR Nabisco buyout, created tremendous wealth for investors and society as a whole. During the 1980s, the Dow Jones Industrial Average tripled from 1,000 to 3,000 and the real value of public firms' equity more than doubled from $1.4 to $3 trillion. Selling shareholders alone received $750 billion in gains (measured in 1992 dollars) from restructuring transactions between 1976 and 1990. Millions of new jobs were created in the process.

Radical change always produces major dislocations with winners and losers, and the 1980s were no exception. The restructuring revolution's biggest winner was the innovative and entrepreneurial investment banking firm of Drexel Burnham Lambert, particularly its high-yield or, as it was more popularly known, junk-bond department headed by Michael Milken. Drexel, which through its high-yield bond department became the financier of many of the big restructuring transactions of the 1980s, including the RJR Nabisco buyout, went from nowhere to being the most successful investment banking firm on Wall Street. Michael Milken in turn went from obscurity to become one of the richest men in America. Drexel's and Milken's success, however, created bitter enemies. First there were the displaced investment bankers who found themselves increasingly irrelevant as Drexel and Milken became more and more dominant. Then there were senior management of corporate

America who now were faced with the choice of doing a better job or being unceremoniously dumped from office following a Drexel-financed takeover. Approximately 10 percent of the Fortune 500 in existence in 1980 disappeared entirely as a result of restructuring transactions. Through their lobbying arm, the Business Roundtable, the management establishment, together with the displaced investment banks and other opponents of change such as labor unions, formed a powerful interest group dedicated to waging holy war against Drexel, Milken, and the other players in the restructuring revolution that was threatening their very existence.

The Need for Restructuring and the Modern Corporation

In 1932, Adolph A. Berle and Gardiner C. Means published their classic work, *The Modern Corporation and Private Property*, without question the most influential book on corporate America ever written. Berle and Means's central thesis was that the large corporation of the twentieth century differed markedly from its nineteenth-century predecessors. Historically, corporations were small-scale ventures in which the shareholders, whom Berle and Means referred to as the "owners," were the decision makers. Because they bore the consequences of their decisions, they had every incentive to work hard and try their best. If they didn't, the only people hurt would be themselves.

But this all changed when corporations grew increasingly large by raising money from thousands of outside investors who had no involvement in running the business. Control now rested with professional managers, not with the true "owners" of the corporation. Worse still, the real owners no longer even had the ability to hire or select who would be in control. Rather, the managers themselves, not the shareholders, nominated the candidates to serve as directors. The owners' role is limited to rubber-stamping this self-perpetuating scheme by casting a vote, typically by proxy, in favor of whomever is nominated by those in control.

Managers in the modern corporation, in Berle and Means's view, no longer have a reason to perform well. The firm's owners benefit if the corporation is profitable, but those in control care much less about performance precisely because they are not owners. And, since their domination of the voting machinery makes it next to impossible for them to be replaced, they have no reason to exert themselves to maximize profitability. Better to be lazy and enjoy the perks of office. Formulated during the Great Depression, Berle and Means's pessimistic assessment of the modern corporation seemed right on target.

The small-scale firms idealized by Berle and Means worked fine so long as the wealth of the owners was sufficient to conduct business. For business ventures where more capital was required, money could be borrowed from a bank. But for some large business ventures such as, for example, building a nationwide system of railroads, more capital is required than can realistically be borrowed from a bank. In these situations, entrepreneurs can raise funds from investors worldwide in exchange for a share of the profits. This is in essence a description of the modern publicly held corporation, in which investors provide firms with needed funds to pursue investment projects for which large amounts of capital are required. Whatever their flaws, large corporations are necessary for economic growth in a modern society.

Still, Berle and Means were on to something. Because in large corporations investors and decision makers are not the same people, conflicts of interest are inevitable. Managers who are performing poorly, or whose skills have become obsolete, have no incentive to fire themselves. While investors have the theoretical ability to nominate their own slate of directors and wage a proxy fight to oust the incumbents, this rarely occurs. In most cases shareholders, just as Berle and Means said, are too dispersed and uninformed to coordinate effectively for a proxy fight.

The difficulty of implementing radical corporate change became, if anything, greater in the decades after *The Modern Corporation and Private Property* was published. Stock ownership of officers and directors in the corporations they managed, never high to begin with, declined steadily after the 1930s. This made it even less likely that senior management would favor investors' interests over their own when there was a conflict between the two. At the same time, laws such as the Glass-Steagall Act of 1933, which prohibited banks from owning stocks, and similar laws, which restricted stock ownership by insurance companies and mutual funds, reduced the influence of large, sophisticated institutional investors. These laws also gave corporate managers greater discretion to pursue their own objectives at investors' expense. Finally, corporations simply became larger, again making it harder for atomistic and dispersed investors to monitor performance in any meaningful way.

One strategy widely used by corporate managers to increase size was to enter new and unrelated lines of business. This process of conglomeration, frequently accomplished by acquisition, became increasingly common after World War II. With the conglomerate merger wave of the 1960s, growth through diversification became the dominant strategy of American business. Giant firms, such as ITT, Esmark, and Northwest Industries, engaged in multiple and unrelated lines of business, seeming to represent the way of the future. Acquisitions in the 1970s and early 1980s such as Marathon Oil by U.S. Steel, Montgomery Ward by Mobil, and Hughes Aircraft by General Motors, demonstrated that few firms could resist the conglomeration temptation.

If Berle and Means were writing a sequel in 1980, these developments would have provided powerful additional ammunition for their original thesis. Growth through diversification created obvious benefits for corporate managers. Bigger firms meant more resources and staff under their control, which in turn usually meant greater security and prestige, as well as increased compensation. But how did shareholders benefit from conglomeration? They received none of the increased power and prestige associated with increased size. Nor did shareholders need their corporations to diversify because they could accomplish the same objective themselves at far lower cost. From shareholders' perspective, there was no reason for corporation A in the steel business to pay a lot of money to acquire corporation B in the clothing business. A shareholder who wanted to diversify and invest in the two businesses could simply buy shares in both. With the development of diversified mutual funds in the 1970s, shareholders could invest in the entire market at trivial cost.

The diversification explanation for conglomeration now seemed little more than a rationalization for managers increasing their salary and perquisites at investors' expense. But what could shareholders, the same powerless investors identified by Berle and Means, do to reverse the trend of continuing corporate expansion, frequently into unrelated lines of business? Investors, of course, could refuse to buy on those extremely rare occasions when established corporations attempted to raise additional funds by selling new equity. Alternatively, they could sell their existing shares, but this accomplished little to send management a message. The price someone else was willing to pay reflected the firm's business prospects. At most, one powerless shareholder was substituted for another.

The Restructuring Revolution

Approaching the 1980s, corporate America was badly in need of a change. American firms had become larger and more diffuse in their operations. Corporate accountability to shareholders was weak, and shareholders had little or no ability to force those in control to maximize profitability. The Dow Jones Industrial Average, reflecting these unfortunate realities, was mired in a long-term slump.

The restructuring boom of the 1980s—the wave of hostile acquisitions, tender offers, leveraged buyouts and recapitalizations, divestitures, spin-offs and the like—dramatically altered the economic landscape. What occurred was nothing less than a revolutionary change in corporate structure, a radical shift in power from managers to shareholders. Berle and Means never even imagined that such a fundamental shift could occur without regulatory intervention.

The boom occurred when it did because of six overlapping and interrelated major developments. First, the energy crisis of the 1970s caused a tenfold increase in the price of crude oil from 1973 to 1979, with expected continued large increases in the 1980s. The profitability of energy firms exploded, triggering a race to increase drilling and development efforts and find substitute energy sources. The energy crisis also had big spillover effects as firms and households changed their behavior to economize on energy costs by, for example, migrating to the Sunbelt states, insulating their houses, or buying small, fuel-efficient cars. When the expected increases in energy prices in the 1980s did not occur, and oil prices fell instead, the industry crashed, forcing a major contraction.

Second, unprecedented improvements in information processing and telecommunications technology in the 1970s and 1980s produced innovations such as the development of personal computers and the wireless telephone. These innovations created industries of their own, but their impact was much broader. Tasks previously performed by large numbers of individuals at corporate headquarters could now be handled by many fewer employees who could work at decentralized locations. As the technology improved and the costs of computing capacity fell during the 1980s, the work patterns of every industry had to adjust.

Third, competition intensified dramatically in many sectors as markets became increasingly globalized. Japan and Germany, whose economies recovered rapidly after World War II, became major international economic powerhouses. American firms now had to compete in a way they never had to before in such basic industries as automobiles, steel, tires, and electronics. Financial markets also became increasingly international. The high nominal inflation of the late 1970s, itself related to the energy crisis, caused investors to search the world for attractive investment alternatives.

Fourth, major regulatory developments in the late 1970s and early 1980s created new entrepreneurial opportunities. Deregulation of the oil and gas, airline and transportation, financial services, and broadcasting industries occurred during this time. These developments were in turn related to external events that made existing regulatory schemes obsolete. The energy crisis of the 1970s and the resulting high nominal inflation, for example, ended the viability of price controls on oil and gas and interest-rate ceilings that could be paid to depositors by financial institutions. Similarly, the advent of cable television immediately rendered the regulation of the broadcasting industry obsolete. Regulation, like industry, had to be modernized.

Fifth, the election of President Ronald Reagan in 1980 resulted in a major relaxation of U.S. antitrust policy. Transactions could now go forward without government intervention on antitrust grounds unless clearly anticompetitive. This in turn facilitated restructuring because it enabled assets and businesses to be readily combined and transferred among firms without regulatory interference.

Sixth, the dramatic growth of the high-yield bond market made it possible for takeover entrepreneurs who themselves otherwise lacked sufficient funds to make credible threats to acquire firms of virtually any size. The investment banking firm of Drexel Burnham, and particularly Michael Milken, the head of its high-yield bond division, was primarily responsible for this development. Drexel and Milken established contacts with the emerging class of takeover entrepreneurs—T. Boone Pickens, Carl Icahn, James Farley, Sir James Goldsmith, Ronald Perelman,

Saul Steinberg, Kohlberg Kravis Roberts & Company, among others—who routinely came to Drexel to finance takeover attempts knowing that Drexel had a stable of institutional clients interested in investing in Drexel deals. Drexel became known as a firm that could, if necessary, finance a takeover bid by raising billions of dollars within a matter of hours. Its reputation was so formidable that a Drexel-backed deal for billions of dollars could go forward even if no money had been raised. All that was necessary was a letter from Drexel announcing that it was "highly confident" the funds would be available when needed. These Drexel "highly confident" letters became the scourge of corporate America.

The coalescence of these six developments created a window of opportunity to restructure American business. Restructurings tended to be concentrated in industries such as oil and gas, financial services, and insurance, where firms had failed to adapt to changing economic and regulatory conditions. Restructurings also occurred in industries where there had been rapid technological change, such as tires and broadcasting. Finally, inefficiently run firms, particularly conglomerates that had grown too large by acquiring other firms in unrelated lines of business, were another prime source for restructurings. Firms in each of these categories needed a major shake-up, a fundamental change in business strategy.

Restructurings facilitated such fundamental change by altering target firms' organizational and financial structure. Reorganized firms typically had much more concentrated equity ownership and higher leverage than before. More concentrated equity ownership meant that senior management and large shareholders had a greater incentive to focus on profitability. The better job they did, the more money they made. Streamlining and cutting back on unprofitable business lines also became more attractive as an option. The perquisites of office were terrific so long as someone else was paying. Now that senior management had to pay more of the tab themselves, perks became much less indispensable. If downsizing and streamlining operations meant a smaller office and staff, greater wealth from increased stock values was a nice consolation.

Leverage also was an agent for change. When purchases of outstanding equity were financed with debt, shareholders immediately received a significant return on their investment. And the obligation to repay the debt forced firms to contract. Funds that had previously been used to finance unprofitable investment projects or acquisitions now had to be paid out to lenders. To pay down debt faster, firms frequently sold peripheral businesses to third-party buyers who specialized in those areas. Throughout corporate America there was a renewed emphasis on focus, on developing core businesses and reversing the post–World War II trend toward conglomeration.

Restructurings made it possible to do something about mismanaged firms as never before. The much maligned leveraged buyout transaction of RJR Nabisco was a perfect example. RJR Nabisco was formed in 1985 when R. J. Reynolds Industries, a tobacco company founded in 1875, merged with Nabisco Brands, a food company. In 1986, F. Ross Johnson, formerly CEO of Nabisco, became CEO of RJR Nabisco. Johnson's tenure was marked by disastrous business decisions coupled with personal extravagance. He invested $400 million in the development of a smokeless cigarette that consumers hated. To gain market share, he introduced and heavily marketed discount cigarettes, which hurt profitability by diverting customers from RJR's more profitable lines, Winston, Camel, and Salem. At the same time, Johnson tried to manipulate reported earnings to convince investors that nothing was amiss. Johnson, for example, adopted a practice of loading cigarettes on its already well-stocked distributors by selling to them at discounts just before scheduled price increases went into effect. While RJR was able to report higher sales and earnings, it payed a big price. Management forfeited future sales at higher prices, accelerated the payment of excise taxes, and alienated smokers who wound up purchasing stale cigarettes.

Johnson was also a man who enjoyed the perks of office. He built ostentatious new corporate headquarters filled with expensive art, acquired a fleet of corporate jets for personal use, and purchased exclusive residences for weekend retreats. Because of his fondness of being seen with celebrities, particularly sports stars, he spent millions to hire them as "consultants."

Not surprisingly, the market was less than thrilled with RJR Nabisco under Johnson's tenure. In 1987, the year before the buyout, RJR's stock price fell 8.6 percent while that of Philip Morris, its closest competitor, increased 19 percent. RJR Nabisco, in short, was ripe for a change of direction, a restructuring. This is exactly what KKR's leveraged buyout of RJR Nabisco accomplished. Equity ownership was concentrated, leverage increased, and Johnson was thrown out as CEO.

These changes achieved their desired result. Under new ownership and leadership, RJR Nabisco became a far more profitable company. Costs were reduced immediately by eliminating excesses such as thirty luxury apartments, seven of eleven corporate jets, thirty athletes on retainer, and thousands of unneeded positions. Many low-profit product lines were sold, while spending on research and development, and marketing and sales for high-profit businesses was increased. Loading, the smokeless cigarette, and the discount-brand strategy were all eliminated. New successful products, particularly Teddy Grahams snack food, were introduced. Debt was quickly paid down using proceeds from asset sales and the sale of new equity. By the end of 1991, the RJR Nabisco buyout created more than $10 billion of value for investors. The critics, like *Time*, who predicted the buyout would threaten American survival and lead to anarchy could not have been more wrong.

Senior corporate management across America were forced by the restructuring wave to be more responsive to investors' desires for efficient performance and high securities prices. Those who did not were only inviting a hostile tender offer or leveraged buyout. Better to make necessary, even if painful, changes than be out of a job. If a hostile bid was made or anticipated, the best defense frequently was to copy the prospective acquirer's strategy and hope that was good enough.

Goodyear Tire & Rubber Company was a case in point. Faced with declining prospects in the tire industry, Goodyear decided to diversify by acquiring the Celeron Oil company for $800 million in 1983. Goodyear's equity value declined by almost $250 million as a result, because investors saw no benefit in the combination of tires and oil. In 1986, Sir James Goldsmith began purchasing Goodyear shares aggressively with the announced intention of reversing the company's diversification program. Alarmed by the threat of a hostile takeover posed by Goldsmith, Goodyear launched a debt-financed share repurchase, paying $2.2 billion to acquire Goldsmith's shares and an additional 36.5 percent of the outstanding stock. Remaining shareholders, including senior management, now owned a larger share of a more leveraged company. The company's disastrous diversification efforts were at an end. Investors approved. Goodyear's equity value increased by more than $750 million on a market-adjusted basis during the time from Goldsmith's investment to the leveraged recapitalization.

What Goldsmith did for Goodyear, Boone Pickens did for much of the oil industry. During the first half of the 1980s Pickens, through his company Mesa Petroleum, launched takeover bids for Cities Service Company, KN Energy Corporation, Gulf Oil, Phillips Petroleum, and Unocal. Almost single-handedly, Pickens forced a major and needed contraction in the oil and gas industry. Cities Service, for example, was trading at $35 when Mesa began purchasing shares. When Cities Service was bought shortly thereafter by Armand Hammer's Occidental Petroleum for $53 a share, Mesa and other Cities Services investors made a huge profit. Pickens then turned his sights to Gulf. After Gulf refused his demand that it spin off some of its oil reserves into a trust for shareholders, Pickens decided to wage a proxy fight to throw out Gulf's directors.

Pickens lost the proxy fight but won big in the marketplace. Gulf stock had been trading at approximately $38 when Mesa began accumulating its shares. Pickens had put Gulf in play, and there was no turning back. Chevron eventually acquired Gulf in a $13.3 billion deal at $80 per share. For Mesa and other Gulf shareholders, it was hard to imagine a better outcome. The chain of events triggered by Pickens's demand that Gulf return the value of some of its oil reserves to its shareholders had caused Gulf's stock to rise by more than forty points, doubling its value. And the deal also accomplished Pickens's objective of forcing the industry to contract. When Chevron acquired Gulf, $13.3 billion that could have been used for unproductive drilling and expansion programs was returned to shareholders instead.

Within a few months, Mesa struck again, this time launching a tender offer for Phillips, located in Bartlesville, Oklahoma. Although Pickens was born in Oklahoma, Bartlesville regarded him as anything but a favorite son. Memories were still too fresh of what happened to Cities Service's Oklahoma operations after Pickens forced the sale of Cities Service to Occidental Petroleum. The company downsized and thousands of workers lost their jobs. Bartlesville was determined to fight Pickens to prevent the same thing from happening again. Special church services were organized for the sole purpose of asking God to help Phillips and the people of Bartlesville to defeat Pickens.

Phillips's management and their investment bankers ultimately decided more than divine intervention was needed. They decided to buy victory by purchasing Mesa's shares for $53 per share and pay Mesa an additional $25 million for "expenses." For Mesa, which began purchasing Phillips shares in the high 30s, this deal was too good to pass up. Phillips was rid of Pickens, but its troubles were not over. Carl Icahn immediately began threatening a takeover attempt, publicly criticizing Phillips for having bought out Mesa in what was commonly referred to as a greenmail transaction. Eventually, Phillips solved the problem by repurchasing almost half its shares at $53, the same price paid to Mesa, financed by $3 billion of new debt. The required retrenchment followed inevitably, as Phillips now had to sell assets and avoid unprofitable investments to pay down its debt, just as Mesa or Icahn would have had to do if either of them succeeded in their bids.

Mesa had taken on a series of bigger, better-known oil companies and made money every single time, almost $500 million in total profits. In each case, bellicose posturing by company executives about the need to continue with business as usual had been followed by capitulation. Now the industry was out to crush Pickens, but Pickens was undeterred. He decided to make a bid for Unocal, another large oil company.

After acquiring 14 percent of Unocal stock in the open market, Pickens announced a two-step $8.1 billion offer to acquire the remaining shares. Mesa said it would pay $54 in cash to acquire 37 percent additional shares and then acquire the remaining shares by paying $54 in high-yield debt securities underwritten by Drexel. Unocal countered by offering to purchase 29 percent of its outstanding shares by paying other high-yield debt securities valued at $72. The catch was that Unocal's offer was structured so that Mesa, a 14 percent shareholder, was ineligible to participate in the $72 exchange offer. When the Delaware Supreme Court upheld Unocal's exclusionary offer, Mesa was beaten. Unocal stockholders had no reason to sell to Mesa for $54 when they could exchange their stock for $72 in debt securities.

The press viewed Mesa's defeat as a victory for Unocal and its chairman, Fred Hartley, but with a big price tag. Although Unocal and Hartley "won," the *Wall Street Journal* reported, "Unocal hardly came out of the war unscathed." By having to "quadruple" its long-term debt to $5.3 billion to finance its $72 exchange offer, Unocal would have to cut back on its operations "for years."

Hartley's gloomy assessment, shared by the *Journal,* was that this retrenchment certainly wasn't "anything to brag about."

Hartley and the *Journal* had it exactly backward. Pickens's efforts made Unocal a vastly more profitable company. Prior to Pickens's arrival on the scene, Unocal was a company with little debt and lots of cash, which it spent on major expansion and exploration ventures. In the five years preceding its leveraged recapitalization, Unocal announced five such major investments in a declining industry, which had the combined effect of reducing shareholder value by $640 million. In the years following the recap, the company, now disciplined by its increased debt, announced no further new investments. Unocal's forced reversal of its expansion program resulted in investors regaining much of the value previously lost by bad management decisions.

The 1980s had many similar success stories: the restructurings of CBS and ABC in response to pressure from Ted Turner; the end of conglomerates like Beatrice and Northwest Industries, which were acquired and restructured by KKR and Jim Farley respectively; and the restructuring of Allegis Corporation, parent of United Airlines, after a takeover attempt by Coniston Partners. The restructuring of Allegis alone, which involved a leveraged stock buyback coupled with the resignation of the chairman, who during his tenure had made a series of value-destroying diversifying acquisitions, caused Allegis's stock to rise in value by more than $1.5 billion on a market-adjusted basis.

Of course not every transaction during the 1980s was a success story. Some restructurings failed; some other firms that would have benefited from change avoided restructuring altogether. Overall, however, the successes vastly outnumbered the failures. Firms involved in restructurings were typically leaner, more profitable operations as a result, and corporate managers now had to be sensitive to the bottom line as they never had before. Corporate accountability was restored.

Insiders Versus Outsiders

The restructuring of corporate America in the 1980s involved more than abstract economic issues of business strategy. The fight was also about power and the struggle between old money and new money. The big stakes involved explain the passion with which the defenders of the establishment attacked the challengers to the status quo.

Michael Milken and the takeover entrepreneurs he financed were for the most part self-made men who made it as outsiders. Few came from privileged backgrounds. Boone Pickens, a distant relative of Daniel Boone, started with nothing growing up in Holdenville, Oklahoma. In 1956 he was able to scrape together $2,500 to start what eventually became Mesa Petroleum. Carl Icahn was born and raised in Brooklyn, the son of a schoolteacher and an unsuccessful lawyer. William Farley's father was a mailman and his mother a funeral-home receptionist. He grew up in a working-class neighborhood in Pawtucket, Rhode Island; his first full-time job after completing his education was selling encyclopedias door-to-door. These men and others like them had little chance of rising through the ranks of Fortune 500 companies or old-line investment banks. They simply lacked the right pedigree. The only way they could break into the establishment was to blast in, paying little regard to the sensibilities of those they might offend.

Milken himself personified the new-money challengers to the establishment. His father, Bernard, was a polio victim who spent much of his youth in an orphanage before ultimately becoming an accountant. After he got married, Bernard changed the family name from Milkevitz to Milken. Like many of his generation, Bernard opted for a simpler name, one that was less obviously Jewish. Bernard Milken, with his triumph over adversity, was fiercely loyal to America, a loyalty that turned out to be somewhat ironic given what happened to his son.

After a modest but comfortable upbringing in Southern California, Michael enrolled at the University of California at Berkeley, where he graduated summa cum laude. He then attended the Wharton School of Business. He accepted his first full-time position in 1970 at a third-tier investment bank, Drexel Harriman Ripley. Drexel was near bankruptcy at the time, but it did have a strong research department. In 1973 Drexel merged with another third-tier firm, Burnham & Company. Neither Michael nor anyone else could possibly have imagined the phenomenal success that he and Drexel were soon to experience.

While at Wharton, Milken became fascinated with corporate bonds, particularly low-rated bonds. After reading Braddock Hickman's classic study of the performance of corporate bonds between 1900 and 1943, Milken became convinced that the market, particularly ratings services such as Moody's and Standard & Poor's, did not understand the true riskiness of bonds. He believed that, in deciding which firms' bonds were entitled to an investment-grade rating, these services overrated the importance of historical track record and physical assets and placed insufficient weight on other, more important factors such as talent and the firm's future prospects. If investors only understood that below-investment-grade bonds were less risky than their ratings implied, a big market could be created. It looked to him like there was a lot of money to be made.

Milken preached the same message at Drexel. He was a great salesman and a tireless worker, routinely putting in fifteen-hour days throughout his entire career. Drexel turned out to be a great place for Milken to work. Since it was such a weak firm without any significant institutional client base, it was more than willing to commit resources to an area in which none of its competitors were interested. Drexel did high-yield bond deals because those were the only deals it was able to do.

Until he was brought down by the government, Milken lived the American dream. Starting with nothing, he negotiated a deal after the Drexel merger in 1973 that was ultimately to make him one of the richest men in America. Drexel paid him a salary of $52,000 per year and a bonus of 35 percent of the profits from the firm's high-yield bond operations for distribution to himself and his employees in any way he saw fit. This compensation formula would not be changed during Milken's entire career at Drexel. As profits soared from high-yield bonds, so did his compensation. In 1987 alone, Milken was paid $550 million.

Drexel also flourished. The Drexel Burnham of 1975 had seventy-three investment banking clients, engaged in twenty-two investment banking transactions, and earned an estimated paltry $1.2 million in corporate finance fees. In 1976 Drexel Burnham Lambert was created when Drexel acquired Lambert Brussels Witter, which specialized in securities research. Drexel first entered the original-issue high-yield debt market in April 1977 with a $30 million subordinated-debenture issue for Texas International, a highly-leveraged oil and gas company. Drexel did six other high-yield bond deals in 1977. The firm was on the move, literally and figuratively. In 1978 Milken moved Drexel's high-yield bond-trading operation from New York to Century City, California, and then to Beverly Hills.

By 1983 Drexel's revenues exceeded $1 billion, a new company record, with profits at an estimated $150 million. Drexel acted as lead underwriter for well over half of the public high-yield bond issues that year. Drexel now employed 5,300 people, up from 3,000 in 1979. But this was just the beginning. In November 1983, Drexel decided to extend its high-yield bond niche into the mergers and acquisitions area. The Drexel network was now committed to financing takeover attempts with high-yield bonds. This fateful decision made Drexel the most profitable investment banking firm on Wall Street. By 1986, the high point of its success, Drexel had revenues of over $4 billion, with profits of $545.5 million. At year-end, Drexel had more than ten thousand employees. The key to its success was still its high-yield bond department, which also grew dramatically but numbered no more than four hundred employees. The high-yield bond department was responsible for all of Drexel's profits.

Drexel's success was accompanied by the parallel success of the companies and entrepreneurs it financed. With Milken's support, whole industries—including gambling, telecommunications, and health care—were financed in significant part with high-yield bonds. So too were various minority-run businesses. Reginald Lewis became the first black CEO in the Fortune 500 after Milken financed his $985 million buyout of Beatrice Foods. It is no coincidence that minority leaders and organizations were among Milken's strongest supporters. As outsiders themselves, they were appreciative of someone who gave them a chance.

Others were appreciative as well. William Farley was able to realize his lifelong dream to be rich when, in 1985, Ben Heineman decided to sell Northwest Industries, the conglomerate he had put together over several decades. After an initial purchaser could not raise the necessary financing, Farley, with Drexel backing, appeared out of nowhere and made a $1.4 billion bid. Heineman had never heard of Farley and at first did not take him seriously. But Milken made good on his promise to raise funds by selling high-yield bonds, and the deal was closed.

Drexel financing had made real what a few years earlier would have been considered impossible. With Drexel's support, Farley, a mailman's son, a former door-to-door encyclopedia salesman, was able to pay over a billion dollars and take over an old-time established company. And this was far from an isolated event. At the same time Drexel and Milken were backing Farley, they did the same for, among others, Carl Icahn, who acquired TWA; Ronald Perelman, who acquired Revlon; and Nelson Peltz, who acquired Triangle Industries. Anyone with Drexel and Milken's support became a potent threat. When Walt Disney ended Saul Steinberg's Drexel-financed takeover threat by repurchasing Steinberg's shares at a big premium in June 1984, the parties entered into a standstill agreement in which Steinberg agreed not to purchase Disney shares and Drexel agreed not to finance any acquisition attempts for ten years. Standstill agreements with potential acquirers were common during the 1980s. But it was unusual to require an investment bank to agree not to finance someone else. From the perspective of Disney's management, however, the deal made perfect sense. Incumbent management in the 1980s could feel a lot better about their job security if Drexel were out of the picture. Drexel and Milken had become that powerful. Once outsiders, by the mid-1980s they had taken over the playing field.

By the time old-line Wall Street figured out just how profitable Drexel had become, it was too late. Drexel had established such a dominant position in trading and underwriting high-yield bonds that it was difficult for other firms to compete. And Drexel did nothing to make it easier for its rivals. Instead Drexel and Milken strove to protect their near-monopoly position, flouting Wall Street etiquette in the process. Instead of the usual practice of setting up syndicates of investment banking firms to spread risk and share fees, Drexel typically attempted to sell all the bonds in a deal by itself. When a client insisted on it, Drexel went through the motions of forming a syndicate, but then it gave its comanagers virtually no bonds to sell.

Drexel never apologized for its success. When old-line Wall Street complained about what it called "ruthless competitive practices," Drexel viewed it as jealous whining. As Robert Linton, Drexel's then-chairman and chief executive officer observed in 1985, "The club is being replaced by what might be called a meritocracy." Drexel never cared about being liked or accepted. Being richer and more successful was more than enough.

The establishment hated them for it. Nicholas Brady, the head of the investment banking firm of Dillon, Read, was one of the most impassioned defenders of the corporate establishment against the Drexel onslaught. Brady, unlike Milken, was a person of privilege. He grew up on a four-thousand-acre estate in Far Hills, New Jersey. After graduating from the Harvard Business School in 1954, he accepted a position at Dillon, Read. This came as no surprise to anyone. Brady's father was a friend of the firm's then-chairman, C. Douglas Dillon, and the Dillon estate was next door to the Bradys' in Far Hills. Brady, with major assistance from wealthy family friends who sent him deals, steadily rose through the ranks. In 1971, he was appointed to head Dillon, Read. He was equally prominent in established social circles, a member of the Bohemian Club, the exclusive California enclave and hunting club for corporate executives. By the mid-1970s, Brady became chairman of the Jockey Club, the elite society entrusted with the critically important task of registering thoroughbred horses.

During Brady's tenure Dillon, Read, like many other old-line Wall Street investment banks, avoided involvement with hostile takeovers and leveraged buyouts for fear of offending its blue-chip corporate clients. When these transactions became the biggest game in town, Dillon, Read and its blue-chip clients were left on the sidelines. For the first time in his life, Brady, the quintessential insider, was on the outside looking in. Unable to compete in the new economic environment, Brady was forced to engineer the sale of Dillon, Read in 1986 to the Travelers Corporation, a giant insurance company.

Brady never overcame his contempt for Drexel, Milken, and the takeover entrepreneurs who had placed corporate America under siege. He became a relentless and public critic of takeovers, debt financing, and financial innovation. Brady preached the same message after his longtime personal friend and new president George Bush chose him to be secretary of the treasury. Although he was uniformly regarded as one of the least effective treasury secretaries in recent history, Brady, in at least one important sense, viewed his tenure as a huge success. As treasury secretary, he was able to turn down a last-minute appeal from Drexel for help to avoid bankruptcy. Watching Drexel declare bankruptcy and Milken plead guilty and go to jail shortly thereafter was for Brady a dream come true. Nothing could have been sweeter.

Brady was one of the most militant defenders of the establishment, but he was far from alone. He was joined by other displaced investment bankers, most notably Felix Rohatyn of Lazard Frères and Henry Kaufman of Salomon Brothers. Both of these men were media figures who had earlier achieved great prominence but were also pushed off the stage by Drexel and Milken during the 1980s. Like Brady, they were active participants in the campaign to regain their lost position and crush Drexel and Milken along the way. Corporate management of the Fortune 500 also had an obvious incentive to join the campaign. For many, hostile takeovers were the first threat to their job security they had ever experienced. Through their lobbying arm, the Business Roundtable, they devoted massive time and resources to preserve their positions.

Big labor was the final piece of the puzzle. Organized labor thought debt-financed hostile takeovers and leveraged buyouts meant inevitable plant closings, relocations, and layoffs. They also were willing to do what was necessary to preserve the status quo. United in their opposition to Drexel, Milken, and the takeover entrepreneurs they financed, these defenders of the establishment extended the fight from the marketplace to the press and the political and regulatory arena.

The Overleveraging of America and Other Takeover Myths

Establishment defenders recognized that, to marshal public support, they had to characterize the restructuring boom as a threat to America, not just to themselves. Andrew Sigler, the CEO of Champion International and the leading spokesman for the Business Roundtable, led the public assault on takeovers, claiming that "the unfettered buying and selling of U.S. corporations solely for the purpose of financial speculation and profit is one of the most destructive phenomena of the 20th century." Lane Kirkland, president of the AFL-CIO and the leader of organized labor, agreed. "I think," Kirkland opined, that "corporate raids are an outrage and a bloody scandal." Fred Hartley, the CEO of Unocal, was even more dire in his assessment: "[T]his speculative binge, this chain letter, must eventually collapse, leaving wreckage of ruined companies, lost jobs, reduced U.S. oil production, failed banks and savings and loans, and Government bailouts, not to mention unemployment and empty buildings . . . "

Capitalizing on the public's fear and ignorance about debt, particularly high-yield bonds, was central to the publicity campaign against takeovers and restructurings. Felix Rohatyn's op-ed article in the *Wall Street Journal* on April 18, 1985, titled "Junk Bonds and Other Securities Swill," was illustrative of the campaign. Rohatyn urged the public to "pay attention" to the "raids and takeovers . . . financed with junk bonds" because, he warned, "in the last analysis the public always pays." One week later Nicholas Brady continued the campaign with a piece in the *New York Times* titled "Equity Is Lost in Junk-Bondage." Brady pronounced that he was "opposed" to "today's takeover frenzy, financed by junk bonds, which increasingly endangers our savings institutions and our system of corporate enterprise." "[T]hese activities," Brady concluded, "represent an abuse of the system that is among the most serious I've seen in 30 years. Speculative, highly leveraged financing techniques, involving junk takeover bonds, if unchecked, will leave misery in their wake."

These claims, and many others like them, were heavy on rhetoric but short on analysis. Contrary to popular claims, the restructuring wave and the explosive growth of high-yield bonds did not result in the "overleveraging of America." In fact it is far from clear whether there was *any* significant increase in corporate leverage during the 1980s. The critics who harped on the increased use of debt financing neglected to mention that the market value of equities also skyrocketed during the 1980s. Without a corresponding increase in the amount of debt, there would have been a major deleveraging of corporate America. When the increase in the market value of equities is taken into account, there was no dramatic increase in corporate leverage during the 1980s. In fact, the ratio of the market value of debt to the market value of assets remained remarkably constant during the 1980s. Corporate leverage during the 1980s also remained at all times lower that it was in the mid- to late 1970s:

Market Value Debt-to-Asset Ratios: 1970–1988

Year	Ratio for Average Company
1988	30
1987	30
1986	30
1985	30
1984	30
1983	29
1982	31
1981	32

Market Value Debt-to-Asset Ratios: 1970–1988 (cont'd)

YEAR	RATIO FOR AVERAGE COMPANY
1980	29
1979	34
1978	35
1977	34
1976	30
1975	32
1974	37
1973	27
1972	24
1971	25
1970	26

And with all the talk about debt hurting American competitiveness in the world, corporate leverage remained low by international standards. For example, corporate leverage was higher in Japan, the country that America supposedly could not compete against.

The form of corporate borrowing did change during the 1980s even if corporate leverage remained relatively constant. The expansion of the high-yield bond market gave corporations the ability to borrow directly from investors rather than borrowing from banks. But this additional financing alternative was a benefit, not a detriment. It was particularly unfair to disparage high-yield bonds by labeling them "junk" or "securities swill." The riskiest high-yield bond was still safer, and thus less "junky," than the stock of the same firm. But the establishment defenders never referred to "junk equity"; their objective was not conceptual clarity but inflaming public opinion.

It seemed as if any claim about debt financing, no matter how illogical, could be made with a straight face. Andrew Sigler, for example, warned of the "billions in equity taken off corporate balance sheets" by successful acquisitions. The inevitable consequence of withdrawing equity, Sigler concluded, was to weaken companies and leave them unable to compete. But equity does not "disappear" when one firm acquires another. The target may cease to exist as an independent entity, but its assets remain intact and are simply transferred to the acquirer. Nothing is lost. And when measured by market value, the total value of corporate equities increased dramatically during the 1980s.

For others, debt financing was nothing short of magic. Martin Lipton, the nation's most prominent takeover defense lawyer, claimed that an acquirer could profitably pay virtually any price for any company by using debt financing. Lipton offered this example to illustrate the point:

> [I]f the equity of a target is selling in the market for 5 times after-tax earnings of $50 million, or a total of $250 million, and money can be borrowed at a 15 percent interest cost, a raider can pay $500 million, or a 100 percent premium over market, for the target and, assuming no goodwill or increased depreciation, still show $12.5 million after-tax earnings—$50 million earnings less $37.5 million after-tax interest cost on $500 million at 15 percent . . .

Debt financing in this example seems to enable the impossible. The bidder invests none of its own money and yet, by borrowing, is able to pay twice the market price to the target's shareholders and still have $12.5 million left over for itself. Was it really this easy to take over companies and make money by borrowing? Many thought that it was.

But they were wrong. Lipton's example is nonsense. No lender would lend an amount twice the market value of the target on the terms he suggests. If equity is selling at five times earnings, then investors are demanding a 20 percent rate of return on their investment secured by all of the assets of the target. Lipton assumes lenders will demand only a 15 percent rate of return for investing in the same target with the same security. This is implausible; both types of investors will demand the same rate of return, causing the profits in the example to disappear. And Lipton also ignores the need to repay the principal of the loan. Even assuming the bidder could borrow at 15 percent, the $12.5 million remaining after payment of interest would not be profit but would have to be returned to the lender to repay the principal.

Another common claim was that restructurings were contributing to the "short-termism" of corporate America, which was destroying our ability to compete. Andrew Sigler warned that "this kind of game-playing imposes short-term attitudes and strategies on companies which are just the opposite of what is needed if this country is to remain competitive." Business professor Peter Drucker concurred: "A good many experienced business leaders I know now hold takeover fear to be a main cause of the decline in American competitive strength in the work economy. . . . It contributes to the obsession with the short term and the slighting of tomorrow in research, product development and marketing, and in quality and service—all to squeeze out a few more dollars in next quarter's bottom line."

This excessive focus on the short term, no matter how unfortunate, was not nearly as bad, many emphasized, as succumbing to a debt-financed takeover bid. Anything was justified to prevent raiders and speculators from gaining control of established and successful companies and then selling off their assets, piece by piece, to pay down the debt. The message to corporate executives was clear. "If a company wants to avoid being taken over and busted up," Martin Lipton advised, "it must sacrifice long-term growth and future profits. It must use the maximum amount of leverage and operate with the primary objective of short-term profitability."

This rhetoric again bore no relationship to reality. The notion that successful and well-managed companies had to forsake needed long-term planning because of takeover fear was a complete myth. Critics never could explain why managing a firm badly was a rational strategy to avoid a takeover bid. The premise seemed to be that the market, particularly institutional investors, only cared about quarterly performance and penalized companies that invested for the long term. But this premise is false, as is obvious from everyday experience. Companies go public routinely with no track record of performance; the stocks of biotechnology and computer companies frequently sell for the highest multiples of current earnings precisely because the market does value projects with future payoffs.

The reality is that companies that were targets of takeover or restructuring bids were poorly performing firms, frequently in declining industries. For these firms, the much maligned "bust-up" that followed a restructuring was more accurately described as a needed downsizing and streamlining of operations. If increased leverage facilitated this greater efficiency, so much the better. There is no natural law that requires corporations to remain the same bloated size forever. If a company can make more money by selling off assets than by operating them itself, that is exactly what it should do.

Firms can invest excessively in research and development, just as they can grow too large by acquisition. In the energy industry, for example, drilling and expansion programs that were justified when oil prices soared in the 1970s were no longer worthwhile when prices collapsed in the 1980s. One study of the effect of research and development expenditures concluded that the market reacted positively with the notable exception of such investments by energy firms in the early 1980s. Contraction was required in light of changed industry conditions, and this was accomplished by the restructuring of the industry.

Organized labor's complaint that restructurings led to fewer jobs at lower wages confused cause and effect. Mature firms in declining industries, or firms facing intense competitive pressures from foreign entrants or because of deregulation, had to adjust and economize. One source of savings was labor costs, particularly in unionized industries with fat labor contracts. Restructurings hastened the process of adjusting wage and employment levels to changed economic conditions and resulted in some highly publicized fights such as Carl Icahn's demands for major union concessions as part of his takeover of TWA. But the givebacks and layoffs would have occurred in any event, with or without restructurings. For the decade between 1979 and 1989, the Fortune 100 lost over 1.5 million jobs. Firms such as AT&T, Exxon, and General Electric made dramatic cutbacks in employment levels without ever having been faced with a takeover threat.

America as a whole, however, gained millions of jobs during the 1980s. Total employment increased dramatically as the job losses in certain sectors were swamped by job gains in other sectors, particularly small and medium-sized businesses and in new high-technology fields. There is an important general point here. Innovation always produces dislocation, which requires adjustment. Restructurings were part of this process of redeploying assets, including human resources, required by changed economic conditions. Without the restructurings of the eighties the process would have been slower and less efficient, and fewer overall jobs would have been created.

When all else failed, critics of the restructuring wave could always raise the specter of bankruptcy. In the late 1980s, many firms that had previously been involved in restructuring transactions—firms such as Revco, Macy's, Allied Stores, Federated Department Stores, and Campeau—wound up in bankruptcy. These bankruptcies, the critics crowed, proved that the earlier restructurings were a failure.

This was yet another myth. The vast majority of restructurings did not result in bankruptcy. And when bankruptcy did occur, the results were different from what was commonly assumed. Bankruptcy does not cause a firm's assets to disappear or evaporate. Ownership of the assets typically changes, but the assets remain in place. The company's debts are renegotiated, and losses are spread out fairly among its creditors. Nor does the fact of bankruptcy, contrary to popular perception, mean that a restructured firm was mismanaged or performed poorly. Campeau Corporation's acquisition of Federated Department Stores in early 1988, for example, was rated by *Business Week* as among the ten worst deals of the 1980s. *Fortune* went further and called it the "biggest, looniest deal ever." When Federated and Allied Stores Corporation, also controlled by Campeau, declared bankruptcy in January 1990, less than two years after the acquisition, these gloomy assessments of the deal appeared to have been confirmed.

But the reality was different. After Campeau's acquisition, which was financed almost exclusively by debt, Federated made substantial cuts in overhead and capital expenditures and divested businesses in leveraged buyout transactions. The increased debt also provided Federated with additional tax benefits. Overall, the value of Federated increased by about $2 billion after the Campeau transaction. Campeau, however, paid a debt-financed premium of more than $3 billion to acquire Federated, with Federated's assets pledged to secure the debt. After the acquisition, the operating cash flow from the unsold Federated divisions was not sufficient to meet required debt service, and bankruptcy resulted. Yet values of Federated's assets were soon to *increase* even further as a result of the rearrangement of ownership claims in the bankruptcy process.

Campeau was a loser in the Federated transaction because it paid too much. Creditors of Federated who got paid less than one hundred cents on the dollar also lost out. But from a social perspective, the transaction was a major success, creating $2 billion of additional value captured primarily by the Federated shareholders who had cashed out in the acquisition. Federated's eventual bankruptcy did not destroy this new value or cause it to disappear. Rather, the bankruptcy, properly understood, was the final chapter in the success story because the value of Federated's assets increased even more.

Another benefit of debt and bankruptcy is that losses from mismanagement are minimized. A firm with a capital structure of 80 percent equity and 20 percent debt can squander up to 80 percent of its value before ownership claims and management policies are altered by bankruptcy. But if the ratios are reversed, bad management can cost the firm only 20 percent of its value. Early bankruptcy in this situation conserves value that would otherwise have been lost.

But ultimately, none of these realities made the nightly news. To many, the takeover entrepreneurs and their financiers were evil, a tax on society. Pejorative labels such as "raiders," "looters," "speculators," "junk-bond artists," "bust-up specialists," and "destroyers of established businesses" captured journalistic imaginations. But name-calling was one thing; stopping takeovers that made economic sense and created value was another. For this, the establishment needed assistance.

The Cry for Help

Getting the government on your side when you are facing a tough fight in the marketplace is a time-honored technique in American economic history. The usual approach is to equate the competitive threat to you with injury to society, exaggerate the magnitude of the danger beyond recognition, and then claim regulation is the only solution. Whether the fight is between domestic versus foreign producers, railroads versus truckers, or optometrists versus ophthalmologists, the approach is always identical. And the same was true in the clash between the establishment defenders and the takeover entrepreneurs.

Martin Lipton, who became phenomenally wealthy and successful from defending takeover targets, was one of many who called for legislative intervention. His rhetorical strategy was to make it seem as if America was hanging on by a thread to its status as a world economic power. All would be lost, if it were not already, unless legislation was enacted to stop takeovers and junk bonds. Lipton's plea for urgent legislation combined breathless hyperbole with a repetition of virtually every economic fallacy ever uttered about restructurings:

> Our Nation is blindly rushing to the precipice. As with tulip bulbs, South Sea bubbles, pyramid investment trusts, Florida land, REITs, LDC loans, Texas banks and all the other financial market frenzies

of the past, the denouement will be a crash. We and our children will pay a gigantic price for allowing abusive takeover tactics and boot-strap, junk-bond takeovers. We are overleveraging American companies and forcing them to focus on short-term stock market results. Research, new product development and capital investment are no longer the keys to business success. To the contrary they have become the invitation to a junk-bond, bust-up party. While the rest of the industrialized world is investing for the future, we are squandering our assets in a speculative binge of junk bonds . . . and the other games of today's financial market casinos. The only remedy is effective legislation. Perhaps it is already too late.

Hundreds of bills were introduced in Congress during the 1980s to curb takeovers and junk bonds. Congress held extensive hearings on these bills, and speaker after speaker testified about the evils of debt-financed restructurings and the need for legislative action. Congress listened sympathetically but did nothing. No general antitakeover bills were enacted into law.

Antitakeover legislation at the federal level was doomed by the ambivalent attitude of the Securities and Exchange Commission and the outright opposition of the Reagan administration, swept into power in 1980 on a platform that included government deregulation as one of its major objectives. The Reagan transition-team report advocated scaling back the size of most federal agencies, including the SEC, by about one-third over three years. The report further recommended scrapping the SEC's venerable Division of Enforcement. Under chief Stanley Sporkin in the 1970s, the SEC had led a controversial crusade for greater corporate morality, attacking payoffs to foreign governments and political payments, areas that previously had been thought to have nothing to do with the securities laws. Reaganites viewed this effort as, at best, a waste of time. For them, corporations could do the most good for society by making the most money. The SEC, under this view, should worry about eliminating unnecessary and oppressive regulations and concern themselves with policing only that hard-core fraud that could not be adequately handled by the states.

To implement these objectives, President Reagan chose John S. R. Shad, vice-chairman of E. F. Hutton, successful Reagan fundraiser, and head of his New York campaign, to be chairman of the SEC. Shad, a Wall Street insider who worked his way up from the bottom before his career peaked when he was passed over to head E. F. Hutton, was more than willing to take the job. Once in office, Shad was confronted with the firestorm about takeovers, and he had to decide what position to take.

This was no small problem. Shad was a practical and well-meaning man who wanted to do the right thing. But he had limited ability, with neither the academic training nor the experience to understand the economic forces underlying the restructuring wave. His instincts were vaguely free-market-oriented and suspicious of sweeping regulatory proposals. But at the same time, he had many friends and contacts on Wall Street who were pressuring him to take a stand against takeovers. Lacking any understanding of why takeovers were occurring, Shad found it difficult to respond. He didn't want to support a legislative ban on takeovers but was unable to articulate the reasons why such action would be harmful.

Predictably, the result was indecisiveness and confusion. Bowing to congressional pressure, Shad in early 1983 created the SEC Advisory Committee on Tender Offers "to examine the tender offer process and . . . to recommend to the Commission legislative and/or regulatory changes the Committee considered necessary or appropriate." The committee's report, which came out in July 1983, was a political compromise that ultimately pleased nobody. After beginning with the observation "that there is insufficient basis for concluding that takeovers are either per se beneficial or detrimental to the economy or shareholders," the report then made fifty recommendations, including many proposals for greater regulation of the takeover process. The committee, however, refused to support a legislative ban on takeovers, because of its belief in "free market solutions."

For two members of the committee, Gregg Jarrell, the SEC's chief economist, and then-professor Frank Easterbrook of the University of Chicago, this intellectual muddle of expressing preference for free-market solutions, calling for increased regulation, and concluding with no opinion on the desirability of takeovers was too much to bear. Easterbrook and Jarrell wrote a separate statement making the obvious but powerful point that the need for increased regulation required a theory of the costs and benefits of takeovers, precisely what was lacking from the committee's report. Easterbrook and Jarrell argued that all federal regulation of takeovers be repealed. Not surprisingly, the compromise position of the Advisory Committee Report, subjected to ridicule by its own members, quickly sank into oblivion.

In June 1984 Chairman Shad decided to go public with his
views on takeovers and the need for regulation. He chose a speech
to be delivered to the New York Financial Writers Association as
the forum. Normally, Shad's speeches were so inarticulate and
lacking in substance that they were instantly forgotten. Not this
time. In a speech titled "The Leveraging of America," Shad
attacked takeovers and debt financing and predicted that the
inevitable result of leveraged takeovers and buyouts would be
more bankruptcies and less long-term planning. "In today's corporate world," Shad proclaimed, "Darwin's 'survival of the fittest' has
become 'acquire or be acquired.'" The only difference between
Shad's speech and the party line of the Business Roundtable was
that Shad professed to believe in "the evolutionary response of the
marketplace" to address the problem rather than "less flexible laws
and regulations."

Still, Shad's speech, which was excerpted in the *Wall Street
Journal* the next day, June 8, 1984, was a stunner. No high-ranking
official from the Reagan administration had ever attacked takeovers
so publicly. Shad's disclaimer notwithstanding, his speech was perceived as a big boost for the chances of passing antitakeover legislation. Maybe even the laissez-faire Reagan administration was now
on board.

This speculation did not last long. On September 25, 1984, just
three months after Shad's "Leveraging of America" speech, the
Reagan administration made its position known. Secretary of the
treasury Donald Regan sent a letter to Congress communicating
the administration's opposition to additional takeover regulation.
Takeovers, Regan wrote, "perform several beneficial functions in
our economy. First, they provide a means—sometimes the only
feasible means—of policing management in widely held corporations. Second, they help identify undervalued assets and . . . help
realize efficiencies by reallocating capital and corporate assets into
more highly valued uses."

With the administration's position now clear, Shad never publicly attacked takeovers again. Without support from the administration or the SEC, the chances of enacting major new takeover
regulation dimmed considerably.

The stock market crash on October 19, 1987, ended any possibility of a new federal ban on takeovers. On October 13, 1987, a
bill was introduced in the House Ways and Means Committee

that would have limited the tax deductibility of interest expenses incurred to finance takeovers and leveraged buyouts. The bill was approved by the committee on the evening of October 15 with the stated purpose of preventing hostile acquisitions:

> The House Ways and Means [C]ommittee believes that corporate acquisitions that lack the consent of the acquired corporation are detrimental to the general economy as well as to the welfare of the acquired corporation's employees and community. The committee therefore believes it is appropriate not only to remove the tax incentives for corporate acquisitions, but to create tax disincentives for such acquisitions.

The stock market declined in value from Wednesday, October 14, to Friday, October 16. On Black Monday, October 19, the Dow Jones Industrial Average dropped 508 points, or 22.6 percent, and the New York Stock Exchange lost $1 trillion in value. Many feared that Black Monday was a repeat of the stock market crash in 1929, which signaled the Great Depression of the 1930s. Nobody wanted history to repeat itself, and Congress did not want to be blamed for causing the collapse of financial markets. Support for antitakeover legislation, which was perceived as a contributing cause of Black Monday, disappeared. Critics of takeovers and restructurings would have to try new tactics and look for help in other ways.

CHAPTER 2

The War Against Insider Trading

Attempting to legislate takeovers and high-yield bonds out of existence was not the only way to attack the new financial entrepreneurs. Another and in many respects far more effective strategy was to mobilize the power and resources of the government to step up its enforcement efforts to stamp out "abuses" in financial markets.

The advantages of this alternative enforcement strategy were obvious. For one thing, it did not require any controversial legislation, which would surely be opposed by a Reagan White House still committed to a free market in takeovers. And for John Shad, stepping up enforcement was the perfect solution. He could continue to champion free markets, criticize broad new legislative initiatives, and still do something for his friends on Wall Street. There were other benefits as well for Shad and the SEC. A legislative ban on takeovers would reduce the SEC's regulatory domain. But beefing up enforcement would have the opposite effect. The SEC could now plausibly claim, the Reagan proposed budget cuts notwithstanding, that the agency needed more power, budget, and staff to do its job.

And the enforcement strategy was popular with the public. Unlike the esoteric and morally ambiguous debates on the economic benefits of takeovers and high-yield bonds, there could be no debate about "abuses." It was a simple matter of right and wrong, of playing by the rules or not. Given the distrust of speculators and money changers existing since biblical times, the public was all too willing to believe the worst about those who were successful in financial markets. There was another force at work—envy. The public may have never had a clue what Michael Milken did for a living, but they certainly understood, because of the relentless efforts of the government and the press to make them understand, that he made $550 million in a single year. The message was obvious: Nobody could make that much money without being a crook.

Predictably, Felix Rohatyn, Nicholas Brady, the Business Roundtable, and the other losers in the restructuring revolution were the biggest supporters of a government enforcement crackdown. Government enforcement, particularly criminal prosecutions, could solve all their problems. Convicted felons are not very effective competitors. Felix Rohatyn went so far as to liken "excesses" in the financial markets to a "cancer":

> As the revelations of illegality and excesses in the financial community begin to be exposed, those of us who are part of this community have to face a hard truth: A cancer has been spreading in our industry, and how far it will go will become clear only as the Securities and Exchange Commission and federal prosecutors pursue the various investigations currently under way. . . . Those who break the law must be punished.

But what laws were broken? Restructuring companies, borrowing money, selling off assets, renegotiating labor agreements, and firing corporate executives, no matter how distasteful to some, was not illegal. Without illegal conduct, there could be no enforcement crackdown.

One obvious candidate for an enforcement crackdown was insider trading. This is exactly what John Shad promised when he was appointed chairman of the SEC, declaring that he intended to "come down with hobnail boots" on insider traders "to give some shocking examples to inhibit the activity." Shad's newly appointed head of the Division of Enforcement, John Fedders, who came to the agency from the prestigious Washington law firm of Arnold & Porter, also publicly declared his commitment to prosecuting inside traders. Fedders was forced to resign shortly thereafter because of his admitted and highly publicized wife beating. He was replaced by Gary Lynch, who if anything was an even more zealous enforcer. The war against insider trading became the top priority of the SEC and its ally, the U.S. Attorney's Office for the Southern District of New York, headed during much of the 1980s by the politically ambitious Rudolph Giuliani.

The government was assisted in its efforts by a cast of characters and events straight out of a Grade B movie. One such character was Dennis Levine, a young investment banker of mediocre ability who, in his words, grew up "selling aluminum siding to niggers." Levine financed his expensive lifestyle by trading on advance knowledge of takeovers and stashing the profits in a secret bank account, which held over $10 million when he was turned in by the bank in 1986. Levine never felt what he did was wrong, believing it was no different from the behavior of a person who works at a deli. As he reportedly said, "You take home pastrami every night for free. It's the same with information on Wall Street." Levine was the perfect villain, a caricature of everything perceived to be wrong with America in the 1980s.

Martin Siegel was another investment banker who, like Levine, had an insatiable desire for the finer things in life. Annual compensation in the millions of dollars wasn't nearly enough. To supplement his income, Siegel provided Ivan Boesky with information and tips. He arranged to be paid by receiving suitcases full of cash brought by anonymous messengers in the lobby of Manhattan's Plaza Hotel. Siegel received between $700,000 and $800,000 in this way for the trading profits he generated for Boesky. When the scheme was exposed, the public was shocked. The stories of the rendezvous at the Plaza and the suitcases full of $100 bills even shocked the financial community.

But once again, appearances were deceiving. From its inception, the war against insider trading was beset by legal and conceptual problems. During the entire decade of the 1980s, the government never developed a theory of why insider trading was harmful or a rationale for deciding whom and when to prosecute—or even of what, exactly, insider trading was. Neither the SEC, Congress, nor the courts have yet, up to the present day, been able to define what constitutes insider trading. The popularity of the war against insider trading masked this intellectual bankruptcy, but to anyone who looked, the problems remained. When all was said and done, the country would have been better off had the war against insider trading never been fought.

What's Wrong with Insider Trading?

The 1980s were filled with emotionally charged rhetoric denouncing illegal insider trading in the strongest and most unequivocal moral terms. Those who engaged in this evil practice were despicable white-collar criminals, thieves in three-piece suits. Insider trading had to be stopped, the SEC emphasized, to restore "public confidence" in the nation's securities markets.

This simple moral story, so frequently told, is a complete fairy tale. For most of American history, there has been virtually no regulation of insider trading. It was not until 1962 that the SEC in its *Cady Roberts* decision even asserted authority to regulate trading by corporate insiders possessing valuable information, and this view was not accepted by the courts until 1968. There is no evidence that investors had less "confidence" in our securities markets before 1968 than after.

Even today, the term "illegal insider trading" is a misnomer. Corporate insiders are not prohibited from trading in shares. In fact, insiders routinely buy and sell shares, and their trades are publicly reported and even published in the financial sections of newspapers. Several investment advisory services also track insider transactions. Investors follow insiders' investment decisions because they believe insiders know the most about the fortunes of their firms. If investors know whether insiders are buying or selling, they can do the same.

The law prohibits only those trades made while in possession of "material" information. This materiality requirement precludes trading by insiders with knowledge of specific, concrete undisclosed events such as earnings or merger announcements. But sometimes corporate insiders will have valuable information that is not so concrete. Maybe the insider believes that a planned reorganization of a company's sales force is going better than expected or knows that a key executive is distracted by health or marital problems. Corporate insiders are permitted, even encouraged, to trade on this type of informed hunch. And what if insiders, because of their superior information, decide not to purchase or to sell, thereby avoiding a loss they might otherwise have incurred? There is no prohibition against *refusing* to trade. Insiders also may trade the stocks of competitors with impunity. Insider trading is pervasive, even today, in the sense that corporate insiders routinely benefit from possession of valuable information gleaned from their contacts in an industry and their expertise.

Insider trading is pervasive because it is frequently beneficial. Sometimes corporate executives want to disclose information but cannot do so directly. Disclosure can cause information to lose its value. A firm may not be able to disclose the details of a promising new technology, for example, because it does not want to share this information with competitors. If corporate executives in possession of the information purchase shares and make a vague or partial disclosure ("We have good news but can't say just what"), stock prices will move in the right direction. Investors who see corporate executives putting their money where their mouths are are more likely to believe what they say.

Insider trading is also a powerful incentive device in some circumstances. An entrepreneur who is developing a new invention, for example, will be more inclined to pursue it if he will be rewarded on success. By trading, the entrepreneur is able to bet on himself and not depend on the willingness of others to pay him a higher salary or bonus for his efforts.

Differences in the knowledge and insight of buyers and sellers are universal in all markets, not just securities markets. If someone wants to buy farmland because he believes the land contains valuable mineral deposits, he can do so without saying anything about it to the farmer. The law imposes no duty on him to disclose his knowledge or belief. The no-disclosure rule allows the farmland to be purchased cheaply and thus facilitates the transfer of assets to higher-valued uses. If the law prohibited informed trading, requiring the buyer to reveal the probable existence of mineral deposits, the incentive to search and innovate would be effectively eliminated.

Corporate takeovers present an analogous situation in financial markets. Potential acquirers must engage in research, and take risks, to determine the gains that may be realized from the acquisition of a particular target corporation. Perhaps the management of the target is inept, or combining two firms may create economies or efficiencies, in which case the whole is greater than the sum of the parts. Whatever the source, gains from an acquisition can only be realized if potential acquirers are rewarded for their efforts.

To provide the necessary reward, the law allows acquirers to purchase shares of potential targets in the open market or in privately negotiated transactions without disclosing their identity or the sources of gains. The Williams Act of 1968 alters this nondisclosure principle in two important respects. First, it requires that a party acquiring 5 percent of the outstanding shares of a firm must file a 13(d) statement with the SEC ten days after crossing the 5 percent threshold. During the ten-day window, however, the acquiring party can continue to purchase additional shares with no disclosure. Second, if the acquirer decides to make a tender offer, the Williams Act requires it to disclose to the shareholders of the target corporation voluminous information including identity, source of financing, and future plans if the offer is successful. Even in this situation, however, the acquirer can accumulate a large block of shares at low prices before announcing its tender offer to the public.

The party acquiring shares secretly in this way is clearly engaging in "insider trading." Takeover bids typically offer a target's shareholders a premium of approximately 50 percent over the current market price for their shares. Other traders would very much like to know that an acquirer is purchasing shares in the marketplace prior to announcing a premium tender offer. If other traders knew this information, they could refuse to sell until the tender offer was announced or even buy shares along with the acquirer. But the law does not require that an acquirer disclose its own secret purchases, no matter how "material" other investors might find that information, because it would eliminate the rewards for search. It would deprive the acquirer of the fruits of his labor.

Of course, informed trading is not always beneficial. A homeowner cannot sell to an unsuspecting purchaser without disclosing that the house is full of termites. There is no reason to reward the homeowner for keeping secret this type of information. Similarly, corporate executives cannot trade in advance of major earnings or other corporate announcements. After all, there is no need to reward insiders for just being in the right place at the right time.

Sometimes informed trading goes beyond just being in the right place at the right time and actually harms the corporation and its shareholders. A corporate executive who buys shares in advance of a planned corporate stock repurchase plan in the hope of selling the shares at a higher price is clearly behaving improperly. The executive is both obtaining unauthorized compensation and risking injury on the corporation by driving up the price for its shares in advance of the repurchase. Insider trading is also undesirable when it leads to bad business decisions. If the possibility of gain from selling in advance of bad news, that is, shorting the corporate stock causes executives to undertake a secret plan to depress corporate value, for example, the corporation and its shareholders would be harmed.

Any legal system must establish rules to distinguish between desirable and undesirable informed trading. This is precisely what the government failed to do in its war on insider trading. No matter how many times the government talked about the need to restore "public confidence" in securities markets, no one was ever able to say what this meant. And how could this meaningless test be applied? How could anyone know when investors did or did not have "confidence"?

In fact, it is impossible for government regulators to make all traders equal. Some traders will always know more than others. Even if corporate insiders were prohibited from all trading, other market professionals would take their place. Why would "investor confidence" be greater if ordinary investors traded against informed market professionals rather than informed corporate insiders? And if somehow all traders were made completely equal, the result would be a disaster. The securities markets would cease to exist because no one would have any incentive to search for valuable information if they could no longer profit by trading on it. Differences in information and judgment are precisely what creates the possibility of gain in the market. These differences, and the ability to trade on them, are what distinguish a market where goods and services are allocated, and their value determined, from a gambling casino or a lottery. Presumably not even the government wanted to turn our securities markets into pure games of chance.

But none of these esoteric arguments made any difference. The government recognized that its campaign to restore "confidence" by making everyone equal was very much in sync with the rich-bashing, "decade of greed" rhetoric of the 1980s. Throughout history demagogues have proposed radical egalitarian schemes to tap into the public's distrust and envy of the rich. The 1980s were no exception.

The Government's Setbacks in *Chiarella* and *Dirks*

The "investor confidence" rationale for the war on insider trading was a nice-sounding slogan, but without any content. It gave the government no clue whom and when to prosecute, or what theory to use when a case was brought. In two important Supreme Court decisions in 1980 and 1983, the government was told that it would have to do better in coming up with a justification for the war on insider trading.

The first case was *Chiarella* v. *United States,* the first criminal insider-trading case ever brought. Vincent Chiarella was a printer who was hired to print documents used by acquirers when making tender offers. Such acquirers typically take steps to preserve the secrecy of the offer and identity of the target prior to acquisition. If leaks occur, the target, now forewarned, may erect defensive measures to defeat the offer. Also, other bidders may enter the scene once a target is identified. The price of the target's shares will almost certainly rise in anticipation of the offer. All this may make the offer more costly and less likely to succeed.

For these reasons, offerers when dealing with printers such as Chiarella conceal the identity of the target corporation until the last possible moment. Preliminary drafts leave the name of the target blank or use a code. Chiarella's employer, Pandick Press, swore all its employees to secrecy. Trading was strictly prohibited. Chiarella knew well that his job was to print the documents and do nothing more.

But Vincent Chiarella was clever, as well as dishonest. He cracked the code used to disguise the identity of prospective targets and proceeded to trade in their shares prior to the acquisition announcements. After being caught, he entered into a consent judgment with the SEC, gave up his trading profits, and was fired. He was then criminally prosecuted and convicted. The appellate court affirmed the conviction, then the Supreme Court decided to hear the case.

It is hard to imagine a less sympathetic defendant in an insider-trading case than Vincent Chiarella. Nobody argued that he was anything other than a thief. Nevertheless, the Supreme Court reversed his conviction. The Court rejected the SEC's contention that the public has a right to equal access to information in securities markets. Rather, they said, each trader is free to trade, no matter how great his informational advantage, unless there is a relationship of trust and confidence—known in law as a fiduciary relationship—with the party on the other side of the transaction. Chiarella wasn't in a fiduciary relationship with the target's shareholders, and therefore he could trade as he pleased. The Court also ruled that Chiarella was not prohibited from trading on the grounds that he breached a duty owed to his employer because the government had not properly presented this argument to the jury.

The Supreme Court rejected the government's position again in *Dirks* v. *SEC* when faced with a radically different set of facts from that of *Chiarella*. Raymond Dirks was a securities analyst with an extensive network of contacts. One of these contacts, a Ronald Secrist, a former employee of an insurance company, Equity Funding Corporation, told Dirks that Equity Funding was perpetrating a massive fraud on its policyholders and the investing public. After a thorough investigation, Dirks confirmed the accuracy of Secrist's information and reported it to the press and the SEC. Both ignored Dirks, believing him to be a crackpot. How could Dirks be right when everyone knew that Equity Funding was one of the most successful and reputable insurance companies around? Dirks had more success, however, when he spoke with his institutional investor clients. They sold their Equity Funding stock in response. Eventually, an investigation revealed that Dirks was right. Equity *was* engaged in fraud, and the price of Equity Funding's shares plummeted. Dirks's clients had, of course, already gotten out while the getting was good.

For his prescience in spotting and his efforts in exposing the fraud, one might have thought that Dirks would have been commended. Instead, the SEC censured Dirks for engaging in illegal insider trading by tipping to his clients material inside information received from Secrist. The Supreme Court then agreed to hear the case, recognizing its importance.

The SEC's position in *Dirks* was that Dirks had acted improperly because the securities laws "require equal information among all traders." The Supreme Court rejected this contention, just as it had done several years earlier in *Chiarella*. The Court ruled that the key question was whether Secrist received a "personal benefit" in exchange for giving the information to Dirks. Since Secrist acted out of a desire to expose a fraud rather than merely to make money for himself, the Court held that Dirks acted lawfully.

Taken together, *Dirks* and *Chiarella* were a nightmare for the SEC. Both Dirks and Chiarella unquestionably profited by their possession of valuable nonpublic information, yet the Supreme Court held that neither engaged in insider trading. Both cases made clear that the SEC's broad assertion that a trader threatened "public confidence" in securities markets would not establish a case of unlawful insider trading.

The two cases created even more fundamental problems for the SEC. By emphasizing the role of Dirks and his clients in exposing the fraud at Equity Funding, the Court went further than declaring that Dirks's conduct was not illegal. It was beneficial. The possibility of financial gain, in fact, had created the incentive for Dirks to ferret out the company's fraud to begin with. Dirks's fees, and the trading profits of his clients, were their reward for discovering and uncovering the fraud. No reward, no discovery. Dirks, in short, was no different from the party who purchases farmland with knowledge that it contains mineral-ore deposits or the bidder who buys up shares in advance of making a tender offer.

Furthermore, in *Dirks* the Court recognized that "insider trading" is not always bad. Sometimes trading while in possession of valuable nonpublic information is desirable; other times it is not. But the SEC had no theory that admitted the existence of "good" insider trading nor any theory to distinguish it from "bad" insider trading.

Even where trading clearly fell on the "bad" side of the line, the Court in *Chiarella* held that it was not necessarily illegal under the securities laws. What was the SEC to do? And worse still, if Chiarella could not be prosecuted, as reprehensible as he was, how could the SEC use the insider-trading laws as a weapon against the upstart financial entrepreneurs who so many thought were wreaking havoc in financial markets?

The War Continues: Rule 14e-3 and the Misappropriation Theory

The government's defeats in *Chiarella* and *Dirks* were short-lived. Just months after *Chiarella* was decided in 1980, the SEC adopted Rule 14e-3, which intended to prevent informed trading in advance of tender offers. The rule makes unlawful "the purchase or sale of a security by one who is in possession of material information relating to [a] tender offer which information he knows or has reason to know is nonpublic and which he knows or has reason to know has been acquired directly or indirectly" from an acquirer or target.

By adopting Rule 14e-3, the SEC attempted to nullify *Chiarella* and go even farther. Before the rule, trading by market professionals in advance of tender offers was not unlawful because, as

Chiarella held, the trader had no fiduciary duty to the target's shareholders. Rule 14e-3 eliminated this fiduciary-duty requirement and also any distinction between those like Chiarella who stole information and those who acquired it by consent.

But did the SEC have the authority to enact Rule 14e-3 to begin with? The SEC as an administrative agency has the power to enforce and interpret law but not to make it. Only Congress can do that. The SEC claimed that Rule 14e-3 was authorized by a 1970 amendment to the Williams Act that made it unlawful for any person "to engage in any fraudulent, deceptive, or manipulative acts or practices" in connection with a tender offer. But the Supreme Court had just held in *Chiarella* that Congress did not intend to prohibit informed trading absent a breach of fiduciary duty. Not all trading with knowledge was supposed to constitute securities fraud. How could the SEC, on its own initiative, broaden the definition of securities fraud beyond what Congress, as interpreted by the Supreme Court, had intended? The SEC also never explained how voluntarily giving someone information, also prohibited by Rule 14e-3, could ever possibly constitute a "fraudulent, deceptive or manipulative act."

Rule 14e-3 makes sense only when viewed as an antitakeover measure. Critics had tried and failed to persuade Congress to enact legislation making it impossible for an acquirer to purchase shares in the marketplace before announcing a public tender offer. Rule 14e-3, which did not require congressional action, was the next best thing.

Sometimes an acquirer may want to alert third parties such as arbitrageurs, who bet on the outcome of takeovers, of its plans. Arbitrageurs are skilled at assembling and selling large blocks of shares, facilitating successful takeovers. The more arbitrageurs know, the better they can do their job. And the target's shareholders are in no way injured by this information transfer. It makes no difference to them whether an acquirer itself purchases shares quietly—which is perfectly legal—or whether someone else trades on the same information. Rule 14e-3 does not protect shareholders. It hurts them because it makes value-increasing takeovers, and the increases in wealth they create, less likely.

The SEC also developed another legal innovation to get around *Chiarella*. Chiarella was never charged with misappropriating information from his employer or the acquirer, so the Supreme Court refused to affirm his conviction on this ground. Chiarella went free, in other words, because the government screwed up by charging him with the wrong offense. The government did not make this same mistake twice. Misappropriation became the government's pet theory of prosecution.

The misappropriation theory revolutionized the law of insider trading. It was now no longer relevant that a trader breached no duty owed to traders on the other side of the transaction so long as the information was obtained somewhere in the vicinity of a fiduciary duty owed to someone. For this reason, the theory gave the government a hook to prosecute a wide array of characters including lawyers, investment bankers, psychiatrists, and others who allegedly obtained and traded on information without the consent of their clients.

The misappropriation theory was tailor-made for regulatory overreaching. The injured party under the misappropriation theory was whomever the information was taken from, not shareholders trading in the marketplace. Under the securities laws as interpreted by the courts, trading is always permitted if it is preceded by public disclosure. The legal obligation is to disclose or abstain from trading, not to preserve secrecy, which is the point of misappropriation and breach-of-fiduciary-duty theories. Thus, the two laws—securities law and fiduciary obligation—are at loggerheads. Complying with the full-disclosure imperative of securities law exacerbates any injury from misappropriation. If there was a misappropriation, then the civil and criminal laws on theft of intangible property should have been consulted, not the securities laws. But this proposal had no appeal to securities regulators anxious to expand their turf at every opportunity.

There is a second, and even more troubling, implication of the misappropriation theory. If trading on the basis of misappropriated information is improper, it follows that trading is proper if there is no misappropriation. This implies, for example, that firms could opt out of insider-trading regulation by adopting a policy allowing insiders to trade. No insider who traded in compliance with firm policy could be said to have misappropriated the underlying information. The SEC has never acknowledged, let alone explained, this tension between the misappropriation theory and its regulatory regime.

In fact, theft and misappropriation had little or nothing to do with the policy and perceived ethical, or economic, harm of insider trading. It was only a legal technicality that the government grasped at, after *Chiarella*, as an all-purpose rationale for prosecution. But when the misappropriation rationale became inconvenient, the government was more than willing to discard it. The government's goal was to prosecute participants in the restructuring revolution, not to stop misappropriation. This explains Rule 14e-3, which prohibits consensual transfers of information prior to tender offers. It also explains many of the government's bizarre prosecutions that were to follow.

Takeovers, Insider Trading, and Run-ups

Although Rule 14e-3 and the misappropriation theory were major weapons for the government in its war against insider trading, many believed they barely made any difference. Illegal insider trading, particularly prior to takeover announcements, was too pervasive, and too profitable, to be stopped.

The cover story of *Business Week* dated April 29, 1985, captured this public perception of rampant criminality on Wall Street. Provocatively titled "Insider Trading: The Wall Street Epidemic That Washington Can't Stop," the story breathlessly described the world of the "shadowy side of Wall Street," where insider trading was "running rampant." As support, the story cited anecdotal evidence and the results of a *Business Week* study on stock-price run-ups of target companies prior to public announcement of takeover attempts. The study demonstrated that in 72 percent of 229 cases surveyed, the target's stock rose prior to any public takeover announcement. The cause of these unexplained run-ups was obvious: "The odds are overwhelming, that inside information is what made those stocks move." The takeover boom, it seemed, was inextricably linked with criminality.

Echoing conventional wisdom, the story concluded that the corruption was so widespread that individual investors had lost confidence and were being driven from the market. Only more vigorous governmental prosecutions to clean up the mess could bring them back. Insider trading in corporate-control contests just had to be reined in.

This conventional wisdom was fundamentally flawed. For one thing, it ignored the role of government regulation itself in creating the climate in which trading was profitable. Prior to the passage of the Williams Act in 1968, takeovers could be consummated quickly and in secrecy. There was no problem of insider trading or run-ups. The waiting periods and disclosure requirements of the Williams Act radically changed the takeover game and actually encouraged and generated insider trading. In the many states that enacted anti-takeover statutes that went far beyond the Williams Act, these problems were even worse.

The effect of federal and state regulation of takeovers was to create uncertainty. The mandatory waiting periods and disclosure requirements gave incumbent management and rival bidders the ability to defend when none existed before. Would incumbent management react to the filing of a 13(d) or a hostile takeover attempt by engaging in defensive tactics to defeat the bid? Would a rival bidder make a competing offer? Would the target enter into a friendly acquisition with a white knight? Would the initial bidder react to any of these strategies by making a preemptive high first bid, or did it plan on making a higher bid later?

This new uncertainty about takeover outcomes had made the lure of tremendous trading gains irresistible. Since takeover bids were commonly at premiums of 50 percent or more relative to the target's pre-offer price, one could make a fortune by being able to predict when bids would be made and when they would be successful. But the risk involved also was formidable. The volatile nature of takeover stocks meant that fortunes could be lost as well as made. The risks involved, and the sophistication required, meant that speculating on takeover stocks was not suitable for the typical individual investor.

The market's response was the creation of a new professional specialty, takeover arbitrage. Those who engaged in this practice bought and sold securities based on their predictions of takeover outcomes. By doing so, they provided a valuable service to both acquirers and investors. Acquirers benefited because the arbitrageurs' accumulation of large share blocks, which could then be transferred, lowered the cost of acquisitions. Investors benefited because they had the option of transferring the risk of their investment in takeover stocks to arbitrageurs once a takeover contest developed. If the takeover failed to materialize, the shareholder might not have another opportunity to sell at such high prices for a very long time. The presence of market professionals willing to bear takeover risks gave investors options, which is all to the good.

At the same time, however, the possibility of large trading gains or losses in volatile takeover stocks caused arbitrageurs to have a tremendous demand for information. Any information, no matter how seemingly trivial, might be worth a fortune. Sometimes an acquirer or its investment banker would give arbitrageurs this information voluntarily, although Rule 14e-3 made this practice illegal. Other times arbitrageurs would make trading decisions after canvassing their network of contacts to determine who was buying shares, who was meeting with whom, and by doing their own study of industry conditions and potential acquisitions.

Still other times, arbitrageurs, like Chiarella the dishonest printer, would trade after learning of upcoming takeover announcements in violation of confidentiality agreements. Arbitrageurs had no monopoly on dishonesty. Sometimes investment bankers like Dennis Levine, attorneys, and others who came into contact with takeover-related information traded when they knew it was forbidden to do so. Finally, some arrangements were simply hard to categorize. This was true of the case of Ivan Boesky and Marty Siegel, despite the infamous suitcases full of cash handed over at the Plaza Hotel. Unlike Levine, Siegel did not use confidential information while disregarding his client's interests. Siegel's problem was profiting by serving his clients too well.

On August 26, 1982, Bendix Corporation announced a $1.5 billion hostile tender offer for Martin Marietta, a big defense contractor. Martin Marietta then hired Siegel, then an investment banker at Kidder, Peabody, to head its defense. Siegel in turn advised his client to adopt what became known as the PacMan defense—launching its own offer for Bendix. Siegel, to accomplish this objective, told arbitrageur Boesky about the pending offer for Bendix. Boesky began accumulating Bendix stock, as Siegel had hoped, and profited when Bendix eventually was acquired by yet another firm, which evidently agreed that Bendix itself made an attractive target. Boesky made money, and Siegel, who was given credit for the PacMan defense, was hailed as a genius. Siegel never told Kidder about tipping off Boesky, and he never paid taxes on the cash he received from Boesky. So Siegel was a crook, but at least he had his client's best interests in mind.

The takeover boom of the 1980s certainly had its share of unsavory and dishonest characters. Dennis Levine, Martin Siegel, and Ivan Boesky were the best known, but they were not alone. These individuals arose in response to the uncertainty and the market for information, legal and illegal, created by the federal and state regulation of tender offers. Yet ironically, without government intervention in financial markets, these individuals never would have been able to do what they did in the first place.

Exactly how much illegal insider trading occurred during the 1980s is impossible to say. Similarly, we do not know to what extent stock-price run-ups before takeover announcements are due to illegal insider trading. Studies on this question have been inconclusive, and all we do know is that some unknown combination of illegal insider trading and legitimate market activity explains run-ups. Part of the problem is distinguishing legal from illegal behavior. Voluntary and consensual transfers of information prior to tender offers were legal until the SEC adopted Rule 14e-3 but illegal thereafter.

Plus, what does "material inside information" mean, exactly? A trader might have firsthand detailed knowledge of an imminent offer at a specified price. Or, at the other extreme, he might know nothing. But what about the situations between these two extremes? What if an arbitrageur finds out after making a series of phone calls to market makers that a well-known acquirer is secretly buying shares of a firm publicly rumored to be a target? What if he learns, in idle conversation with a limousine driver, that a well-known acquirer has been holding secret meetings with a rumored target? Are these types of information "material" under the securities laws? There is no clear answer.

Many contemporary observers, however, were untroubled by these complexities and were content simply to jump to the dire conclusions served up by journalists at newsmagazines. Insider trading, like AIDS, was an "epidemic," and takeovers were instruments of corruption, investment banker enrichment, short-term job loss, and shocks to the status quo. Few bothered to think through the real relationship between illegal insider trading and takeovers. Stock-price run-ups prior to takeover announcements indicate that information about the prospective acquisition has leaked into the market. This raises the cost to the acquirer of achieving its toehold position in the target and may raise the price of a bid once an offer is made. Contrary to conventional wisdom, therefore, run-ups did not cause takeovers. The opposite was true. Run-ups reduced the number of hostile takeovers because they made acquisitions more costly.

Uninformed target shareholders who sold prior to a public takeover announcement, far from being the victims of stock-price run-ups, as the newsweeklies and the SEC claimed, were nothing but beneficiaries. The typical pattern of stock-price movements prior to a takeover announcement was:

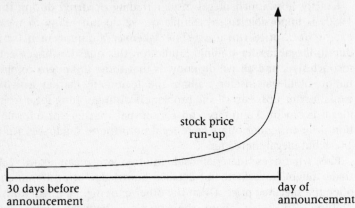

stock price
run-up

30 days before
announcement

day of
announcement

According to *Business Week* and the SEC, investors would have more "confidence" in the market if the typical pattern had been:

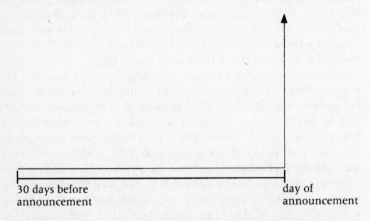

30 days before
announcement

day of
announcement

Which way are selling shareholders better off? With run-ups, selling shareholders sell for increasingly higher prices until the day of the offer. With no run-ups, by contrast, selling shareholders receive the same low price until the day of the offer. Shareholders clearly benefit, quite tangibly, from run-ups. The only class of selling shareholders who are arguably hurt by run-ups are those tape watchers who see the price increase, sell in response, and miss out on the higher tender price. These sophisticated investors, typically takeover arbitrageurs or other market professionals, are likely betting that a rumored takeover would be defeated or never materialize. They are hardly representative of the ordinary, unsophisticated investor idealized by the SEC. The notion that uninformed investors were being victimized by run-ups caused by insider trading, or by takeovers themselves, therefore, was based on sheer misconception. From shareholders' perspective, the more run-ups the better.

Congress Increases the Penalties for Insider Trading But Cannot Define the Practice

Yet Congress made this common misperception into a crusade. Two major pieces of legislation in the war against insider trading were soon enacted: The Insider Trading Sanctions Act of 1984 (ITSA) and the Insider Trading and Securities Fraud Enforcement Act of 1988 (ITSFEA).

The ITSA was initially proposed by the SEC in 1983. Increased penalties for insider trading were needed, the commission argued, because "insider trading in publicly traded securities undermines the expectations of fairness and honesty that underlie public confidence. . . ." Moreover, the "potential for immense profits" from trading in anticipation of mergers and tender offers "is a powerful lure to this illegal activity." Something had to be done to preserve "the investing public's legitimate expectation of honest and fair securities markets where all participants play by the same rules."

These rotund phrases, however, gloss over all the hard questions about the function of the market and the nature of insider trading. They were also a rehash of the government's arguments rejected by the Supreme Court in *Chiarella* and *Dirks*. But the wisdom of resurrecting a theory found to be intellectually incoherent by the Court as new, statutory laws did not trouble Congress, which enthusiastically enacted the ITSA. The act substantially increased the penalties for insider trading by giving the SEC the authority to recover a civil penalty of three times the amount of profit gained or loss avoided by any person who trades on inside information in violation of the securities laws. Also, the act increased the maximum criminal fine for illegal insider trading from $10,000 to $100,000 and made it illegal to trade in options or other derivative instruments while in possession of inside information.

The ITSFEA was enacted in 1988 against a background of perceived "serious episodes of abusive and illegal practices on Wall Street." This "scandal" was so serious that it had created a national emergency. Congress had to act decisively, and thus declared the practice of insider trading "guilty on all counts."

The ITSFEA contains a variety of provisions designed "to provide greater deterrence, detection and punishment" of insider-trading violations. For example, the maximum term of imprisonment for individuals criminally convicted of securities-law violations was increased from five to ten years. The act also increases the maximum criminal fine for individuals from $100,000 to $1 million; for corporations the increase is from $500,000 to $2.5 million. Civil remedies are increased as well. The ITSFEA also authorizes the SEC to seek civil penalties against people who "recklessly . . . failed to take appropriate steps to prevent" other people from engaging in unlawful insider trading, expanding the range of personal responsibility far beyond one's own behavior to those who are thought to have something more than no control over the situation. Here the penalties are remarkably harsh—up to the greater of $1 million or three times the profit gained or loss avoided from the trade.

The act also permits investors who traded "contemporaneously" with and on the opposite side of the market from the inside trader to sue for damages. Congress never explained, however, why this right to sue should exist. A trader in, say, New York who decides to sell is not harmed if another trader somewhere else in the country is buying the same stock while in possession of inside information. The two trades occurring through different brokers are totally unrelated. The remedy Congress chose made no sense.

Finally, the ITSFEA grants the SEC the authority to award bounty payments to persons who provide information leading to the successful prosecution of insider-trading violations. The commission has the discretion to award up to 10 percent of the penalty imposed. This bounty system, like the draconian penalties of the ITSFEA, was a major victory for the opponents of the restructuring revolution. It gave jealous competitors, incumbent management threatened with a takeover, and others facing displacement a powerful weapon to use against unwelcome aggressors. The bounty provisions enabled them to protect their turf, collect financial rewards, and be called heroes by the SEC to boot.

The philosophy underlying the ITSA and particularly the ITSFEA was that no penalty was too harsh for those who engage in the sinister practice of insider trading. The consensus was so clear that the ITSFEA sailed through Congress, passing by a vote of 410–0 in the House and by a voice vote in the Senate. In light of this unanimous condemnation, one might have thought that Congress would have no difficulty in defining what the term meant and who would be subject to the new enhanced penalties. But this Congress was unwilling, or unable, to do.

The fuzziness of the very term "insider trading" first surfaced in 1984 during hearings over the ITSA. A few witnesses testified that Congress could not increase penalties for insider trading yet not even bother to define the practice. Predictably, the SEC opposed efforts to define the term, emphasizing the dangers of "freezing into law either a definition which is too broad, or too narrow to deal with newly emerging issues." It preferred to maintain total prosecutorial discretion over what it might deem a violation. Congress ultimately agreed, saying that any statutory definition would leave "gaping holes" that would be "large enough to drive a truck through."

The ITSFEA raised the same concern again. The act's stiff civil and criminal penalties for insider trading made it even more important to provide clear guidelines about what was allowed and what was not. Chairman John Dingell of the House Committee on Energy and Commerce vigorously opposed any clear definition, arguing that to define the criminal behavior would inevitably be underinclusive and provide a "roadmap for fraud." In explaining why the ITSFEA contained no definition, Chairman Dingell's committee merely waved its hands, saying that it "did not believe that the lack of consensus over the proper delineation of an insider trading definition should impede progress on the needed enforcement reforms encompassed within this legislation." The inability to define insider trading, in other words, is no reason not to increase the penalties faced by those who engage in the practice, whatever it might be!

The ITSFEA thus gave regulators and prosecutors maximum power and discretion to prosecute whomever they choose for essentially whatever reasons they might choose. This, of course, suited the turf-building goals of the regulators and prosecutors. But creating unbridled governmental power and discretion is not a good way to govern. It lends itself to politicized prosecutions of unpopular people with strong enemies—people such as repeat players in hostile takeovers who had a role in booting powerful but poorly performing corporate executives out of multimillion-dollar sinecures.

Perhaps this is what the SEC and Congress had in mind when they argued that any definition of insider trading should be avoided because it would be "underinclusive." Nothing should permit any targets of the government's wrath to escape.

Prosecutors, Courts, and the War Against Insider Trading

Criminalizing an activity without defining it runs counter to powerful traditions in American law. Defendants have a constitutional right to fair notice that behavior is criminal. Unlike certain highly repressive Communist or other dictatorial nations, America has no tradition of common-law crimes, where courts can declare conduct criminal on a case-by-case basis. The Supreme Court declared such common-law crimes unconstitutional more than 150 years ago. Even Congress has no power to decree that individuals can be criminally prosecuted for conduct that was not criminal at the time it occurred. To ensure that criminal defendants receive their constitutional right of fair notice, courts enforce a rule of lenience: Criminal statutes are construed narrowly. Novel and expansive interpretations of criminal statutes are discouraged.

Prosecutors are sworn to protect the rights of the accused as well as prosecute them. Their job is to do justice, not just rack up convictions. When prosecutors abuse their discretion, courts are there as safeguards. The system is structured so that defendants can only be convicted of real crimes after receiving a fair trial.

Unfortunately, the system broke down during the 1980s when defendants were accused of insider trading. The lack of a definition of insider trading gave prosecutors maximum discretion to charge whomever they chose. Prosecutors such as Rudy Giuliani exploited this discretion for maximum personal advantage. Similarly, no court has yet found troubling the absence of a statutory definition of insider trading. Novel and expansive prosecutions were routinely approved by the courts, making the crime of insider trading very much in the forbidden tradition of common-law crimes. The rights traditionally accorded to criminal defendants were simply deemed to be inapplicable in insider-trading prosecutions. At the same time, courts and prosecutors, seduced by the general public hysteria over the "decade of greed," abandoned any pretense of objectivity about insider trading. Doubtful legal authority or ambiguous facts would not be allowed to stand in the way of the government's enforcement crackdown.

1: **The Robert Freeman Guilty Plea.** Robert Freeman was head of arbitrage at Goldman, Sachs until he was arrested for insider trading on February 12, 1987. After KKR announced its planned leveraged buyout of Beatrice, Freeman, like other arbitrageurs, began investing heavily in Beatrice stock. When rumors began to circulate that the deal might collapse, Freeman got nervous and began calling around to people who might have information. Freeman became more concerned after hearing that the deal was in trouble from another arbitrageur, Bernard "Bunny" Lasker. Freeman then decided to sell before the anticipated plunge in Beatrice's stock price that would occur if KKR's offer were withdrawn. To be sure he was making the right decision, Freeman then contacted Marty Siegel at Kidder, Peabody, who was working on the deal. When Freeman relayed that Bunny Lasker had told him the Beatrice deal was in trouble, Siegel responded, "Your bunny has a good nose." Ultimately, it turned out that the rumors were wrong and the Beatrice deal was not in trouble; arbitrageurs who, unlike Freeman, bought and held made a fortune. Freeman, whose "bunny" gave him what turned out to be incorrect information, did not.

Based on these facts, Freeman, who after his arrest had lost his job and was subjected to a several-year investigation, eventually pled guilty to mail fraud and received a sentence of four months in jail. His "crime" was contacting Siegel, who was working on the deal at Kidder, to confirm what Bunny Lasker had told him. Freeman misappropriated no information, had decided to begin selling before talking to Siegel, and the information about the Beatrice deal being in trouble was simply the confirmation of a public rumor, which turned out to be wrong anyway. But none of this made any difference.

Freeman's guilty plea had terrifying implications for Wall Street because Freeman seemed to be only doing his job. What was

Freeman supposed to do? Having heard rumors that the deal was in trouble, Freeman called around to get additional information. Anyone else in the business was professionally obliged to do just that. The stakes in takeovers are far too high to act in ignorance when making major trading decisions, but nothing less seemed to satisfy the government. It was beginning to look like the government wanted the securities markets to resemble lotteries or gambling casinos after all, at least where takeover specialists were involved.

2: *Carpenter* v. *United States.* R. Foster Winans was a reporter for the *Wall Street Journal.* Because of his position, Winans was privy to information about upcoming stories about particular stocks in the *Journal's* "Heard on the Street" column. When the column was published, the stocks that were reported upon frequently moved in price. Winans was under a duty of confidentiality to the *Journal* not to disclose the contents of the column to outsiders until the column appeared.

Notwithstanding this confidentiality pledge, Winans told a ring of accomplices, Kenneth Felis and David Carpenter, the names of stocks included in upcoming "Heard on the Street" columns. Winans, Felis, and Carpenter bought and sold securities based on this advance information. They were then caught, criminally prosecuted, and convicted of securities, mail, and wire fraud. The Court of Appeals affirmed the convictions, and the Supreme Court decided to hear the case.

The case was a difficult one for the Court. What Winans and his accomplices did was clearly wrong but not obviously criminal. For one thing, the Court had never endorsed the misappropriation theory of liability, notwithstanding the eager acceptance of the theory by the SEC and lower courts following the earlier *Chiarella* decision. And *Carpenter* presented a very different situation from *Chiarella.* In *Chiarella* the unauthorized trading created the risk of direct economic injury to the acquirer by raising the price of shares to be acquired. In *Carpenter,* by contrast, the *Journal* had no interest in the shares traded and suffered no direct economic injury from the unauthorized trading. Similarly, the *Journal,* unlike the acquirer in *Chiarella,* was not an actual or potential purchaser or seller of securities. The wrongdoing in *Carpenter* was a breach of an employment agreement that caused no direct economic injury to the employer and had little, if any, connection to the securities marketplace. At most, the *Journal* suffered a reputational injury that might have caused its readers to have less confidence in the "Heard on the Street" column. Labeling this conduct criminal securities fraud would be novel, to say the least.

Perhaps recognizing these difficulties, the Court did not affirm the securities-fraud convictions, pronouncing itself equally divided on this issue. But the Court did unanimously affirm the mail- and wire-fraud convictions, reasoning that Winans's scheme constituted "embezzlement," which is part of the "concept of fraud." What Winans did, under the Court's view, was no different from embezzlement or other type of theft.

But it was different. Theft of tangible property has always been properly viewed as within the domain of the criminal law. Unauthorized possession of a car, for example, deprives the rightful owner of its use. The economic injury to the owner is clear. The same is not true for unauthorized possession of intangible property such as information or ideas. An idea, unlike a car, can be in the possession of, and used by, multiple people simultaneously. And because ideas can be created by different people independently, it is frequently difficult to determine whether possession is unauthorized or the product of one's own efforts. For these reasons, theft of information or ideas has never been viewed as a violation of the criminal laws except in the most extreme cases such as espionage. In the typical case, the injury to the victim is too indirect and the risk of punishing those who legitimately develop ideas on their own too great.

Carpenter dramatically expanded the scope of the criminal law. No case previously had ever criminalized a breach of an employment agreement where the direct economic injury to the employer was as remote as in *Carpenter*. Does *Carpenter* mean that all breaches of the employment agreement involving information are now criminal? What about the unauthorized use of customer lists, or Rolodex contacts, or daily business information? If anything, this conduct is a stronger candidate for criminal sanctions than what Winans did because of the greater potential economic injury to the employer. The law, however, has always treated unauthorized use of customer lists as a civil matter, and a relatively minor one at that. Winans should have been treated the same way.

But Winans was different because he was engaged in conduct that was perceived as part of the "insider-trading scandal" on Wall Street. The courts were becoming deeply politicized on the issue. Whether or not such traders actually violated existing securities laws and precisely how those laws should be interpreted was a detail—the mail- and wire-fraud statutes were good enough reason to bring a prosecution. Legalistic arguments may have saved Vincent Chiarella in 1981 before the public hysteria about insider trading and corruption on Wall Street. By 1987, however, it was hard to find any court, at any level, that was willing to let anyone accused of the heinous offense of "insider trading" off the hook.

3: *United States* v. *Chestman.* Robert Chestman was a stockbroker who in 1982 was hired by Keith Loeb to consolidate his and his wife's holdings in Waldbaum, Inc. From 1982 to 1986, Chestman executed various transactions in Waldbaum stock for Loeb. From these dealings, Chestman learned that Loeb's wife, Susan, was a granddaughter of Julia Waldbaum, a member of Waldbaum's board of directors, the wife of its founder, and the mother of its current president, Ira Waldbaum.

On November 21, 1986, Ira Waldbaum agreed to sell Waldbaum to Great Atlantic and Pacific Tea Company in a tender offer, with the offer to be publicly announced several days later. Ira then told his children and his sister, Shirley Witkin, Susan Loeb's mother, about the sale but told them confidentiality was essential until the offer was announced. Shirley then told Susan, who in turn told her husband, Keith Loeb, Chestman's client. Every communication was accompanied by an admonishment that the information was confidential.

Keith Loeb then telephoned Chestman at 8:59 A.M. on November 26 and left a message that Chestman should call "ASAP." According to Loeb he spoke with Chestman later that morning and told him that he had "some definite, some accurate information" that Waldbaum was about to be sold at a "substantially higher" price than its market value. Loeb did not reveal the source of this information or state that it was confidential. During the remainder of the day, Chestman purchased Waldbaum shares for his own accounts and for his clients' discretionary accounts, including the Loeb account.

Chestman was then indicted for trading on misappropriated information and for violating Rule 14e-3 by trading on material nonpublic information in advance of a tender offer. At trial, Chestman denied ever having spoken to Loeb on the morning of November 26 and claimed that his purchases were based on his own research. In support, Chestman pointed to his previous purchases of Waldbaum stock and other retail food stocks, stories in trade publications, and the unusually high trading volume of the stock on the day prior to his purchases, indicating Waldbaum was a possible takeover target. The jury nevertheless convicted Chestman on all counts, at least in part based on the testimony of Loeb, who agreed to cooperate with the government and was not criminally prosecuted. The Second Circuit Court of Appeals, the same court that had earlier affirmed the convictions of Foster Winans and his accomplices before the Supreme Court heard the case, affirmed Chestman's convictions.

The Second Circuit's decision in *Chestman* is very troubling. The court ruled that the SEC could adopt Rule 14e-3 in the interests of prohibiting securities fraud. But to delegate the creation of crimes to an administrative agency destroys the traditional constitutional right of defendants to have criminal statutes be construed narrowly. *Chiarella* had held that a trader could not be criminally convicted of securities fraud if he did not breach a fiduciary duty. Chestman violated no fiduciary duty under the law as defined by Congress and the courts and should not have been prosecuted. His conviction was inconsistent with some of the most basic elements of Anglo-American jurisprudence.

The *Chestman* decision also is deeply disturbing because it blurs the line between normal market activity and criminal conduct. Chestman was an analyst who followed and routinely traded Waldbaum stock. On the day before Loeb contacted Chestman, there had been an unexplained increase in the trading volume of the stock. This usually signals market participants that something unusual may be happening. Chestman, a market professional, was sure to notice this increase, and he so testified. Even if the conversation between Loeb and Chestman occurred (as Loeb testified but Chestman denied), its significance is unclear. Since Loeb by his own testimony did not tell Chestman the source of his information, relevant details such as the identity of the bidder or the offer price, or even that the information was confidential, Chestman may therefore have reasonably viewed the communication as nothing more than a rumor based on public information. Chestman also had no way of knowing the information was misappropriated.

Finally, *Chestman* is distressing because of how prosecutorial discretion was exercised. Loeb was the one party who knew the information was confidential in the case, though all he did was break a promise to his wife to keep it confidential. However trivial, this is the kind of peg prosecutors usually feel they need to hang their hat on. The government, however, declined to prosecute Loeb and instead went after Chestman, the presumptively unsavory stockbroker involved in the takeover game, who broke no promises and misappropriated from no one. Such sophistical and opportunistic prosecutorial decisions were an everyday occurrence in America's campaign to restore "confidence" in the nation's securities markets during the "decade of greed."

4: *United States* v. *Teicher.* Victor Teicher was a takeover arbitrageur. His job was to trade stocks of companies involved in takeover contests. Thus, Teicher routinely analyzed market information, industry trends, trading patterns, and takeover rumors. The government charged Teicher with buying stocks after receiving tips of imminent acquisitions.

At trial, Teicher admitted that he received tips but testified that he did not rely on them in making his trading decisions. Teicher claimed that the tips were nothing more than unsubstantiated rumors given to him by individuals trying to impress him so that they could become arbitrageurs themselves. Even under the government's theory of the case, much of the information Teicher received was vague, equivocal, and ultimately incorrect. For example, Teicher was allegedly told of a possible takeover attempt of American Can Company by Triangle Industries, which "would occur, if at all, within six months." This information turned out to be wrong. Similarly, Teicher supposedly was told of an imminent acquisition by BAT of American Brands, but the acquisition never occurred. Other tips informed him of meetings in conference rooms with no communication of the subject matter discussed. Moreover, Teicher's trading activity showed that he often traded against the tips. Sometimes he purchased and sold when, under the government's theory, he should have just purchased; another time he sold a rumored target short, demonstrating that he believed the tip of an imminent takeover to be false.

Yet the government argued, and the court agreed, that all this was irrelevant. The court instructed the jury that the government to convict didn't have to show that Teicher bought or sold because of tips. All the government had to show to win was that Teicher made any kind of trade after receiving valuable information:

> The government need not prove a causal relationship between the misappropriated material nonpublic information and the defen-

dants' trading. That is, the government need not prove that the defendants purchased or sold securities because of the material nonpublic information that they knowingly possessed. It is sufficient if the government proves that the defendants purchased or sold securities while knowingly in possession of the material nonpublic information.

With this sweeping instruction, the jury, not surprisingly, convicted Teicher on all counts. The conviction was affirmed on appeal by the Second Circuit.

Teicher is the ultimate victory for the government in its campaign to use the criminal laws to attack takeover arbitrageurs. It establishes what was only implied by Robert Freeman's guilty plea. By making mere possession of inside information a crime for any actively trading broker, *Teicher* effectively makes the whole industry of takeover arbitrage illegal. Arbitrageurs are in the business of ferreting out and interpreting information. They routinely came into contact with nonpublic rumors and other bits of information of varying degrees of reliability. This process is continuous, and investment decisions are made accordingly. A clever and ambitious prosecutor, aided by the testimony of government witnesses granted immunity, will always be able to allege that any arbitrageur who makes a profit from trading must have possessed "material" nonpublic information. After *Teicher*, this is all that is necessary to prove criminality. *Teicher* makes all arbitrageurs criminals waiting to be charged.

Arbitrageurs today literally have no way to protect themselves other than to quit the business altogether. Given the current state of the law, it's the only sure way to stay out of jail. What is certain is that the effectiveness of takeover arbitrageurs in facilitating hostile takeovers has been severely crippled. It may be that this was the goal of the government's war against insider trading all along.

Was the war on insider trading worth the effort? What was accomplished? Some white-collar criminals such as Dennis Levine and Ivan Boesky were caught, prosecuted, and sent to jail. This was all to the good, although Levine and Boesky could and should have suffered the same fate even if there were no laws against insider trading. Levine was guilty of tax fraud and theft, among other crimes. In fact, these crimes much better describe Levine's wrongdoing than insider trading does because they properly identify the victims of Levine's acts: his employer, the acquiring company, and the U.S. Treasury. Boesky was also guilty of theft and participating in Marty Siegel's tax fraud. Still, if the war on insider trading had focused solely on characters like Levine, Boesky, and Siegel, it may have been worthwhile.

But given the vagaries of the law, this would have required prosecutorial discretion near saintliness, and self-interested prosecutors like Rudy Giuliani were anything but saints. The intellectual incoherence of the war on insider trading only compounded the problem. By justifying its actions in moral terms and meaningless cliches such as the need to restore "investor confidence," all the hard questions were avoided and, ultimately, the decision to prosecute was made in accordance with the politics of the moment, not law.

It should have been obvious that something was seriously out of whack. How else could the government simultaneously claim that Vincent Chiarella, the dishonest printer, was engaging in the same illegal behavior as Raymond Dirks, the analyst who single-handedly uncovered one of the biggest frauds in history? How else could the SEC enact Rule 14e-3, which treats stealing information with being given it voluntarily as the same thing? How else could individuals like Robert Freeman be prosecuted for only doing their job? And how else could Congress and the courts serve as cheerleaders while penalties were increased for an offense that nobody could define in violation of the most basic rights traditionally guaranteed to criminal defendants?

Crazy or not, the government understood perfectly well how an unholy alliance between the left and the right supported its crackdown on players in the takeover game. On the right, the Nick Bradys of the world, the Business Roundtable, and organized labor cheered the government's efforts to preserve the status quo. On the left, the "decade of greed" rich haters were thrilled with the spectacle of the humiliation and degradation of wealthy and powerful financiers. This was all the support the government needed. By waging the war against insider trading, the government became the ally of the losers in the restructuring revolution. These losers never were able to regain their lost prominence by competing in the marketplace, but they didn't need to. The government did their work for them.

CHAPTER 3

The Criminalization of Regulatory Offenses

The government's attack on Wall Street was not limited to the war on insider trading. During the 1980s it repeatedly used the criminal laws to prosecute alleged violators of technical regulatory offenses. The highly publicized prosecutions of Drexel Burnham, Michael Milken, Boyd Jefferies, John Mulheren, Paul Bilzerian, and others were all based primarily, if not exclusively, on just such alleged technical violations.

The government did what it could to create an atmosphere of crisis to justify its regulatory zeal. Gary Lynch, the SEC's director of Enforcement, warned that regulatory offenses such as stock parking were "as serious as insider trading" and would be treated accordingly. William McLucas, Lynch's deputy, agreed that the government had to intervene because these offenses were "further weakening the industry's ability to command investor confidence." As with the war on insider trading, the government's efforts were primarily directed against participants in the takeover game. Stock-parking schemes, according to the SEC, were "corrupting the whole takeover process."

Indeed, the parallels to the war on insider trading were striking. Once again, the government radically expanded the scope of the criminal law to attack conduct that it could not and would not define. Routine trading practices were suddenly redefined as criminal, blurring the line between permissible and impermissible activity. The government reveled in sensationalized prosecutions challenging actions that harmed nobody and were either innocuous or economically beneficial to investors. What commentators referred to as a "wave of corruption" sweeping Wall Street would have been more accurately characterized as a wave of trivia, and perhaps not even that.

The government's reliance on the shopworn "investor confidence" rationale for prosecuting technical regulatory violations should have been a tip-off. The less reason the government had to act during the 1980s, the more it fell back on this meaningless slogan as its all-purpose justification.

Stock Parking and the Fischbach Transaction

Beginning in 1987, the *Wall Street Journal*, periodicals such as *Time*, *Newsweek*, and *Business Week*, and various legal trade journals all became fascinated with the new offense of stock parking. Stories with titles such as "Stock 'Parking' Becomes Big Factor in Insider Scandal," "Should Stock Parking Be a Criminal Offense?" and "Stock 'Parking' Schemes Have Become Controversial" appeared with regularity. This was no accident. Virtually every case the government brought against Wall Street firms or individuals contained allegations of stock parking. When Ivan Boesky pled guilty in October 1986, he pled guilty not to insider trading but to engaging in an illegal stock-parking scheme. For his crimes he was sentenced to three years in prison, ordered to pay a $100 million fine, and banned from the securities industry for life.

What is stock parking? The term is nowhere defined in the securities laws. Nor is there any other law that defines, let alone criminalizes, the "parking" of stock. Under common usage, stock parking occurs when a nominee purchases securities from or on behalf of the true owner on the understanding that the securities will be later bought back by the owner, who bears the risk of gain or loss. The purpose of the practice is to conceal the owner's identity. There is nothing necessarily illegal about stock parking. In fact, sophisticated investors routinely attempt to disguise their identity and the size of their transactions by utilizing the services of multiple brokers and other nominees. If investors learn that somebody smart is buying in large amounts, they often conclude that the shares are a bargain and refuse to sell or buy themselves. But if they have no idea that a big player is buying, they won't take any of these steps. Smart investors can then transact on more advantageous terms. Such "stock-parking schemes" are an everyday occurrence in securities markets.

In fact, such "schemes" are an everyday occurrence in all markets. Renowned art experts do not show up at auctions because their actions reveal too much information to others deciding whether and how much to bid. It makes more sense for experts to use anonymous agents to bid for them with the understanding that the agent is paid for his services but does not bear the risk of gain or loss. Stock-parking "schemes" are no different.

Sometimes, however, stock-parking arrangements can be used to evade specific regulations. For example, broker-dealers are heavily regulated by the securities laws. They must meet minimum net-capital requirements, maintain extensive records, and are often prohibited by the margin requirements from using credit. Broker-dealers who park clients' stock may run afoul of each of these requirements.

The enactment of Section 13(d) of the Williams Act in 1968, which requires a filing with the government when you acquire 5 percent or more of a company's stock, created a new use for parking arrangements. By entering into a stock-parking arrangement, and thus not counting the shares being held by your nominee, a potential acquirer can postpone, or even avoid, a 13(d) filing. This may enable the potential acquirer to purchase stock in secrecy at lower prices for a longer time if the public filing causes an increase in market price.

Historically, regulators have never viewed alleged stock-parking schemes as major offenses or given them a high priority. Violations of net-capital, margin, and record-keeping regulations accomplished by alleged parking schemes historically have either been ignored or treated as minor, technical infractions. Nobody had ever suggested that such technical violations should be treated as major crimes. Even parking schemes allegedly designed to avoid compliance with the disclosure requirements of the Williams Act and Section 13(d) were viewed as civil regulatory violations with the penalty being a slap on the wrist. In the typical case, the potential acquirer was ordered to file a revised 13(d) statement disclosing all nominee shares. In an unusual case that was considered a major breakthrough at the time, the SEC successfully sued the Belzberg family of Canada to disgorge their profits obtained from parking stock with Bear, Stearns, which caused the filing of a 13(d) statement to be delayed, and thereby allegedly allowed the Belzbergs to purchase shares at lower prices. But having to give back illegal profits in a civil case is not the same as being accused of being a felon and subjected to criminal prosecution.

The historical reluctance of regulators to treat stock-parking arrangements as serious offenses is understandable. Such schemes are hard to prove because the agreements creating the repurchase obligation and allocating the risk of gain or loss are typically oral and informal. For this reason, they are also very hard to distinguish from routine accommodations between parties with a long-term course of dealing. A broker-dealer firm might be willing to reimburse a good client for losses suffered as a result of following its recommendations, or it may be willing to provide the client with other services at reduced cost to maintain good relations. Such accommodations may be routine marketing expenditures, or they may be evidence of an unlawful arrangement. It is often impossible to distinguish between the two potential scenarios. And when it is difficult to distinguish legitimate from illegitimate behavior, society tends to avoid use of the criminal laws. The danger of convicting innocent people is simply too great.

Also, stock-parking schemes, because of their informal and ambiguous nature, never completely shift market risk because whatever agreements are reached cannot be enforced. There is always the risk that if market prices change unexpectedly one of the parties may renege. If a nominee purchases a security and its price rises dramatically, for example, the nominee may decide to keep the profits and refuse to sell the security back to the supposed true owner at cost. Similarly, the supposed owner may refuse to purchase if the security falls in price, leaving the nominee to absorb the loss. Parking schemes thus never allocate ownership and the risk of gain or loss definitively. At most, parking arrangements are expectations of what will occur enforced by the reputations of parties with ongoing relationships.

Finally, parking schemes typically have no victims. They enable investors to capitalize on profitable investment opportunities by not disclosing their identity. It is hard to justify use of the criminal law to punish traders who engage in wealth-creating activities and harm no one.

None of these reasons for treating stock parking as a minor, technical offense mattered during the frenzied atmosphere of the 1980s. Now no penalty was perceived as too severe for those who profited from "abuses" on Wall Street. Under the new regime, stock parking became the government's favorite theory of criminal prosecution during the 1980s.

If stock parking was the government's pet theory of criminal prosecution, then Fischbach was their favorite transaction. Story after story in the *Wall Street Journal* and elsewhere in the 1980s detailed how the government was focusing on the events leading up to the takeover of Fischbach Corporation by Victor Posner as the most evil of all the criminal parking schemes. For their role in this single transaction, Ivan Boesky, Drexel Burnham, and Michael Milken all pled guilty to felonies. In a separate proceeding, Judge Milton Pollack, who abandoned any pretense of impartiality and became a recognized leader of the government's lynch mob, barred Victor Posner and his son from serving as directors of a public company for life because of their role in the Fischbach transaction.

What happened in Fischbach? In January 1980, Pacific Engineering Corporation ("PEC"), a public company controlled by Victor Posner, began accumulating shares in Fischbach Corporation, an electrical and mechanical contracting company traded on the New York Stock Exchange. Soon thereafter, PEC filed a Schedule 13(d) statement disclosing that it had purchased slightly over 10 percent of Fischbach's outstanding common stock. Fischbach's management reacted with hostility to the disclosure and threatened to retaliate.

In August 1980, Fischbach and Posner resolved their differences by entering into a standstill agreement. Under the agreement, PEC could not acquire more than 24.9 percent of Fischbach's outstanding common stock for a five-year period unless some other party unaffiliated with PEC or Posner filed a Schedule 13(d) indicating ownership of over 10 percent of Fischbach's stock, or made a tender offer to acquire control. The agreement, in effect, allowed Posner through PEC to increase his holdings in Fischbach to 24.9 percent without opposition but prevented Posner from acquiring control unless some other party acquired a large block or made a tender offer.

Pursuant to the agreement, PEC increased the size of its holdings of Fischbach to 24.8 percent as it disclosed in an amended Schedule 13(d) filed in September 1981. In February 1983, the parties extended the standstill agreement for an additional five years, until August 1990. At the same time, Fischbach revealed its nervousness about a possible takeover attempt by announcing that ten top executives had been awarded lucrative "golden parachute" contracts. These contracts provided that top management would receive approximately $7 million in the event of a change in control.

Later that year such a change in control seemed a distinct possibility when Executive Life announced that it had acquired a 14.4 percent ownership interest in Fischbach. This announcement, made on December 30, caused the price of Fischbach shares to rise significantly, from $50 to $54, as investors anticipated a possible takeover attempt. Just a few days later, on January 9, 1984, however, Fischbach ended the threat by purchasing Executive Life's entire interest. Investors were disappointed by the announcement, and Fischbach's stock price declined back to $50 as a result.

A dispute then arose as to whether the Executive Life filing of its 14.4 percent ownership interest ended the standstill agreement. Because of a technicality in securities regulation, insurance companies like Executive Life file 13(g), not 13(d) schedules, and so the standstill agreement, which referred specifically to 13(d) schedules, arguably still remained in effect. At least this was Fischbach's position. Posner disagreed, and he had a strong argument. It turned out that Executive Life had made a 13(d) filing as well as a 13(g), although it was under no obligation to do so. And Fischbach's management was sufficiently nervous about a takeover attempt that they attempted to entrench themselves further by having the company adopt a series of antitakeover measures. The effort failed in February 1984 when shareholders refused to go along.

Immediately thereafter, Ivan Boesky called Michael Milken asking for investment advice about Fischbach, and Milken responded by encouraging Boesky to accumulate Fischbach stock. By July of 1984, Boesky announced that his company, Ivan F. Boesky, Corp., had acquired more than a 10 percent ownership position and had so disclosed in a series of 13(d) filings. The press speculated that Boesky was motivated by the possibility of a greenmail transaction—selling his stock back to Fischbach at a premium over the market price. Since Fischbach purchased Executive Life's stake within a week after learning about it, maybe it would do the same for Boesky. Whatever Boesky's motivation, his 13(d) filings disclosing a greater than 10 percent ownership position broke the standstill agreement, ending any ambiguity about whether

Executive Life's earlier filings had the same effect. Posner was now free to seek control of Fischbach.

Disaster struck immediately after the Boesky group disclosed its greater than 10 percent ownership position in July 1984. On July 19, 1984, a federal grand jury in Philadelphia indicted Fischbach for rigging bids on electrical construction projects. The Justice Department then expanded the criminal investigation to other allegedly illegal practices by Fischbach. A series of criminal convictions and guilty pleas resulted. In the second half of 1984, Fischbach's stock price fell from over $50 to the low $30s as the weight of the government's criminal investigations weakened Fischbach's business. Boesky, who had paid over $50 for his shares, was now stuck with a major loss, for which he blamed Milken. Eventually in early 1985, Boesky sold his Fischbach stock to Posner for $45 per share in a transaction on the London Stock Exchange at a time when it was trading at $36. Posner was willing to pay this premium over the market price because the block purchase facilitated his obtaining control of Fischbach, which he subsequently did. Drexel and Milken arranged financing for the transaction.

The government's theory of prosecution went as follows: Posner bought Fischbach as a result of a conspiracy between Posner, Drexel, Milken, Boesky, and possibly Executive Life (although it was never charged), which enabled Posner to break the standstill agreement. When Boesky purchased Fischbach shares, he was acting as Milken's agent, because Milken had guaranteed him against loss. Because Boesky did not disclose the stock-parking scheme in his 13(d) filings, he committed a crime, and Milken aided and abetted this crime. And because Drexel did not record Milken's alleged guarantee against loss of Boesky in its books and records, it committed a crime as well. Boesky, Drexel, and Milken admitted as much by their guilty pleas. Posner denied being part of the conspiracy, but Judge Pollack after a bench trial in which Boesky and Milken both testified, concluded the opposite.

The guilty pleas and Judge Pollack notwithstanding, there is considerable doubt as to whether any stock-parking arrangement ever existed. In fact, the evidence reveals that the primary "abuse" that occurred in Fischbach was by the government. Nothing that any of the participants did compared with the government's abuse of prosecutorial discretion.

The government's theory of what occurred in Fischbach relies on the premise that Posner used Milken to break the standstill agreement, and to do so Milken enlisted Boesky and guaranteed him against risk of gain or loss. If on the contrary Boesky did bear the investment risk, his purchases legitimately terminated the standstill agreement and his 13(d) filings disclosing his stock accumulations were accurate and lawful. The understanding between Boesky and Milken is critical, therefore, in determining whether there was a stock-parking scheme.

Both Boesky and Milken have testified about that understanding. Boesky, who pled guilty to a felony in connection with the Fischbach transaction and became a cooperating government witness as part of his plea agreement, has explained his arrangement with Milken as follows:

> Q. How soon before you bought your first share of Fischbach did you have the conversation, your first conversation with Milken about Fischbach?
> A. I believe it was very soon before I began buying.
> Q. OK. And did Milken say to you in that conversation that he would guarantee you against loss?
> A. Those were not the words, never were the words.
> Q. It's the code you were talking about, the Wall Street code?
> A. I never used that word either. It was an understanding.
> Q. OK. What are the words that you remember Milken using, not your understanding, I want to know the words you remember Milken using in that first conversation?
> A. "Just buy it, don't worry about it," something to that effect . . . I've forgotten the exact language or the specific conversation.

Incredibly, the multiple criminal prosecutions that arose from Fischbach were based on this vague "just buy it, don't worry about it" statement, which Boesky did not even definitively remember or describe. What he did recall was that Milken *never* guaranteed him against loss. Boesky's self-serving and vague recollection in hindsight was instead that Milken told him not to "worry" about his Fischbach purchases. He just went along with the government's idea that maybe the conversation could be construed to have insured him against any losses he might suffer in reliance on Milken's recommendation.

Boesky's testimony regarding the rest of his conversations with Milken was equally ambiguous. When the price of Fischbach plummeted in the second half of 1984, Boesky testified that he expressed "concern" to Milken. Boesky testified that the conversations with Milken "weren't particularly lengthy or weighty or meaty conversations. I might just say, you know, something like, 'Gee, it's down quite a bit.' And he would say, 'Don't worry about it.' " This was the best Boesky could do to support the government's theory that Milken was the real purchaser, parking Fischbach stock with Boesky and guaranteeing him against any loss.

Finally, Boesky testified that Milken, through Drexel, made good on his promise to guarantee him against loss in connection with his Fischbach investment. Ultimately, Boesky, who bought Fischbach in the low $50s and sold at $45, lost approximately $2 million. This loss, Boesky claimed, was borne by Drexel:

Q. Were you eventually compensated for these losses?
A. Yes, I was.
Q. Who compensated you?
A. The firm of Drexel Burnham.
Q. How did Drexel Burnham do this?
A. Well, we had had a variety of trades with one another that were being kept a record of and this was one of them and it was an offset to other profits and losses between us, and in the netting out of these transactions at a point in time this was taken into account.

Milken, who also pled guilty to a felony in connection with his role in Fischbach but never became a cooperating government witness, gave a strikingly different characterization of what transpired. When Milken was asked whether he encouraged Boesky to purchase Fischbach, Milken testified that "I mentioned to him that I thought the investment had little or no downside risk, yes." Milken testified that he based this opinion on Fischbach's strength as a company, its willingness to repurchase its stock from Executive Life, and Posner's declared intention to acquire control of Fischbach. "For an arbitrageur like Boesky," Milken testified, "this was the ideal situation to invest in."

Milken further testified that Boesky began complaining incessantly when Fischbach's stock price fell in the second half of 1984. Milken responded that while he did not expect Boesky to lose money, he would "make good" on any losses Boesky incurred:

Q. And it's true that after Mr. Boesky began his purchasing of Fischbach securities he eventually exceeded a 10 percent position in that security, is that not correct?

A. Yes, it is.

Q. Am I correct that thereafter as the price of Fischbach began to drop Mr. Boesky began to call and to repeatedly tell you that Drexel was responsible for his losses and that he expected Drexel to make good on those losses?

A. Well, not in those exact words, but yes, to that effect.

Q. In words or substance, right?

A. Yes.

Q. What did you say to Mr. Boesky at that time in response to those repeated requests for assurance?

A. Well, the first few times that he called to complain, I told him, "Don't worry about it." I did not really respond to his complaints. And sometime I believe at the end of the year, either in November or December, I assured him that we would make good on the fact that he would not lose any money, if he did lose money. At that time I did not expect him to lose any money.

Milken testified that he wanted to keep Boesky happy because he was a valued customer who paid large fees to Drexel in connection with various financings and restructurings of Boesky entities. He also testified that he never expected to have to make good on the guarantee because he believed Boesky's Fischbach stock would be sold for a large premium in a takeover. Moreover, even if there was a loss, it wouldn't cost Drexel anything. When Drexel did make good on Boesky's $2 million loss, it did so not by writing a check, but by recommending other profitable investments to Boesky. It was nothing more than a routine accommodation for a good client. When asked to reconcile his version of events with his felony guilty plea, Milken testified that he committed a record-keeping violation because "there was no documentation—which is why I pled to it—of my guarantee of making up the loss."

While Boesky and Milken's characterization of the relevant events differ dramatically, their description of the events themselves is quite similar. Both agree that Boesky purchased

Fischbach based on a recommendation by Milken, that Milken told Boesky that Drexel would cover any losses, and that Drexel later made good on this promise by providing Boesky with valuable investment recommendations. They differ only in their claimed subjective understanding of the events at issue. Boesky testified that he understood Milken's statement not to "worry" about Fischbach to be a guarantee against loss; Milken testified that the same statement meant that there was little or no downside risk in purchasing Fischbach stock. Boesky testified that he believed Milken's assurance in late 1984 that Boesky would not lose money was a recognition of his earlier guarantee against loss; Milken testified that he believed this assurance was an accommodation to a valued client who was complaining about receiving bad advice.

Either way, however, no one ever claimed that there was any mechanism, such as an explicit stock-parking arrangement between Milken and Boesky, that would enforce a guarantee against loss. Nor did Boesky ever indicate that he intended to give Drexel his profits, as Milken's nominee, if he made money on Fischbach, which would have been the case had it in fact been a stock-parking situation. So how can Boesky plausibly be charged with a major criminal felony by failing to disclose Milken's alleged guarantee of his arrangement with Milken in a 13(d)? Or Milken for failing to record a guarantee in Drexel's books and records? Such ambiguous disputes, based solely on parties' different subjective understandings of relevant events, should not be the basis of criminal felony prosecutions.

Apart from the ambiguity of the events, the other notable aspect of the Fischbach transaction is its complete insignificance. At worst, assuming Posner was involved in a conspiracy with Boesky and Milken, there was a breach of the standstill agreement between Posner and Fischbach. Undoing takeover defenses such as standstill agreements may harm the executives of a particular company who wind up losing their jobs in a takeover, but shareholders usually are the beneficiaries.

It is certainly hard to feel sorry for Fischbach's management, the supposed victims of Posner, Boesky, and Milken's stock-parking scheme. They did everything they could to entrench themselves. They negotiated the standstill agreement, they awarded themselves golden parachutes, they purchased Executive Life's stock, causing Fischbach's stock price to plunge, and they attempted to block a hostile takeover attempt but were thwarted because of shareholder opposition. The company also lost half its value during their tenure as a result of their illegal bid-rigging price-fixing activities. Under these circumstances, their ouster by takeover specialists was hardly cause for aggressive prosecution under the criminal law.

Why then did Judge Pollack ban Posner and his son for life from ever serving as director of a public company? Nominally, Judge Pollack, who has publicly expressed his contempt for Milken, concluded that Posner and his son were involved in a scheme to break the standstill agreement with Milken and Boesky. But this was a fabrication. There was no evidence suggesting that Posner was involved in any such scheme. Not even Boesky could implicate Posner, which explains why Posner was never prosecuted.

The real reason was different. Victor Posner is a well-known takeover specialist, a corporate "raider" who, according to popular myth, "loots" companies. He has been in repeated skirmishes with the SEC and, even prior to Fischbach, had twice been charged by the SEC for violations of the securities laws. In both of these cases, Posner settled the charges by agreeing not to violate the laws again. In 1982, he was charged with criminal tax fraud in a ten-count felony indictment. He entered a plea of *nolo contendere*, a fancy way to plead guilty, after the trial judge declared a mistrial and set aside a jury verdict convicting him. Summarizing these events, the SEC told Judge Pollack that Posner's involvement with public companies "has been marked by self-dealing, lavish perquisites for himself and his family, the use of corporate funds to pay personal expenses, and subordinating the interests of public shareholders to his own."

Judge Pollack banned Posner and his son for life from running public companies because he accepted this characterization. But this had nothing to do with Posner's role in Fischbach, which was innocuous. Moreover, Posner's overall record is not all one-sided. Like other maligned takeover specialists, Posner created wealth for investors and society as a whole. His track record during the early 1980s was particularly impressive (he hasn't done as well in recent years). But Judge Pollack wasn't interested in a fair assessment of Posner's overall career. Posner and his son did business with Drexel and Milken. Thus, they had to be purged. While they got a raw deal, at least they didn't wind up in jail.

Fischbach was far from the only highly publicized stock-parking prosecution of the 1980s. Another was the government's prosecution of Boyd Jefferies, which resulted from Ivan Boesky's guilty plea and his agreement to cooperate and implicate others in exchange for a lighter sentence. Based on information supplied by Boesky, the government alleged that Boesky and Jefferies through their companies, Seemala Corporation and Jefferies & Company, both regulated broker-dealers, entered into a series of reciprocal stock-parking arrangements to avoid minimum capital, margin, and record-keeping requirements.

Under governing regulations, brokers must maintain sufficient net capital. Securities owned are subject to "haircuts," meaning that their value for regulatory purposes is less than their market value. Purchasing securities with cash, therefore, causes regulatory capital to fall even if the securities are purchased at market value. The government alleged that Jefferies & Company and Seemala routinely purchased securities as nominees for each other to avoid falling below the required level of net capital. Because these parking transactions can be viewed as extensions of credit by the nominee to the owner without collateral, the government also charged Jefferies with criminal violations of the margin rules. And because the parking arrangements were not recorded, the government also charged Jefferies with criminal books-and-records violations.

Even if there had been an arrangement between Jefferies and Boesky, precisely as alleged, this had always before been considered a minor, technical regulatory violation. Such an arrangement made it possible for Boesky and Jefferies to evade the net-capital rules and make profitable investments. The violations were temporary, and there was no possibility of harm to anyone. The understanding was that the securities purchased by the nominee would be repurchased by the true owner when it was again in compliance with the net-capital rules. Otherwise, no repurchase would occur and the nominee would be stuck with the security.

Technical violation or not, Jefferies quickly became another scalp in the government's trophy belt. Once implicated by Boesky, Jefferies decided to give up without a fight. He pled guilty to margin violations and aiding and abetting Seemala's books-and-records violations.

The government's campaign to criminalize stock parking could only be described as a rousing success. It resulted in guilty pleas by some of the biggest names on Wall Street. So if they hadn't committed any crimes, why did they plead guilty? For Boesky, his plea copped him a deal by which he avoided prosecution on the far more serious offenses of his insider-trading ring with Dennis Levine and Martin Siegel, including the infamous suitcase full of cash. Jefferies probably overestimated the strength of the government's case as well as Boesky's credibility as a witness, whose lack thereof had not yet been exposed.

Jefferies no doubt was also influenced by the sweet deal he got from the government. He spent no time in jail, and he was allowed to keep his ownership interest in Jefferies & Company, the leading after-hours market maker and block-trade specialist. While banned from participating in the securities industry, he was given the right to seek reinstatement after five years. There was only one catch. Jefferies had to do what Boesky did—implicate others. This he was more than willing to do. He was to become a star government witness.

For Milken, the decision was the most complicated of all. Perhaps he too overestimated the strength of the case. Or, perhaps, he concluded he could not win, no matter what. As the ultimate symbol of the "decade of greed," he may have believed the government would stop at nothing to convict him, break him, or both. In this, as subsequent events would confirm, he was surely right.

Stock Manipulation and the Prosecutions of John Mulheren and James Sherwin

Stock manipulation was another favorite government theory of prosecution during the 1980s. As with stock parking and insider trading, the government radically expanded the scope of the criminal laws and blurred the line between legitimate and illegitimate trading practices in the process. Once again, the primary targets of the government's wrath were arbitrageurs and other players in the takeover game.

Manipulation, like insider trading and stock parking, is not defined in the securities laws or other regulatory statutes. The term is commonly understood to be conduct intended to cause securities to trade at "artificial prices." Such conduct distorts securities markets by "interfering with the free play of supply and demand."

Certain manipulative practices are no different from fraud. If an underwriter interested in selling a newly issued security to the public "paints the tape" by recording a series of transactions at high prices that are in fact not occurring, a fraud is committed. The investing public is misled into believing there is intense interest in the stock. The phony trades are manipulative because they cause prices to trade at "artificial levels" by interfering with the "free play of supply and demand." Frauds involving such phony trades or fictitious sales have always been considered unlawful manipulative practices. Historically, the government has always prosecuted people who engage in such fraudulent schemes.

But none of the well-publicized stock-manipulation prosecutions of the 1980s involved allegations of this type of violation. Instead, the government prosecuted traders who were alleged to have traded with improper "manipulative intent." Under the government's new view, trading with manipulative intent was no different from lying or recording phony transactions to defraud investors.

But how can you tell a trade made with bad intent from one that is not? Everything turns on the trader's state of mind. Trading for investment purposes is fine, but trading to force prices to "artificial levels" is prohibited. But what is an "artificial" price? Philosophers and theologians have struggled with this question for centuries and have yet to come up with an answer.

How can trades intended to move prices to "artificial" levels be identified if there is no way to define "artificial" prices? Proving intent is a universal problem in the law, but it is usually inferred from objective evidence. If I buy a gun under an assumed name, lure my enemy to a secluded spot, and then fatally shoot him, it is reasonable to infer that I intended to commit murder. Similarly, if I record a series of phony transactions, it is reasonable to infer that I intended to fool investors into believing a stock is hot.

But in the government's new theory of manipulation, there is no improper conduct from which illegal intent can be inferred. All that is observable is a trade indistinguishable from other trades. This is true even if there is a price reaction following a trade. The price reaction may be caused by other factors such as a movement in the overall market or news about the firm. Even if the trade causes the price movement, the trader may still have been motivated by legitimate investment objectives.

Finally, any price reaction may be temporary due to the bid-ask spread. Market makers earn a living by the spread between what they are willing to pay (the bid) and what they are willing to sell for (the ask). If the spread is $10/$10.50, and the last trade was a purchase by the market maker at $10, then the next trade will be at $10.50 if it is a purchase from the market maker. Obviously, the observed price increase from $10 to $10.50 reflects the bid-ask spread and not manipulation.

Nor can improper intent be inferred from trading practices such as trading at the end of the day or short selling. Trading is typically heaviest at the end (and at the beginning) of the day. Prior to the market's closing, traders must decide whether to close out their positions or take a position overnight until the next day. Because the stakes are higher, trading is heavier. Similarly, short selling is a way for those who believe that the price of a security will fall to express those beliefs. Like trading at the end of the day, short selling is a perfectly legitimate trading practice. Neither practice is evidence of manipulation.

There is another problem with the government's expanded view of manipulation—the difficulty of profiting from the alleged unlawful scheme. Frauds are committed for financial gain. If there is no possibility of financial gain, there will be no fraud. In manipulation cases involving actual trades, the trade is supposedly made to move prices to artificial levels. Once made, the manipulator then has to somehow get rid of his holdings. If this second trade causes prices to return to their original level, the manipulation has accomplished nothing. Indeed, the alleged manipulator is worse off because he has paid double brokerage commissions and borne other costs to accomplish the transaction, such as the risk of price fluctuations during the holding period. Sometimes this risk can be substantial. When the Hunt brothers allegedly attempted to manipulate the silver market in the late 1970s, they went bankrupt as a reward for their efforts. This difficulty of making money, coupled with the inability to distinguish between legitimate and improper trades, should have made the government skeptical of its new expanded view of manipulation.

But perhaps this misses the point. Maybe the government's objective was not to punish wrongdoers and deter harmful conduct, but rather to have maximum discretion to use the criminal laws against whomever they chose. For this purpose, the conceptual problems with the expanded view of manipulation, like the similar problems with stock parking and the refusal to define insider trading, were a plus. The inability to distinguish manipulative from nonmanipulative trades made it possible for the government, with the aid of a cooperating witness, to accuse traders of criminal wrongdoing for essentially routine trading practices, whenever it chose.

Once again Ivan Boesky is at the center of the story. When Boesky pled guilty to stock parking in Fischbach, he agreed to cooperate fully with the government in exchange for lenience. He then implicated John A. Mulheren, Jr., the chief trader and general partner of Jamie Securities Company, in multiple illegal activities including the manipulation of Gulf + Western Industries' stock price in 1985.

Mulheren was a Wall Street phenom whose skill as a trader and arbitrageur had made him rich beyond his wildest dreams. Although he lived lavishly, commuting to and from work in a private helicopter, Mulheren was also generous with his wealth. He gave millions to charity and to educational institutions. When the mood took him, as it often did on Christmas Eve, Mulheren would go to a poor section of New York and hand out tens of thousands of dollars in hundred-dollar bills.

Mulheren was known as one of Ivan Boesky's few friends on the street. The two attended each other's major family events; Mulheren served as trustee for Boesky's children and hosted a tribute dinner for Boesky at the Jewish Theological Seminary. Boesky and Mulheren also had a close professional relationship. They spoke frequently, and each respected the acumen of the other.

In the mid-1980s, Mulheren was on top of the world and didn't have to work another day in his life. Yet he decided to start up a new investment firm, Jamie Securities. It was an immediate success. Mulheren did have one major problem—he was a diagnosed manic depressive and needed to take medication to control his extreme mood swings. Sometimes, however, the medication didn't work or he forgot to take it. His behavior was unpredictable, but even this was not all bad. Mulheren felt his mental condition made him a better trader.

Mulheren's world changed when Boesky pled guilty in the fall of 1986 and began to implicate others as his plea agreement required. When it became clear the government was planning to indict him, Mulheren's lawyer, Otto Obermaier, encouraged him to cop a plea, as Boesky and others had done. Obermaier believed he could work out a deal where Mulheren would plead to a minor, technical offense and avoid incarceration. Obermaier was convinced that if Mulheren refused to plead, he would likely be indicted, convicted, and sentenced to jail. In laying out the options and recommending that his client plead guilty, Obermaier was following the conventional wisdom of the 1980s.

But Mulheren was no conventional criminal defendant. He was convinced of his innocence. The more Obermaier urged him to plead, the less Mulheren trusted him. Distrust became paranoia, fueled by his manic depression, and Mulheren became increasingly distraught. After Mulheren told his wife, Obermaier, and others that he wanted "to kill" Boesky or commit suicide, Obermaier tipped off the U.S. attorney. Mulheren was arrested while in possession of a loaded semiautomatic rifle and other weapons, which meant he was in deep trouble. Mulheren was to remain in custody for almost three months, first in jail and then in a private psychiatric hospital.

During Mulheren's time in custody, the government played hardball with him. While in jail, he was kept in holding cells for hours on end in anticipation of court appearances that never materialized. The government opposed his transfer to a private psychiatric hospital and objected to visits by Mulheren's own psychiatrist. Some observers thought the government was trying to "break" Mulheren in retaliation for his refusal to cooperate.

All the while Mulheren remained in custody, Obermaier continued to recommend a guilty plea. Mulheren refused. Increasingly, he felt that Obermaier was more interested in good relationships with the government than in representing him. Eventually, Mulheren fired Obermaier, replacing him with Thomas Puccio, another well-known criminal lawyer. Mulheren felt his suspicions were confirmed when Obermaier was chosen shortly thereafter to be U.S. attorney for the Southern District of New York.

Obermaier too found some vindication. As he had predicted, the government eventually grew tired of Mulheren's stonewalling. In June 1989, the government indicted Mulheren on forty-two counts, based on the securities laws. Among the allegations, the government charged that Mulheren conspired to and did manipulate the price of Gulf + Western Industries' ("G+W") common stock by purchasing seventy-five thousand shares on October 17, 1985, for the purpose of raising its price to $45 per share.

At trial, the evidence showed that Ivan Boesky's companies purchased approximately 3.4 million shares of G+W's common stock, approximately 4.9 percent of the outstanding shares. Carl Icahn, another prominent arbitrageur, also accumulated a sizeable position. In September and October 1985, Boesky and Icahn had discussions with Martin Davis, G+W's chairman, in which they expressed interest in taking over the company through a leveraged buyout or, alternatively, purchasing additional shares and obtaining representation on G+W's board of directors.

When Davis rejected these proposals, Boesky proposed on October 1, 1985, that G+W buy back his 4.9 percent stake at $45 per share. Davis did not reject the idea but would not commit to a price. After the close of trading on October 16, Boesky contacted Davis and renewed his offer to sell at $45 per share. Davis responded that G+W would purchase his shares but only at the price at which G+W stock last traded on the New York Stock Exchange at the time of the transaction.

During this same period Mulheren also contacted Martin Davis. Unlike Boesky, however, Mulheren expressed no interest in seeking control of G+W. Rather, Mulheren wanted to know whether G+W would join with other investors in an attempt to acquire CBS. These talks went nowhere. On October 16, 1985, the same day that Boesky contacted Davis to renew his offer to sell out of his stake at $45, Mulheren decided to sell twenty-five thousand shares of G+W short, after another broker asked him if he was willing to sell. By agreeing to sell shares he did not own, Mulheren obligated himself to purchase the shares sometime in the future to cover his short position. If, as he was betting, the price of G+W shares fell, his profit per share would be the difference between G+W's price at the time of the short sale and the price at the time of the later purchase.

The critical events occurred on the next day, October 17. Sometime before 11:00 A.M. that morning, Boesky called Mulheren. The discussion focused on G+W stock. When asked at trial by the government what was said in that conversation, Boesky answered:

A. Mr. Mulheren asked me if I liked the stock on that particular day, and I said yes, I still like it. At the time it was trading at forty-four and three-quarters. I said I liked it; however, I

would not pay more than forty-five for it and it would be
great if it traded at forty-five.

Q. What if anything did he say to you?

A. I understand.

Mulheren testified about the same conversation. According to
Mulheren, Boesky called him that morning to ask what
Mulheren's position was in G+W. He testified that he told Boesky
that he took a short position in G+W the day before, and Boesky
responded, "I think it's the kind of stock you want to be in," suggesting that Boesky believed it was a mistake to be short in G+W.
Mulheren further testified that Boesky's recommendation
changed his view of the stock: "The one thing I was definitely
going to do was cover my short, because I had a real smart guy
telling me not to be short in the stock, be long in it." On the $45
price, Mulheren testified that G+W was "up a lot the day before
and I didn't think I would pay higher than forty-five . . . and he
said 'I wouldn't pay higher than forty-five either.'"

As with Fischbach, the parties' testimony differed, not so much
in what occurred but in their subjective understandings of what
occurred. Boesky testified that he thought he was telling
Mulheren to buy so as to cause G+W to move up a notch and
trade at $45. Mulheren, by contrast, testified that he thought
Boesky was advising him to be long in the stock, not short, but
not to pay more than $45. Under both versions, Boesky recom-
mended that Mulheren purchase at any price up to $45.

That is exactly what Mulheren did. Between 11:04 and 11:10
A.M., Jamie, Mulheren's firm, bought seventy-five thousand
shares of G+W at prices of $44 $3/4$ (the closing price the day
before), $44 $7/8$, and $45. At 11:17 A.M., just seven minutes later,
Boesky and Icahn sold their G+W stock—6,715,000 shares
between them—back to the company at $45 per share. The stock
closed at $43 $5/8$ that day; Jamie sold its position at the end of the
day at a loss. Mulheren testified that when he learned of Boesky
and Icahn's sale, he felt "pissed off" and that he had been "used"
by Boesky, who was a "son of a bitch."

What are we to make of the cryptic conversation between
Boesky and Mulheren? It was ambiguous at best. Boesky's testimony that he told Mulheren that it would be "great" if G+W
traded at $45, if believed, was consistent with Boesky's admission
that he was guilty of manipulation. Boesky obviously wanted the

stock to trade at $45 so that he could get out at the target price he had demanded of Martin Davis. But how does this incriminate Mulheren? Even Boesky admitted that he never revealed to Mulheren his plan to sell at $45. Mulheren had no reason to know of Boesky's attempted manipulation. And if manipulation were Boesky's plan, why would he tell Mulheren that he liked G+W but "would not pay more than $45 for it"? The higher the price, the greater Boesky's profits. This fundamental contradiction in Boesky's story cast further doubt on whether Mulheren could reasonably have inferred Boesky's manipulative scheme.

Boesky carried considerable baggage as a witness. He was testifying as a friendly government witness who received a lighter sentence in exchange for his cooperation. Plus, he wasn't great on the witness stand. Under cross-examination, he freely admitted lying on numerous occasions and violating prison rules. When asked about his personal finances and his prior wrongdoing, he repeatedly weakened his credibility by saying he couldn't remember. He "could not recall," for example, whether he transferred assets out of his name to limit his exposure to creditors just prior to taking his plea.

Finally, there was one other reason to like Mulheren's chances of avoiding conviction. Boesky and Icahn made $42 million in profit between them when they sold their stock back to G+W at $45. Mulheren, in contrast, lost $64,000 on Boesky's manipulation of him. Yet Boesky and Icahn weren't charged. Mulheren was. This result seemed not just unfair, it raised doubt about the whole theory of the government's case. Why would anyone *knowingly* participate in an illegal scheme and lose money while others made $42 million?

The jury apparently was unimpressed with any of these points, for they convicted Mulheren of stock manipulation. Perhaps the jury reached a compromise verdict; after all, they did not convict Mulheren on any of the other charges. But the manipulation case was weak to the point of nonexistence. What happened?

Jurors are human. They are not immune from relentless propaganda in the culture about the need to stop the rampant criminality on Wall Street. Perhaps Mulheren's enormous wealth or his odd behavior during the trial rubbed the jury the wrong way. Mulheren always came to court dressed as if he were going to a barbecue. He neglected to act with respect. He tended to treat the judge, Miriam Cederbaum, whom he had regarded a tool of the government, with imperious contempt. The situation got so bad that the judge had to admonish Mulheren's attorneys for his refusal to stand when she entered the courtroom, the obligatory sign of respect for judges. Finally, his demeanor on the witness stand must have appeared bizarre, a symptom, his lawyers claimed, of not taking his medication for his manic depression.

Usually defendants, no matter how full of bravado beforehand, quickly adopt an attitude of contrition and remorse after being convicted. To display these emotions reflects conventional legal wisdom on how to get a lighter sentence. Not Mulheren. The government recommended a stiff prison sentence of more than five years, calling him "brazen," "arrogant," and a man who had "demonstrated contempt" for the legal system. Mulheren had acted so uninterested at his sentencing hearing that it looked as if he were dozing off. When the judge asked him whether he wanted to make a statement before sentencing, he declined and sat down instead. In Mulheren's view, he just refused to grovel. Judge Cederbaum then sentenced him to a prison term of a year and a day and a fine of $1.7 million.

Mulheren then hired a new set of lawyers who specialized in appellate practice to appeal his conviction. The chances for success seemed small since the appeal was to the Second Circuit, the same court that had affirmed the convictions of Carpenter, Chestman, and Teicher. But this time the government's case was just too weak. The Second Circuit threw out the conviction, expressing "doubt about the government's theory of prosecution" and concluding that "no rational trier of fact could have found the elements of the crimes charged here beyond a reasonable doubt."

For once the system worked, but at a big cost. Mulheren's conviction was reversed, but he had had to endure the ordeal of the investigation, trial, three months in jail and a mental hospital. Jamie Securities, Mulheren's firm, was also a casualty, liquidated as a result of the prosecution.

As weak as the government's case against Mulheren was, its case against James Sherwin in *United States* v. *GAF Corporation* was, if anything, even weaker. This time the government's main witness was Boyd Jefferies. Following in Boesky's footsteps, Jefferies plea bargained in exchange for agreeing to play along with the prosecution and implicate others. Jefferies fingered James T. Sherwin, former child prodigy and chess champion, the vice-chairman of GAF Corporation.

The background of the case again grew out of an attempted takeover, GAF's unsuccessful tender offer for Union Carbide in December 1985. In October 1986, the parties entered into a standstill agreement prohibiting GAF from acquiring any Union Carbide shares in addition to the ten million it already owned, at which point GAF looked to sell. Sherwin was retained to find a buyer. He solicited bids from leading investment banks, including Jefferies's, eventually succeeding in selling five million of GAF's Union Carbide shares, half of what it owned, in a negotiated transaction to Jefferies on November 10, 1986.

Based on information provided by Jefferies, the government alleged that Sherwin and Jefferies deliberately manipulated the price of Union Carbide stock from $21 $7/8$ to $22 so that GAF could sell its shares for a higher price. For this supposed $$1/8$ "manipulation," Sherwin was charged with multiple felonies. He was tried three times. The first trial ended in a mistrial due to government misconduct; the second in a hung jury; and the third in a conviction. The Second Circuit once again reversed the conviction. Finally the government gave up and decided not to retry Sherwin a fourth time, but what is remarkable about *United States v. GAF Corporation* is that it took so long for the government to reach this conclusion. Prosecutors don't often make multiple efforts to retry even meritorious cases when faced with mistrials and hung juries.

The case against Sherwin rested entirely on Jefferies, who testified that on October 29, 1986, when Union Carbide was trading at $21 $7/8$, Sherwin called Jefferies, asked him to "close" the stock at $22, and guaranteed him against loss. On October 29 and 30, Jefferies & Company purchased approximately 100,000 Union Carbide shares near the close of trading on the New York and Pacific stock exchanges, and the price closed at or above $22 on both days. These shares were then sold at a loss by Jefferies on November 3 and 4 after Union Carbide's stock price fell.

Jefferies's testimony was full of holes and inconsistencies. Jefferies & Company, like any investment firm, routinely traded Union Carbide stock and also, like other traders, was more likely to trade at the end of the day. Small price increases, like the $$1/8$ increase in Union Carbide from $21 $7/8$ to $22 on October 29, are routine, particularly at the end of the day. The purchases on October 29 and 30 therefore resembled any number of other purchases of Union Carbide by Jefferies during the months of

October and November 1986 that had nothing to do with Sherwin. For instance, in a pattern identical to the questioned trades on October 29 and 30, Jefferies bought an additional twenty thousand Union Carbide shares on November 6 and 7 and sold these shares a few days later, between November 10 and 12.

The original indictment alleged that the purchases and sales by Jefferies in November were also part of the manipulative scheme. But then Jefferies changed his story in the third trial, testifying that the second set of trades in November were undertaken to limit his company's losses incurred from the purchases on October 29 and 30. Jefferies's new version of events, in addition to weakening his credibility by changing his story, made no sense. If Jefferies, as he testified, believed he was guaranteed against loss by Sherwin, why would he attempt to recoup his own losses by purchasing additional Union Carbide shares on November 6 to 7 and then selling these shares between November 10 and 12? The second set of November trades made sense only if Jefferies was trading for its own account and did not believe it was guaranteed against loss.

The government's case made no sense on an even more fundamental level. The alleged motive for the manipulation on October 29 and 30 was Sherwin's desire to obtain a higher price when GAF sold its Union Carbide shares in a negotiated transaction in November. But how could a temporary price increase from $21 7/8 to $22 on October 29 have any effect on the price of a negotiated transaction eleven days later? And what about Jefferies's sales on November 3 and 4 and 10 through 12? If the goal of the manipulative scheme was to increase the trading price of Union Carbide stock by purchases, wouldn't the effect of Jefferies's purchases be nullified by the sale of these same shares? The government had no arguments responding to any of these problems.

Faced with a weak case, the government adopted a desperate, win-at-any-cost strategy to save face. It spent millions of taxpayer dollars trying Sherwin three times, and finally wound up crossing the fine legal line between zealous advocacy and unethical behavior. For example, the prosecution withheld expert reports they were required to turn over to the defense. This resulted in the first mistrial. One of the government's cooperating witnesses, James Melton, Jefferies's head trader, may not have testified truthfully, as evidence uncovered at the third trial revealed. Melton testified that he spoke to Sherwin at specific times to confirm the trades. Phone records discovered by the defense, however, contradicted Melton's testimony and indicated that none of these conversations had taken place. No trade confirmation by telephone had ever taken place. It is therefore possible that Melton's entire story about these trades was false. The government has an ethical obligation to investigate the veracity of testimony to ensure that an innocent defendant is not wrongly convicted. The prosecutors in *United States* v. *GAF Corporation* conducted no such investigation. Instead, they told the jurors to ignore the phone records in reaching a verdict.

And there was the issue of Jefferies's November trades. When the government changed its position after the second trial, it also amended its bill of particulars against Sherwin to drop its objections to the trades made after October 30. The defense at the third trial then attempted to introduce the earlier version of the bill of particulars against Sherwin, which included the second set of November trades, to show the government's change of position. The defense wanted to show that if the government now agreed that Sherwin was not responsible for the November trades, Sherwin also should not be held responsible for the October trades, which were identical. But the government objected to the introduction of the earlier bill of particulars, and the judge sustained the government's position. And when the defense tried to focus the jury on the November trades, the prosecutors told the jury that the defense was creating a "smokescreen" that had nothing to do with "what this case is about." The jury was never told that until the third trial, the November trades, according to the government, were exactly what the case was about.

After the jury convicted Sherwin in the third trial, the next step was sentencing. Judge Mary Lowe was clearly troubled by the weakness of the government's case, its hardball tactics, and her doubt as to whether Sherwin could really be viewed as a criminal in the situation. She spoke movingly of Sherwin as a "good man" who, along with his family, had suffered the "agonizing" experience of three trials. She noted the support for Sherwin marshaled "by people from all walks of life," attesting to his unblemished record of integrity, his self-effacing character, and his lifelong commitment to helping the less fortunate. Unable to "remember a case that had caused [her] more anguish," she nevertheless sentenced Sherwin to six months in prison. Because of the "wide attention" the case had received, it was necessary, the judge emphasized, to send a message to those who were corrupting our financial markets.

Justice was finally served when Sherwin's conviction was reversed by the Second Circuit. Fittingly, the government's win-at-any-cost tactics were the basis for the reversal. The Second Circuit ruled that the jury should have been told about the government's compromising change of position and the earlier bill of particulars, including the November trades. By withholding this information from the jury, the trial judge had denied Sherwin a fair opportunity to defend himself.

For James T. Sherwin, a proud man who consistently refused to plead guilty even to a misdemeanor because he wanted to clear his name, victory was bittersweet. While he no longer faced criminal charges, the three trials had left him disillusioned. Returning to the status quo was unthinkable. Rather than attempting the impossible task of putting the pieces together, Sherwin left GAF and decided to get a fresh start by moving to Europe.

Like Mulheren, Sherwin learned that there was no winning if you were accused by the government of being a crook during the "decade of greed." It was only a matter of how badly you lost.

False 13(d) Statements and the Prosecution of Paul Bilzerian

During the 1980s Paul A. Bilzerian was, like Victor Posner, a much vilified "raider," an acquirer of public companies. In 1985 and 1986, Bilzerian launched hostile takeovers of two companies, Cluett, Peabody & Company and Hammermill Paper Company, both of which were eventually acquired by white knights. Shareholders of both companies made huge profits as Bilzerian and the white knights bid up the price of the targets' shares. The government went after Bilzerian with a vengeance, indicting him on multiple counts for filing false 13(d) statements. The case was widely described as a "landmark" because 13(d) had never before been used as the basis for a criminal prosecution. There were also stock-parking allegations, furnished, once again, by Boyd Jefferies to hold up his end of his plea bargain.

The government asserted that Bilzerian's recitation in his 13(d) filings that he had acquired his shares with "personal funds" was a lie. In fact, said the government, Bilzerian had got a group of wealthy investors to finance the purchases through a series of trusts under Bilzerian's control in exchange for half the profits and a guarantee against loss. The government also charged Bilzerian with illegal stock parking by purchasing through a nominee, Jefferies, who testified that Bilzerian guaranteed him against loss.

Bilzerian testified in his own defense. It was true, he said, that he had used trusts in the takeover, but he regarded such funds under his direction and control to be, in effect, "personal funds." The reason for the trusts, he explained, was to protect his investors from lawsuits that routinely occur when targets resist hostile acquisitions. Bilzerian flatly denied Jefferies's allegation of stock parking, saying that while Jefferies and Bilzerian made routine accommodations for each other, Jefferies had never acted as his nominee.

The jury convicted Bilzerian on all counts. At sentencing, the government did everything it could to ensure that Bilzerian would receive the maximum penalty. "Bilzerian's unlawful conduct," the government emphasized, "defrauded thousands of innocent shareholders, undermined investor confidence in the securities markets, and impeded important functions of government." Moreover, Bilzerian had the temerity to continue insisting he was innocent. This, the government thundered, showed Bilzerian's "contempt for the legal system," before which he displayed "absolutely no contrition or remorse." Bilzerian, it charged, had gone so far as to question the "good faith" of the government in prosecuting him. He needed to receive a stiff sentence "to deter other wrongdoers in the financial community." "Wall Street," the government warned, "will be watching this sentencing very closely." Judge Robert Ward agreed. Bilzerian was sentenced to four years in prison, a sentence longer by a year than that received by Ivan Boesky. The Second Circuit then affirmed the conviction.

True, Bilzerian was defiant until the end and refused to express any remorse or, in John Mulheren's words, "to grovel." It is also true that Bilzerian, by all accounts, is personally arrogant and abrasive, a man with few friends and many enemies, who was constantly involved in disputes. Even those who believed that Bilzerian received an unfair sentence after an unfair trial before the notoriously progovernment Judge Ward felt little sympathy for him personally. Bilzerian was just not the type of person that anyone felt sorry for.

But did he in fact commit a crime? Was it necessary to convict him and go for maximum punishment to restore "investor confidence" and "deter" other wrongdoers? It is hard to believe the shareholders of Cluett and Hammermill felt, as the government claimed, that they had been "victimized" by the sudden escalation in the value of their shares. They might easily regard Bilzerian a hero. Shareholders of these firms made tens of millions of dollars from the bidding contests that resulted from Bilzerian's takeover attempts. The government didn't need to take any action to restore *these* shareholders' "confidence."

Investors couldn't have cared less that Bilzerian's 13(d) disclosures referred only to "personal funds," without detailing that those funds were contributed in part by others. Investors may want to know the source of funds if there is a chance they won't get paid. But this was not the case with Bilzerian. The cash was in hand and everyone got paid. And Bilzerian's legal argument, while aggressive, was plausible. Because he was in control of the cash, and there was no lender who could call a loan and get the money back, Bilzerian believed he could legally refer to the cash as "personal funds." Even if he was wrong to reach this conclusion, his decision harmed no one. On the contrary, investors only benefited from his actions.

Bilzerian's justification for the trusts made, in fact, a lot of sense. Tender-offer filings are routinely criticized for disclosing no information of any real value to investors, particularly to those who sell their shares for cash. This useless 13(d) information, however, can be of tremendous value to a target's management and its lawyers because they are alerted to a possible offer and can then adopt a plan of resistance including filing lawsuits challenging the accuracy of any disclosures made. Bilzerian's investors were less willing to proceed due to this litigation risk. By overcoming their reluctance, Bilzerian was able to go forward, to the benefit of the target's shareholders.

While the government's arguments about the severity of Bilzerian's conduct were clearly wrong, the prosecutors were correct when they told Judge Ward that "Wall Street will be watching this sentencing very closely." The message, however, was different from what the government told Judge Ward. It was not that "wrongdoers" who "defrauded innocent investors" needed to be punished. Rather, it was that anyone in the takeover game could step on a land mine at any time. Any infraction, no matter how technical or inconsequential, would be vigorously prosecuted whether or not there was any motive or reason to believe that the underlying conduct was criminal. After what happened to Paul Bilzerian, anyone would have to think twice before launching another hostile tender offer.

CHAPTER 4

Rudy Giuliani's Reign of Terror

In June 1983, Rudolph Giuliani resigned his position as associate attorney general of the United States to become the United States attorney for the Southern District of New York. It was to be the best career move he ever made. Forty years earlier, another high-profile U.S. attorney for the Southern District of New York, Thomas Dewey, had used the position to launch a political career that culminated in Dewey's unsuccessful 1948 presidential campaign against Harry Truman. Giuliani's four-and-a-half-year tenure as U.S. attorney was much in the same mold, eventually leading to his election as mayor of New York in 1993 after narrowly losing an election for the same post four years earlier.

Popular and press accounts of the 1980s routinely depict Giuliani as the tough cop and prosecutor—the Eliot Ness of the financial markets—who had the courage to fight the powerful financial interests and clean up the corruption on Wall Street. In truth, Giuliani was much more the pawn of special interests than their conqueror. The losers in the restructuring revolution needed someone like Giuliani to snuff out their competitors and restore them to their prior positions of dominance. Giuliani fit the bill perfectly. It is no coincidence that top officials at Dillon, Read, Lazard Frères, and other establishment investment banks in New York were among Giuliani's biggest campaign contributors and strongest supporters in his mayoral bids.

Of course Giuliani was far from an unwilling player in the game. Once he figured out that becoming publicly identified as the crusader against greed and criminality on Wall Street was his ticket to national fame and political success, Giuliani was all too happy to play the part. It seemed like every other day he was on television, announcing another arrest or just denouncing the wave of corruption among the privileged few who were running the nation's financial markets. While critics complained of Giuliani's shameless self-promotion and his prosecutorial ethics, few really cared. Giuliani understood that he could do no wrong with the public by prosecuting Wall Street speculators because there was no constituency to defend them. Everyone likes to see the mighty fall.

There was more than a little irony in Giuliani's priorities as U.S. attorney. While serving as associate attorney general under President Reagan, Giuliani was a probusiness Republican who criticized the white-collar prosecutions by his Democratic predecessors. He felt such prosecutions were a waste of time that diverted scarce resources and attention away from going after organized crime, drug dealers, and other hard-core criminals. He had no use for prosecutors who were "chasing rainbows, spending two or three years chasing a white-collar case they can never make." "The previous administration had one priority, and that was white-collar crime," Giuliani complained in 1982. "I think there was almost a McCarthyism to it. It had gotten to the point where these people had become zealots rather than prosecutors." Giuliani's critics would later use almost the exact same words to describe the U.S. attorney's office during his tenure.

Giuliani's upbringing prepared him well for a career as a prosecutor. He was an only child who was born in Brooklyn, New York, where his father ran a bar and restaurant after leaving his job as a plumber. Wanting a better life for his son, Giuliani's father moved the family to Garden City, New Jersey, when Rudy was seven. Even after moving, Giuliani's father commuted to Brooklyn every day to work where he was able to make a modest living. But his life was not easy. In addition to the usual problems of making money in a neighborhood business, Giuliani's father had to fight off the mob's continual demands for protection money. Rudy was taught how to box when he was two years old so he would be prepared for similar experiences as an adult.

After attending parochial schools through college, Rudy was torn between entering the priesthood or becoming a lawyer. He chose the latter career and went to New York University Law School. After graduating in 1968, Giuliani clerked for a federal district court judge for two years and then began his career as a prosecutor in the U.S. attorney's office. During his five-year stint there, Giuliani quickly made a name for himself as an effective trial lawyer in several high-profile government and police corruption cases. He was even portrayed in a movie, *Prince of the City*, for his role in the Knapp Commission investigation of police corruption in New York. Giuliani was the prosecutor who broke the investigation by convincing the government's key witness, Robert Leuci, to confess to all of his crimes. Giuliani always had a knack for being in the right place at the right time.

Giuliani left government for private practice during the time the Democrats controlled the U.S. attorney's office. But he made a big enough impression when he served to be selected as associate attorney general, the number-three man in the Justice Department, when President Reagan was elected in 1980. In his new position, he was in charge of all U.S. attorneys. When a vacancy developed in 1983 in the Southern District of New York, Giuliani, who was recently divorced and remarried to Donna Hanover, a television personality with career opportunities in New York, decided to take it himself.

In his early years as U.S. attorney, Giuliani focused on organized crime. He cultivated publicity from the beginning, but he was largely unknown nationally, and even in New York he was far from a household name. This all changed in the spring of 1986 when opportunity fell into his lap. He was to make the most of it.

Back in May 1985, the compliance department at Merrill Lynch in New York received an unsolicited letter from Caracas, Venezuela. The letter, written in badly broken English, reported that two brokers from the Caracas office were "trading with inside information." Somewhat ominously, the letter also revealed that "[a] copie with description of their trades so far has been submittet to the S.E.C. by separate mail." The letter triggered an investigation by Merrill Lynch, and then by the SEC, which ultimately led to the downfall of Dennis Levine.

When Levine began his trading in takeover stocks in 1980, he opened an account under an assumed name, Mr. Diamond, at Bank Leu in the Bahamas. All Levine's trades were routed through this bank. Levine's banker at Bank Leu then routed Levine's trades through a broker in New York. Unknown to

Levine, however, the banker and the broker themselves began trading for their own accounts by copying Levine's trades. The broker also tipped two brokers at the Caracas branch of Merrill Lynch, who also began copying Levine's trades. Two other brokers who were excluded from the scheme then complained to Merrill Lynch.

Merrill Lynch notified the SEC of the letter, and the investigation intensified. The trades were quickly traced to Bank Leu in the Bahamas, but Swiss secrecy laws (the bank was a subsidiary of a Swiss bank) prevented U.S. investigators from learning Mr. Diamond's real identity. Ultimately, Bank Leu's lawyer, Harvey Pitt, decided to disclose Levine's identity in exchange for immunity for the bank.

On May 12, 1986, almost one year to the day after the letter from Caracas, Dennis Levine was arrested. On June 5, 1986, just twenty-three days later, he pled guilty to four felonies for insider trading, income-tax evasion for failing to report his $11.6 million in trading profits, and perjury for having given false testimony to the SEC. Levine also settled SEC charges on the same day, agreeing to disgorge the $11.6 million in trading profits, give the government certain other possessions including his new Ferrari, and to be barred from the securities business for life.

The Levine case attracted intense publicity during the short period between his arrest and guilty plea. Giuliani saw a chance to seize the spotlight, and he took it. In a nationally reported press conference on the day of Levine's guilty plea, Giuliani heralded the government's success and strongly hinted that Levine was just the beginning. Levine was cooperating with the government, Giuliani announced, and this cooperation was going to be "very fruitful and very valuable" in the ongoing investigation of Wall Street corruption.

The press conference was vintage Giuliani. He had nothing to do with cracking the Levine case. In fact, for all the fanfare surrounding the war on insider trading, Levine's trading activities had gone undetected for almost six years. It was not until Merrill Lynch turned over the Caracas letter to the SEC that the governmental investigation began, and even then the SEC, led by Gary Lynch, the director of Enforcement, did all the work. Giuliani's office was totally uninvolved until the very end when Giuliani's assistant, Charles Carberry, negotiated the terms of Levine's guilty plea. But none of this stopped Giuliani from holding a press conference to grab the headlines for himself. It was a spectacle to be repeated many times during Giuliani's tenure as U.S. attorney.

Giuliani's genius was his insight that the unholy alliance between the threatened establishment business community and the "decade of greed" rich-haters would support his high-profile assault on Wall Street, no matter how unprincipled. Conventional wisdom is that the rich have an advantage in the criminal justice system because of their influence and ability to hire the best lawyers. But this advantage becomes a disadvantage when the fact of being wealthy and successful is what makes you a target. And the most talented lawyers in the world can do little when the government decides to criminalize routine business practices and declare them to be major felonies.

Giuliani embraced the criminalization of such vague and undefined offenses as stock parking, insider trading, and stock manipulation because it maximized his flexibility to prosecute whomever he chose. Those prosecuted faced the choice of pleading guilty and cooperating by implicating others or going to trial. Few had the intestinal fortitude to fight, and most of those who did lost. The Second Circuit ultimately reversed many of these convictions, but this did not occur until long after Giuliani had left office. During his tenure, he was close to invincible. Each success only emboldened him further.

The more Giuliani expanded the scope of the criminal laws, trampling civil liberties in the process, the more popular he became. Not even the American Civil Liberties Union was willing to take him to task. Still, Giuliani did not escape criticism completely. Ironically, he was first criticized for being too soft in allowing Ivan Boesky to plead guilty in a negotiated deal announced in November 1986. He did not make this mistake twice. Later, some observers, particularly the editorial-page writers of the *Wall Street Journal*, became increasingly critical of Giuliani's hardball tactics and self-aggrandizing behavior during his reign of terror.

The Government's Deal with Ivan Boesky

Ivan Boesky was the richest and most powerful arbitrageur on Wall Street during the first half of the 1980s. On Friday, November 14, 1986, after the close of trading, Rudy Giuliani and

John Shad announced that Boesky's career as an arbitrageur was over and a new one had begun—as a cooperating government witness. To settle SEC charges of insider trading and securities-law violations, Boesky agreed to pay $100 million, consisting of a $50 million fine and disgorgement of another $50 million in illegal profits. Boesky also agreed to plead guilty to one felony for his role in the Fischbach transaction and cooperate fully in the government's ongoing investigation. Boesky himself also issued a statement admitting his guilt and strongly hinting that the whole takeover process was corrupt. "I know that in the wake of today's events," Boesky declared, "many will call for reform. If my mistakes launch a process of re-examination of the rules and practices of our financial marketplace, then perhaps some good will result."

The events of November 14 shocked the country, making the Levine arrest and guilty plea look trivial by comparison. No one in the history of Wall Street up to that time had ever flown as high or crashed as hard as Ivan Boesky. He grew up modestly in Detroit, the son of a Russian immigrant who owned and operated several delicatessens. A mediocre student, Boesky attended three different colleges without getting a degree. He then attended Detroit College of Law (which didn't require a college degree), where he took five years to graduate instead of the usual three. With such an undistinguished academic record, Boesky was unable to land a job with any of the major Detroit law firms. After a short and unsuccessful stint as an accountant, Boesky moved to New York in 1966 to begin his career on Wall Street.

His early career showed little promise. He was fired from one job on his first day for making one big losing trade. He left several other jobs because he was given little responsibility or opportunity to do arbitrage. In 1972 Boesky was hired as head of the arbitrage department of a small brokerage house but lost this job when the firm went bankrupt in 1975.

Boesky's career was in trouble, but fortunately for him, he had married into money. Back in 1962, Boesky married Seema Silberstein, the daughter of a wealthy Detroit real estate developer. Throughout Boesky's career travails, he always lived well by taking liberally from his father-in-law, who referred to Boesky as "Ivan the Bum." Boesky's economic fortunes improved again when his mother-in-law died in 1975, leaving $700,000 to Seema. Boesky now felt secure enough to start his own company rather than looking for yet another job. On April 1, 1975, Boesky took the $700,000 and opened Ivan F. Boesky & Company, an investment limited partnership devoted to risk arbitrage.

Boesky's new firm was spectacularly successful. In the four years between 1976 and 1979, the firm had investment returns of 97 percent, 95 percent, 18 percent, and 51 percent. The firm's worst year was 1980, but it still made 6 percent. The success of Ivan F. Boesky & Company made Boesky and his investors wealthy. His $700,000 original investment was now worth $90 million.

In 1981 Boesky dissolved Ivan F. Boesky & Company and began raising funds for a new firm, Ivan F. Boesky Corporation. The new firm also focused on takeover arbitrage, but on a much larger scale. With the increase in the number and size of megatakeover transactions, Boesky had more opportunities to bet on the outcome of particular transactions. He routinely took massive positions and became the dominant arbitrageur on Wall Street. Sometimes he lost big, such as when he invested heavily in Cities Service in anticipation of a takeover by Gulf that never materialized. But more often he won, making huge profits in the process. His success, and the sheer size of his investments, gave him access to a vast network of takeover entrepreneurs, investors, and investment bankers, which he used to maximum advantage in seeking information about actual or potential deals. Nobody would refuse to take his call. In the summer of 1984, *Fortune* ran a feature story about Boesky that lauded his accomplishments but also ominously mentioned how "Boesky's competitors whisper darkly about his omniscient timing." It was a portent of things to come.

Before the roof fell in, Boesky had amassed hundreds of millions of dollars in wealth. His vast real estate holdings included a 163-acre estate in Mount Kisco, New York, where he lived, and a luxury apartment in Manhattan. Travel by chauffeured limousine and private jet was the normal routine. But wealth was not enough for Boesky. He also craved respectability and prestige.

Embarrassed about his own undistinguished academic background and support from his wealthy wife, Boesky sought to remake his image in a more flattering light. He portrayed himself publicly as a self-made man, a modern-day Horatio Alger who worked his way up from the bottom and conquered Wall Street. To improve his image further, he made large donations to Harvard University, which entitled him to membership in the Harvard Club in New York, which he frequented regularly. Acting like a Harvard man to the outside world was clearly better than advertising that he never graduated from college. Boesky also became active with various Republican, Jewish, and cultural causes as a donor and fund-raiser. In appreciation of his generosity, he was named a trustee of the Jewish Theological Seminary, Brandeis University, New York University, and the American Ballet Theatre, among others. He was on top of the world.

Boesky's fame put him in great demand as a public speaker, and in his speeches he extolled the virtues of takeover arbitrage, capitalism, and the pursuit of wealth. He even wrote a book on these subjects, appropriately titled *Merger Mania,* subtitled *Arbitrage: Wall Street's Best-Kept Money-Making Secret.* He said he wrote the book for all those people who "may be inspired to believe that confidence in one's self and determination can allow one to become whatever one may dream." At a commencement speech for the graduates of the business school of the University of California at Berkeley on May 18, 1986, Boesky defended himself against the charge that he was motivated solely by greed. After describing his personal success story, Boesky told the graduates that "greed is all right, by the way. I think greed is healthy. You can be greedy and still feel good about yourself." Many in the audience no doubt agreed and dreamed that their careers could turn out as well as Boesky's.

Unknown to the graduates, Boesky's life was already falling apart at the time of his speech. Dennis Levine had been arrested six days before his speech, and Levine began cooperating almost immediately. Levine's cooperation led to a rash of guilty pleas from a series of minor figures in the takeover game—Ira Sokolow from Shearson Lehman; David Brown from Goldman Sachs; Robert Wilkis from Lazard Frères; Randall Cecola, a student who had worked at Lazard; and Ilan Reich, a lawyer from Wachtell, Lipton. Levine's cooperation also led to the downfall of Ivan Boesky.

In a routine debriefing session, Levine told government regulators and prosecutors that he and Boesky had entered into an explicit agreement whereby Boesky would pay Levine for tips. The agreement began in early 1985, shortly after Levine joined Drexel Burnham in February 1985. Under the agreement, Levine would receive 5 percent of Boesky's profits from Levine's tips if Boesky owned no stock prior to the tip and 1 percent if Boesky already owned shares. Any losses from tips would be deducted from payments owed to Levine. No payments were ever made pursuant to the agreement, although Levine claimed the two had agreed that Levine was entitled to $2.4 million.

Because no payments were made and the agreement was never reduced to writing, the government decided to investigate further rather than immediately charge Boesky. In early August the SEC sent Boesky a series of wide-ranging subpoenas for information based on information provided by Levine. Boesky then retained Harvey Pitt, the same lawyer who had represented Bank Leu and disclosed Levine's name to the SEC, to represent him in responding to the subpoenas. Boesky's choice of Pitt was more than a little ironic. Pitt had skillfully saved Bank Leu by turning in Levine, who in turn fingered Boesky. By hiring Pitt, Boesky placed his future in the hands of the man who triggered the chain of events that led to his current predicament.

As a former general counsel of the SEC, Pitt had tremendous credibility with the agency. Clients frequently hired him to benefit from this credibility in negotiations with government regulators. This was no doubt Boesky's motivation when he authorized Pitt to respond to the subpoenas by initiating immediate settlement negotiations with the SEC. Pitt had one trump card in negotiations. Boesky was a big fish but not the biggest. Drexel Burnham and Michael Milken had that distinction. Pitt tried to duplicate his earlier triumph representing Bank Leu by offering up Drexel and Milken in exchange for the government granting Boesky immunity from prosecution. But this was now impossible after Dennis Levine had just pled guilty to four felonies. There was no way Giuliani could let Boesky, a much more important figure, get off with nothing.

Having decided to reach the most favorable deal possible rather than fight, Pitt did the best he could. By September 1986, just one month after the receipt of the subpoenas, the basic deal was struck. Boesky agreed to plead guilty to one felony, pay $100 million, be banned from the securities industry for life, and become a cooperating government witness. The parties agreed to delay public announcement of the deal so that Boesky could accumulate more evidence. He agreed, for example, to wear a wire in conversations with Michael Milken to induce him to say something incriminating. Boesky, like other cooperating government witnesses, hoped that he would ultimately receive a lighter sentence for his crimes if he could deliver on his promise to provide incriminating evidence. Although Boesky's taped conversations with Milken ultimately produced nothing of value to the government, nobody knew that at the time. Boesky used the prospect of Milken incriminating himself on tape to bluff the government into giving him major concessions. For example, Boesky was given permission to sell the takeover stocks in his arbitrage fund secretly during the delay before public announcement of his deal with the government when he was supposedly accumulating evidence.

When the deal was publicly announced two months later, it was a bombshell. The press immediately recognized that the implications of what had occurred went far beyond Boesky himself. His plea and agreement to cooperate meant that the government's investigation was expanding. Speculation abounded that the noose around Drexel's and Milken's neck was tightening and that the takeover boom might be over. As one trader told *Business Week* about the significance of Boesky's plea, "One day the takeover wars had to end. Was this the day?" *Time* elaborated on the connection between the Boesky plea and takeovers:

> Like tremors signaling great shifts in the earth's strata, the Ivan Boesky insider-trading scandal heralds a fundamental change in the takeover game. Deals will now be seen in a wholly new light, and the government may change the rules for raiders and traders. To many, the disclosure that arbitrageur Boesky was using stolen information from Drexel Burnham Lambert investment banker Dennis Levine proves what was long suspected: that millions in takeover profits have been going to those who rigged the game. . . . The takeover surge of the past few years is now suspect.

The market fell sharply in response to concerns that takeovers, particularly Drexel-financed takeovers, were going to slow down. In the first two trading days after news of the Boesky deal, the Dow Jones Industrial Average dropped more than fifty-five points. Particularly hard hit were stocks of rumored takeover candidates and stocks of companies that were clients of Drexel:

Takeover Candidates

COMPANY	DECLINE IN STOCK PRICE NOV. 14–19	
	DOLLARS	PERCENT
Borg-Warner	$5.63	13.2%
Federated Dept. Stores	12.88	12.9
Gillette	10.00	14.8
Goodyear	5.50	11.6

Takeover Candidates (cont'd)

COMPANY	DECLINE IN STOCK PRICE NOV. 14–19	
	DOLLARS	PERCENT
J. C. Penney	5.63	6.6
Johnson Controls	7.38	11.0
Lear Siegler	13.00	14.1
Stop & Shop	10.00	16.7
Time Inc.	7.50	9.7
USX	2.63	11.2
Winn-Dixie	7.00	13.4

Companies Identified as Drexel Clients

COMPANY	DECLINE IN STOCK PRICE NOV. 14–19	
	DOLLARS	PERCENT
Columbia Savings & Loan	$1.38	10.7%
First Executive	2.13	11.8
Horn & Hardart	3.00	18.3
Lorimar-Telepictures	1.50	7.27
Revlon Group	2.25	15.3
Texas Air	2.13	5.7
Triangle Industries	2.75	9.9
Wickes	.50	11.1

When the news leaked out that Boesky had been allowed to sell his takeover stocks before public announcement of his guilty plea, the public was irate. Why did the government give Boesky this favored treatment? The government's position seemed hopelessly inconsistent. On the one hand, the government claimed that Boesky broke the law and hurt investor confidence by purchasing stocks of takeover targets after receiving tips from Dennis Levine. But if this was true, how could the government allow Boesky to sell his takeover stocks after he agreed to plead guilty, knowing that the prices would fall when the plea was revealed? In both cases, Boesky benefited from possession of inside information material to the prices of the securities he traded. To many, it appeared as if the government allowed Boesky to pull off one of the biggest insider trades of his career.

When confronted with the obvious hypocrisy of allowing Boesky to trade on his own inside information, Giuliani blamed the SEC. "That was the SEC's decision," Giuliani stated somewhat defensively. "They decided how to announce the Boesky settlement, the effect it would have on the market and the way innocent investors would be harmed by it." Taking the credit for success, even if undeserved, and blaming others when problems arose became a pattern Giuliani would develop during his tenure as U.S. attorney.

Other criticisms of the Boesky deal Giuliani had to cope with personally. Boesky was allowed to plead guilty to only one felony while Levine, a far less important figure, had earlier been forced to plead to four. And then it came out that Boesky had negotiated the ability to choose his own sentencing judge. When Boesky chose the notoriously lenient Morris Lasker, many believed that Giuliani, the tough, no-nonsense prosecutor, had gone soft.

Then on November 24, 1986, the *Wall Street Journal* reported that Boesky had made over $200 million in illegal insider profits from information provided by Levine. Now it seemed like Boesky's $100 million fine, which Giuliani had so proudly announced just one week earlier, was just a pittance. The press wanted to know how Giuliani could have been outmaneuvered so badly.

Giuliani responded by highlighting the difficulty of convicting Boesky had he not come forward and the value of his cooperation. Giuliani was at least partially correct. At the time Boesky decided to plead guilty, the case against him was extremely weak. Levine told prosecutors about the compensation that Boesky promised him, but there was no corroboration. If Boesky denied the existence of the agreement, the government would have had to rely exclusively on the testimony of Levine, who had an obvious incentive to implicate others falsely in exchange for more lenient treatment.

The government would have had a hard time proving the existence of the agreement from Boesky's trades. Levine told the government that he provided Boesky with information about many of the big companies involved in takeovers and restructuring transactions—American Natural Resources, Nabisco, Houston Natural Gas, FMC, Union Carbide, and General Foods, among others. But the government knew that Boesky's trading records were ambiguous. Boesky bought and sold takeover stocks for a living, so his investments in these stocks proved nothing. He also typically bought after public rumors of a possible takeover

attempt, consistent with normal business practice for an arbitrageur. And even though he made a lot of money in the stocks
identified by Levine, the timing of his trading decisions was
inconsistent with his being perfectly wired. For example, he frequently bought after price run-ups and sold before higher offers
or other events causing stock prices to move even further.

Boesky also lost money investing in other takeover stocks. The
nature of his business was to take big positions and big risks. He
won most of the time, but this was predictable because of the
risks involved. Boesky could have made these points forcefully in
denying that he traded on inside information. Even under
Levine's version of the agreement, there was a penalty clause for
losing trades. Why did Boesky have to worry about deducting
losses from profits made if Levine were really giving him inside
information?

Even assuming the truth of the government's allegations that
Boesky agreed to pay Levine for stolen information, Boesky still
would have had a defense. In *Chiarella* the Supreme Court held
that trading on stolen information did not constitute a crime so
long as the trader did not owe a fiduciary duty to investors on the
other side of the transaction. This was precisely Boesky's situation.
Ultimately, the Supreme Court held in *Carpenter* that misappropriation of information violated the mail- and wire-fraud statutes,
but *Carpenter* had not yet been decided when Boesky pled.

Because of the legal and factual problems with the government's
case, there was at least "a realistic chance," as Giuliani said in
defending the government's actions, "that Boesky never would've
been convicted had he not agreed to plead guilty." Boesky's decision
under these circumstances to give up without a fight was a coup for
the government, and for Giuliani. Nor did Boesky ultimately receive
a light sentence. The supposedly lenient Judge Lasker, perhaps himself stung by the criticism of allowing Boesky to pick the sentencing
judge, gave Boesky a three-year sentence. It was by far the longest
prison sentence ever given to anyone involved in the government's
enforcement crackdown up to that time.

The real problem with the government's deal with Boesky was
that the cure was worse than the disease. What critics should
have asked Giuliani was why the stock market, and takeover
stocks in particular, collapsed in response to the Boesky
announcement. If the government was right that it was catching
crooks and restoring investor confidence in the market, stock

prices should have gone up, not down. And takeover stocks should have gone up the most. Apprehending those who were stealing confidential information about actual or contemplated offers should make those offers more, not less, likely to succeed. If this is what the government was doing, the press would have been filled with stories predicting an increase in the number of takeovers now that the thieves were caught. But the press stories said the opposite, predicting the end of takeovers. That's why takeover stocks and the Dow Jones Industrial Average fell when the Boesky deal was announced. Whatever the details of Boesky's conduct, investors correctly perceived that the government's enforcement crackdown was directed against those who had facilitated the restructuring revolution of the 1980s.

Why else would Boesky's plea lead the government to intensify its investigation of Drexel Burnham and Michael Milken? Under the government's theory that Levine stole confidential information while a Drexel employee and sold it to Boesky, Drexel was a victim, not a perpetrator. No one in the Winans case accused the *Wall Street Journal* of wrongdoing when Foster Winans violated his employment agreement and tipped the contents of forthcoming "Heard on the Street" columns. And no one in the Chiarella case accused Pandick Press, the dishonest printer's employer, of wrongdoing when Chiarella violated his employment agreement. The *Wall Street Journal* and Pandick Press weren't charged because they were harmed by the wrongful conduct of their employees. The same was true of Drexel. Levine harmed Drexel by hurting its reputation for integrity and ability to maintain confidentiality. Under the government's theory, Drexel should have been entitled to compensation from the $50 million of Boesky's fine dedicated to compensating victims. Instead, it became the primary target of the government's continuing investigation. And because the government viewed Drexel as a violator and not a victim, the stocks of Drexel clients also fell sharply in the aftermath of the Boesky announcement. If Drexel's stock were traded (Drexel's stock was privately held and not listed), it would have crashed.

This was not lost on Drexel's competitors. Much of Wall Street supported the widening government investigation. The most enthusiastic supporters, the *Nation* reported, were "the old-line investment houses" who were "glad" to see "the upstarts" put in their place by government prosecutors. The government may have hurt investors by causing stock prices to fall, but frustrated

competitors were a different story. For them, Giuliani was a god-
send who created opportunity for them where none existed
before. No wonder they were so supportive when Giuliani asked
them to return the favor when he ran for mayor.

The Arrests of the Giuliani Three

Martin Siegel knew he was finished the day Boesky's deal with
the government was announced. Unlike Levine, Siegel had actually received cash payments from Boesky in the rendezvous at the
Plaza Hotel. When Siegel received government subpoenas seeking
information about his arrangement with Boesky, the jig was up.
Even if Siegel could somehow justify the receipt of suitcases full
of cash, he didn't pay taxes on the money. He was guilty of tax
fraud, at the very least. Siegel, faced with no good options, did
the best he could for himself. He hired Jed Rakoff, a first-rate
attorney with an impeccable reputation, and immediately made
clear to the government that he was willing to cooperate and
implicate others. Following in Levine's and Boesky's footsteps,
Siegel capitulated without a fight.

Siegel had one major problem in negotiating a favorable deal
for himself—who else to implicate. Drexel was the government's
primary target, and Siegel, like Levine, worked there. But Siegel
had been at Drexel for only a short time. He was lured away from
his prior position as head of arbitrage at Kidder, Peabody in early
1986, just before Levine's arrest in May. From then until Boesky's
deal with the government was announced in November 1986,
nothing happened. The pressure of the government's expanding
investigation was too great. Siegel couldn't help the government
get Drexel.

Siegel told the government he still had something to offer.
While he was head of arbitrage at Kidder, Siegel claimed, arbitrageurs from Kidder regularly swapped inside information about
the takeover developments with their counterparts at Goldman
Sachs. Siegel provided the government with the names of individuals who traded on inside information and the particular transactions involved. On February 13, 1987, Siegel pled guilty to two
felonies and simultaneously settled charges brought by the SEC.
Sentencing was deferred because of the possible need for Siegel to
testify as a witness.

Giuliani was ecstatic. The Wall Street types he was now prosecuting behaved differently from the hard-core criminals he had
prosecuted most of his career. For organized crime figures, the
risk of incarceration was a fact of life, an occupational hazard.
They could not be easily intimidated by the threat of prosecution,
which was more a badge of honor than a source of shame. And
only rarely did they offer to implicate others to get more lenient
treatment for themselves. To do so might be tantamount to signing their own death sentence.

But those accused of financial crimes were nowhere near this
tough. The criminal justice system with its routine of arrest, fin-
gerprinting, mug shots, arraignment, bail, trial, and prison was
totally alien to them. They were mortified by the prospect of
being publicly labeled as criminals but still did not have the stomach to fight. Levine, Boesky, and Siegel proved as much. Giuliani
had never seen anyone give up as easily or be so desperate to
cooperate to save themselves. Wall Street types were easy prey
because they were so soft. Or, as Giuliani put it, investment
bankers and their ilk "roll easier"—become government witnesses
against their former friends and associates—than any other type
of defendant he had ever prosecuted. It seemed as if all Giuliani
had to do was arrest someone, sometimes just send them a subpoena, to get them to confess and become a cooperating government witness.

Armed with information provided by Siegel and feeling invincible, Giuliani decided to order more arrests. He first ordered the
arrest of Timothy L. Tabor, a former arbitrageur at Kidder, on the
evening of February 11, 1987. Tabor was arrested at night at
home to make it impossible for him to arrange bail. When Tabor
refused to confess and cooperate, he was forced to spend the
night in jail. The following day, Richard Wigton, Siegel's successor
as head of arbitrage at Kidder, was arrested at his office, handcuffed, and led away in tears before waiting television cameras.
Also on February 12, Robert M. Freeman, head of arbitrage at
Goldman Sachs, was arrested and handcuffed on the trading floor
of Goldman Sachs.

The handcuffed arrests were front-page news across the country. In a series of press conferences, interviews, and national television appearances after the arrests, Giuliani touted the strength
of the government's case against the three arbitrageurs and others
in its expanding investigation. He also defended the arrests as

"the way people are commonly arrested. . . . We handcuff and frisk to make sure you don't have a weapon or knife to harm yourself or someone else." The message to the financial community was chilling. Could the United States attorney really believe that the heads of arbitrage of such respected firms as Goldman Sachs and Kidder, Peabody were no different from violent criminals who needed to be frisked for weapons and handcuffed? How would they be treated in jail? The only hope for those like the three arrested arbitrageurs was to cooperate against others. "If they had common sense and some sense of morality," Giuliani told the *Wall Street Journal*, "what they would do is cooperate and try to help the U.S. Government clean up this mess."

Within days of the arrests, Giuliani informed representatives of Kidder, Peabody that the firm was now under criminal investigation because Kidder was responsible for Siegel's criminal acts. General Electric Company, which had recently acquired an 80 percent stake in Kidder, decided the best way to avoid an indictment was to clean house. Eventually, Kidder's lawyer, Gary Naftalis, the SEC, and Giuliani worked out an agreement, which required Kidder to pay a $25 million fine to the SEC, replace its top management, quit the business of takeover arbitrage, agree to SEC supervision of its internal controls, and cooperate in the government's continuing investigation. Kidder also agreed to suspend Robert Wigton and refuse to pay his or Tabor's legal expenses. Wigton was also informed that if he refused to plead guilty and cooperate with the government and was later found guilty, GE would sue him to recover the $3 million that Wigton was paid for his GE stock. In exchange, Giuliani agreed not to indict Kidder.

Naftalis skillfully saved Kidder from the certain demise that would have occurred had Kidder been forced either to plead guilty or risk criminal conviction at trial. But Kidder's deal with the government also placed maximum pressure on Wigton and Tabor. Without Kidder's support in building and paying for a defense, they were cast adrift. The easy thing for them to do, and what Giuliani expected based on his past experience, was to plead guilty and cooperate against Freeman. But they refused and asserted their innocence. For the first time, Giuliani actually had to prove allegations against defendants who refused to roll over.

The government's case was in trouble right from the start. Freeman, Wigton, and Tabor were arrested based on a complaint that accused Freeman of giving Siegel inside information about

Unocal's planned defensive strategy in response to Mesa's announced tender offer in April 1985. The complaint then detailed how Siegel contacted Wigton and Tabor who then, along with Siegel, sold put options based on the inside information. When the indictment was returned on April 9, 1987, however, the government abandoned the original arrest accusations regarding the Unocal transaction. The indictment made no mention of any confidential communication in April 1985 and placed the sale of Unocal options in May, not April. This discrepancy was important because Unocal's defensive strategy was publicly announced by May. Trading after public disclosure was inconsistent with the government's claim that Freeman, Wigton, and Tabor were guilty of insider trading.

Recognizing the problems with the government's case, the three defendants, who continued to assert their innocence, pressed for a speedy trial. Judge Robert Stanton granted the request, setting a trial date of May 20, 1987, three months after the arrests and slightly more than one month after the original indictment. The government's case was hanging by a thread, and Giuliani knew it. After milking the arrests for as much national publicity as possible, he now had to put up or shut up and admit the arrests were improper.

Giuliani decided to try to buy time and save face. On May 11, 1987, just nine days before the trial was to begin, the government requested a two-month continuance so that the old indictment could be superseded by a new one with expanded allegations. Judge Stanton denied the request for continuance, ruling that the delay would violate defendants' right to a speedy trial on the existing indictment. The government then had no choice but to dismiss the indictment.

Giuliani still refused to admit that he made a mistake in ordering the arrests. Instead, he went on a public relations offensive in continuing to insist on the strength of the government's case. The earlier indictment had to be dismissed, Giuliani insisted on a national news program, because it was just "the tip of the iceberg." Giuliani also told the *Wall Street Journal* that the government had granted immunity from prosecution to critical witnesses who were now expected to testify against Wigton, Freeman, and Tabor. At every opportunity, Giuliani promised that an expanded, new indictment with additional counts and allegations of criminal acts was imminent.

Time passed, but nothing happened. There was no superseding indictment because the government had no case. In desperation, the government even offered immunity to Tabor if he would corroborate Siegel's accusations against Wigton and Freeman. Lacking any incriminating information to provide, Tabor courageously declined. The situation was finally resolved in August 1989, almost two and a half years after the initial arrests, when Freeman finally pled guilty to one felony count for hearing Siegel's "your bunny has a good nose" comment about the Beatrice transaction. Charges against Wigton and Tabor were dropped.

The government tried to cast Freeman's guilty plea in the best possible light. Benito Romano, Giuliani's handpicked successor as United States attorney, defended the government's handling of the investigation and Freeman's guilty plea, which, Romano announced, was to "a very substantial criminal charge." Romano also defended Siegel's contribution: "We wouldn't have gotten to where we are today, with the charge and the plea, if we thought that Siegel was a liar."

The government stuck by Siegel until the end. On April 13, 1990, Freeman was sentenced to serve four months in prison for his role in the Beatrice deal. In June, it was Siegel's turn. The government in its presentencing memorandum praised Siegel as a "credible and reliable witness" who cooperated fully in the government's investigation. On June 18, 1990, Siegel was sentenced by judge Robert Ward, the same judge who threw the book at Bilzerian. This time, however, Judge Ward saw things differently. Hailing Siegel's cooperation, the judge announced that Siegel should receive "a sentence less than imposed on Mr. Freeman." Siegel was sentenced to serve two months in prison.

The whole episode revealed the worst aspects of the government crackdown on financial markets, and the tactics of Rudy Giuliani. Martin Siegel, in an attempt to get more lenient treatment for himself, falsely incriminated three men, Robert Freeman, Richard Wigton, and Timothy Tabor. Giuliani accepted the information at face value and ordered the handcuff arrests of the three in February 1987. When it became clear that Siegel had sold the government a bill of goods, the government refused to concede its error. Instead, Giuliani, who reveled in the press coverage generated by the arrests, only intensified his accusations of guilt. When he was running for mayor, Giuliani eventually did acknowledge that he ordered the arrests "too hastily." But he never apologized to Wigton, Freeman, and Tabor for publicly humiliating them, or for causing irreparable injury to their careers and reputations.

For his role in the debacle, Siegel was treated as a hero by the government and the sentencing judge. That he falsely incriminated innocent people to save himself was treated as irrelevant. The message from the government's behavior was obvious—better to cooperate and lie than insist on your innocence even if you are in fact innocent. And if a target of the government's investigation decided not to cooperate, he or she better be prepared to experience the full brunt of the government's wrath.

What about Robert Freeman's guilty plea? This made the government look even worse. The "crime" Freeman pled guilty to—insider trading based on hearing Siegel say "your bunny has a good nose"—was a joke. At most, Siegel confirmed a public rumor that Freeman had heard and acted on independently and that later turned out to be incorrect. Freeman never admitted to anything else and, even when he pled guilty, he refused to cooperate and implicate others. Given what he went through, Freeman's decision to end the fight is easy to understand.

Freeman's career as the head of arbitrage at the prestigious Goldman Sachs ended the day the government arrested him in February 1987. For almost the next two and one half years, he did little other than work on his defense. But the government, first Giuliani and then Romano, would never clear his name. The government had to have something to show for its efforts following the sensational arrests. When Freeman decided he wasn't willing to spend the rest of his life fighting, he allowed the government to claim victory and let Wigton and Tabor off the hook.

Freeman's guilty plea proved that when the government wanted to get somebody badly enough, it usually could. In other cases, the government at least gave the accused a chance to defend against allegations in a trial. While the vague and amorphous offenses of insider trading, stock parking, and manipulation made trials hard for defendants to win, at least there was a beginning and an end to the process. Freeman and the others, by contrast, were subjected to the legal system's version of Chinese water torture—arrests, public humiliation, and continued accusations of guilt with no opportunity for exoneration in a trial.

Under these circumstances, Freeman's guilty plea proves more about the effectiveness of the government's unethical tactics than it does about Freeman's guilt.

Princeton/Newport and Lisa Jones

The months surrounding the Wigton-Freeman-Tabor fiasco in early 1987 were depressing times in the United States attorney's office for the Southern District of New York. For the first time Giuliani's tactics were openly questioned by the press. Even within his own office there was dissension. Giuliani's chief deputy, Charles Carberry, resigned, a decision widely perceived to be linked to the public criticism of the government's actions toward the three investment bankers. Still, Giuliani refused to apologize for the overly harsh and grandstanding behavior of his office. Instead, he and Carberry's successor, Bruce Baird, a prosecutor of drug crimes with no experience or understanding of financial markets, decided to get even tougher. Giuliani always believed that the best defense was a good offense.

Giuliani then ordered his office to redouble its efforts to find some new ammunition that could jump-start the government's ongoing investigations. Some new cooperating witness was needed to trigger a fresh round of dominoes-style guilty pleas. Soon the government found the perfect man for the job—William Hale.

While investigating Freeman, the government learned that Freeman maintained a close relationship with Jay Regan, his old college roommate. Regan ran Princeton/Newport Trading Partners, a little-known but highly successful trading firm with offices in Princeton, New Jersey, and Newport Beach, California. The government also learned that the firm's cohead was Edward Thorp, a former math professor of Michael Milken. Princeton/Newport and Drexel had a business relationship as well, with Drexel executing a series of trades for Princeton/Newport that the government wanted to investigate. The Princeton/ Newport employee who executed the trades was William Hale; his counterpart at Drexel was Lisa Jones, trading assistant to Bruce Newberg.

When the government contacted Hale, he was unemployed and living in London. He had long ago been fired from Princeton/Newport after working there for fourteen months. But Hale was smart enough to know how to deal with the government.

He hired a close friend of Giuliani to represent him who quickly got Hale immunity in exchange for cooperation. Hale then told the grand jury that he was fired from Princeton/Newport because he complained about the company's illegal stock-parking scheme with Drexel. The government's assault on Wall Street was back in business, and Giuliani decided it was time to make his next move, a move that would make the handcuff arrests of the three investment bankers look modest by comparison.

On December 17, 1987, fifty federal marshals possessing a search warrant, carrying guns, and wearing bulletproof vests burst unannounced into the offices of Princeton/Newport Partners. While stunned employees watched in fear, the marshals seized records, files, and boxes of taped phone conversations. The same night in Los Angeles, a government investigator, Thomas Doonan, the same man who signed the arrest warrants against Wigton, Freeman, and Tabor, was sent to see Lisa Jones. Doonan, knowing that Jones as a junior assistant trader for Drexel had to be up for work before dawn the next morning, arrived at Jones's apartment at 10:00 P.M. that night. Doonan also knew that Jones was then only twenty-four and would likely be terrified by the sight of a government investigator with a badge knocking on her door late at night. Doonan's tactics were obviously calculated to bludgeon Jones into joining Hale as a cooperating government witness against Princeton/Newport and Drexel. But Jones didn't buckle. After answering a few preliminary questions, she refused to talk further and demanded to contact an attorney. Disappointed, Doonan handed her a subpoena compelling her to testify before the grand jury.

Jones gave her grand jury testimony the following month in January 1988. Frustrated by Jones's refusal to cooperate, the government gave her immunity to compel her to testify. When the government immunizes a witness, the witness cannot invoke the Fifth Amendment privilege against self-incrimination. Unknown to Jones, the government was in possession of a tape-recorded conversation seized in its raid of Princeton/Newport in which she and Hale appear to be discussing how a security will be sold from Princeton/Newport to Drexel and then back again at the original market price with Drexel being paid a commission for its role in the transaction. The government expected Jones, now testifying with immunity, to confirm the trades and, with any luck, to incriminate her superiors at Drexel.

The government was wrong again. Jones admitted executing trades with Hale but denied knowledge of any agreement requiring that Drexel purchase securities from Princeton/Newport and then sell them back. She also testified that she had no knowledge of any stock-parking scheme or other illegal arrangement. Furious, the government prosecutor, Jess Fardella, warned her that she was committing perjury, but she stuck to her story. In the ensuing months, she refused to recant her testimony even after the government invited her to do so. Exasperated, prosecutors decided to use their trump card and summoned Jones to listen to the recorded conversation with Hale discussing the terms of the sale and resale of securities between Princeton/Newport and Drexel. Jones then admitted that the conversations occurred but continued to insist that she believed the trades to be routine, legal transactions. No matter what the government did, Jones simply refused to cooperate.

Prosecutors badly underestimated Jones's loyalty to Drexel. In 1978 Jones, not yet fourteen, ran away from home in New Jersey and traveled to California. By lying about her age, she was able to get hired as a bank teller in Los Angeles and rent an apartment. For the next several years, she lied about everything—her age, education, background, work experience—in filling out credit card, job, and other applications. As she later explained, she had no husband or family to support her. It was either do what she could to make an honest living, including lying to get in the door, or turn to crime, most likely drugs and prostitution.

In 1980 Drexel, which had an affinity for underdogs like Jones, hired her in a clerical position. In Hollywood fashion, she rose through the ranks to become a trader's assistant working directly for Bruce Newberg, one of Drexel's head traders. By the time of her grand jury testimony in January 1988, she was earning more than $100,000 a year, a fortune to a young woman in her midtwenties with no formal education. Jones, against all the odds, had made something of herself. Nothing could make her turn against Drexel, the firm that rescued her from the wrong side of the tracks. She was to remain loyal until the end, no matter what the government threatened to do to her.

Prosecutors had no more luck with Princeton/Newport. The government had the tapes and the testimony of Hale, who would say anything to save himself. But Hale's credibility was suspect. He was, after all, a disgruntled former employee who had been fired several years earlier. He only came up with the story about the illegal trades between Drexel and Princeton/Newport in exchange for immunity. The government wanted more before going forward. Prosecutors were particularly hopeful about Regan, whom they believed could incriminate both Drexel and Freeman. They knew that if Regan and the other principals of Princeton/Newport could be broken, the government's investigation would really take off. As Bruce Baird reportedly told defense lawyers, "We have no real interest in Princeton/Newport . . . but Princeton can help us with Drexel Burnham and others. . . . If you cooperate, fine. If you don't, we are going to roll right over you to get where we want to go." Regan and the others decided to call the bluff. They refused to plead guilty, and rejected any promise of leniency in exchange for cooperation.

Giuliani was more than a little frustrated. His threats and bullying tactics had produced no more results with Lisa Jones and Princeton/Newport than they had with Wigton, Freeman, and Tabor. Another fiasco and public relations nightmare loomed as a distinct possibility, but Giuliani, with his honed jugular instinct, decided to up the ante and raise the stakes one more time.

On August 4, 1988, the government indicted Jay Regan and four other officers of Princeton/Newport for violating the Racketeer Influenced and Corrupt Organizations Act, popularly known as RICO. Also indicted was Bruce Newberg, Lisa Jones's boss at Drexel. The indictment was a watershed because it was the first time the antiracketeering law was invoked as part of Giuliani's attack on Wall Street. The defendants were accused of illegally operating Princeton/Newport, then one of the most successful securities firms, as a "racketeering enterprise" and of engaging in a "pattern of racketeering" activity by participating in an unlawful stock-parking scheme designed to generate phony tax benefits for themselves.

The same day, Giuliani announced that the government would seek to confiscate the value of the defendants' partnership interests and salaries—what the government referred to as "ill-gotten gains"—from participation in a "racketeering enterprise." As if this were not enough, the government also requested and was granted a temporary restraining order freezing Princeton/Newport's assets to prevent them from being dissipated. Terrified, the firm's largest financial backers and investors, including the Harvard University endowment fund, decided to pull out to avoid the risk that their own funds might be seized. The effect on Princeton/Newport was devastating. Deprived of financial backing, and stigmatized as a "racketeering enterprise," Princeton/Newport could not survive. In December 1988, long before there was any trial, the firm ceased operations and decided to liquidate.

Giuliani's use of RICO to bludgeon Princeton/Newport into submission was a radical departure from precedent. No securities firm had ever before been accused of being a "racketeering enterprise," and for good reason. RICO was enacted into law in 1970 as part of the Organized Crime Control Act. Congress made clear in RICO's preface, as is obvious from the name the Racketeers Influenced and Corrupt Organizations Act, that its purpose was to prevent the infiltration of legitimate businesses by organized crime:

> The Congress finds that (1) organized crime in the United States is a highly sophisticated, diversified, and widespread activity that annually drains billions of dollars from America's economy by unlawful conduct and the illegal use of force, fraud, and corruption; (2) organized crime derives a major portion of its power through money obtained from such illegal endeavors as syndicated gambling, loan sharking, the theft and fencing of property, the importation and distribution of narcotics and other dangerous drugs, and other forms of social exploitation; (3) this money and power are increasingly used to infiltrate and corrupt legitimate business and labor unions and to subvert and corrupt our democratic processes. . . .
>
> It is the purpose of this Act to seek the eradication of organized crime in the United States by strengthening the legal tools in the evidence-gathering process, by establishing new penal prohibitions, and by providing enhanced sanctions and new remedies to deal with the unlawful activities of those engaged in organized crime.

To achieve its objective of preventing the infiltration of legitimate businesses by organized crime, RICO gave the government sweeping new powers, including the power to freeze a defendant's assets at the time of indictment and confiscate them after conviction. Traditionally, criminal defendants are presumed to be innocent and face punishment only after conviction. RICO, by allowing the government to seize entire businesses connected even indirectly with a defendant at the time of indictment, before any proof of guilt, is a major exception to this general principle. The government is authorized, in effect, to act as prosecutor, judge, and jury in the same case. The government under RICO is also able to make it more difficult for the accused to wage a defense by, for example, seizing the funds that a defendant would have used to hire an attorney. And if a defendant is convicted, RICO provides for onerous criminal penalties.

RICO's enhanced powers and penalties were clearly intended to be used only in exceptional circumstances involving mob violence and other similar antisocial behavior. In fact, an early version of RICO made it "unlawful to be a member of the Mafia, Cosa Nostra or other criminal organization." But this language had to be dropped because of concerns that it would penalize status in an organization, rather than unlawful acts, and would therefore be unconstitutional. Instead, Congress defined the crime as engaging in a "pattern of racketeering activity" in connection with a "racketeering enterprise." But Congress could not, and did not, clearly define the meaning of "pattern," "racketeering activity," or "enterprise."

RICO's vague, almost meaningless, statutory language requires prosecutors to exercise maximum caution to prevent the law from being misused in ways that Congress never intended. But instead Rudy Giuliani saw RICO's amorphous language as a potent weapon to rubber-hose and coerce guilty pleas and punish those who refused to cooperate. He had already pioneered the criminalization of such standardless offenses as insider trading, stock parking, and manipulation. Now the government could claim that the same underlying conduct that supposedly provided the basis for these standardless offenses also constituted a "pattern of racketeering activity" that justified a RICO prosecution. By this bootstrapping logic, Giuliani was able to drop the equivalent of a nuclear bomb on any target, at any time, no matter how trivial or harmless the underlying conduct.

This is exactly what Giuliani did to Princeton/Newport. Before its encounter with Giuliani, Princeton/Newport was known for its hedging trading strategies using complex computer programs. The basic idea was to purchase a convertible security and simultaneously sell the underlying security short. The firm made these trades after identifying abnormal price relationships between the two sides of the hedged position. The strategy was successful, but the firm had a problem because both sides of the hedge were not taxed in the same way. Gains (or losses) produced by the long side of the hedge, if held for the required holding period, were treated as long-term, while gains (or losses) produced by the short side of the hedge were always treated as short-term. Because of this anomaly in the tax laws, the hedge could result in a tax liability without any underlying economic gain.

During 1984 and 1985, Princeton/Newport engaged in fifty-nine "tax trades" for the purpose of matching the tax treatment of both sides of its hedge transaction. The firm sold securities that had earlier been purchased as one side of a hedge to another securities firm, frequently Drexel, with the understanding that the securities would be repurchased after one month at the original sales price plus a commission. The goal was to avoid the tax mismatch and have both sides of the hedge taxed as short-term capital gains (or losses).

The fifty-nine tax trades constituted a tiny fraction of Princeton/Newport's total trades during 1984–1985. The total tax savings accomplished by the trades was also relatively small, approximately $400,000 for a firm with over $1 billion in assets. Moreover, when Princeton/Newport's entire tax returns for the 1984 and 1985 years were audited, it turned out, and the government conceded, that the firm had *overpaid* its taxes by $1.6 million. Even if the tax trades were improper, which was far from clear, Princeton/Newport was still entitled to a tax refund of over $1 million. Under these circumstances, normal practice would have been for Princeton/Newport and the IRS to reach a quick out-of-court settlement of amounts in dispute without the need for even a civil proceeding. Instead, Rudy Giuliani decided to use a law directed at mob violence and organized crime to drive Princeton/Newport out of business before those indicted had a chance to defend themselves in a trial.

Giuliani's destruction of Princeton/Newport could not have come at a better time for him. After being embarrassed by the Wigton-Freeman-Tabor fiasco, Giuliani had now reasserted his power to destroy those who refused to play his game by pleading guilty and implicating others. It was a message heard loud and clear by Drexel Burnham and Michael Milken, the primary targets of the government's investigation. The message was also not lost on Robert Freeman, who ultimately decided to plead guilty to the ridiculous "your bunny has a good nose" charge rather than contine to fight. It was no accident that Freeman pled guilty in August 1988, the month of the Princeton/Newport RICO indictment, and Drexel did the same in December 1988, the month Princeton/Newport went out of business.

Giuliani was still not satisfied. In November 1988, the government indicted Lisa Jones for perjury based on her grand jury testimony about the tax trades. Her trial in early 1989 was a massacre. Prosecutor Mark Hansen told the jury that Jones lied to the grand jury to conceal Drexel's involvement in the criminal tax trades because she wanted to protect Drexel and her comfortable lifestyle. Jones "made the wrong choice," Hansen insisted, when "she chose to protect the criminal conduct of others." When Jones took the witness stand to testify in her own defense, she was confronted with the inconsistency between her grand jury testimony denying knowledge of any arrangements between Princeton/Newport and Drexel and the tapes of her conversations with Will Hale. Her attempts to explain that she believed her grand jury testimony was truthful at the time rang hollow when prosecutor Hansen forced her to admit in excruciating detail her lifetime pattern of lies about her education and background. She was quickly convicted and sentenced to serve eighteen months in prison.

The Princeton/Newport trial began a few months later in late June 1989. The defense strategy was to admit that the tax trades took place and explain why the defendants believed them to be legal. Jay Regan, one of the two founders of Princeton/Newport and its managing partner, was the key defense witness. He testified that he believed the tax trades as structured were legitimate to generate tax losses based on advice from his accountants, a report of the Tax Section of the New York City Bar Association, and his own study of tax laws and regulations. The defense tried to bolster Regan's testimony by attempting to introduce evidence of how the relevant tax laws and regulations had been interpreted in the past. The defense also offered the testimony of leading tax experts who were prepared to testify that Regan's interpretation of the rules was reasonable.

The trial judge, however, refused to allow the defense to offer this evidence or expert testimony. Prosecutor Mark Hansen, who had just successfully convicted Lisa Jones, diverted the jurors' attention away from the complicated tax issues in the case even further. Hansen assured the jurors that they didn't need to worry about technical nuances of tax law to convict under RICO. "You don't need a fancy tax-law expert because common sense tells you it's fraudulent, it's phony," Hansen proclaimed. "If it sounds sleazy, it's because it is sleazy." With this appeal to the basest anti-financier, "decade of greed"–hating mentality so prevalent in the popular media, Hansen convinced the jurors that guilt under RICO depended on whether complex trading practices were "sleazy." Whether the defendants had in fact complied with the tax law became irrelevant in a case where they were accused of tax fraud. The jury convicted the defendants on substantially all of the charges.

Giuliani had finally gone too far. During the trial, the Justice Department adopted a major policy change making it practically impossible to base future RICO cases on tax offenses. The accompanying statement, in a thinly disguised slap at Rudy Giuliani, made clear that a change was required to prevent overzealous prosecutors from converting routine civil tax disputes into major criminal RICO prosecutions. The goal, in short, was to guarantee there would never be another Princeton/Newport.

The Justice Department's policy change had a major impact on the Princeton/Newport defendants. Judge Robert Carter, the trial judge in the case, inferred from the government's new position that the "likelihood that future tax fraud cases being brought as RICO violations" was "remote." While he refused to overturn the convictions, Judge Carter ruled that RICO's forfeiture provisions allowing the government to confiscate the defendants' entire ownership interest in Princeton/Newport because of the tax trades were too onerous and therefore unconstitutional. On appeal, the Second Circuit finished the job and threw out the convictions for the tax trades altogether. This was at least a Pyrrhic victory for the Princeton/Newport defendants, although not much more than that. Personal and professional reputations were irreparably harmed by the ordeal of the trial and conviction as racketeers. And Princeton/Newport itself, the firm that Jay Regan cofounded and built up into one of the most successful securities firms, was completely destroyed, having been RICOed out of existence by Rudy Giuliani.

The Lisa Jones story had an even more unhappy ending. Jones testified falsely (although maybe unintentionally) before the grand jury, but this was not the reason why she was prosecuted. The government went after Jones because she refused to cooperate and, instead, defended the tax trades. At the time of her trial, however, there had been as yet no proof that the trades were illegal. This was to be determined later at the Princeton/Newport trial. But once the Second Circuit overturned the convictions of the Princeton/Newport defendants, the government could no longer claim that the tax trades were criminal. The result was that Lisa Jones was prosecuted and convicted for covering up "crimes" that were never proven. Sadly, Jones was unable to get her conviction overturned. The best she could do was have her prison sentence reduced from eighteen to ten months. Excluding Dennis Levine and Martin Siegel, who were employed by Drexel only a short time, Jones was the only Drexel employee, other than Michael Milken himself, who ever spent time in jail.

When asked in a national television interview whether the government's treatment of Jones was too harsh, prosecutor Hansen unrepentantly responded, "In the search for justice, blood gets spilled and that's an unfortunate fact of life." What the government did was "unfortunate," to be sure, but not for reasons having anything to do with "justice." The prosecutorial excesses in the government's witch-hunt, and the damage to the people who refused to play the government's game, were the real misfortune. Of all of those whose lives and careers were wrecked, Lisa Jones, the teenage runaway who improbably made something out of her life, was perhaps the most pathetic victim of Rudy Giuliani's reign of terror.

CHAPTER 5

The End of Drexel

From the time Ivan Boesky's deal with the government was first announced in the fall of 1986, it was obvious that Drexel and Milken were the ultimate targets. And if anyone forgot, they were reminded by the constant stream of leaks from "reliable government sources" or "people familiar with the government's investigation" that indictments were inevitable. The news department of the normally probusiness *Wall Street Journal* was by far the worst offender. Week after week, reporters James Stewart, Daniel Hertzberg, and Laurie Cohen breathlessly reported how the government had "unearthed substantial evidence to support charges of criminal violations of securities laws by Michael R. Milken and Drexel Burnham Lambert Inc." Acting more like press spokespeople for the prosecutors than objective reporters, Stewart, Hertzberg, and Cohen wrote one front-page story after another that read like prosecutorial briefs explaining to the public why Drexel and Milken were guilty of major crimes. These stories continued without interruption for the next several years.

These press leaks to friendly reporters were designed to weaken Drexel and Milken's resolve to resist. When Levine, Boesky, and Siegel gave up without a fight, there were no leaks. The government kept negotiations secret to maximize the value of their cooperation. But with Drexel and Milken, there was no secrecy. The government hoped that by repeatedly publicizing allegations of criminal conduct before any charges were filed, Drexel and Milken would realize that trying to defend themselves was hopeless.

The ceaseless drumbeat of negative publicity made Drexel an attractive target for its enemies. In February 1987, Staley Continental filed a $200 million lawsuit accusing Drexel of racketeering, extortion, and stock manipulation by attempting to coerce Staley's management to participate in a Drexel-led leveraged buyout in November 1986. The suit charged Drexel with secretly buying Staley stock pursuant to a "scheme whereby a company is selected as a takeover candidate and Drexel and its associated persons thereafter embark upon a planned pattern of conduct designed to place the target in a position of being taken over." When Staley refused to cooperate with Drexel's leveraged buyout plans and planned a major stock offering instead, James Dahl, a key Drexel official, supposedly threatened Staley's management: "It is very important for us to sit down and talk before you do something that hurts me and before I do something that hurts you. . . . The next thing that happens is someone files a 13(d) . . . and management is thrown out." Staley's stock offering was unsuccessful, the suit charged, because Drexel's presence made its shares so "tainted" that investors didn't want to buy them.

The Staley suit was widely reported as an exposé of Drexel's "financial gangsterism" and "Cosa Nostra tactics." What the suit really showed was that even the most ridiculous accusations would be taken seriously in the feeding frenzy to destroy Drexel. Staley's stock price had been depressed for some time because of poor performance, making it an ideal takeover candidate. Staley's stock price rose from $27 to $34 $1/2$ within a few weeks after Drexel and its clients began accumulating shares. When Staley's management rebuffed Drexel's leveraged buyout proposal and tried to sell additional stock instead, its stock price again fell below $30.

The stock price fell, and the attempted stock offering was unsuccessful, because investors lost confidence in Staley's management and were disappointed that the potential takeover transaction was frustrated. Dahl's supposed "threat" to Staley's management (which he denied making) appears to be nothing more than a statement that Drexel would launch a hostile takeover and throw out Staley's management if they persisted in harming investors, including Drexel, which owned a large block of Staley stock. Staley's investors would have only benefited if a takeover or other restructuring transaction occurred, as Staley's earlier stock-price rise demonstrated. But by now hostile takeovers and leveraged buyouts had become dirty words, and this perspective was totally lost. Drexel's competitors, who clearly knew better, were still all too willing to feign outrage and mail copies of the Staley suit to potential clients.

Drexel's mounting problems began to take a toll. Revenues plunged from $4 billion in 1986 to $3.2 billion in 1987, while profits fell from $545.5 million to approximately $125 million. The decline in profitability was due, at least in part, to the setting aside of large reserves against possible damages arising from the government's civil and criminal investigations of the firm and related private suits. It was also partly due to Drexel's decision to de-emphasize financing hostile takeovers while the government's investigation was pending.

Nineteen eighty-eight only brought more problems. In April Congressman John Dingell convened a congressional hearing for the sole objective of publicly embarrassing Drexel and Milken. The stated purpose of the hearing was to investigate Drexel employee partnerships that invested in high-yield bonds underwritten by Drexel. But Dingell's opening statement made clear that his real purpose was to launch a tirade against takeovers and junk bonds:

> Inefficiency and diversion of funds in this market are of serious concern to the subcommittee and the Nation. . . . [C]ompanies which have existed for decades, which have carried the brunt of our national defense through two World Wars, which have provided employment in the heartland of America, no longer exist. They have been victims of takeovers, financed through the junk bond market. Research and development budgets have suffered as millions of dollars have been diverted to pay high interest rates on junk bonds. In short, the competitiveness of the United States in the international market, indeed, our balance of trade and the future of this country, is impacted by junk bonds.

Dingell called Michael Milken as the hearing's first witness. Milken, as Dingell knew all too well, was under grand jury investigation and had informed the committee through his lawyer, the famed criminal defense attorney Edward Bennett Williams, that he would take the Fifth Amendment and refuse to answer questions. Dingell compelled him to appear anyway and go through the humiliating spectacle of taking the Fifth Amendment before Congress. While the privilege against self-incrimination is a fundamental constitutional right guaranteed to all Americans, the natural inference is that it is only valuable to those with something to hide. When Milken was forced to take the Fifth Amendment and did not respond to Dingell's tirade against junk bonds and hostile takeovers, it seemed as if everything that Drexel and Milken did was corrupt.

Fred Joseph, Drexel's CEO, was the next witness, and he only made matters worse. When grilled about the evils of takeovers and junk bonds, Joseph responded lamely that financing takeovers was only a small part of Drexel's business. And when asked about the employee investment partnerships—which Congressman Dingell referred to as "insider accounts" to conjure up the evil image of insider trading—Joseph resorted to confusing legal technicalities to explain why the partnerships were not illegal.

Joseph should have gone on the offensive and told Congress how the existence of the employee investment partnerships proved the value of high-yield bonds as an investment. Why else would Drexel employees want to buy them? One reason why Drexel was so successful selling high-yield bonds to investors, Joseph should have said, is that its employees were willing to use their own money to make the same investments themselves. But Joseph made none of these points, apparently concluding that such aggressive responses would offend Congressman Dingell. Instead, Joseph retreated, and said that the partnerships' investment practices must be monitored to avoid even "the possible appearance of unfairness."

In a "supplemental submission" to the committee shortly after the hearing was concluded, Joseph communicated Drexel's new "firm policy which discontinues investment by employee accounts in public offerings of debt securities underwritten by Drexel." If Joseph thought he was going to win Congressman Dingell over by this appeasement strategy, he was badly mistaken. Joseph's decision to cave after facing congressional pressure was widely interpreted as a public admission of guilt.

The next public relations debacle was the publication of Connie Bruck's book, *The Predators' Ball*, in the spring of 1988. Hailed by reviewers as a brilliant exposé of the excesses of the 1980s, the book describes how Drexel and Milken were the masterminds of a sinister cabal of financiers, corporate raiders, and arbitrageurs. In fact, the book, written by a journalist with no appreciation of the economic significance of the restructuring revolution she was describing, was nothing more than an expanded version of the Drexel- and Milken-bashing articles that appeared regularly in the *Wall Street Journal*. Even the transactions described were the same. But Bruck knew what the public wanted to hear. Instead of

analyzing the role of takeovers and high-yield debt in the economy, she described how Drexel allegedly hired prostitutes at its
annual high-yield bond conference ("the Predators' Ball") for the
pleasure of its morally depraved high-roller clients. And to give
her account an aura of ultimate truth, Bruck charged that Drexel
and Milken had attempted to buy her off to prevent the book's
publication. It seemed like Drexel and Milken were willing to do
anything to cover up their illegal and immoral deeds.

By June of 1988, the *Wall Street Journal* was reporting that the
SEC had decided to file a massive securities-fraud action against
Drexel and Milken but that formal charges would be delayed until
the U.S. attorney completed the criminal investigation. Drexel and
Milken had been tried and convicted in the press but had no
opportunity to defend themselves because no charges had yet
been filed. The government wanted to thoroughly poison public
opinion before Drexel and Milken had a chance to respond. This
strategy was devastatingly effective but repugnant. By leaking confidential information to the press the government was, in effect,
exploiting its own "inside information" to make it impossible for
Drexel and Milken to get a fair trial. The press never questioned
how the government had the moral standing to accuse others of
abusing inside information when it was guilty of the same practice. Instead, the press, with almost no exceptions, were eager participants in the campaign to destroy Drexel and Milken.

The SEC Sues Drexel

In September 1988, the shoe finally dropped when the SEC filed a
183-page securities-fraud suit against Drexel, Milken, and others.
Legal analysts were surprised that the SEC would sue before the
criminal investigation had concluded because the suit gave the
defendants a preview of the government's evidence. But the SEC
was more than willing to bear this risk. The government's allegations had been so extensively leaked that the SEC's suit didn't
reveal anything Drexel and Milken didn't already know. Also, the
SEC had succeeded in bypassing the usual lottery system for
assignment of judges and had its suit assigned to Judge Milton
Pollack, the government's most loyal ally on the bench.

Judge Pollack immediately ordered that Drexel would not be
allowed to defend itself against the SEC's charges by subpoenaing

witnesses or documents. To allow Drexel and Milken access to the government's evidence, Judge Pollack reasoned, would prejudice the government's continuing criminal investigation. A more impartial judge would have concluded that the government shouldn't have filed its civil suit if it was concerned about prejudice to its criminal investigation. Having decided to file the civil case, the government could not now complain if the defendants wanted to defend themselves. But Judge Pollack had no interest in being impartial, or in preventing prejudice to Drexel and Milken, who were now in the position of being formally accused of securities fraud without any ability, once again, to respond to the charges.

Drexel recognized that being before Judge Pollack was a no-win situation. When Drexel lawyers discovered that Judge Pollack's wife expected to receive $30 million from a Drexel-financed investment, they made the controversial decision to file a motion for disqualification, which Judge Pollack angrily denied. Ordinarily, judges are not supposed to hear cases when they or a member of their immediate family is a major investor in a transaction connected to one of the parties. For this reason, most judges in Judge Pollack's position would have disqualified themselves. But it was also obvious that the real reason Drexel wanted to get rid of Judge Pollack had nothing to do with his wife's profitable investment, which, if anything, should have made the judge sympathetic to Drexel. The real reason was that Judge Pollack was so progovernment and anti-Drexel that there was no hope of receiving fair treatment. Judge Pollack also understood Drexel's motives for trying to disqualify him, and this only made him hate Drexel even more.

Drexel appealed Judge Pollack's refusal to disqualify himself, and the entire Second Circuit decided to hear the case. The court ruled against Drexel, but three judges, a small minority but still an extraordinary number under the circumstances, believed Judge Pollack should have disqualified himself. Drexel fought until the end, unsuccessfully appealing the disqualification issue all the way to the United States Supreme Court. Now Drexel was stuck with Judge Pollack, which from its perspective was truly unfortunate. A fairer judge might have made a difference.

The SEC's 183-page complaint was skillfully drafted to create the impression that Drexel and Milken had defrauded investors, their clients, and were guilty of insider trading. In reality, what the

SEC's complaint revealed was an incredibly weak case. The SEC's key allegation was that Milken and Boesky entered into a "secret arrangement" in early 1984 under which both would purchase and sell securities on behalf of the other. The "secret arrangement," the SEC's sinister name for what was more commonly referred to as a stock-parking scheme, lasted until 1986 when "Milken and Boesky agreed to reconcile their outstanding profit and losses." This led, the SEC charged, to the payment by Boesky to Drexel of $5.3 million in cash, which was "falsely described" in an invoice (which the government called the "smoking gun" document) as payment for "consulting services." The bulk of the complaint describes the transactions entered into under the "secret arrangement" that allegedly led to the $5.3 million payment.

The government's case rested on a very fine line. If Milken and Boesky had not entered into a definitive (but unwritten) agreement in 1984 to act on each other's behalf, their subsequent actions could be viewed as routine reciprocal accommodations to preserve good client relationships. And if the favors ran more in one direction than the other, it is hardly surprising there would ultimately be some reconciliation. To have any hope of disproving this innocent explanation of what occurred, the government would need to rely heavily on Boesky's testimony as an admitted felon. This in itself was a problem for the government given Boesky's shaky credibility. The last thing the government needed was a repeat of the Wigton-Freeman-Tabor fiasco in which the three men were arrested based on false information provided by Martin Siegel.

And even if Boesky were believed, there was still the problem of demonstrating who was harmed by the stock-parking scheme, or "secret arrangement." Maybe Drexel and Boesky committed books-and-records violations by not reporting all securities under their control, but so what? One might think that if the "secret arrangement" was as bad as the SEC claimed, it would have no trouble coming up with some victims who were injured. But none were identified.

When the specific transactions described in the complaint are analyzed, the absence of victims is even more striking. This is clear from the Fischbach transaction, the most prominent transaction in the complaint. The extremely ambiguous evidence of what occurred between Milken and Boesky in Fischbach casts considerable doubt on whether any "secret arrangement" ever existed. But even if the government's claim that Milken instructed Boesky to purchase Fischbach shares to void the standstill agreement between Posner and Fischbach is accepted as true, there is still no injury. Rather, Fischbach's investors only benefited from invalidation of the standstill agreement.

Other transactions in which Drexel and Milken supposedly acted unlawfully demonstrate nothing more than Milken did what he could to help his clients. For example, Golden Nugget, a Drexel client, purchased shares of MCA in 1984 in anticipation of a possible takeover attempt. Golden Nugget, on Milken's advice, then decided not to go forward and sell its shares instead. On October 12, 1984, the *Wall Street Journal* quoted Stephen Wynn, Golden Nugget's CEO, as saying he intended "to sit" on the MCA investment. But this is not what Wynn did. In the following weeks, Golden Nugget sold its MCA shares to Boesky through Drexel. The SEC alleged that Boesky's purchases were made at Milken's direction under the "secret arrangement" and were illegal because not properly recorded in Drexel's and Boesky's books and records. Whether such a violation occurred depends, as in Fischbach, on the fine line between Boesky acting at Milken's direction as his agent, or independently for whatever reason, including in response to Milken's recommendations. At worst, however, there was a technical reporting violation that harmed no one. And Golden Nugget, Milken's client, benefited by being able to unload shares to Boesky that it no longer wanted to own.

In other transactions, the SEC did accuse Drexel and Milken of using the "secret arrangement" to defraud their clients, but their allegations made no sense. For example, the SEC accused Drexel and Milken of defrauding their client, Maxxam Group, in connection with Maxxam's takeover of Pacific Lumber. The SEC charged that Milken instructed Boesky to purchase Pacific Lumber shares under the "secret agreement" at prices in excess of Maxxam's original tender price to force Maxxam to raise its bid. But Pacific Lumber's stock price immediately rose above Maxxam's original tender price when the bid was first announced because the market expected a higher offer. For Boesky to purchase any shares, he, like all other investors, had to pay more than the tender price, so Boesky's purchases at the market price prove nothing. The SEC also ignored Boesky's many sales of Pacific Lumber stock, which were obviously inconsistent with the claim that Boesky was directed by Milken to purchase. The SEC simply could muster no evidence that Drexel and Milken had injured anybody.

The SEC's insider-trading allegations were equally weak. In early 1985, Drexel's client, Occidental Petroleum Corporation, was negotiating a merger with Diamond Shamrock Corporation. After trading in the two stocks was halted pending a major public announcement of the merger, Boesky began purchasing Diamond Shamrock shares and selling Occidental short. The SEC charged that these decisions were ordered by Milken pursuant to the "secret arrangement" while he was in possession of material inside information. But as the SEC was forced to admit, the merger never occurred and Boesky suffered large losses. If Milken was abusing inside information, why didn't he tip Boesky that the merger was not going to happen? The SEC offered no explanation why Milken, who under the SEC's theory was required to reimburse Boesky, had any motive to use the "secret arrangement" to inflict losses on himself.

With so much advance buildup from the never-ending leaks, the SEC's suit was a big anticlimax. The press should have been filled with stories about how the suit showed the emperor has no clothes, but few, if any, such stories appeared. Instead, the *Washington Post* reported that the SEC had filed "the most sweeping securities fraud case against a major Wall Street firm in the agency's history." Similarly, the *New York Times* reported that the government's accusations were "stronger than expected." Others, including the *Wall Street Journal*, reported that the suit had exposed widespread corruption on Wall Street and it was just a matter of time until Drexel and Milken were criminally indicted. The stage was set, and now it was Giuliani's turn to apply the pressure. He was to make the most of the opportunity.

Drexel Pleads Guilty

Rudy Giuliani realized, even if the public did not, that the case against Drexel was less than overwhelming. But he also knew that the government still had the ultimate weapon, the ability to charge Drexel and its key employees with violations of RICO and move to seize all their assets. Using RICO had worked so well with Princeton/Newport in August 1988, just one month before the SEC's suit against Drexel and Milken. There was no reason it wouldn't be equally effective again.

Giuliani also realized prosecutors would have even more leverage if they could find additional cooperating witnesses besides

Boesky. This proved to be no problem. Faced with the threat of a RICO prosecution, several key Drexel employees were more than willing to cooperate in exchange for immunity. Charles Thurnher, a Drexel employee who reportedly had knowledge of Boesky's supposedly phony payment of $5.3 million to Drexel for "consulting services," was the first to cooperate. Then James Dahl, Milken's top bond salesman, testified before the grand jury and was given immunity. In early December 1988, Cary Maultasch and Terren Peizer reached agreements to turn state's evidence. The *Wall Street Journal* reported how the rush to cooperate against Drexel and Milken had "turned into a stampede." Maultasch's testimony, according to the *Journal*, was particularly damaging, making the indictments of Drexel and Milken a virtual certainty.

Giuliani, having created the impression that the rats were bailing out of the ship, then demanded that Drexel plead guilty or face a RICO indictment. Giuliani's insistence that Drexel would have to not only plead guilty but also cooperate against Milken split the firm. On one side against any deal stood Milken's supporters, who included many younger executives and traders who worked with Milken in Beverly Hills. Leon Black, Drexel's head of mergers and acquisitions, and two of Milken's top allies, John Kissick and Peter Ackerman, were also in this group. Arguing that it was immoral to help Giuliani convict Milken, the man most responsible for Drexel's success, these Milken supporters opposed acceding to Giuliani's demands. Kissick especially was vehemently against turning on Milken. Others within Drexel, particularly older executives based in New York who were not part of the high-yield bond division, were in favor of a deal to avoid a RICO indictment.

Fred Joseph was in the middle. Joseph, like Milken, came from a modest background. He grew up in Boston, the son of a taxi driver. An amateur boxer when he was younger, Joseph had the same outsider, underdog mentality so common at Drexel. But Joseph, much more than Milken, also craved acceptance and respectability. This trait, as the congressional hearing on the employee investment partnerships revealed, made him weak and indecisive. He would vacillate between a willingness to fight and an eagerness to please Drexel's accusers. During the tense negotiations with Giuliani in December, Joseph told others at Drexel that he was confident things would work out because "Rudy likes me." Joseph's lack of insight into Giuliani's agenda was to prove very costly. He never learned, even after being burned by Congressman Dingell, that with those bent on destroying you the appeasement strategy never works.

Conflicted between wanting to fight and wanting to work out something with Giuliani, Joseph could not figure out what to do. On December 19, 1988, the Drexel board of directors followed Joseph's recommendation and voted unanimously to reject any deal with Giuliani. That night at the Drexel Christmas party, Joseph gave a rousing speech to thunderous applause announcing the board's decision and vowing to fight until the end no matter what the consequences. Observers reported that many in the audience, particularly those loyal to Milken, broke down and cried.

Unfazed, Giuliani called Joseph the next day, December 20, and delivered the final ultimatum. Unless Drexel agreed to Giuliani's terms immediately, the firm would be indicted under RICO at 4:00 P.M. on December 21. Joseph, who had talked so tough the night before, panicked. After around-the-clock meetings, Giuliani made some minor concessions and the deal was done by 4:30 P.M. on December 21. Drexel agreed to plead guilty and settle the SEC lawsuit. The Drexel board voted 16–6 to approve the deal, with Joseph in the minority. But nobody within Drexel was fooled. Joseph's vote against the deal that he himself had negotiated and signed was seen for what it was—a cynical ploy to ease the sense of betrayal that so many felt.

When the dust settled, the extent of Drexel's capitulation became clear. Drexel would plead guilty to six felonies and pay a record penalty of $650 million in fines and restitution. In addition, the firm agreed to fire Milken and deny him his anticipated compensation for 1988, expected to be around $200 million. Lowell Milken, Milken's brother, would also be let go and be denied one-half his bonus for 1988. At Giuliani's insistence, Drexel did more than fire Milken and his brother. The firm was also required to cooperate in the government's continuing criminal investigation of the Milkens. Drexel also agreed, as the government demanded, that its employees would be prohibited from discussing any firm-related business transaction with Michael or Lowell Milken.

The post-Milken Drexel was to be run as a quasi government agency. Drexel was forced to hire and pay for "compliance officers" and an SEC-approved accounting firm to monitor its actions, including every high-yield bond trade, to detect any possible wrongdoing. These new government-ordered monitors were to report to a new oversight committee, consisting of three new outside directors who also had to be approved by the regulators. In perhaps the most demeaning move of all, Drexel was forced to hire John Shad, the former chairman of the SEC who presided over the initial regulatory investigation of the firm, as its new chairman.

Drexel's deal with the government guaranteed the firm would never again be a factor on Wall Street. By pleading guilty to six felonies, the firm was disgraced. Few understood that the felony charges were for acts that were, at worst, the same hypertechnical books-and-records-type offenses alleged in the SEC's civil complaint that nobody had ever thought constituted crimes. The $650 million that Drexel was forced to pay in fines and restitution to victims of its illegal conduct was also unbelievably harsh. During the entire investigation, the government never identified anyone who was harmed by any of Drexel's supposed "crimes."

The other provisions of the deal were, if anything, even worse. What authority did the government and Drexel have to refuse to pay the Milkens the compensation they were owed for 1988? The Milkens at that time had not been accused, let alone convicted, of any crime. In fact, the government never claimed that Drexel itself engaged in any illegal acts in 1988 or that the money the Milkens were owed was compensation for anything other than lawful activity. What Drexel did, in effect, was to confiscate the Milkens' property without any hearing or trial so that their money could be used to help pay Drexel's $650 million obligation. At the same time, the government required Drexel to keep cooperating witnesses like Jim Dahl and Terren Peizer on the payroll and pay them millions of dollars notwithstanding their diminished role.

Drexel's agreement to fire the Milkens and assist in the government's continuing criminal investigation of them added insult to injury. Also offensive was Drexel's agreement that none of its employees could even talk to Michael or Lowell Milken about a business transaction. The government apparently saw no problem with Drexel discussing business strategy with real criminals like Ivan Boesky or Dennis Levine, but the Milkens were another matter. It was obvious that Drexel was now in the business of doing the government's bidding. The firm that rose to prominence by brazenly defying the establishment was a thing of the past.

The government also made sure Drexel would never be able to have a change of heart and return to its old ways. The government-installed compliance officers, accounting firm, and outside directors would prevent any backsliding. And if the regulators still weren't satisfied, John Shad, the regulator arguably the most responsible for Drexel's predicament, would take care of the problem. Joseph tried to put the best face on government oversight of its operations, claiming that Drexel was guaranteed to remain "squeaky clean." Another Drexel employee was closer to the mark, however, when he predicted that Drexel was now "going to die a slow death."

Joseph did secure one concession in his negotiations with the government. Instead of the normal guilty plea where the defendant is required to acknowledge guilt, Drexel was permitted to plead by declaring it was "unable to contest" the government's charges. But if Joseph thought this fig leaf would impress anyone, he was badly mistaken. Congressman Markey, reflecting public reaction to Drexel's plea, immediately announced, "We now know that the single most successful firm on Wall Street during the 1980's largely built its fortune on a foundation of criminality." And Congressman Dingell, whom Joseph tried to win over by discontinuing investments in new issues by the employee investment partnerships, threatened to hold more congressional hearings on why Drexel's punishment was so light.

For Rudy Giuliani, there was nothing more he could accomplish as a prosecutor. He had destroyed Drexel, and Milken's indictment was now just a matter of time (Milken was indicted in April 1989). It was time to move on. In January 1989, Giuliani resigned his position as United States attorney to run for mayor of New York.

Joseph's Christmas Eve capitulation was the beginning of the end for Drexel. Did he do the right thing by agreeing to such draconian penalties? It is easy to argue he had no choice. Giuliani was relentless and unscrupulous, willing to use any tactic, including unleashing the RICO monster, to obtain his desired outcome. Earlier in December 1988, Princeton/Newport had been forced to liquidate after its principals were indicted under RICO. The defendants' claims of innocence were not enough to prevent nervous investors from withdrawing their funds to avoid the government's asset freeze. Drexel may well have suffered the same fate even if the firm were ultimately proven innocent. Any investment firm, including Drexel, would find it close to impossible to survive after a RICO indictment. A guilty plea would at least give the firm a chance to survive, and some chance of survival was better than none.

And what chance did Drexel have of winning at trial? Probably very slim. Megasuccessful corporations are never very sympathetic defendants, and Drexel, the symbol of the excesses of the "decade of greed," would be the least sympathetic of all. Since the public had been brainwashed into believing that hypertechnical books-and-records violations were the white-collar equivalent of murder, a jury would likely share these same views. There would surely be no shortage of cooperating government witnesses. It was simply a question of how many witnesses the government wanted to immunize in exchange for cooperation. Few could be counted on to refuse to cooperate at the risk of being indicted under RICO themselves. A jury, faced with a parade of ex-Drexel employees testifying about the magnitude of the firm's crimes, would have to be impressed. If a conviction was inevitable anyway, Drexel might as well plead guilty and avoid the ordeal and expense of an even more prolonged investigation and trial.

Joseph, in short, had no good options. He faced the ultimate catch-22. He could either plead guilty or continue to fight. If he chose the latter course, Drexel would likely be driven out of business before a trial and probably convicted at trial. For these reasons, Joseph's decision to plead guilty and pay the obviously extortionate $650 million penalty was a rational response to the government's police-state tactics. Allowing Drexel to be placed under government control was less justifiable, but maybe Joseph believed the shackles would be only temporary. He and the other Drexel directors had to weigh the sacrifice in profitability resulting from government control against the prospect that the firm would no longer exist if it refused to plead guilty. This was still a decision primarily about money.

But Joseph's decision to sell out Milken and his brother by agreeing to fire them, withhold their compensation, and cooperate against them was a singular act of cowardice. Corporations are legal fictions; they are not people. A corporation convicted in a criminal trial cannot be sent to prison. Drexel only faced financial penalties, no matter what happened. Michael Milken and his brother, on the other hand, faced personal ruin and imprisonment. What Joseph and the other directors did in their deal with the government was make a bargain with the devil. They were allowed to save their jobs and high salaries, at least temporarily, in exchange for helping the government convict the Milkens and send them to prison. That Michael Milken was the man most responsible for the very success and high salaries that Joseph and the other Drexel directors were trying to protect for themselves made the decision that much more morally bankrupt.

There was an important practical consequence as well. Joseph had to lead a crippled Drexel into an uncertain future without Milken's help. Time would prove that Joseph, who sold Drexel's soul to protect himself, was not up to the task.

Drexel Cannot Survive

Just before Drexel's guilty plea, Joseph sent a memo to Drexel employees updating them on the status of the government's investigation. He told them that the investigation had cost Drexel $1.5 billion in potential revenues and $175 million in legal fees and other direct expenses. He also expressed the opinion that these losses could be turned around by making a deal. When Drexel in December 1988, the same month as its guilty plea, was named the lead high-yield bond underwriter for Kohlberg Kravis Roberts's $25.07 billion leveraged buyout of RJR Nabisco, Joseph seemed like a prophet. And for all its problems with the SEC suit and the guilty plea, 1988 turned out to be an incredibly good year. In the first six months alone, earnings totaled $110.7 million and, for the year, Drexel continued to rank number one in high-yield bond underwriting with a 42.8 percent market share, up from 40 percent the year before. Maybe Drexel had finally overcome its legal problems and could now go forward.

It didn't turn out that way. The RJR Nabisco deal was Drexel's last major hurrah. Even before the guilty plea, Drexel's competitors had been fighting to gain market share in the highly lucrative high-yield bond business. Rival investment banks even began marketing a product superior to Drexel's "highly confident" letter, which had given Drexel a virtual monopoly on junk-bond financing for hostile takeovers. That product was the bridge loan. A "highly confident" letter meant that Drexel believed outside investors would be willing to invest in a deal by purchasing high-yield bonds. But there was still some risk that Drexel was wrong and the money could not be raised. With a bridge loan, the investment bank committed its own capital to finance a deal. If the investment bank couldn't convince investors to purchase high-yield bonds after it made the bridge loan, it was stuck with the bonds—but the borrower still had its financing. All the risk fell on the investment bank.

So long as Milken was around, Drexel's rivals' new aggressive practices made little difference. Milken's reputation for being able to raise funds from his network of investors once Drexel committed to a deal made the "highly confident" letter the functional equivalent of the bridge loan. But after the guilty plea and Milken's departure, everything was different. Without Milken, potential borrowers didn't have the same confidence in Drexel. And there was the additional problem that Drexel was now an admitted felon, making the firm, as one competitor smugly asserted, "radioactive." Some longtime Drexel clients such as Stone Container Corporation publicly declared that they would no longer do business with the firm. Government entities and public pension funds had a particularly hard time doing business with Drexel. Immediately after the guilty plea, New York City excluded Drexel from participation in two bond offerings and New Jersey announced that the firm would be temporarily banned from financing gambling casinos. Drexel was badly wounded, and its competitors smelled blood. For Drexel to retain its dominant position in the high-yield bond market, it now had to take greater risks than it was ever willing to take before.

With Milken gone, others had to generate deals. Peter Ackerman, a former top Milken aide, first proposed that Drexel raise $43 million to finance the purchase of Paramount Petroleum Corporation, a fifty-year-old bankrupt refinery. When investors showed no interest in the deal, Drexel decided to go forward anyway by putting its own funds at risk. Drexel then tried to sell high-yield bonds or find an acquirer to recoup its investment but with no success. Meanwhile, the refinery was losing money, making it even harder to attract new investors. Eventually, Drexel lost its $43 million investment when it was forced to put Paramount into bankruptcy again. Other Ackerman deals also flopped. When Drexel committed $385 million for the leveraged buyout of JPS Textile Group by Odyssey Partners, an Ackerman client, the firm again could not attract sufficient interest from outside investors. Drexel wound up investing close to $200 million of its own money in the deal. By December 1989, Ackerman was out of the high-yield bond business, having moved to London to write a book on international relations.

Leon Black did no better trying to fill Milken's shoes. In April 1989, Black committed Drexel to finance William Farley's $1 billion takeover attempt for West Point-Pepperell, a textile company Farley desperately wanted to acquire. Once again, Drexel could not raise sufficient capital by selling high-yield bonds to get the deal off its books. It wound up with $250 million dollars of its own funds invested and a big loss.

Drexel was also the victim of bad market timing. Just as Drexel was doing riskier deals, committing more of its own funds in bridge loans and getting stuck with high-yield bonds it couldn't sell, the market collapsed. Beginning in the summer of 1989, the high-yield bond market nosedived for the first time since Drexel grew to prominence in the late 1970s. The crisis began when Integrated Resources, a major Drexel client and issuer of high-yield bonds, defaulted on its commercial paper obligations in June 1989. In the summer of 1989, Congress enacted the Financial Institutions Reform, Recovery and Enforcement Act (FIRREA), which required savings and loans to liquidate their high-yield bond portfolios. As a result, Drexel had one fewer category of buyer for the bonds it was trying to sell. And as thrifts dumped their inventories of high-yield bonds on the now jittery market, the value of existing bonds fell in response.

The fall of 1989 brought more depressing news when Campeau, a highly leveraged retailer with $2.6 billion of high-yield bonds outstanding, experienced severe financial problems and ultimately declared bankruptcy. Other major high-yield bond issuers such as Southland also announced similar bad news. Bond prices of speculative issues plunged by more than 20 percent, and liquidity in the secondary market disappeared. There was more bad news in October 1989 when a proposed buyout of United Airlines's parent corporation, UAL, collapsed because of inability to sell new high-yield bonds. Drexel incurred $25 million of arbitrage trading losses on the deal.

Drexel was forced to retrench, but this only made its diminished status all the more apparent. Before Integrated Resources defaulted on $1 billion of short-term paper, it went to Drexel for help. Integrated's debt was held primarily by other Drexel clients, and Integrated hoped Drexel would be able to work something out. If Integrated's lenders were willing to exchange long-term for short-term debt, or if new investors could be found, default could be averted. After all, this is what Milken, with his credibility and vast network of contacts, used to do routinely when a Drexel client got into trouble. But Milken wasn't around anymore, and investors, including Drexel's clients, were nervous. Even Drexel was nervous, first promising and then refusing to lend Integrated the needed funds to pay off its short-term creditors. And when Integrated desperately sought out other lenders, it got nowhere. If Drexel wasn't willing to help its own client, no other lender would either. Having run out of options in its frantic search to survive, Integrated defaulted.

The Integrated default was a watershed event in Drexel's ultimate demise. It showed that Drexel was no longer able or willing to resuscitate a troubled high-yield-bond client. As one observer told *Business Week,* Drexel's display of weakness "was the most confidence-shattering event I've seen in the high-yield market." The old Drexel would have figured out some way to step in and bail out the company. Added the same observer, "Their franchise was riding on that."

Drexel paid the price for the Integrated default. When Integrated couldn't repay its outstanding obligations, the losers were the firm's creditors, many of which were also Drexel clients that had been encouraged by Drexel to invest in Integrated. When Integrated defaulted, they were stuck with worthless paper. To avoid alienating its clients even further, Drexel wound up guaranteeing its clients that it would make good on any losses incurred by having invested in Integrated's commercial paper.

Some observers attributed Drexel's problems in 1989, and the decline in the overall high-yield bond market, to Milken's absence. "Many investors," *Fortune* reported in November 1989, now "long wistfully for the stability that Michael Milken brought to the junk market. . . . Without Milken, the market seems to lurch from one crisis to another." Milken built up a vast network of high-yield bond purchasers and sellers, which included issuers, takeover specialists, money managers, and certain savings and loans and insurance companies. When an issue got into trouble, Milken was always seemingly able to find some way to avoid a crisis. Sometimes he would find new investors for a deal; other times he would arrange securities swaps trading preferred shares for the troubled high-yield bonds. His track record of success in solving problems and the loyalty clients had to him was the envy of the industry.

But Milken was still only one person, not Superman as some of his partisans claimed. The high-yield bond market would have experienced problems in 1989–90 even if he had not been driven from the market. The early success of restructuring transactions financed by high-yield bonds attracted new investors who wanted a piece of the action. By the late 1980s, too much new money was chasing too few good deals. Many transactions after 1985 were overpriced or inefficiently structured, with investment bankers and promoters taking out too much money up front regardless of the deal's success. A market correction was needed, and in fact was already occurring by 1989. There were fewer deals and less reliance on high-yield bond financing. Had Milken been present, there may have been fewer bad deals and less of a need for a market correction. But some market shake-out, the type that occurs periodically in all markets, was inevitable.

Government regulatory policy, however, made the problems of the high-yield bond market much worse. The FIRREA eliminated an important category of high-yield bond purchasers, savings and loans, from the market and forced them to be involuntary sellers instead. By enacting the FIRREA, Congress told investors that there was something inherently wrong with high-yield bonds and that investors that purchased them should do so at their peril. The government's assault on Drexel conveyed the same message. By bringing Drexel to its knees, the government also crippled high-yield bonds' leading market maker, decreasing liquidity at the precise time when liquidity was needed the most.

Nineteen eighty-nine turned out to be a disastrous year for Drexel. The firm reported an operating loss of $40 million for the year, its first loss ever. It ended the year at about half its former size, reducing its number of employees from approximately 10,000 to about 5,200. The signs of Drexel's deteriorating financial condition were becoming obvious to all. At the end of November 1989, Standard & Poor's downgraded Drexel's commercial paper to A-3, the lowest rating of any major Wall Street firm. In January 1990, Drexel's biggest high-yield bond customer, Executive Life, announced a $515 million charge for the fourth quarter of 1989 because of losses suffered in its high-yield bond portfolio. Drexel's biggest customer now seemed on the brink of collapse, and Drexel itself could not be far behind. Not that Drexel was likely to receive any sympathy. In December 1989, John Phelan, chairman of the

New York Stock Exchange, informed Drexel that the exchange intended to seek tens of millions of dollars in penalties for the firm's transgressions.

Everything was falling apart, but Joseph refused to acknowledge that Drexel's demise was imminent, or even that the firm was in trouble. At year-end 1989, Joseph was faced with the problem of bonuses for key Drexel employees. Back in September, Drexel had proposed a bylaws change to compel its employees to wait before cashing in their stock upon retirement or departure. Nearly two dozen large employee shareholders quit the firm in protest, taking their capital with them.

In December, conflict erupted again as senior officials bickered over who should get the biggest bonus. Rather than take a hard line because of the firm's precarious financial situation, Joseph caved. Leon Black demanded and received over $15 million while John Kissick, Milken's successor as head of the high-yield bond department, received $7 million. Overall, Joseph and John Shad decided to pay out $270 million in bonuses, about $200 million of which was to be paid out immediately in cash with the rest given in Drexel stock. The move was yet another public relations disaster, prompting a new round of regulatory and congressional investigations. But Joseph defended the bonuses as necessary to preserve morale and motivate Drexel's key people to face the challenges of the 1990s. It was not as if Drexel was in any trouble, Joseph insisted. As he told the *Wall Street Journal* on February 5, 1990, "I see daylight. The worst is behind us."

Joseph was wrong again. Within two weeks of Joseph's ill-timed statement, Drexel would be forced to declare bankruptcy. The end came suddenly, but the seeds of destruction had been apparent for some time. By the third quarter of 1989, Drexel was forced to carry more than $1 billion of bridge loans and unsold high-yield bonds. Drexel had committed these funds to its clients, and it now had to come up with the money. Beginning in September 1989, Joseph had tried to recruit another Wall Street firm as a merger partner, but none were interested. Drexel's liabilities and its potential civil liability from suits filed after its guilty plea scared off all potential suitors. Drexel's only option was to borrow.

But borrowing was becoming increasingly difficult. When Standard & Poor's lowered Drexel's credit-quality rating in November 1989, the firm's access to the commercial paper market, the traditional source of corporate short-term borrowing, was severely impaired. Drexel's banks were also getting skittish. It didn't take a genius to figure out that the bridge loans and high-yield bonds that Drexel could not sell to the public were not worth much as collateral. Drexel needed money badly, and it was running out of places to go. Richard Wright, Drexel's chief financial officer, flew to Paris on an emergency trip to plead with Groupe Bruxelles Lambert, the European investors who were Drexel's largest shareholders, to make a capital infusion. They refused, citing Drexel's potential civil liability and declining profitability. There was no sense throwing good money after bad.

Drexel had only one option left: itself. As was common in the industry, Drexel was set up as a holding company with a broker-dealer subsidiary. The firm also had a separate commodities-trading unit. The need for cash was at the holding-company level, because that's where the bridge loans and unsold high-yield bonds were. During 1989, the firm had borrowed $650 million from its commodities-trading unit. This arrangement worked well until Drexel could no longer raise funds by selling commercial paper and pay the commodities group back on demand. Drexel then turned to its broker-dealer subsidiary, which still had capital well in excess of regulatory requirements. But there was one important wrinkle that eliminated this source of money. Broker-dealers are regulated by the SEC and the New York Stock Exchange, which had the power to prohibit transfers of funds to the holding company. On Thursday, February 8, 1990, Drexel was told that the firm could no longer withdraw funds from its broker-dealer subsidiary without express SEC approval.

Drexel's situation was now desperate. The firm had another $30 million of commercial paper obligations due the next Monday and another $200 million more due two weeks after that. Friday and the weekend were spent frantically trying to raise money to avoid a default. Joseph proposed a sweeping restructuring plan to save the firm, which required Drexel to sell off assets, including its high-yield bond portfolio. But this obviously could not be done over the weekend. Drexel's last hope was regulatory intervention. If regulators could only nudge the banks to lend Drexel some money for a short time, the firm would be able to implement its restructuring plan. The regulators were contacted and told that Drexel would be meeting with the banks on Monday, February 12.

The Monday meeting went nowhere. The banks viewed Drexel as a firm on the verge of imminent collapse with no good collateral to offer. The banks had reached the same conclusion, as did Drexel itself, when Integrated had come begging in June of the previous year, just eight months earlier. Now it was Drexel's turn. Far from being pressured by regulators to bail Drexel out, the banks decided to pull the plug instead. They would do nothing to prevent Drexel from defaulting on all its loans.

At 1:30 A.M. on Tuesday morning, a conference call was set up between Joseph, Richard Breeden, the SEC chairman, and Gerald Corrigan of the New York Federal Reserve. Joseph was hoping for a miracle, but none was forthcoming. Breeden and Corrigan told Joseph that they had conferred with treasury secretary Nicholas Brady and Fed chairman Alan Greenspan and had reached a decision. If Drexel did not declare bankruptcy later that day, it would be seized by the government as insolvent. Breeden and Corrigan gave Joseph until 7:00 A.M. that morning to decide. The die was now cast, and Joseph knew it. On Tuesday February 13, Drexel declared bankruptcy.

Of all Joseph's miscalculations, his hope that Drexel would be saved by Nick Brady, Drexel's vanquished former competitor at Dillon, Read, and other regulators was perhaps the worst. True, Joseph had done everything they asked. He complied with the government's demand that Drexel plead guilty, pay $650 million in extortion money, and turn on the Milkens. He had even agreed to place the firm under de facto government control and hire the SEC's former chairman as Drexel's chairman. Joseph kept all his promises but got nothing in return. He never understood that the regulators, like Drexel's competitors and the corporate establishment, wanted Drexel dead and nothing less would satisfy them. It was impossible to curry favor with the regulators, as Joseph should have learned when he unsuccessfully attempted to placate Congressman Dingell by abandoning the employee partnerships. The appeasement strategy that Joseph followed from the time of the guilty plea until the end only made him and Drexel seem weak. When Drexel was vulnerable and needed the regulators the most, they had no hesitancy in moving in for the kill.

While Joseph was surprised by the regulators' and the banks' insensitivity to Drexel's plight, others were more realistic. As one executive commented, "We were tough on the way up. We never made any friends. We stole business from other firms. We made the banks look silly. This was payback time. The establishment finally got us."

Drexel's demise was also greeted with little sympathy by contemporary observers. What was remarkable, however, was the virtually complete absence of any discussion of exactly what Drexel did wrong to warrant the punishment it received. It was sufficient that Drexel symbolized the excesses of the 1980s. *Newsweek*, for example, reported that Drexel was the firm "that championed the junk bond and drove takeover fever on Wall Street." Its bankruptcy, *Newsweek* concluded, was "the latest testimony to the excess of the '80s." *Time* agreed, reporting that "The collapse of Drexel Burnham marks the end of a money-mad era of hostile takeovers, lavish living and heedless disregard for debt." Wall Street economist Pierre Rinfret added, "The era of extravagance and insanity has come to an end. This is a breath of fresh air. Drexel got what it deserved. These guys could destroy the country. There was no rhyme or reason for what has been going on."

For pure vitriol, however, none could match Benjamin Stein, who wrote a story in *Barron's* comparing Drexel's fall with the defeat of Nazi Germany:

> Today, in February 1990, the Drexel empire looks like the Thousand Year Reich in May of 1945. Like an imprudent householder, Drexel has entered the protection of Chapter 11 of the Federal Bankruptcy Code. It has defaulted on at least $100 million of short-term debt. Thousands of staffers are seeking new jobs. The company has no credit on Wall Street. That most anomalous of situations has happened: A securities company whose capital was largely in its own issues has had to admit the worthlessness of its own issues.

Rudy Giuliani must have read these stories with glee. Nobody blamed him for triggering the chain of events that drove Drexel, which at its peak employed ten thousand people, out of business. Few (with the notable exception of Gordon Crovitz and the other editorial-page writers of the *Wall Street Journal*) even questioned his use of RICO to bludgeon Drexel into pleading guilty. Rather, Drexel was to blame for its own demise because it championed high-yield bonds and hostile takeovers. This was its crime, not "stock parking" and the other noncrimes that earlier had gotten so much attention. At least now the cards were finally on the table.

Drexel's Demise, the High-Yield Bond Market, and the Recession of 1990

Drexel's demise also triggered speculation about the future of the high-yield bond market. For many, the answer was simple. Since the market was an artificial product of Drexel and Milken's financial machinations, it would not survive. *Business Week,* for example, proclaimed that the high-yield bond market was now "dead," its earlier success the result of "magic" and "sorcery":

> The junk bond market, at least as we have come to know it, is dead. For the past half-dozen years, it has been a creature less of rational financial precepts than of wishful thinking, artful promotion, and, above all, illusion and magic. Instead of free interaction of buyers and sellers, the market was ruled tightly by sorcerers—Michael Milken and his apprentices at Drexel Burnham Lambert Inc. The magic began to fade last year when several big junk deals fell apart.
>
> Now, with Milken facing a new federal indictment and Drexel in bankruptcy court, most of the sorcery has vanished.

Benjamin Stein, who compared Drexel's bankruptcy with the fall of Nazi Germany, went even further. Stein equated the growth of the high-yield bond market and Drexel's success with a giant Ponzi scheme that collapsed when Drexel and Milken were driven from the market:

> This, then, is my scenario. Drexel/Milken was largely a vast scam based upon myths about bond valuing skills and bond value, kept going by a vast Ponzi controlling markets, prices, reputation and data about defaults, offering the kind of profits that a decade-long scam involving tens of billions of dollars of phony bonds would offer. . . . [W]ithout Milken there to keep the game going, everything fell apart remarkably quickly. . . . [W]ithout him, the subordinated debt market learned the truth, dried up, and blew away.

Stein's assessment struck a responsive chord with many who viewed high-yield bonds as the incarnation of evil. Ponzi schemes are named after Charles Ponzi, who in 1920 raised $7.9 million from investors by promising them 50 percent interest for the use of their funds for forty-five days. Ponzi told potential investors that he was going to profit from exchange-rate differences by buying International Postal Union coupons abroad and redeeming them for U.S. stamps in the United States. When Ponzi was arrested in August 1920, only $61 worth of stamps and postal coupons were found on the premises.

Ponzi's scheme and all similar schemes that now go by the same name have certain common features: (1) investors are promised spectacular returns for investments that are by definition worthless; (2) the scheme can last as long as new investors can be found to invest funds, which are used to pay off earlier investors; and (3) when new investors fail to grow sufficiently rapidly to pay off earlier investors, the scheme collapses. Once potential investors learn that current investors are not being paid, the supply of new investors dries up, with the most recent investors bearing the brunt of the loss. The trick for Ponzi scheme perpetrators is to pocket the proceeds and disappear before investors learn the truth. If they don't, they will be caught and sent to jail.

Did this pattern describe Drexel and the high-yield bond market in the 1980s? According to Stein and other critics, it did. Drexel and Milken defrauded purchasers into investing in junk bonds by lying about their profitability and risk of default; the proceeds from new junk issues were used to pay off earlier investors; and the market collapsed when investors learned the truth about the junkiness of the bonds and Drexel's and Milken's misdeeds. But this simple tale is contradicted by the most cursory review of the evidence.

Investors in high-yield bonds never were promised or experienced the too-good-to-be-true returns characteristic of Ponzi schemes. High-yield bonds outperformed long-term treasury bonds in certain years, for example, but not in others. In 1981 and 1983, high-yield bonds had returns of 7.56 percent and 21.8 percent versus .48 percent and 2.23 percent for long-term treasuries. But when high-yield bonds returned 32.45 percent in 1982 and 22.51 percent in 1985, they were outperformed by long-term treasuries, which had returns of 42.08 percent and 31.54 percent in those respective years. Moreover, Drexel, even when it was the most dominant, was never the sole underwriter of original-issue high-yield bonds. Merrill Lynch, Bear Stearns, Shearson Lehman, Paine Webber, First Boston, and other firms all competed with Drexel. The proponents of the image of Drexel as Ponzi scheme operator had no explanation for these other firms offering the same product. Were they all conspirators? And when Drexel or these other firms raised funds by selling high-yield bonds, the proceeds typically were not used to repay old investors. Rather, the funds financed restructurings and the expansion of growing industries such as health care, pharmaceuticals, cellular telephones, and gambling. This too was inconsistent with the classic Ponzi scheme.

The collapse of the high-yield bond market beginning in the second half of 1989 also bore no resemblance to the end of a Ponzi scheme. In a Ponzi scheme, investments become worthless when investors learn the truth about their lack of any underlying value. This never happened with the high-yield bond market, which never became worthless. Despite the highly publicized defaults of such high-yield bond issuers as Integrated Resources, Southmark, Lomas Financial, Seaman Furniture, and Braniff, and the news of severe financial problems at Resorts International, Interco, Southland, Payless Cashways, USG, and Campeau's Allied and Federated Stores, most high-yield bond issuers did not default. In 1989 $8.11 billion of the bonds defaulted, or about 4.3 percent of the total market. In 1990 defaults increased to $18.35 billion, or 10.1 percent of the market. But still, even in 1990, its worst year, 90 percent of the market did not default.

Nor were all the defaults of Drexel-underwritten issues. For example, the Campeau deal, which *Fortune* dubbed the "looniest deal ever," was underwritten by First Boston, not Drexel. Overall, Drexel's share of defaults of the total number of all high-yield bonds underwritten between 1977 and its guilty plea at the end of 1988 was 43.6 percent, slightly less than its market share of 46.8 percent. In contrast, Salomon Brothers' share of defaults (18.3 percent) was three times its market share (6.1 percent), First Boston's share of defaults (18.5 percent) was 2.3 times its market share (8.1 percent), and Lehman Brothers' share of defaults (3 percent) was 1.4 times its market share (2.1 percent). Drexel's "junk" was better than the products of many of its jealous rivals.

Default statistics are also misleading because defaults do not measure investment performance. High-yield bonds pay higher interest rates and typically have shorter maturities than high-grade bonds, which results in a much quicker return on investment. And even when default occurs, the bonds usually retain some value. If sufficient value is retained, and if interest payments are received for a long enough period, defaulted bonds still may be profitable investments.

Of course some high-yield bonds were not profitable investments, but this is to be expected. The bonds offered high yields for a reason, their greater risk. The riskier an investment, the greater the risk of loss in certain periods. For example, the return on small-company stocks in 1990, the same year as the greatest decline in the value of high-yield bonds, was -21.6 percent. In 1991, IBM stock lost almost 50 percent of its value, declining in market value by over $30 billion, an amount greater than the total decline of the high-yield bond market in its worst year. Does this mean that small stocks and IBM, or for that matter all assets that sharply decline in value, are also Ponzi schemes? Of course not. The decline in value is simply the realization of a risk, which explains why the higher yields are paid to investors in the first place. With the high-yield bond market, the decline in value was also attributable to the government's regulatory policies such as the FIRREA and the assault on Drexel itself.

But the most damning evidence against the Ponzi scheme claim is what has happened in the high-yield bond market since 1990. Unlike Ponzi schemes, which end when they are discovered, the original-issue high-yield bond market surged back after its decline. High-yield bond returns were a phenomenal 40.2 percent in 1991, 21.2 percent in 1992, and 18.2 percent in 1993, far outperforming returns generated by other bond investments or the stock market. Moreover, the highest returns were concentrated in the lowest-quality issuers. The most speculative bonds, which lost 20 percent of their value in 1989–1990, had eye-popping returns of 61.2 percent in 1991, followed by returns of 25 percent and 22.9 percent in 1992 and 1993.

This strong resurgence of the high-yield bond market demolishes the Ponzi scheme hypothesis. The government succeeded in driving Drexel and Milken out of business, but it did not demolish the high-yield bond market. That market survives because there is a need for non-investment-grade borrowers to have access to the public debt market. Drexel's competitors, who were Rudy Giuliani's biggest cheerleaders and the first to dance on Drexel's grave, have been more than willing to step in and fill the void created by Drexel's demise.

The resurgence of the high-yield bond market does not mean that government regulatory policy toward high-yield bonds had no effect on the economy. High-yield bonds were an important source of financing for the new and growing non-Fortune 500 companies that accounted for all of the 12.5 million net new jobs created during the 1980s. They also played a major role in the restructuring of many of the Fortune 500 companies, increasing their efficiency and profitability as well. The regulatory attack on Drexel and the high-yield debt market temporarily all but eliminated this important source of credit, which put the brake on economic growth.

The U.S. economy entered into a recession in 1990 with real GNP falling 1.6 percent in the fourth quarter alone. This recession lasted well into 1992 and was widely believed to have contributed to Bill Clinton's victory over President George Bush that year. The government's attempted purge of the high-yield debt market created a "credit crunch"—the inability of borrowers to obtain financing for profitable investments—which contributed to the length and severity of this recession. This credit crunch was experienced primarily by non-investment-grade borrowers, the source of America's boom during the 1980s. Between 1989 and 1990, new capital raised in the public high-yield debt market fell by 95 percent, from $28.8 billion to $1.4 billion. During this same period, the size of the investment-grade debt market declined by less than 15 percent.

The government's elimination of Drexel and Milken from the market and the FIRREA were only part of the picture. In 1990 the insurance industry, fearing passage of a FIRREA-type law applicable to insurance companies, enacted guidelines limiting insurers' ability to invest in high-yield bonds. Several states also enacted laws to the same effect. The regulatory siege on the high-yield debt market also extended to commercial banks, money market funds, and pension funds. The Federal Reserve Board, the Federal Deposit Insurance Corporation, and the Comptroller of the Currency enacted regulations restricting commercial banks' ability to finance highly leveraged transactions (HLT's), a euphemism for corporate restructurings. Not to be outdone, the SEC adopted new regulations reducing the amount of lower-grade commercial paper that money market funds could hold. State pension-fund regulators also jumped on the bandwagon, enacting initiatives preventing funds from investing in high-yield bonds, which financed hostile takeover transactions. The cumulative effect of these regulatory decisions attacking the high-yield debt market was to halt, at least temporarily, the innovative financing device that had so contributed to the increased corporate efficiency and economic growth during the 1980s.

The regulators should have known better. A sharp reduction in the availability of credit to non-investment-grade borrowers contributed to the length and severity of the Great Depression during the 1930s. The same was true during the severe recession of the 1970s, when soaring inflation and interest rates made it difficult for small and medium-sized businesses to borrow. By attacking the high-yield debt market at the end of the 1980s, government regulators again reduced the supply of credit to worthy borrowers at precisely the wrong time. But sound economic policy was not the government's objective. The government was far more interested in appearing responsive to the demagogic attacks against junk bonds, which many viewed as the symbol of what was wrong with America during the "decade of greed."

CHAPTER 6

Was Milken Guilty?

Drexel's guilty plea in December 1988 triggered a new round of press stories describing Milken's legal woes. Milken had received a target letter back in September 1988, informing him that he was likely to be indicted. Now that Drexel agreed to cooperate against him as part of its plea agreement, Milken's indictment was a foregone conclusion. Milken didn't have to wait long. In March 1989, the government filed a ninety-eight-count indictment against Milken and his brother Lowell accusing them of racketeering, and securities, mail, and wire fraud. In April 1990, Milken pled guilty to six felonies and agreed to pay $600 million, consisting of a $200 million fine and an additional $400 million for creation of a restitution fund to compensate "victims." In November 1990, he was sentenced by Judge Kimba Wood to serve ten years in prison. Before and after his guilty plea and sentencing, Milken was condemned as one of the worst, if not the worst, white-collar criminals in history. This view is still frequently expressed, even today.

That a view is widely held, however, does not make it correct. The blanket denunciations of Milken as a hard-core criminal must be based on evidence, not on a visceral dislike of the perceived excesses of the 1980s nor on envy of Milken's success. The legal proceedings involving Milken and those with whom he dealt are now largely over. There is now a considerable record making it possible, for the first time, to analyze definitively what Milken actually did in relation to the crimes he was charged for. It is now possible to begin to answer the question that will long be debated by historians: Was Milken guilty?

Milken was a tough and formidable competitor who was despised by the Wall Street and business establishment he displaced. His success also made him the envy of many, both in and out of the financial world. He was an outsider who made it big by ignoring the unspoken rule that outsiders must know their place and not rock the boat. But did he commit serious crimes or, for that matter, any crimes? There is no evidence that he did, and certainly no evidence that he engaged in any conduct that had ever before been considered criminal. After the most thorough investigation of any individual's business practices in history, the government came up with nothing. In fact, the government never established that Milken's "crimes" were anything other than routine business practices common in the industry.

The Indictment and Guilty Plea

The government's ninety-eight-count indictment of Michael and Lowell Milken contained little new of substance. The basic allegations detailing the supposedly unlawful dealings between the Milkens and Boesky were already well known from the SEC's earlier civil suit against Drexel, Drexel's guilty plea, and the extensive press leaks. But the indictment did contain one piece of new information, which the government knew would capture the public's attention. On page 2 of the 110-page indictment, the government revealed for the first time that "Michael R. Milken's direct compensation from Drexel was approximately $45,715,000 in 1983; $123,805,000 in 1984; $135,324,000 in 1985; $294,779,000 in 1986; and $550,054,000 in 1987." On page 3, the indictment disclosed that "Lowell J. Milken's direct compensation from Drexel was approximately $10,180,000 in 1984; $16,674,000 in 1985; $27,209,000 in 1986; and $48,059,000 in 1987."

The government understood that by disclosing the Milkens' spectacular wealth right up front, the rest of the indictment almost didn't matter. The Milkens' compensation was sufficient to prove their guilt. As the *New York Times* reported, "The indictment of Michael R. Milken stunned even the most jaded Wall Street professionals—not for its legal implications, but for its revelation of the income paid to the junk bond pioneer." Milken's $550 million compensation in 1987, the *Times* continued, was "incomprehensible" even during the "decade of greed." Milken's establishment critics were quick to jump on the bandwagon. David Rockefeller, for example, the retired chairman of Chase Manhattan Bank and a scion of one of the nation's most prominent old-money families, commented, "such an extraordinary income inevitably raises questions as to whether there isn't something unbalanced in the way our financial system is working." Apparently Rockefeller, who had a net worth of over $1 billion largely due to inheritance, was untroubled by the wealth of those, like himself, who obtained spectacular wealth from having the right family name.

The government's strategy of using the indictment to inflame public opinion against the Milkens by pandering to the rich-hating mentality of the 1980s was fundamentally wrong. Financial success is not a crime. The government never even claimed that Michael Milken's compensation was attributable to his alleged crimes. But the government recognized that the public didn't care how or why Milken made so much money. Nor did anyone care that Milken never engaged in any of the ostentatious conspicuous consumption so common among the newly rich. He always lived relatively modestly, remaining with his family in the same house he bought in 1978 when he first moved to California. His modest lifestyle notwithstanding, Milken's staggering compensation still symbolized the "decade of greed."

The furor over the Milkens' compensation obscured some difficult issues. For instance, why was the government prosecuting Milken in the first place? Drexel had just pled guilty for the same offenses and paid the record $650 million penalty. It was not as if Drexel and Milken were two separate people who were involved in different criminal acts. The opposite was true. Drexel, like all corporations, was a legal fiction that had already pled guilty and paid the price for Milken's supposed crimes. Why punish Milken again for the same "crimes"? And if the government wanted to punish Milken for his own conduct, what was the possible rationale for the earlier prosecution of Drexel? Other than vindictive piling on, there was no reason for the government to prosecute both the corporation and the individual for the same underlying conduct.

Another problem for the government was that its case was still remarkably weak. For those who got past the sensational disclosure of the Milkens' compensation and read the rest of the indictment, it was obvious the government's case still rested almost entirely on Milken's supposed unlawful agreement with Boesky. The two-and-a-half-year investigation, the cooperating witnesses, and even

Drexel's cooperation had seemingly produced next to nothing. Finally, there was the issue of Lowell Milken, who had no involvement in any of the claimed illegalities described in the indictment. The government defended its racketeering and securities-fraud accusations against Lowell Milken as justified by the evidence. But more cynical observers recognized that the government was using Lowell as a bargaining chip to coerce Michael into pleading guilty. The government was willing to do anything, no matter how unethical, to bring Milken down.

Michael Milken responded to the indictment by issuing a statement declaring his innocence and commitment to fight: "In America an indictment marks the beginning of the legal process, not the end. After two and a half years of leaks and distortions, I am now eager to present all the facts in an open and unbiased forum. I will plead not guilty to the charges and vigorously fight these accusations. I am confident that in the end I will be vindicated." Milken and his team of lawyers, led by the renowned Arthur Liman of the Paul, Weiss firm in New York (Edward Bennett Williams had died of cancer), immediately began to prepare for what was expected to be the trial of the century. But it would never happen. Almost exactly one year after the indictment, Milken entered his guilty plea and forever lost any chance to "be vindicated."

Milken ultimately decided to abandon the fight for vindication for a number of interrelated reasons. During 1989 he and his lawyers began to lose confidence that he could win. That was the year that prosecutor Mark Hansen ruthlessly but effectively demolished Lisa Jones, the former Drexel employee, in her criminal trial. The conviction of the Princeton/Newport defendants in the summer of 1989 was even more troubling. The Princeton/Newport defendants were convicted of engaging in illegal tax trades with Drexel after prosecutor Hansen told the jurors to ignore technical issues of tax law and focus instead on the defendants' "sleaziness." If jurors were willing to convict low-level employees like Jones of covering up for her superiors at Drexel, and the Princeton/Newport defendants who did business with Drexel for being "sleazy," what chance did Milken have? Many believed Milken's conviction was a foregone conclusion for no other reason than that he made $550 million in a single year.

And what if Milken was acquitted, what then? By the end of 1989, Milken was being blamed for some widely publicized savings and loan failures. Milken faced the possibility of being indicted and tried again for his role in the savings and loan crisis. Prosecution by various states was also a concern. The double-jeopardy clause of the Constitution protects a defendant from being tried by the federal government twice for the same offense. But it provides no protection against successive prosecutions by the federal government and state governments. Typically, successive prosecutions are not a problem because governments have limited resources. But Milken was different because destroying him was such a high priority. The government would never relent until it realized its objective. Milken was facing multiple criminal trials that potentially could last into the indefinite future. He had no assurance that he could win any of these trials, let alone all of them.

Other events also wore Milken down. Faced with unrelenting negative publicity, Milken hired a public relations firm to tell his side of the story. His extensive history of charitable and philanthropic activities were also publicized for the first time to improve his image. These efforts backfired as the press now denounced him for trying to buy and manipulate public opinion. "Milken is hardly the first buccaneer of business to seek rehabilitation in acts of charity and social concern. But he has taken magnanimity in the face of adversity to new heights," the *New Republic* sniped. His newfound "commitment to such causes as Jewish scholarship, minority business development, and handicapped and deprived children," the magazine concluded sarcastically, was "almost heartbreaking."

Nothing Milken did worked, and the pressure of the government's investigation was unrelenting. It wasn't just that Milken himself was being pursued by the full resources of the United States government. His own brother was also a target, and Drexel, the firm he had built, had turned on him and was assisting in the government's effort. People with whom he had close working relationships, Jim Dahl and Terren Peizer, and who became rich from his efforts, were also cooperating. Plus, Milken worried about the effects of all the negative publicity on his children, who had serious health problems, and on his wife, Lori. When the government sent the FBI to interview Milken's ninety-two-year-old grandfather about what he knew, Milken was at the breaking point.

In late 1989, a new round of press stories began appearing announcing that the government was about to issue a superseding indictment against Milken with new and expanded accusations. Now Milken and his lawyers didn't even know what charges they were defending against. The threat of a superseding indictment also gave the government additional leverage in plea-bargaining negotiations. Michael either had to plead guilty to the existing indictment, prosecutors said, or be reindicted on expanded charges with the process starting all over again. Milken, with his resolve weakened from the excruciating three-year investigation, began to waver for the first time.

Eventually, the government gave Milken an ultimatum just as they had done with Drexel in December 1988. Prosecutors told Milken he could avoid a superseding indictment only if he pled guilty to six felonies and agreed to pay the $600 million. In exchange, the government would drop all charges against Lowell and guarantee that Michael would face no further prosecutions. Prosecutors further agreed not to recommend any specific sentence of incarceration and that Michael would have no obligation to cooperate in the government's continuing investigation until after sentencing.

Now it was up to Michael to decide, and he was genuinely torn. The government's deal offered finality, an end to the ordeal. Exoneration for Lowell was important because Lowell was never more than a pawn in the government's war against Michael. And not having to cooperate was an additional plus. Nobody could say that Michael was like Levine, Jefferies, Boesky, and Siegel, who all were more than willing to incriminate others, whether fairly or not, in exchange for more favorable treatment for themselves. Finally, the prosecutors' willingness not to recommend any specific sentence meant that Michael might be treated leniently. Still, no matter how the government's deal was analyzed, it required Michael to plead guilty to six felonies. He would never again be able to credibly claim that he was an innocent man. If he took the deal, his legacy would be as an admitted felon.

Nobody, including Michael's lawyers and family, knew what he was going to do. Michael himself couldn't decide. Predictably, the advice he received was conflicting. Ironically, Lowell, who had the most to gain from the deal, was its strongest opponent. Lowell told Michael that a guilty plea would ruin his life. Others were concerned that Michael ultimately couldn't take the pressure of continuing a fight he probably couldn't win in any event. Michael, with all his power, wealth, and ability to hire the best legal talent, was still no match for the government, which was dedicated to destroying him. Michael went back and forth until the last minute, when he decided to take the deal and plead guilty.

Four of the six felony counts to which Milken agreed to plead guilty involved his dealings with Ivan Boesky. The first count was a general conspiracy allegation that Milken, Boesky, and a money manager named David Solomon agreed "to engage in a series of unlawful securities transactions." Counts two through four were the specific stock-parking transactions engaged in pursuant to the conspiracy. In count two, Milken admitted to unlawfully aiding and abetting Boesky's filing of a false 13(d) statement in the ever-present Fischbach transaction. Similarly, Milken admitted in count three to unlawfully "inducing" the Boesky organization to purchase MCA stock "for the purpose of concealing from the market that Golden Nugget was selling its MCA common stock." Count four focused on Drexel's purchase of Helmerich & Payne Corporation from the Boesky organization "with the assurance" from Boesky that Drexel would be guaranteed against loss. Milken admitted in count four to "subsequently confirming this assurance."

Counts five and six dealt with Milken's dealings with Solomon. In early 1984 Drexel had organized Finsbury Group Ltd., a fund that enabled foreign investors to invest in high-yield securities. Shares of Finsbury were sold by Drexel salespeople, to whom Drexel paid a fee of 1 percent of Finsbury's net asset value in addition to regular commissions. Drexel then charged Milken and the high-yield bond department for the 1 percent fee in its internal accounting system to offset the expected profits to the department from Finsbury's purchases and sales of high-yield securities. David Solomon, on Milken's recommendation, became one of Finsbury's two money managers. When Solomon failed to do enough business with Milken to generate the profits necessary to offset the 1 percent fee the department was being charged by Drexel, Milken and Solomon struck a deal. They agreed to adjust transaction prices within the bid-ask spread on all high-yield securities transactions between Finsbury and Drexel slightly in Drexel's favor to enable Milken to recoup more of the 1 percent fee. In count five, Milken admitted to "unlawfully failing to disclose" this agreed-upon adjustment in trade confirmations sent to Finsbury.

In December 1985, Solomon wanted to generate some short-term capital losses to offset other short-term capital gains to reduce his personal 1985 federal income tax liability. Milken helped Solomon accomplish his goal by having Drexel sell Solomon two illiquid investments and then buying them back at a much lower price. Solomon's loss was Drexel's gain, and Milken promised to return the favor by finding Solomon some profitable investments in 1986, which he did. Milken agreed in count six that he acted unlawfully by "aiding and assisting" Solomon's filing of a false tax return in 1985.

The deal was done, and all that remained for Milken was to formally enter his guilty plea in court. Tuesday, April 24, 1990, was the fateful day. Judge Kimba Wood went through the usual routine whenever a defendant pleads guilty, having Milken state on the record that he was not on drugs, that his plea was voluntary and not the result of any promises or threats, that he understood that he could be sentenced to a maximum of twenty-eight years in prison, and that by pleading guilty he was giving up the chance of being found innocent by a jury even if he was in fact guilty.

Milken then read a statement, known as an allocution, admitting that he "transgressed certain of the laws and regulations that govern the securities industry" and that he was "wrong" to have done so. While formally admitting his guilt, Milken also suggested that his plea had less to do with his acts than with the ordeal of the investigation. Choking back tears, he described how "This investigation and proceeding are now in their fourth year. This long period has been extremely painful and difficult for my family and friends as well as myself. I realize that by my acts I have hurt those who are closest to me." Now openly sobbing, he stopped, took a drink of water, and concluded his allocution with the obligatory apology: "I am truly sorry. I thank the Court for permitting me to add this apology and for its fairness in handling this complex case."

When he was finished, Judge Wood asked him, "Mr. Milken, how do you plead?"

Milken paused and then responded, "Guilty, Your Honor." Milken was now a convicted felon.

The government seized upon Milken's public admission of guilt as a vindication of its entire investigation. Richard Breeden, chairman of the SEC, immediately called a press conference to give the government's perspective on Milken's plea. "Mr. Milken has been portrayed as wrongly accused and as having simply devoted himself to the financing of small or emerging businesses. Despite the efforts to mold public opinion, his admissions today demonstrate that he stood at the center of a network of manipulation, fraud, and deceit."

Breeden's statement could not have been more wrong. None of the six felonies that Milken pled guilty to demonstrated that he was "at the center of a network of manipulation, fraud, and deceit." Breeden would have been closer to the truth if he had said that there was still no basis for concluding that Milken committed any crimes, using the common understanding of what it means to commit a crime, even after he pled guilty to six felonies.

Counts one through four covered the stock-parking agreement under which Boesky and Milken supposedly failed to record and disclose the true beneficial owner of various stocks in their books and records and certain public filings. The unlawful agreement was proven, prosecutors claimed, by Boesky's $5.3 million payment to Drexel after receiving the allegedly phony invoice that the money was owed for "consulting services." In reality, prosecutors said, the $5.3 million payment represented the net amount owed by Boesky after the gains and losses on all illegal securities transactions where Boesky or Milken transacted for the benefit of the other with a guarantee against loss.

The very evidence that the Boesky organization provided to the government, however, undermined the government's theory. The Boesky organization produced ledgers of gains and losses from securities trades relating to Drexel. These ledgers included some of the trading in securities like Fischbach, which the government challenged as illegal, but also included trading in many securities that the government conceded to be perfectly legal. Moreover, there were multiple ledgers, some in Drexel's possession, listing varying transactions and amounts which themselves could not be reconciled. The ledgers provided no support for the government's claim that Boesky and Milken entered into an unlawful stock-parking scheme and then kept track of gains and losses on those trades both knew to be illegal. In reality, the $5.3 million payment was simply the value that Drexel and Boesky placed on all reciprocal favors and accommodations, including consulting services, that had occurred up to that time. But even if the government's explanation for the $5.3 million payment is accepted at face value, Milken pled guilty to participating in an arrangement with Boesky to commit books-and-records violations by not properly documenting the ownership of stock. Unlike most felonies like theft or fraud, where the harm to the victim is obvious, the government never could identify any comparable injury to anyone resulting from the trading in Fischbach, MCA, or Helmerich & Payne.

Count five, which deals with Milken's agreement with David Solomon to recoup part of the 1 percent fee that Drexel was charging Milken for promoting the Finsbury Fund, was equally suspect. Solomon presumably agreed to adjust the bid-ask spread on securities transactions with Drexel because he wanted to continue doing business with Drexel and Milken and have Drexel promote the fund. Solomon and Finsbury's investors clearly benefited from Drexel's promotional efforts and Milken's willingness to engage in high-yield securities transactions with the fund, something Milken may have been unwilling to do if he could not recoup the 1 percent fee. If Milken refused to pay the fee, Drexel may have refused to continue to promote the fund. Moreover, the transaction prices, even as adjusted, were always within the bid-ask spread and competitive with the terms offered by other firms. Otherwise, Solomon could have shifted all his business away from Drexel. Disclosure of the agreement between Solomon and Milken would have made no difference because Finbury's investors were not harmed, and may well have benefited, from the deal. Once again, Milken pled guilty to what was more accurately described as a noncrime with no victims.

But the phoniest "crime" of all was Milken's guilty plea to count six, assisting in Solomon's filing of a false 1985 tax return. When Solomon purchased illiquid securities from Drexel and then resold them at a loss, he suffered a real economic loss, which he had every right to claim on his taxes. The government's theory that Milken's statement to Solomon that he would try to find profitable investments in future years created an offsetting gain made no sense. Solomon, as a judge in another case would later state, surely could not have lawfully listed Milken's statement as an asset before any investment was made. Solomon could not, for example, have listed Milken's statement as an asset in applying for a bank loan. But the loss that Solomon claimed on his taxes was a real, realized economic loss. Neither Solomon nor Milken committed any crime when Solomon claimed this loss on his 1985 tax return.

If Milken believed the government would recommend a light sentence because of the trivial nature of his "crimes," he was wrong. SEC Chairman Breeden immediately announced that because of the severity of Milken's crimes "a substantial period of incarceration should be imposed." Milken's lawyers were out-raged by Breeden's comment because it was inconsistent with the spirit, if not the letter, of the government's promise not to recommend any specific sentence. But Breeden's comment was insignificant compared to what was to come. Having won the first major battle when Milken pled guilty, the government now shifted its war against Milken to the sentencing phase of the proceeding.

The Fatico Hearing and Sentencing

When the time came for the government to formally take a position on sentencing, the result from Milken's perspective was chilling. Echoing Breeden, prosecutors John Carroll and Jess Fardella claimed that the six felonies to which Milken pled guilty demonstrated "a pattern of calculated fraud, deceit and corruption of the highest magnitude." Moreover, these six felonies were "but a sampling of the larger pattern of criminal activity that permeated Milken's operation of the High Yield Department." Of the government's 132-page sentencing memorandum 70 pages were devoted to what prosecutors described as "Milken's Other Crimes." The government went so far as to compare Milken to the head of the Mafia or other organized criminal enterprise who used his subordinates to disguise his criminal activities until he was caught:

> Not unlike the Kingpins of other sophisticated criminal enterprises, Milken used his criminal enterprise to insulate himself from detection. For a time he seemed invincible: his corrupt business transactions had the appearance of normality, his illegal securities schemes were often implemented by others, and his criminal cronies adhered to a code of silence. That invincibility ended on April 24, 1990.

Having thoroughly demonized Milken, the government then blamed him for his "persistent efforts to minimize the nature and scope of his criminal conduct." Unlike Levine, Boesky, and Siegel, who had fully accepted responsibility for their crimes and cooperated with the government's continuing investigation, Milken had done neither:

> Milken has not accepted responsibility for all of his crimes; indeed, his self-serving rationalizations . . . undercut any serious claim that he has truly accepted responsibility for even the crimes to which he

has now pleaded. Finally . . . Milken has not taken—and has indicated that he will not take—affirmative steps to clean up the industry he dirtied.

Finally, the government blamed Milken for Drexel's legal problems, culture of greed, payment of excessive bonuses at the end of 1989, and its ultimate bankruptcy:

> There is no question that the excesses in Drexel's corporate culture that Milken fathered hastened the collapse of the company, corrupted many young professionals and occasioned the loss of thousands of jobs. Were it not for the lawlessness of Milken's High Yield Department there would not have been grand jury and SEC investigations. Even after the investigations, moreover, the greedy habits of the Milken years led to the payment of tens of millions of dollars in 1989 bonuses and compensation as Drexel spiralled toward bankruptcy.

In sentencing, prosecutors urged, Judge Wood should consider not only Milken's monstrous misdeeds, but also the effect on the financial community and the public who "will use this case to measure the quality and even-handedness of our justice system." Taking everything into account, the government recommended that "Milken be sentenced to a period of incarceration that reflects the enormity of his crimes."

As an advocacy document and appeal to popular passions and prejudices, the government's sentencing memorandum was a tour de force. But as an objective presentation to the court, it was an outrage. The government knew, but the public did not, that the "crimes" Milken pled guilty to were, at most, hypertechnical regulatory violations and not serious offenses. Comparing Milken to "kingpins of organized crime" went beyond the pale of normal advocacy. And the government's claim that Milken should receive harsher treatment than Boesky, Levine, and Siegel was also a cheap shot. True, Milken, unlike Siegel, had refused to falsely incriminate others and ruin their lives to benefit himself, but this was hardly something that could fairly be used against him. Blaming Milken for the government's witch-hunt, which led to Drexel's demise, was the ultimate outrage. Milken wasn't even around when Drexel paid the controversial 1989 year-end bonuses, having been forced out a full year earlier as a condition of Drexel's guilty plea.

The excesses in the government's sentencing memoranda were in a sense completely predictable. For three years the government had done everything in its power, including using its allies in the press, to depict Milken as the ultimate venal and corrupt criminal. It was too late now for the government to admit they never had a case to begin with. Better to continue the campaign of lies and disinformation until the end. The public, which had been duped from the beginning, would never know the difference.

Milken's lawyers did their best to respond, but they were in a difficult position. They had to walk the fine line between explaining why the six felonies were not serious offenses while simultaneously proclaiming that Michael accepted full responsibility for his wrongdoing. To place Michael's guilty plea in perspective, his lawyers highlighted how the offenses "had rarely, if ever, been subject to criminal prosecution at the time of Michael's acts." Prior to Rudy Giuliani's tenure as U.S. attorney, the defense explained, there were no criminal prosecutions for participating in books-and-records violations or for failing to disclose an attempt to recoup commission expenses from money managers. The defense's message was that Michael pled guilty to offenses that really weren't crimes, but this could not be said directly lest Judge Wood conclude that Michael was insufficiently remorseful. Instead, the defense made the noncrimes point while emphasizing to the court that, of course, "the novelty of the charges does not excuse Michael Milken's transgressions." What the defense really hoped was that the "novelty" of the charges would lead Judge Wood to question whether there were any transgressions.

Milken's lawyers were also in an impossible position on the cooperation issue. Either Michael committed six felonies for which he accepted responsibility, or he didn't. If he did, there was no reason why he shouldn't cooperate with the government. But if he didn't, then why did he plead guilty in the first place? Once again, the defense tried to have it both ways. Michael pled guilty and acknowledged his crimes but should not be penalized for his defiance in refusing to cooperate. The inconsistency in the defense's position was obvious.

But the defense was most concerned about the government's seventy-page recitation of Milken's "other crimes." Milken's lawyers knew this issue would come up. In Robert Freeman's sentencing hearing earlier in 1990, judge Pierre Leval ruled that the government's recitation of other crimes that Freeman supposedly commit-

ted but had not pled guilty to were irrelevant for sentencing. Judge
Leval's ruling, while based on the elementary principle of justice that
sentencing should be based on guilt, not unsupported accusations
that have never been proven, was of deep concern to the government at the time of Milken's guilty plea. In fact, prosecutors were so
concerned that they insisted as part of the plea agreement that they
had the right to present Judge Wood with evidence of Milken's other
crimes. The defense's only hope was to persuade Judge Wood that it
was fundamentally unfair for the government, having accepted
Milken's guilty plea for six offenses, to advocate that he be punished
for other offenses for which he had never been proven guilty.

Judge Wood received a flood of letters from the public in addition to the prosecution and defense sentencing memoranda. More
than five hundred letters were sent in Milken's support from
friends, business associates, clients, and those touched by his charitable and philanthropic activities. These letters described Michael's
love for his family, his concern for the sick and underprivileged, his
commitment to education, and his modest lifestyle and disregard of
material possessions. Letters written prior to sentencing always
have to be taken with a grain of salt. The suspicion always exists
that the letters are prompted, and maybe even written by, the
defense lawyers who are trying to get their client the best deal possible. But even the most cynical court observers had to admit that
there was something special about the large number of heartfelt
and intensely personal letters written on Milken's behalf. But by
the same token, many letters were written viciously attacking
Milken as a master criminal who symbolized everything wrong
with America. These letters included requests that Milken be
"slowly executed" or that he be "hung by the balls until death."

Judge Wood, faced with such radically different portrayals of
Milken and the severity of his crimes, decided to invoke a seldom
used procedure known as a Fatico hearing before pronouncing
sentence. The purpose of a Fatico hearing is not to find the defendant guilty or innocent but, in Judge Wood's words, "to educate
the judge about the defendant's character, to help the judge
decide where sentence should be set within the range of penalties
permitted for the crimes that the defendant has admitted." The
hearing is informal with no jury, and there is no requirement that
the government prove facts beyond a reasonable doubt. Judge
Wood decided that the ground rules for the Fatico hearing in
Milken's case were that the government would have twenty

hours to present its evidence of Milken's other crimes. The government then announced it would use the time to present evidence of Milken's criminal conduct in transactions involving the securities of Wickes, Storer Communications, and Caesars World.

The hearing began on October 11, 1990. The government first contended that Milken was guilty of manipulating the common stock of Wickes Corporation on April 23, 1986, from $6 to $6 $1/8$. In April 1986, Wickes had approximately eight million shares of $2.50 convertible exchangeable preferred stock outstanding. The preferred had a redemption feature, which allowed Wickes to redeem the issue of preferred stock if the closing price of Wickes common stock equaled or exceeded $6 $1/8$ per share for at least twenty of thirty consecutive trading days. To avoid redemption, the preferred stockholders had the right to exchange their preferreds into common stock. Wickes, the government contended, wanted to force the preferred stockholders to exchange into common stock to get rid of its obligation to pay the $2.50 dividend. Wickes paid no dividend to its common stockholders.

On March 13, 1986, Wickes common stock closed at or above $6 $1/8$ for the first time since the firm emerged from bankruptcy the previous year. Wickes common then continued to close at or above $6 $1/8$ for eight trading days but then fell below $6 $1/8$ for the next eight days. On April 8, 1986, Wickes announced a takeover of National Gypsum, which the market reacted to favorably. From April 8 through April 22, Wickes closed at or above $6 $1/8$ for eleven consecutive days. Wickes's April 8 announcement also caused Wickes to be placed on Drexel's restricted list, meaning that Drexel could not trade the stock for its account or solicit orders from third parties. Unsolicited trades, however, could still be executed.

At the close of trading on April 22, 1986, Wickes common stock had closed at or above the threshold price of $6 $1/8$ on nineteen of twenty-eight consecutive trading days. A closing price at or above $6 $1/8$ on either of the next two trading days would satisfy the redemption condition and allow Wickes to get rid of the $2.50 dividend on the preferred. To accommodate Wickes, prosecutors said, Milken then caused the Boesky organization to purchase 1.9 million shares of Wickes stock in the last half hour of April 23 at prices ranging from $6 to $6 $1/8$, causing the price of Wickes common stock to close at $6 $1/8$ on that day. Milken's motive for the manipulation was the $2.3 million in fees that Drexel received for underwriting the redemption and the millions of dollars in expected fees from having Wickes as a satisfied investment-banking client.

But once the hearing began, the government produced no witnesses who could link Milken to the alleged manipulation. Cary Maultasch, Drexel's trader, and Michael Davidoff, Boesky's trader, both testified that Milken never asked them to manipulate Wickes, or any other stock for that matter. The only witness who even came close to implicating Milken was Peter Gardiner, a former junior trader at Drexel who admittedly committed perjury before the grand jury but who the government immunized anyway solely for the purpose of having him testify against Milken at the Fatico hearing. Gardiner testified that several times late in the trading day on April 23 when Wickes was trading below $6 $1/8$, Milken directed Gardiner to his Quotron screen and said, "Peter, Wickes six and one-eighth." Gardiner testified that he understood this cryptic comment to mean that Milken was telling him "to use nominees or agents or clients of [Drexel's] to make the stock close at six and one-eighth." Milken, Gardiner continued, also told members of the high-yield department on April 23 that "we are looking for unsolicited buyers of Wickes common stock" to get around Wickes's being on Drexel's restricted list. "Gardiner's testimony," prosecutors told Judge Wood, "conclusively demonstrates that Milken was responsible for the Wickes manipulation."

The truth was that there was nothing "conclusive" about Gardiner's testimony. As Arthur Liman brought out on cross-examination, Gardiner was about to be indicted himself for perjury until he received immunity in exchange for his testimony against Milken. Moreover, even if Gardiner were believed, his testimony was ambiguous at best. Milken's "Peter, Wickes six and one-eighth" statement (which other witnesses who were present denied Milken ever made) could have simply reflected Milken's belief or hope, looking at the pattern of price movements on the Quotron machine, that Wickes would close at $6 $1/8$.

Similarly, Milken's supposed statement that he was "looking for unsolicited buyers" could easily have meant that he wanted to know whether any unsolicited orders came in, not that he wanted his employees to violate the terms of the restricted list. Gardiner also had no explanation for his own behavior, which contradicted the government's manipulation story. For example, Gardiner admitted that he, on Drexel's behalf, had a large short position in

Wickes common stock until Wickes went on the restricted list, which was obviously inconsistent with any scheme to prop up its price. And on April 23, the day of the supposed manipulation, Gardiner executed a large sale trade of Wickes common for First Executive, one of Milken's best clients. Why would Gardiner and Milken be executing large sale transactions at the time they were supposedly manipulating the stock upward? Gardiner's testimony was simply not credible, as Judge Wood herself concluded, and he was the best witness the government had.

The remaining piece of the puzzle is why the Boesky organization bought 1.9 million shares in a series of trades at the end of the trading day on April 23. Prosecutors claimed the only explanation for this pattern of purchases was manipulation. Liman conceded the manipulation but pointed out that wrongdoing by Boesky didn't incriminate Milken. Liman conceded too much. Boesky may well have believed that Wickes, which had recently announced an acquisition attempt for National Gypsum, was a hot takeover stock. Boesky, as a takeover arbitrageur, routinely acquired large positions in takeover stocks. Boesky may also have been betting that the redemption condition was going to be satisfied in any event and that Wickes's common-stock price would rise as a result. This would have been perfectly logical because Wickes believed its investors would benefit if the redemption condition were satisfied, thereby eliminating its obligation to pay dividends, and the odds of that happening were high. Boesky may even have concluded that the elimination of the dividend would have improved Wickes's acquisition prospects because the company would then have more cash. Boesky's purchases by themselves proved nothing.

Storer was the second transaction covered in the Fatico hearing. In 1986, Drexel committed to raise over $1.4 billion in debt and equity to finance KKR's leveraged buyout acquisition of Storer Communications, a cable company. The transaction was the largest LBO in history up to that time. As originally structured, Storer shareholders were to receive cash plus $255 million of PIK preferred stock, pay-in-kind preferred stock where dividends are paid in more stock rather than cash. If Storer shareholders wanted cash instead, they would have had to sell the PIK preferred stock in the secondary market.

The deal was restructured after Comcast Corporation submitted a competing bid for Storer. KKR and Drexel then agreed "to monetize" the preferred by paying Storer shareholders an additional $255 million in cash, which Drexel would raise by selling the PIK preferred to investors. The rest of the $1.4 billion would be raised by selling high-yield-debt securities to the public. As an inducement to investors, KKR agreed to issue warrants, junior equity securities that would be exercisable only if the LBO was very successful. The warrants were assigned a value of $5 million, or approximately 7¢ a warrant. If all the warrants were eventually exercised, the warrant holders would hold 32 percent of the post-LBO firm's common stock.

The deal was set up so that the warrants were owned by a limited partnership called SCI Equity Associates. To purchase warrants, investors had to purchase limited-partnership units in SCI Associates. Ultimately, 80 percent of the limited-partnership interests in SCI, and thus the warrants, were purchased by employee partnerships of Milken's high-yield department. Milken also wound up selling some of the remaining warrants to money managers and executives of Drexel clients and to trusts set up for the benefit of his and Lowell Milken's children. The transactions involving these remaining warrants were accomplished by selling interests in another limited partnership, MacPherson Investment Partners. The employee partnerships, Milken and his family, and Milken's clients eventually made several hundred million dollars on the warrants because the Storer LBO turned out to be a phenomenal success.

The government's basic claim in Storer was that Milken "unlawfully enriched himself" by having the employee partnerships purchase the Storer warrants instead of distributing them to investors in the Storer LBO and then further acted unlawfully by using some of the remaining warrants "to pay unlawful gratuities" to "certain favored money managers." But once again, the parade of government witnesses on Storer—which included, among others, R. Theodore Ammon, a KKR associate who worked on the deal, Fred Joseph himself, and money managers who purchased interests in MacPherson—did not support the government's version of events.

Ammon and Joseph seemingly helped the government by testifying that Milken should have been more candid about his personal involvment in buying and selling the Storer warrants. When Liman confronted them on cross-examination with Milken's role in the Storer transaction, however, Ammon and Joseph told a very different story.

Ammon and Joseph both wanted the Storer transaction to go forward. But when Comcast came along with a competing bid, they had a problem. KKR believed that Storer's board of directors would only approve KKR's bid if Storer's shareholders were guaranteed receiving an additional $255 million in cash instead of the PIK preferred. Drexel and KKR then had to decide who would make up the shortfall if the PIK preferred could not be sold to the public. KKR didn't want to put up any more money, and Drexel in 1986 still had a policy against making bridge loans. The deal was in danger of falling apart until Milken personally guaranteed that the employee partnerships would buy whatever PIK preferred could not be sold to the public. As part of the deal, Joseph agreed that the employee partnerships would then also have the right to purchase the warrants along with the PIK preferred. KKR didn't care who purchased the warrants or the PIK preferred so long as Drexel could raise the money for the deal.

By mid-November 1985, Drexel had sold only about $100 million of the PIK preferred, so the employee partnerships wound up buying the rest. The partnerships, in accordance with the earlier agreement, also purchased 80 percent of the warrants by acquiring that percentage of the limited-partnership interests in SCI Equity Associates. The other 20 percent were purchased by Atlantic Capital Corporation and General Electric Investment Corporation. Eventually, Milken was able to sell all the PIK preferred without having to use the warrants as an inducement. After all the PIK preferred was sold, the employee partnerships still owned the warrants.

But this was perfectly consistent with the deal Milken negotiated with KKR and Joseph. Milken had no obligation to distribute the warrants to investors in the Storer LBO. Rather, Milken bore the risk that the PIK preferred couldn't be sold to the public and got the right to purchase the warrants in exchange. Because Milken agreed to bear this risk, KKR prevailed over Comcast and Drexel received $50 million in fees without having to put up any of its own capital. KKR and Drexel got exactly what they bargained for. From their perspective, the warrants were significant only as an inducement to sell the PIK preferred and raise the $255 million in cash. Once Milken guaranteed that the $255 million would be raised, the identity of the warrant holders became irrelevant.

In fact, the transaction was deliberately structured to allow their identity to remain confidential. SCI Equity Associates was created

in the first place because there was no requirement that purchasers of limited partnership interests be disclosed, even to KKR
or Drexel, as both Ammon and Joseph understood. If Milken
couldn't sell the PIK preferred and had to offer potential purchasers additional inducements beyond the warrants, he would
have had no right to get KKR or Drexel to foot the bill. The reverse
was also true if, as in fact occurred, Milken was able to sell the PIK
preferred without using the warrants as an inducement. As
Ammon was forced to admit at the conclusion of his testimony,
KKR would have behaved in exactly the same way even if it knew
everything about the warrants.

Prosecutors also couldn't prove that Milken paid "unlawful gratuities" to money managers. What happened was that Atlantic
Capital, one of the original purchasers of the PIK preferred and the
warrants, decided against going forward because of regulatory
developments and sold its investment back to Drexel for the same
price it paid, including 7¢ per warrant. The deal was structured so
that these warrants were technically purchased by another limited
partnership, MacPherson Investment Partners. Milken then turned
around and sold the warrants at a price of 8.8¢ per warrant, the
7¢ original price plus a charge for expenses, to a number of his
money manager clients who had earlier purchased the PIK preferred on behalf of the funds they managed.

Prosecutors claimed that the ability to purchase the warrants by
investing in MacPherson personally was a bribe to induce money
managers to buy the PIK preferred on behalf of their funds and
bail Milken out, who otherwise would have been stuck. Not even
the government's witnesses testifying with immunity, however,
supported this simple bribery story. The two money managers
who testified as cooperating government witnesses, Bernalder
Bayse and Richard Grassgreen, both said that their decision to
purchase the PIK preferred on behalf of their funds was made
prior to, and independent of, their personal decision to invest in
MacPherson.

The government's bribery story was also undercut by the relationship between the PIK preferred and the warrants. Financial
inducements paid to money managers are properly suspect
because they create a conflict of interest between the manager and
the fund's investors. The risk is created that the manager is making
a particular investment because of the personal benefit received,
rather than the benefit to the fund. Paying a money manager cash

to make an investment on behalf of the fund creates precisely this risk. But what happened in Storer was different. The warrants were junior to the PIK preferred in seniority, and had value only if the PIK preferred had value. There was no chance that the money managers would benefit personally while the fund would lose.

In this sense, the warrant transactions with money managers created less of a conflict of interest than other routine transactions. Vacation resorts offer free visits to travel agents; law firms wine and dine corporate counsel who decide which lawyers to hire; interest groups give money to politicians for their campaigns and invite them to go on luxury junkets. Each of these arrangements, and countless others like them, creates the risk that the recipients' judgment will be skewed by the personal benefit received. But Storer was different because of the relationship between the warrants and the PIK preferred.

Perhaps the money managers who purchased the warrants can be faulted for not offering or disclosing the existence of the investment to their funds. However, the whole area of separating personal from corporate investment opportunities is fraught with line-drawing problems and has never before been criminalized. At worst, the money managers took an investment opportunity belonging to their funds, but even this is complicated because many of the funds were prohibited from purchasing warrants, which are riskier than common stocks. But whatever the permissible investments for money managers, Milken should not be blamed for what they did. Again, it's difficult to distinguish Milken's role relative to his clients from other routine transactions. For example, airlines award frequent flyer miles to corporate travelers but are not criminally prosecuted if the corporate executive does not credit or disclose the existence of the miles to his or her employer.

In fact, providing investment opportunities to clients has long been common practice on Wall Street. Even Joseph testified that Drexel's policies expressly permitted this practice so long as clients didn't invest at bargain prices or receive "favored treatment." The real value of the warrants at the time of sale, however, was difficult to determine. The warrants were unusual financial instruments, which represented the most junior claim on a new entity that itself had a complex capital structure. They had no marketability, so their market value, as Ammon testified, was not "ascertainable." There was even a chance the warrants could wind up having negative value because, under certain circumstances, holders would have to contribute additional capital. The government tried to establish that the 8.8¢ per warrant paid by money managers was too low but could not do so convincingly. Many contemporary observers believed KKR paid too much for Storer, making the warrants, which only had value if the post-LBO firm turned out to be worth much more than what KKR paid, very suspect investments.

The warrants ultimately turned out to be a great investment, but so did the PIK preferred. The government, once again, could point to no victims of Milken's alleged crimes. Everyone, including investors in the funds that purchased the PIK preferred, benefited from the Storer transaction. Milken, of everyone, was the closest thing to a loser in the sense that he would have done even better if he had kept the warrants for himself as he had every right to do.

Ceasars World, the last transaction covered in the hearing, was an anticlimax. Very little evidence was presented, and both parties by this time seemed to be just going through the motions. Prosecutors accused Milken of purchasing Ceasars World bonds with inside information that the bonds would be exchanged for equity. The dispute centered on a June 29, 1983, meeting that Milken attended with Ceasars World, where a debt-for-equity swap was one of many financing alternatives discussed. Milken purchased Ceasars World bonds in a trade recorded on July 1, but the defense showed that Milken had committed to purchase at an earlier date. The defense also disputed whether Milken learned any inside information at the June 29 hearing, since the debt-for-equity swap was only one of many alternatives discussed and no decisions were made.

The SEC had investigated the same transaction in 1985 and decided against filing even a civil enforcement action. In the intervening five years, prosecutors had uncovered no persuasive new evidence to warrant altering this decision, but they felt they had to charge Milken with insider trading and Ceasars World was the best they could do. This itself spoke volumes about the weakness of the government's case. Milken had been involved in virtually all of the megatransactions of the 1980s. He had greater ability than anyone on earth to trade on inside information. Prosecutors scrutinized every one of these transactions and came up empty.

After all the leaks and accusations, the Fatico hearing exposed the government's case as a bust. This was true even though the government had every advantage. Prosecutors got to choose the three transactions where the evidence was the strongest. But given how weak the evidence was, one can only imagine what would have happened if the government had to prove its accusations in the dozens of other transactions where prosecutors accused Milken of committing other crimes. Prosecutors also had the ability in the Fatico hearing to control who would testify by the use of immunity. Those who the government wanted to testify received immunity; those who the government wanted to keep off the witness stand did not and risked indictment if they testified voluntarily. With all these advantages, prosecutors still didn't come close to proving that Milken engaged in any crimes. And then there was the issue of Ivan Boesky. Having been billed for years as the government's star witness against Milken, he wasn't even called to testify. Prosecutors had seen Boesky's pathetic performance in the Mulheren trial and didn't want a recurrence.

The press should have denounced the government and treated the Fatico hearing as a scandal, an exposé of prosecutorial overreaching. All of the government's actions should have been called into question now that it was clear prosecutors had no case. What right did the government have to drive Drexel Burnham out of business? Why did the government indict Milken on ninety-eight counts of securities fraud and racketeering and compare him to "kingpins" of organized crime? Did Milken's guilty plea, entered to avoid this and other threatened indictments and to save his brother, really prove anything? But the press, whose historic role is to act as a watchdog and safeguard the citizen from the abuse of governmental power, largely remained silent.

For Milken, the Fatico hearing was bittersweet. His lawyer, Arthur Liman, had demolished the government's case, but Milken was still a convicted felon awaiting sentencing. And Judge Wood had said from the outset that the Fatico hearing was to learn about Milken's "character," not to determine guilt or innocence. Guilt had already been established when Milken pled to six felonies. The government may have proved no crimes, but nobody knew what Judge Wood learned about Milken's "character" at the hearing that would play a role in sentencing.

But there were some ominous signs. Judge Wood seemed to be quite interested in the possibility that Milken obstructed the government's investigation based on the testimony of ex-Drexel employees who described Milken's reaction to the announcement of Boesky's deal with the government on Friday, November 14, 1986. Terren Peizer testified that Milken instructed him on the following Monday, November 17, to give a ledger listing all dealings with David Solomon to Lorraine Spurge, one of Milken's closest confidantes. The ledger, prosecutors said, subsequently disappeared, although Spurge denied the episode ever occurred. Peizer also described a conversation with Milken where, in reference to government subpoenas, Milken pointed to his empty desk drawer and said, "You can't turn over what you don't have."

James Dahl testified that Milken called him into the men's room and told him, in hushed tones over running water, that "There haven't been any subpoenas issued, and whatever you need to do, do it." Cary Maultasch testified about a dawn meeting with Milken in a conference room where Milken didn't speak but communicated by writing notes on a legal pad and then erasing them.

No witness testified that Milken ever actually told them to destroy documents or withhold evidence, and prosecutors did not list obstruction of justice as one of the charges they would prove in the Fatico hearing. But prosecutors, by eliciting sinister-sounding testimony from ex-Drexel employees who were all cooperating with the government's investigation, had raised a question about Milken's character. Calling Milken to the witness stand would have been the most effective way to respond. But the defense decided to play it safe and not take the risk of having Milken testify in a hearing about his own character. Instead, the defense attempted to expose the various inconsistencies in the testimony and the obvious incentive of Peizer, Dahl, and Maultasch to protect themselves by incriminating Milken.

When Judge Wood released her findings about the hearing, it seemed like the strategy backfired. "The evidence at the Fatico hearing," Judge Wood announced, "established that Milken engaged in the additional misconduct of attempting to obstruct justice and obstructing justice." On the actual crimes that prosecutors said they were going to prove in connection with Wickes, Storer, and Caesars World, in contrast, Judge Wood concluded simply that "the evidence established neither the government's version of Milken's conduct nor Milken's own version."

Sentencing was set for November 21, 1990, just before Thanksgiving. Predictably, virulent anti-Milken stories began appearing in the press before the fateful day. On November 5, 1990, *Barron's* ran a story intimating that Milken should be sentenced, not for his crimes, but for the excesses of the 1980s. After proclaiming that Milken should not be blamed for "all the ills of the world, or even all the ills of the economy," *Barron's* proceeded to do just that:

> Mr. Milken lent his considerable guile to every dubious investment activity of the Eighties. And he did supply the matches to the savings and loans. He did by any means, often as not foul, push leverage to Corporate America until it grew insatiably addicted, with ruinous results. He trivialized the financial environment. He was Mr. Greed of an historically greedy epoch, for analogs to which one must go back to the Gilded Age or the Twenties.

Milken's other enemies jumped on the same bandwagon. Congressman Dingell, the old Milken nemesis, released documents ten days before the sentencing describing how the Drexel employee partnerships doled out more than $2 billion during the 1980s. The *Wall Street Journal* dutifully reported the story on November 12, complete with a quote from a "top aide" to Dingell's committee that the $2 billion sum was "more than the GNP of half the countries in the United Nations." The timing of the documents' release, and the *Wall Street Journal* story, were clearly intended to further inflame public opinion against Milken. But nothing could top the *Wall Street Journal*'s front-page story on November 20, 1990, the day before Milken's sentencing. Titled "Junk King's Legacy," the story blamed Milken for Drexel's demise, the collapse of the high-yield-bond market, and for misleading investors into believing that high-yield bonds were a good investment. Milken, the *Journal* told its readers, was "wrong," and the "many people who bought into his sales pitch of the early 1980's, thinking it the path to riches, now are chastened and bitter." The clear inference was that Milken had no redeeming qualities and society would be better off if Judge Wood sent Milken to jail and threw away the key.

The sentencing hearing on the following day, November 21, was the time for Judge Wood to finally announce her decision. Arthur Liman spoke first and made an hour plea for leniency. Milken, Liman stressed, had lived a life of good deeds and felt "deep remorse" for his crimes. Liman also read some of the more moving letters written on Milken's behalf, and asked Judge Wood not to be influenced by "the unreasonable passions of the moment." Finally, Liman urged the court to sentence Milken to community service so he could use his considerable talents to help underprivileged children. Next Milken made the obligatory statement of contrition. "What I did violated not just the law but all of my principles and values. I deeply regret it and will for the rest of my life. I am truly sorry."

Then Jess Fardella spoke briefly on behalf of the government to urge, as expected, that Milken receive a sentence of "substantial incarceration." Now all eyes in the packed courtroom were on Judge Wood. All the speculation about what sentence Milken would receive was about to end. Nobody believed Milken would get off with community service, but few expected a sentence of greater than five years. Many thought three years, Boesky's sentence, seemed about right. Everyone was searching for clues about what Judge Wood was going to do as she delivered her address.

Milken, Judge Wood began, should not be a scapegoat for a "decade of greed," but nor should he receive any credit for creating jobs and business opportunities. An overall assessment of Milken's career was a task for a historian, not a court. A judge, in contrast, has to decide what sentence is appropriate to punish the wrongdoer and prevent others from engaging in similar crimes. Here, Milken's crimes were serious because he "repeatedly conspired to violate and violated securities and tax laws in order to achieve more power and wealth for himself and his wealthy clients." And Milken's crimes were "subtle," and "crimes that are hard to detect warrant greater punishment in order to be effective in deterring others from committing them." Having set out the relevant principles, Judge Wood then sentenced Milken to a prison term of ten years. Even the many rabid Milken haters had not expected such a harsh sentence.

The severity of Milken's sentence caused many to second-guess the defense's strategy. Milken had unlimited resources and hired the best lawyers money can buy. How could he have gotten screwed so badly? Why did Milken publicly assert his innocence, and fight the government for years if he was ultimately going to plead guilty? Why did he refuse to cooperate when he did ultimately plead guilty? Why did his lawyers agree to allow prosecutors to argue that Milken committed other crimes beyond his guilty plea? Why didn't his lawyers put him on the witness stand at the Fatico hearing so he could testify about his own "character"? Would Milken have received a lighter sentence if he had defended himself and his accomplishments at a trial, even if he were convicted? There was no obvious answer to any of these questions.

Developments in 1991 made Milken's decision seem even worse. Milken's decision to plead was based in substantial part on the belief that he couldn't win. After all, John Mulheren, James Sherwin, and the Princeton/Newport defendants were all found guilty. Milken's chances of acquittal at the time he pled were remote. But in 1991 the Second Circuit, in a stunning rebuke of the U.S. attorney's office, reversed all of these convictions. The Second Circuit the same year also threw out the conviction of Robert Wallach for his role in the Wedtech scandal, another of Rudy Giuliani's highly publicized prosecutions, because the government had knowingly used perjured testimony.

Hindsight is twenty-twenty, of course. Nobody could have anticipated in 1990 when Milken pled guilty that the Second Circuit would take such a dim view of Rudy Giuliani's convictions. Nor could anyone have anticipated that after all the buildup, Ivan Boesky, Milken's chief accuser, was such an unreliable witness that the government wouldn't even call him to testify in the Fatico hearing. But still Milken had to wonder in the months after he began his ten-year prison sentence on March 3, 1991, in Pleasanton, California. Those who fought and stood for principle had ultimately prevailed. They were all free men while Milken, who just several years earlier was one of the most successful and powerful private citizens in the world, was incarcerated facing a long prison term. How could everything have turned out so badly? What did Milken do to deserve this fate? Once again, there were no obvious answers to these questions.

The press ignored Milken's plight. No stories appeared describing the irony of Milken's ten-year prison sentence and Drexel's demise in light of the Second Circuit's repudiation of the prosecutorial tactics that led Drexel and Milken to plead guilty in the first place. If anything, the press attacks on Drexel and Milken intensified. In the fall of 1991, James B. Stewart, the *Wall Street Journal* reporter who had written so many of the front-page anti-Drexel and Milken stories since 1986, published his long awaited book, *Den of Thieves*. Milken's crimes, Stewart wrote, were "far more complex, imaginative and ambitious than mere insider trading" and placed him at the center of "the greatest criminal conspiracy the financial world has ever known." Stewart's 587-page book described, in his words, "the full story of the criminals who came to dominate Wall Street" and the "heroic efforts of underpaid, overworked government lawyers who devoted much of their careers to uncovering the scandal."

The book was an instant success. Michael Thomas, another well-known Milken hater, wrote a front-page review in the *New York Times Book Review* describing the book as "tremendously important" and one of the best books on Wall Street ever written. Other similar tributes appeared throughout the country. When Harvard Professor Alan Dershowitz, who had been added to the defense team after Milken's guilty plea, publicly attacked the book as anti-Semitic—making the same mistake that Drexel made in creating additional publicity for Connie Bruck's *The Predators' Ball* four years earlier—sales skyrocketed. *Den of Thieves* became the number-one best-selling book in the country.

In reality the book was hopelessly biased. Stewart, for example, spends page after page detailing Milken's supposed massive crimes without mentioning that prosecutors could not even prove in the Fatico hearing that one such crime occurred. In fact, the whole subject of the Fatico hearing is ignored by Stewart altogether, except for a brief mention in one footnote. Worse than Stewart's bias, however, is his treatment of the restructuring transactions of the 1980s:

> To dwell on the ill-gotten gains of individuals, however, is to risk missing the big picture. During this crime wave, the ownership of entire corporations changed hands, often forcibly, at a clip never before witnessed. Household names—Carnation, Beatrice, General Foods, Diamond Shamrock—vanished in takeovers that spawned criminal activity and violations of the securities laws.
>
> Others, companies like Unocal and Union Carbide, survived but were nearly crippled. Thousands of workers lost their jobs, companies loaded up with debt to pay for the deals, profits were sacrificed to pay interest costs on the borrowings, and even so, many companies were eventually forced into bankruptcies or restructurings. Bondholders and shareholders lost many millions more. Greed alone cannot account for such a toll. These are the costs of greed coupled with market power—power unrestrained by the normal checks and balances of the free market, or by any fears of getting caught.

Stewart's lack of understanding of what occurred in the 1980s is astonishing, particularly for a *Wall Street Journal* reporter. One would never know from Stewart's account of "vanishing" and "crippled" companies with investors "losing many millions" of dollars that the Dow Jones Industrial Average tripled during the 1980s, and investors made close to $1 trillion from restructuring transactions. But probably few would have cared in any event. It was easier to believe that Milken's accomplishments were worthless, just as it was easier to believe that he masterminded the "greatest criminal conspiracy the financial world had ever known." After all, why else was Milken in prison for ten years? Perception had triumphed over reality.

Faced with this hostile environment, Milken and his lawyers had to decide what to do. They contemplated, and rejected, attempting to withdraw Milken's guilty plea or appealing the ten-year sentence. The probability of success for these options was just too low, and the risk of alienating Judge Wood too great. Better to curry favor with Judge Wood and ask her to reduce Milken's sentence. At Milken's sentencing hearing in November 1990, Judge Wood said that she might reduce the ten-year sentence if Milken cooperated with the government's continuing investigation, something he had refused to do up to that time. Now Milken had to decide whether he was willing to play the same game as Levine, Boesky, Jefferies, and Siegel to get his sentence reduced.

Milken was at least willing to go through the motions. He met with prosecutors and enforcement attorneys dozens of times, but the consensus was these meetings were a waste of time. Either Milken didn't know anything that could incriminate anyone else or, as the government lawyers kept saying, he wasn't telling what he knew. Whatever the reason, the debriefing sessions led to no new prosecutions.

Milken did testify once as a cooperating government witness in the trial of Alan Rosenthal, a former employee of Drexel's high-yield department whom the government accused of being involved in the illegal commission-recouping scheme and tax trades with David Solomon. The stakes were high when Milken was transported from federal prison to take the witness stand. His lawyers had formally requested that Judge Wood reduce the ten-year sentence based on his willingness to testify against Rosenthal. How Milken did as a witness against Rosenthal might well determine whether the request was granted, as well as whether Rosenthal would be convicted.

Milken had every incentive to shade his testimony against Rosenthal, even to lie as so many others had done, but he resisted.

Instead, Milken's testimony was an act of defiance stopping just short of saying that he committed no crimes in his dealings with David Solomon, notwithstanding his guilty plea to two felonies.

He described his agreement with Solomon to recoup the 1 percent fee his department was being charged as the routine receipt of a "sales credit" or, more accurately, a "potential sales credit." The credit was only "potential," Milken explained, because it was something to be used in negotiations to get Solomon to pay a slightly higher price when purchasing securities from Drexel, or take a slightly lower price when selling. There was no guarantee, however, that the ultimate transaction price arrived at would be different from what it would have been without the credit. And the tax trades with Solomon, Milken said, were also innocuous, a simple "account accommodation" for a valued client. For good measure, Milken denied ever having suggested to anyone that they not produce documents or obstruct justice in any way, directly contradicting Judge Wood's finding at the Fatico hearing.

Judge Louis Stanton, the same judge who didn't allow prosecutors to steamroll Wigton, Freeman, and Tabor, was apparently impressed with Milken's testimony. Even before the Rosenthal case went to the jury, Judge Stanton ruled that Rosenthal could not be convicted on the tax trades because the trades were not illegal. Solomon's tax losses were real, Judge Stanton reasoned, and not offset by Milken's promise to find Solomon profitable investments in the future, which was too indefinite to be currently taxed before any investments were ever made. Judge Stanton, with full "understanding of the anomaly" of his ruling that Milken pled guilty to a felony for conduct that was not criminal, gutted much of the case against Rosenthal. The jury did the rest, acquitting Rosenthal on all but one minor count, for which he received probation. Milken's debut as a cooperating government witness was indeed memorable for the damage he did to the government's case.

Milken also testified once as a defense witness when he was subpoenaed by Patsy Ostrander, one of the money managers who purchased limited partnerships in MacPherson for her personal account. Prosecutors accused Ostrander of taking the Storer warrants for herself without disclosing the opportunity to her employer. Milken again did what he could in his testimony to hurt the government's case. He explained that there were no restrictions on who could purchase the Storer warrants and why he was fully justified in selling the warrants to Ostrander. It was a perfectly legitimate transaction involving a risky security, which worked out when the Storer LBO did better than expected. Ostrander made a lot of money, but, Milken said, she could have just as easily lost, as she did in other warrant transactions. Anyway, the fund that Ostrander managed, Fidelity, was barred by regulation from purchasing the warrants. Although Milken couldn't explain why Ostrander failed to disclose this and other investments to her employer as she was required to do, it was hard to tell from Milken's testimony why Ostrander was being prosecuted in the first place.

On cross-examination, the prosecutor attacked Milken's credibility by pointing out that Milken was a criminal who had pled guilty to six felonies. Milken admitted that he pled guilty but all but denied that he ever committed any crimes:

Q. You would admit, Mr. Milken, would you not, that all of those crimes that you pled guilty to were serious crimes?

A. Yes.

Q. Every one of them?

A. Yes.

Q. They weren't just technical violations of the law, were they?

A. I believe that they were violations of regulations, that at the time were not considered criminal in my business.

Q. So in other words, you pled guilty to something that really wasn't a crime?

A. I didn't say that, sir.

Q. Well, I'm trying to get your understanding.

A. The issues that I pled guilty to, most of them no one had ever been prosecuted before in this country. And many of these practices were widespread throughout my industry. That does not diminish what I pled to. I'm just stating at the time that these things were not viewed as criminal by people in my business.

Q. You didn't plead guilty for expediency, did you, Mr. Milken?

A. I obviously entered into an agreement with the government to try to get this part behind me, sir.

If Milken's testimony in *Rosenthal* was an act of defiance, then what he did in *Ostrander* bordered on sabotage. His refusal to cooperate or even acknowledge guilt in *Ostrander* was all the more remarkable because he knew that Judge Wood was due to decide any day whether his sentence would be reduced. Even though Ostrander was ultimately convicted, prosecutors were upset with Milken's performance. They were not likely to be very helpful in recommending to Judge Wood that Milken's sentence be reduced.

On August 5, 1992, two weeks after Milken's testimony in *Ostrander*, Judge Wood announced her decision on sentence reduction. Citing Milken's "substantial cooperation" with the government, Judge Wood reduced Milken's ten-year sentence, ruling that he would be eligible for release in March 1993 after serving twenty-four months. No one really believed that Milken's cooperation was "substantial," but the defense was happy with the ruling whatever the reason. Milken had finally gotten a break.

For Judge Wood, the "substantial cooperation" rationale, even if a sham, was easier than admitting her earlier sentence was too severe. Judge Wood presided over the Fatico hearing, and knew the government couldn't prove that Milken engaged in any crimes. She also now knew that her colleague, Judge Stanton, had publicly stated that one of the six felonies that Milken pled guilty to wasn't even a crime. And she knew that the Second Circuit had reversed a slew of Rudy Giuliani's convictions for the same conduct that Milken was accused of. Perhaps Judge Wood also realized that, no matter what she said at the time, Milken was unfairly sentenced as a symbol of the "decade of greed" and now she had a chance to correct the mistake.

Judge Wood's reduction of Milken's sentence in August 1992 marked the end of Milken's legal problems. Earlier in 1992, Milken and other ex-Drexel employees settled the hundreds of civil lawsuits that had been filed for $1.3 billion, with Milken paying by far the largest share even after he received a credit for the $400 million he already paid. When added to the $200 million penalty he paid as part of his guilty plea, Milken paid over $1 billion to resolve the claims against him. Drexel, Milken and other ex-Drexel employees together paid close to $2 billion, not an insignificant amount considering the complete absence of harm or victims. It was legal extortion, pure and simple, but at least it was over. When Milken was released from prison in March 1993, he was done with the legal system.

Milken's sentence reduction stopped the second-guessing of his defense strategy. All the decisions beginning with the guilty plea itself that looked so bad in November 1990 when Milken was originally sentenced to serve ten years looked much better when Milken emerged a free man in March 1993. But nothing could change the reality that Milken was still an admitted felon and would be for the rest of his life. And for many he remained the incarnation of evil, and this too would never change.

Soon after Milken was released from prison, he announced that he had prostate cancer, which had spread beyond the prostate. While no one can say with certainty, it's likely his condition was only worsened by the medical advice and treatment he received while incarcerated. Still, Milken's disclosure of his life-threatening disease generated no wave of public sympathy. There was more concern that Milken had been treated too lightly because of his wealth and prominence, that he had been let out of prison too soon and allowed to keep too much of his fortune.

Milken did receive special treatment from the legal system, but of a very different type. He was driven out of business and forced to plead guilty to crimes that previously did not exist. Judge Stanton's observation that one of the six felonies that Milken pled guilty to was not a crime was equally applicable to the other five. Milken's downfall proves only that the government, with its unlimited ability to harass and change the rules in the middle of the game, is more powerful than any individual. In all but the rarest cases, the safeguards built into our democratic system of government, including the constitutional rights of the accused, protect the individual against arbitrarily being declared a criminal. But in Milken's case the system didn't work. The unholy alliance of the displaced establishment and the "decade of greed" rich-haters, aided by ambitious but unscrupulous government lawyers like Rudy Giuliani, combined to destroy him. The whole episode is a national disgrace.

CHAPTER 7

Michael Milken and the Savings and Loan Crisis

The 1980s were a disaster for the savings and loan industry. More than one thousand savings and loans failed during the decade, and of the approximately three thousand that survived in 1990, more than half were in weak financial condition. Many of these subsequently failed or can be expected to fail in the future. Current estimates of the ultimate costs to taxpayers from the carnage on a present-value basis range from $150–$200 billion.

Predictably, the savings and loan debacle has fueled a search for villains, someone to blame for what has been called "the worst public scandal in American history." There has been no shortage of suspects. Those most frequently identified in the many popular and press accounts as the culprits include those who supported deregulation of the industry, S&L crooks, derelict accountants and lawyers, corrupt politicians, and, of course, Michael Milken. But to blame Milken, or any of the other popular scapegoats, for the savings and loan crisis is to ignore what really happened.

The savings and loan crisis occurred because unprecedented high interest rates, advances in computer technology and information processing, and increased worldwide competition in financial markets—the same market forces that triggered the restructuring revolution—made the savings and loan industry obsolete. Rather than let the industry fail, the government enacted a series of misguided regulatory policies designed to preserve savings and loans as viable entities even though they no longer served any socially valuable function.

Historically, savings and loans, also known as thrifts, have served as financial institutions that specialize in providing home mortgages. Although savings and loans have existed in some form since the early nineteenth century, they were transformed by federal regulation in the 1930s. The Great Depression had devastated the housing industry, and the government stepped in to help, as it did with other distressed industries. Congress also enacted a comprehensive regulatory scheme to ensure the safety of savings and loans, which were viewed as indispensable to a healthy housing industry. Identification of savings and loans as the vehicle for guaranteeing that ordinary Americans would have access to affordable housing made the industry a sacred cow to government officials, particularly those holding elective office.

The key features of the Depression-era regulatory scheme were the creation of Federal Home Loan Banks, which had the authority to make low-interest loans to member savings and loans, a system of federal chartering that protected institutions from competition, the creation of the Federal Savings and Loan Insurance Corporation (the FSLIC) to provide insurance for depositors, and the creation of a new agency, the Federal Home Loan Bank Board (the FHLBB) to oversee the system. Congress did not regulate the rate of interest thrifts could pay their depositors, which it did for commercial banks by enacting Regulation Q. This changed in 1966, however, when Congress extended Regulation Q to thrifts but still allowed thrifts to pay $1/4$ percent higher than commercial banks to compensate them for their greater specialization in home mortgages.

The thrift industry enjoyed prosperity for much of the next forty years. The key was relatively low short-term interest rates. So long as the short-term rates thrifts had to pay their depositors was comfortably lower than the long-term rates thrifts received on their mortgages, thrifts made money. And because the economy was growing for much of this period, the value of housing rose as well, making defaults extremely rare. Between 1934 and 1979, an average of only three thrifts per year failed in the whole country.

Still, the industry was a time bomb waiting to explode. Thrifts faced extreme interest-rate risk because of the maturity mismatch between their assets and liabilities. Their assets were typically long-term fixed-rate mortgages, while their liabilities were short-term deposits withdrawable on demand. If interest rates rose, thrifts would have to pay more to their depositors or face withdrawals. But thrifts could not offset the effect of increased interest rates on the asset side because rates on their long-term mortgages were fixed. Thrifts were also very undiversified, offering basically one product in a limited geographical area. If anything happened to reduce the value or demand for housing in an area, the effect on thrifts could be devastating. Finally, thrifts were extremely leveraged, so the margin of safety was razor thin. Thrifts typically held only about $5 of assets for every $100 of deposit liabilities.

The time bomb exploded in the late 1970s and early 1980s when interest rates and inflation skyrocketed. These unprecedented interest rates, coupled with advances in computer and information-processing technology, which greatly reduced the cost of financial transacting, spawned a new innovation, money market mutual funds, which payed depositors the market rate of interest. Regulation Q, which limited the interest rate thrifts could pay to depositors to 5.5 percent, became a straightjacket when the new money market funds were offering in excess of 15 percent. As a result, the thrift industry experienced record deposit outflow as consumers switched their funds to obtain market rates. At the same time, thrifts could do nothing about their existing stock of illiquid, low-interest long-term mortgages. Thrifts could meet current liquidity problems by borrowing from the Federal Home Loan Banks, but this didn't solve the basic problem. High interest rates had eroded the market value of thrifts' assets while making it impossible for them to retain their deposit base.

By the early 1980s, the industry was insolvent and the government had to decide what to do. What the government should have done was to reassess the role of thrifts for national housing policy. Much had changed in the fifty years since the 1930s. Savings and loans now had multiple competitors for mortgage originations from mortgage brokers, commercial banks, and other financial intermediaries. The importance of deposits as a source of funds for mortgage loans was also greatly diminished because of the explosive growth of the secondary mortgage market. Thrifts served a function so long as banks and other institutions were unwilling, or unable because of regulation, to hold a portfolio of long-term illiquid home mortgages. But securitization has greatly reduced the need for any institution to specialize in holding these illiquid assets. Investors in the worldwide capital market now invest in mortgage-backed securities and provide a far superior source of funds to finance mortgages than depositors at thrifts. An illiquid asset, home mortgages, has become liquid, much in the same way that high-yield bonds created a liquid market for commercial loans. In fact, during the 1980s thrifts became net sellers of mortgages, selling more mortgages from their portfolios into the secondary market than they generated.

With the savings and loan industry insolvent, the government should have gotten out of the thrift business. Insolvent thrifts should have been closed and deposit insurance phased out for the rest to protect depositors who invested in reliance on the insurance guarantee. Whether thrifts would continue to exist, and in what form, would then be determined by the marketplace. But the government, after intense lobbying by the politically powerful U.S. League of Savings and Loans, rejected this option. Instead, the government adopted policies designed to save the industry from the market forces that had made it obsolete. It was a recipe for disaster, which only made the problems of the industry worse. When the problems became too great for the government to pretend they didn't exist, the search for scapegoats began. Michael Milken, with his highly publicized legal problems, was an obvious target.

The Government Tries to Save the S&L Industry

The massive interest-rate shock between 1979 and 1982 destroyed virtually all of the savings and loan industry. Thrifts suffered losses of $4.6 billion in 1980 and $4.1 billion in 1981. Ninety percent of the industry was losing money, and by the end of 1982, savings and loans had a negative net worth on a market-value basis of over $100 billion. Congress reacted by passing two major pieces of legislation—the Depository Institutions Deregulation and Monetary Control Act of 1980 and the Garn-St. Germain Depository Institutions Act of 1982—to allow the industry to survive in the changed economic environment. Federal and state regulators also adopted major policy changes to achieve the same objective. The major features of these new legislative and regulatory initiatives were:

1: **Elimination of deposit and interest-rate restrictions.** Regulation Q was abolished, allowing thrifts to pay the market rate of interest on deposits. Thrifts were also authorized to expand their deposit base by seeking deposits outside their local geographic area. Finally, thrifts were permitted to offer checking accounts to improve their competitive position relative to commercial banks and the new money market mutual funds.

2: **Reduction of thrifts' exposure to interest-rate risk.** Thrifts were authorized to make mortgage loans with adjustable interest rates. This alleviated the maturity mismatch problem, since thrifts would no longer be locked in to below-market returns on long-term mortgages when rates rose. The relief was only partial, however, because of caps on permissible interest-rate adjustments and customer resistance.

3: **Increased investment powers.** Thrifts were given increased power to make a wide array of commercial, consumer, and real estate loans in addition to home mortgages. Thrifts' authority to make acquisition, development, and construction real estate (ADC) loans was greatly expanded. These loans frequently had equity features, meaning thrifts would share in the profits of the venture if successful. Thrifts were also given the power to purchase high-yield bonds.

4: **Increased level of deposit insurance.** The level of deposit insurance was increased from $40,000 to $100,000. This allowed thrifts to compete for larger deposits.

5: **Reduced capital requirements.** The net-worth requirement for federally insured thrifts was reduced from 5 percent to 3 percent, but even this lower number was illusory. Net-worth requirements relied on historical book value of assets rather than market values, involved five-year averages of assets and liabilities, and had a twenty-year phase-in period before a thrift had to fully comply. Regulators also adopted a series of accounting gimmicks to allow thrifts to report artificially high net worth. For example, the FSLIC issued promissory notes to weak thrifts in exchange for "net worth certificates," which could be used to satisfy minimum capital requirements. Regulators also rewarded acquirers of insolvent thrifts by allowing them to record the negative net worth of the acquired thrift as an asset for accounting purposes, thereby improving the reported financial condition of the acquirer. Similarly, thrifts that sold assets at a loss were allowed to defer recognizing the loss for accounting purposes.

6: **Organizational form changes.**   Thrifts were authorized to convert from mutuals, where the institution is owned by the depositors, to corporatelike entities, where the owners are stockholders. The rules were also changed to allow a single owner to own all of a savings and loan's outstanding stock to encourage corporations and wealthy individuals to acquire thrifts.

The combined effect of these legislative and regulatory initiatives was to eliminate whatever market discipline existed in the thrift industry. Weak or insolvent thrifts, allowed to remain in existence by lowered capital requirements and accounting gimmickry, now could choose among a wide menu of investment alternatives. To finance these investments, thrifts, now free from interest-rate and deposit restrictions, could raise a virtually unlimited amount of funds by offering depositors an above-market rate of interest. And depositors were more than willing to invest in thrifts, no matter how weak, because of deposit insurance. In fact, a whole new subindustry developed, deposit brokerage, to bundle investments in $100,000 amounts, the deposit-insurance ceiling, and place the funds at the savings and loan paying the highest rate. The process was simple because deposit insurance made the underlying health of the savings and loan irrelevant. All that mattered was which institution payed the highest rates.

Thrifts now had incentives to raise large amounts of money and take big risks. This incentive was strongest for those thrifts, particularly stock thrifts, at or near insolvency with little or no capital of their own at risk. These thrifts had nothing to lose by adopting a "shoot the moon" strategy and pursuing the most speculative investment ventures. If the investments turned out well, thrift operators and stockholders got the benefits. But if not, the thrift was effectively no worse off than before—the insurance fund had to make good on the losses.

The consequences of the new regulatory regime were predictable. The insolvent thrift industry needed to contract, or possibly disappear altogether because of its inability to compete. Instead, the industry, responding to the incentives created by the government, experienced explosive growth. But this made the industry sicker because it was the weakest thrifts that were most likely to offer the highest interest rates to attract funds, thereby making it harder for the healthy thrifts to compete. And there was another effect of the government's regulatory policies. A new

breed of thrift owners who saw the value of financing their existing or planned business ventures with government-insured thrift
deposits entered the industry. Many who would later be called
the industry's greatest villains—Charles Keating, David Paul, Don
Dixon, and even Neil Bush, to name a few—became involved
with savings and loans to take advantage of the opportunities the
government created.

Ironically, the government's gamble of allowing the insolvent
thrifts to remain open, hoping that the industry would grow out
of its problems, almost worked. Interest rates fell after 1982,
returning many thrifts to health. Speculative real estate investments also performed well in the early 1980s after Congress
favored these investments in 1981 with tax breaks. But problems
developed when various sections of the country, particularly
Texas, Florida, Arizona, California, and Colorado experienced
regional difficulties. Falling energy prices and the related depressing effect on real estate values had a major impact. Lower energy
prices also reduced the rate of migration to Sunbelt states, slowing
their expected rate of growth. Commercial real estate investments
in general also suffered when Congress in 1986 eliminated many
of the tax breaks for real estate investments that had been created
in 1981. Now the interest rate crisis of the early 1980s had been
replaced by a major credit crisis as thrifts had to deal with a wave
of defaults on their real estate loans. And thrift operators still had
no incentive to scale back their activities because of the perverse
incentives created by deposit insurance.

Many popular accounts of the savings and loan crisis have
blamed the deregulation of the industry for the problems that
developed. This perception is wrong because the industry was
already insolvent before any regulatory intervention. As Richard
Pratt, then chairman of the Federal Home Loan Bank Board,
explained in 1983: "Savings and Loans two years ago [1981] were
in a position of guaranteed atrophy and obsolescence. A set of
financial institutions with severe legislative limits on assets and
severe legislative and regulatory limits on liabilities could not
compete in a highly competitive market against institutions that
had more ability and a greater range of authority. They simply
would have disappeared."

The popularly held view that deregulation caused the savings and
loan crisis is also wrong because what occurred was not deregulation.
Real deregulation would have required eliminating deposit insurance

and letting the industry sink or swim, depending on whether it could survive in the marketplace. What happened was the exact opposite. The government decided to rescue the industry, without consideration of the costs or whether thrifts were still necessary to finance home mortgages. The hope was that the industry would grow its way out of its problems, but the gamble didn't pay off. The perverse incentives created by the regulatory scheme, coupled with adverse regional economic developments, plunged the industry deeper into crisis. But the government couldn't admit that its attempt to rescue the thrift industry had been a failure and it was time to finally let the thrifts go under. Instead, the government began a new campaign to toughen capital requirements, eliminate accounting gimmickry, and increase regulatory oversight to undo the damage it had caused. The government also embarked on a search for scapegoats to deflect as much attention as possible away from its own failed policies.

Scapegoating High-Yield Bonds

After thrifts were authorized to invest in high-yield bonds, several large savings and loans became clients of Drexel Burnham and Michael Milken. Benjamin Stein, the man who compared Drexel's bankruptcy to the fall of Nazi Germany, blames the savings and loan crisis on these client relationships:

> In barely disguised maneuvers in broad daylight, the Drexel machine sucked the blood of its captive S&Ls like a vampire, draining the assets of their depositors dry. Plasma available through the federal deposit insurance blood bank could not even begin to replace their losses and huge transfusions would ultimately have to be drawn from taxpayers. For the Drexel Draculas, it was a feast. For their victims, S&L depositors and American taxpayers, it was an experience from which they would not soon recover.

It would be easy to dismiss this account as the ranting of a crackpot, except that Stein's views became the official policy of the United States government. But official government policy or not, this account is a complete distortion of what occurred.

Thrift investments in high-yield bonds never consisted of more than a tiny fraction of all thrift assets. By June 1988 thrifts' investments in high-yield bonds grew to $13 billion, but total industry assets were $1.3 trillion. High-yield bonds constituted 1 percent or less of thrift assets from the time thrifts began actively investing in 1985 through the end of the decade:

High-Yield-Bond Holdings by Thrifts

DATE	HOLDINGS ($ MILLIONS)	PERCENT OF ASSETS
Mar 85	$5,100	.50%
Jun 85	5,741	.60
Sep 85	5,171	.50
Dec 85	5,587	.50
Mar 86	6,038	.60
Jun 86	6,583	.60
Sep 86	7,221	.60
Dec 86	7,572	.60
Mar 87	8,278	.70
Jun 87	9,971	.80
Sep 87	11,364	.90
Dec 87	12,294	1.00
Mar 88	12,392	1.00
Jun 88	13,136	1.00
Dec 88	12,810	1.00
Dec 89	12,318	1.00
Dec 90	10,730	.90
Dec 91	4,018	.40

Moreover, only about 450 of the approximately 4,000 savings and loans in existence in 1980 ever held any high-yield bonds. Obviously, high-yield bonds cannot even begin to explain why one thousand thrifts failed at a cost to taxpayers of somewhere between $150 and $200 billion.

In fact, high-yield bond investments made the thrift industry healthier. High-yield bonds are a type of securitized commercial loan that enabled thrifts to, in effect, become commercial lenders without having to go through the trouble and expense of setting up and staffing a commercial lending department. High-yield bonds also provided thrifts with valuable diversification. Thrifts now could lend to other industries operating in different parts of the country and were no longer limited to one type of loan, home mortgages, in their local community. Finally, high-yield bonds offered thrifts some income protection in a declining interest-rate market. When rates are falling, as they were during much of the 1980s, home mortgages are frequently prepaid and refinanced at lower rates, frequently without penalty. High-yield bonds, in contrast, provide fixed yields to a specific future date, either the maturity date or an earlier call date. Of course, these fixed yields had to be balanced against the risk of default, but for most of the 1980s, defaults were relatively rare.

These economic realities did not appease the critics who wanted to know why federally insured deposits were being used to purchase junk bonds. For those who wanted to find out, the answer was simple. The government permitted, even encouraged, federally insured thrifts to purchase high-yield bonds because the industry had gone broke by focusing exclusively on home mortgages. And since Congress didn't want to let the industry fail, something had to be done. Allowing thrifts to diversify into commercial lending, which is what thrifts did when they purchased high-yield bonds, was a logical policy response. Of course, the more thrifts diversified away from home mortgages, the less clear it was why a separate thrift industry was needed in the first place. But the government decided to live with this contradiction when it embarked on the campaign to prop up the now obsolete thrift industry.

Popular pressure to stop thrifts from investing in high-yield bonds intensified after November 1986, when Boesky's deal with the government was announced, and Drexel and Milken became the primary targets of the government's Wall Street prosecutions. Beginning in 1987, the FHLBB began to criticize high-yield-bond investments by thrifts as excessively risky. But the FHLBB never presented any evidence that high-yield bonds were riskier than other permissible investments such as ADC real estate loans. The FHLBB also ignored the role of high-yield bonds in diversifying a thrift's portfolio. An institution that held both high-yield bonds and real estate assets was more immune to economic downturns than an institution that exclusively held one type of asset.

The FHLBB should have focused on thrifts' level of capitalization, not their investments in high-yield bonds. The government acts as guarantor of thrifts' obligations to their depositors, and therefore has a strong interest in the likely costs it (taxpayers) will have to bear from thrift failures. But the expected cost from failure is a function of a thrift's current and future net worth, the difference between the value of assets and the value of liabilities. Net worth acts as a "cushion" to protect the government insurance fund from loss. For thrifts with large net worth, both the probability of failure and the expected cost to the government insurer are low. These thrifts also have the incentive to make appropriate investment decisions because the owners, not the government insurer, bear the risk of loss.

The FHLBB had no reason to worry about thrifts with high net worth investing in high-yield bonds. Thrifts with low or negative net worth were a different story whether or not they invested in high-yield bonds. These thrifts had the most perverse incentive to grow the fastest and make the riskiest investments because they had nothing to lose. But they were the same thrifts that the government allowed to remain open by the combination of reduced net-worth requirements and phony accounting. The last thing the government wanted to do was admit its role in prolonging the life of insolvent thrifts. Targeting unpopular high-yield bonds, however unjustified, was a much safer course.

Also in 1987 Congress ordered the General Accounting Office to investigate purchases of high-yield bonds by federally insured thrifts. The GAO released its report in early March 1989. To the surprise of many, the report's principal conclusions were that returns on high-yield bonds had more than compensated for their risk and that high-yield bonds were not responsible for the thrift crisis:

Returns on high yield bonds exceed risks to date
Compared to other fixed income investments, such as Treasury and investment grade bonds, high yield bonds have a higher risk of default. However, studies by academics and investment bankers show that from 1977 to 1987 high yield bonds have provided investors higher net returns than these other investments because their relatively high yields have outweighed the additional losses from default. . . .

High yield bonds have not caused the current thrift industry problems
A review of FHLBB data and discussions with its officials showed only one case in 1985 where high yield bond investments appeared to have been a factor in a thrift failure. However, in that case, mismanagement of the institution's high yield bond portfolio was only one part of a broader pattern of unsafe lending and investment practices leading to the institution's collapse.

The GAO report was immediately relegated to the scrap heap of history, however, when Congress enacted the FIRREA in August 1989 prohibiting savings and loans from investing in high-yield bonds and requiring them to liquidate those bonds currently held.

The FIRREA's prohibition on thrifts acquiring or retaining high-yield bonds was not contained in earlier versions of the bill. When Congress held hearings on thrift investments in high-yield bonds in March 1989, Richard Fogel, assistant comptroller of the GAO, explained why the "widespread assumption" that high-yield bonds contributed to thrift failures "was wrong":

CHAIRMAN HUBBARD: Then your comments and that of GAO that say that a reckless assumption—excuse me, a widespread assumption that reckless investment in junk bonds contributed to the thrift industry crisis is wrong?

MR. FOGEL: Yes, I think that's correct. If you look at the statistics, very few savings and loans have invested in high yield bonds in any significant way. We didn't find that investments of this type were really a contributing factor to the crisis we're facing today in the S&Ls.

CHAIRMAN HUBBARD: Mr. Fogel, is there any evidence that high yield bond investments by savings and loans have contributed in any way to the current thrift insolvency crisis?

MR. FOGEL: Not that we can see on a macro basis. As I noted, there was certainly one institution that really mismanaged a lot of things in their portfolio, and high yield bonds were one of the things. But we haven't got any evidence to support that hypothesis.

CHAIRMAN HUBBARD: Can you go so far as to say that high yield bonds have generally increased the profitability of those S&Ls which have purchased them?

MR. FOGEL: The statistics show that the return on high yield bonds has been fairly significant. We didn't look individually at the portfolios of all of the institutions, but the evidence shows that they have been a fairly good investment for thrifts that have had them in their portfolios over the last several years.

Based on the GAO report and Fogel's testimony, Congress initially concluded that no prohibition was required. But the indictment of Michael Milken later in the same month of March 1989 changed everything. Now the critics of takeovers and high-yield bonds had additional ammunition to use with the public, which already believed the worst.

Representative Byron Dorgan of North Dakota, who was to play a critical role in securing the FIRREA's high-yield bond prohibition, immediately announced on the House floor that the "binge of greed" was over and legislation was needed to stop the use of junk bonds to finance hostile takeovers:

> Mr. Speaker, I have a message today for some folks in Los Angeles. The Predators' Ball is going on this week in Los Angeles. The three thousand Americans attending the Predators' Ball are the speculators, the junk-bond kings, the hostile-takeover artists.
>
> Mr. Speaker, the message to them is that the party is about over. This binge of greed is disgusting America and injuring this country's ability to compete.
>
> These speculators say that this is all about good business. It is not. It is about greed, pure and simple greed. The king of the hill, Mr. Milken, now under indictment, last year made $550 million, $107,000 an hour, selling junk bonds and accommodating hostile takeovers.
>
> Mr. Speaker, some of us are intent on offering legislation to put this country's business back on track. While our competitors are spending their time trying to build better products, our executives all too often are trying to figure out how to attack other companies or how to defend themselves from hostile takeovers. We have got to put this country back on track and get back to business basics.
>
> Some of us in Congress are going to work to pass legislation to curb the use of junk bonds for hostile takeovers.

When the FIRREA came up for debate, Representative Dorgan saw his chance. He introduced an amendment that attacked thrifts' investments in high-yield bonds. "Junk bond investments," Dorgan began, "are a foolish and dangerous game." Although he argued that high-yield bond investments were too risky for government-insured thrifts, his concern once again seemed more about hostile takeovers:

> [T]hrifts have substantially increased their investment in junk debt used to finance the hostile takeover and break-up of some of our country's most productive and successful companies. In my judgment, junk bond financed takeovers threaten the very foundation of American history. I stress my belief that Congress must tell speculators that we will not allow them to pillage our companies for short-term profits at the expense of our national economy. Nevertheless, Congress continues to implicitly reward takeover activity by permitting federally insured savings associations to invest in the same junk issues that fuel much of the takeover market. . . . Again, the first step toward curbing the use of junk bonds is to prohibit all federally insured thrifts from investing in risky junk

bonds. I urge you to join me in this effort to stop thrifts from investing in junk bonds by supporting this amendment.

Opponents of the Dorgan amendment stressed the GAO's conclusion that high-yield bonds were not responsible for the thrift crisis. Others warned of the "calamitous effect" the FIRREA's divestiture requirement would have on the high-yield bond market and the "thousands of pension funds and innocent investors with a substantial stake in high yield bonds." Representative Donald Luken pointed out that the Dorgan amendment would hurt the very thrifts it was supposed to protect, as well as deny companies from using high-yield bonds as a source of financing: "A forced dumping on the high yield bond market of so many bonds could result in massive price decreases for all other holders of high-yield bonds, and huge losses for those thrifts being forced to liquidate. . . . By wiping out 9 percent of the market, the Dorgan amendment will raise the cost of capital for many of the companies leading America's competitive resurgence."

But the opponents of the Dorgan amendment could not compete with the anti–Milken/junk-bond/takeover fervor sweeping the country. Congresspeople recognized there was no public sentiment for allowing savings and loans, which were originally protected by deposit insurance to help ordinary Americans purchase homes, to support investments created by indicted financiers. Representative James Leach captured this populist sentiment perfectly when he argued that the Dorgan amendment should be adopted so that "the little guy" wouldn't have to "stand in line for credit" behind Ivan Boesky and Michael Milken:

> But the question this amendment poses to Congress is simple: Should the U.S. taxpayer subsidize leveraged buyouts, takeover artists, and large corporate mergers? If you think the Federal Government's scarce resources should be stretched for such Wall Street machinations, then you should not support this amendment. If you think the savings and loan industry should help middle-class families finance the purchase of their homes, then you should support this amendment. Every billion dollars that a thrift invests in junk bonds is $1 billion less for families to invest in their homes. Alas, this body and various State legislatures have passed legislation in the past that has turned institutions designed to serve the little guy into the private piggybanks for the well-heeled.
>
> The question before us with this amendment is whether thrifts should be allowed to have governmental subsidies—including

Federal deposit insurance, tax breaks, access to cheap money through Federal Home Loan Banks—for concentration of corporate ownership or for decentralization of home ownership, whether middle-class families should have to stand in line for credit behind Ivan Boesky, R. J. Reynolds, and Mike Milken.

Congress also had another reason to support the Dorgan amendment—fear of scandal. In the spring of 1989, representative Jim Wright, then Speaker of the House, was facing ethics charges for exceeding limits on outside income and accepting improper gifts from a real estate developer with an interest in pending savings and loan legislation. Wright's lobbying efforts on behalf of insolvent Texas thrifts had been highly publicized, and Wright himself symbolized the role of unscrupulous politicians in the thrift crisis. Wright denied all charges and declared he would fight until the end, but nobody believed him. His resignation was believed to be inevitable, and the press openly speculated on his likely successor. The betting favorite was representative Tony Coelho, from California, the House majority whip and former head of the Democratic Congressional Campaign Committee (DCCC).

Coelho himself then became enmeshed in scandal when a series of stories appeared in April and May describing his dealings with Thomas Spiegel, the head of Columbia Savings & Loan and a protégé of Michael Milken and Drexel Burnham. Spiegel was a major donor to the DCCC when it was headed by Coelho. Spiegel also had a keen interest in federal legislative and regulatory matters affecting savings and loans. Columbia was one of the largest thrifts in the country and by far the largest thrift purchaser of high-yield bonds. Starting in 1984, Spiegel and other Columbia officials had cultivated a network of political contacts in Washington, making large campaign contributions and personally lobbying members of Congress and the FHLBB. Their particular interest was making sure the government didn't interfere with Columbia's profitable high-yield bond operation.

In the spring of 1986 Spiegel was having serious problems with the FHLBB. Bank regulatory personnel had challenged Spiegel's $9 million compensation in 1985, the most any thrift executive had ever received. Spiegel defended his compensation, which was set by formula, because Columbia was widely regarded as the most profitable thrift in the country. Eventually, Spiegel compromised by reducing his compensation to $5.1 million, which still left him the best-paid thrift executive in the United States. Spiegel was also concerned about rumblings at the FHLBB and in Congress about the need to limit thrifts' investments in high-yield bonds.

At this exact time in the spring of 1986, when Spiegel was being pressured by the FHLBB to reduce his compensation and the possibility of limiting thrifts' investments in high-yield bonds was being discussed, Coelho supposedly called Spiegel for advice on investments. Spiegel recommended a $100,000 investment in high-yield bonds underwritten by Drexel to finance a hostile takeover. Coelho wanted to make the deal but didn't have any money. Spiegel then agreed to buy the bonds for Coelho and hold them until Coelho could raise the needed funds, which he eventually did by borrowing $50,000 from Columbia and $25,000 from two other banks. Spiegel then transferred the bonds to Coelho at cost even though they had appreciated in value in the intervening period. Coelho failed to report the $50,000 loan from Columbia on his House disclosure forms as required by House rules. Then it turned out that Coelho underreported his gain on the high-yield bonds and had to pay additional taxes.

On May 25, 1989, the *Los Angeles Times* reported that the Justice Department had begun a preliminary criminal inquiry into whether Coelho had received preferential treatment from Drexel and Spiegel in exchange for legislative assistance. Stories then appeared in the next few days describing how Coelho had lobbied the Securities and Exchange Commission on Drexel's behalf and how various savings and loan operators had furnished Coelho with use of planes and a yacht for Democratic fund-raising free of charge. Complaints were filed with the House Ethics Committee, and Democrats feared a repeat of the painful year-long investigation of Jim Wright. Coelho decided to preempt the investigation by announcing his immediate resignation from Congress. Jim Wright's resignation, already a foregone conclusion before the Coelho affair, was announced within days.

The forced resignations of two leading Democrats, the Speaker of the House and the majority whip, with close ties to the savings and loan industry and, in Coelho's case, to Drexel and its high-yield bond investments, rocked Congress. Passage of the Dorgan amendment was now a foregone conclusion as congresspeople wanted to put as much distance as possible between themselves and anything that could be viewed as support for thrifts' investments in high-yield bonds. The amendment passed overwhelmingly and was signed into law.

Congress enacted the FIRREA's high-yield bond divestiture requirement for purely political reasons as part of the backlash against Drexel, Milken, and hostile takeovers. No evidence existed at the time of passage that high-yield bonds had contributed to the savings and loan crisis. The opposite was true, as the GAO had concluded earlier in 1989. As late as August 1989, the same month that the FIRREA was enacted, the *Institutional Investor* reported that Columbia Savings & Loan, which held $4 billion worth of high-yield bonds, about one-third of the total held by all savings and loans, had a "bulletproof balance sheet" because of these investments: "Columbia's shrewd moves in the junk-bond market have helped it put together one of the strongest-looking financial statements in the thrift industry today. By almost any measure, the Spiegels' bank appears solid and well managed." This assessment was widely shared. At year-end 1988, Columbia had assets of $12.7 billion, stockholders' equity of $675 million, and net interest income for the year of $218 million. *Forbes* ranked it for two straight years the most profitable thrift in the country.

But Columbia could not survive the collapse of the high-yield bond market, caused to a significant extent by the FIRREA and the Drexel-Milken prosecutions. Between July 1989, just before the signing of the FIRREA, and October 1989, just three months later, the high-yield market index fell 19.5 percent. Columbia, like CenTrust Savings and other large thrift investors in high-yield bonds, suffered huge losses in 1989, which continued into 1990. In July 1990, Columbia negotiated a sale of its entire high-yield bond portfolio for $3 billion, but the sale was blocked by the government. The problem was the purchase price was to be paid over a ten-year period and if the purchaser walked, Columbia would get the bonds back. The regulators concluded that this possibility that Columbia would wind up holding high-yield bonds violated the FIRREA's divestiture provision and vetoed the deal. Columbia had lost its last chance to survive and was seized by the government in January 1991. The once mighty Columbia became another victim of the government's regulatory policies.

The Government Blames Milken for the S&L Crisis

The government refused to acknowledge its role in making the savings and loan crisis worse by enacting the FIRREA and prosecuting

Drexel and Milken out of the high-yield bond market. Instead, the government decided to blame Milken for the damage caused by its own policies. In a series of lawsuits filed after Milken's guilty plea in April 1990, the government accused Milken of "artificially controlling and manipulating" the entire junk-bond market, which "as a whole was the product of a systematic fraud." Milken, the government charged, then "palmed off" these "unsuitable" risky and fraudulent securities on Columbia and other savings and loans who had no knowledge of Milken's "manipulative and deceptive acts and practices which materially affected the value of the investments." Milken's "wide range of illegal conduct included market manipulation, threats, bribes, coercion, extortion, agreements to control prices and numerous fraudulent misrepresentations about the value and liquidity of junk bonds." The suits sought billions of dollars to compensate the government for the claimed losses of savings and loans from investing in high-yield bonds.

The suits were immediately mired in controversy because of the government's retention of Cravath, Swaine & Moore as outside counsel, probably the country's most successful, skillful, and expensive law firm, to prosecute the suits. In an unusual contingency-fee arrangement the government agreed to pay Cravath's top partners $300 per hour with the understanding that the rate would be retroactively increased to $600 if enough money were recovered. The arrangement was attacked by critics as "scandalous" in terms reminiscent of the government's own attack on Milken. Representative Henry Gonzales, chairman of the House Banking Committee, for example, lambasted the deal: "My judgment is that the Cravath fee is excessive. It's the equivalent of war profiteering." But "profiteering" wasn't a concern when it suited the government's objectives. Cravath's "greed" was fine so long as the government got to confiscate more of Milken's money.

The government's retention of Cravath reeked of hypocrisy for another reason. Cravath, it turned out, itself had a very active role in the high-yield bond market during the 1980s. In fact, Cravath had represented Drexel on a number of high-yield securities offerings that it was now claiming, in its new role as counsel for the government, were illegal. Also, Cravath regularly represented major issuers and other underwriters of high-yield bonds that were sold to savings and loans. In this capacity, Cravath routinely drafted selling and disclosure documents governing thrifts' purchases of high-yield bonds, provided legal advice on the propriety of such purchases, and assisted in the marketing efforts. Nowhere did Cravath advise Drexel or anyone else that there was anything wrong with thrifts purchasing high-yield bonds. Under the government's theory that the whole market was a "fraud" and that high-yield bonds were "unsuitable" for savings and loans, Cravath should have been a witness in the case, if not a defendant itself. Instead, the government hired Cravath to sue Milken for the same conduct that its law firm had participated in and approved. And when Cravath's involvement was challenged because of its obvious conflict of interest, a federal judge ruled that there was no problem with Cravath proceeding with the suit. Nothing was allowed to stand in the way of separating Milken from his money.

But for sheer hypocrisy, nothing could match the government blaming Milken for thrifts' losses from high-yield-bond investments. Lost in the anti-Milken hysteria was the basic fact that the government encouraged thrifts to invest in high-yield bonds to prevent the industry from going under completely. And when Congress, reacting to public pressure, ordered an investigation, the GAO released a study in March 1989 concluding that thrifts benefited from investing in high-yield bonds. Big losses were incurred only after the government enacted the FIRREA and drove Drexel and Milken out of the market. Given the market's rebound, high-yield bonds would have continued to be a source of profitability for thrifts if the government hadn't intervened and caused the collapse in the first place. If the government sued anyone for thrifts' losses from high-yield bonds, it should have sued itself.

The savings and loan suits were not the government's only attempts at revisionist history. In yet another multibillion-dollar suit filed on behalf of the government, Cravath accused Milken of causing Drexel's demise by "concealing his pattern of racketeering activity" and "falsely" denying his guilt. Had Drexel known the truth about Milken's "illegal activities," the suit charged, Milken would have been terminated in the 1970s and the loss of business and other "severe damage" resulting from the prosecution of Drexel avoided. The suit could have been a chapter in George Orwell's *1984*. If Milken had been "terminated" in the 1970s, Drexel wouldn't have had much business to lose. But for Milken's efforts, Drexel would likely have remained the third-tier investment banking firm it was when Milken arrived. Now the government was suing Milken for "destroying" the value that he had created, which would have continued to exist in the absence of the government's baseless and vindictive prosecutions.

Blaming Milken for the savings and loan crisis and Drexel's demise was an outrage, but the government and Cravath were rewarded for their efforts. Milken wanted to resolve all his legal problems and didn't have the stomach to fight. The suits were resolved as part of the $1.3 billion global settlement between the government and Milken and related entities. The government won another "victory," succeeding in blaming Milken for damages caused by its own conduct, with the public never learning the difference.

The FIRREA's Other Scapegoats

The search for savings and loan scapegoats did not end with high-yield bonds. S&L insiders, and their accountants and attorneys, were also convenient targets. According to the Senate report explaining the FIRREA:

> Little doubt exists that fraud and insider abuse contributed substantially to the current crisis. According to the United States Department of Justice, the most prevalent forms of fraud and insider abuse included nominee loans, double pledging of collateral, reciprocal loan arrangements, land flips, embezzlement, and check kiting. In addition, witnesses have told the Committee of extravagant parties, exorbitant spending on frivolous corporate aircraft, lavish office suites, and numerous other squanderings of federally-insured deposit monies. At the very least . . . there was an enormous failure of individuals to exercise their fiduciary responsibilities as managers, directors, auditors, appraisers, and lawyers. . . .
>
> In his testimony before the Committee, United States Attorney General Richard L. Thornburgh estimated that fraud and insider abuse were involved in 25 to 30 percent of all savings and loan failures and caused over $2 billion in losses during 1988 alone. Other witnesses before the Committee estimated an even greater incidence of fraud and insider abuse.

Attorney General Thornburgh's assessment, however, was disputed by other members of the Justice Department. "Regardless of whose numbers one looks at," commented assistant attorney general Lee Rawls, "fraud has not yet been shown to be the 'major' factor in the industry's failures. . . . Blaming all of the S&L losses on 'criminals' may be politically convenient but it is not responsible law enforcement and it is not accurate."

But political expediency was more than enough reason for Congress to blame S&L "crooks" and the lawyers and accountants they hired for the crisis. Between October 1, 1988, and June 30, 1992, the Justice Department charged 3,720 defendants of major financial crimes and obtained 2,603 convictions. Courts ordered thrift-fraud offenders to pay fines and restitution of $450.5 million during this period, but only $25.5 million, or about 5.7 percent, was collected. The government was more successful in collecting revenue from accounting and law firms. Ernst & Young, a large accounting firm that audited many problem thrifts in Texas and elsewhere, alone paid $400 million to the government to settle thrift litigation. Other major accounting and law firms reached major settlements with the government, which in the aggregate totaled hundreds of millions of dollars.

The government's simple fraud and insider-abuse explanation for the thrift crisis defied common sense. Why was there a sudden simultaneous explosion of fraud and criminality at savings and loans across the country? Did a new generation of morally depraved thrift operators just coincidentally appear at the same time? The government provided no answers to these questions, nor did the press, which almost uniformly supported more vigorous prosecution of S&L crooks.

But there were exceptions. On September 28, 1992, *Forbes* published a story titled "What Did Pop Expect to Happen When He Gave the Kid His Credit Card?" *Forbes* forcefully rejected the government's claim that rampant fraud and insider abuse caused the thrift crisis. "To hear the government talk about the S&L losses, you'd think they were all a result of massive fraud and misdealings. . . . That simply isn't so." Rather, *Forbes* stressed how the real cause of the S&L crisis, including the much ballyhooed insider abuse, was the regulatory incentives created by the government:

> This is the S&L crisis. . . . In part I, the federal government in effect lent out its own capital by providing an all but unlimited guarantee of deposits and allowing the deposit takers to speculate with the money. As it turned out, this was equivalent to giving your 14-year-old kid your American Express card and telling him to go out and have a good time. . . . In part II, the government looks for scapegoats. Instead of blaming itself for letting the kid have the

card, it tries to pin the blame on the merchants who sold stuff to the kid.

"It's time for Congress to call off this witch hunt," *Forbes* concluded, "and own up to its own responsibility in causing the disaster."

Forbes was right on target. The widely publicized outbreak of "fraud and insider abuse" was in reality a completely predictable consequence of the government's regulatory policies. Savings and loans, long insulated from market competition and discipline by the Depression-era regulatory scheme including deposit insurance, have always been more susceptible to abuse than other types of firms. But this tendency was greatly accentuated in the 1980s when a new breed of owners, many with existing vast fortunes and lavish lifestyles, entered the industry. It was all too easy for these new owners to finance expenditures remotely related to legitimate business activities but primarily for personal consumption, with government-insured deposits. Use of thrift funds to pay for private airplanes, luxurious foreign trips, and plush vacation retreats all fall within this category. And for those thrifts operating near insolvency, the problem was far worse still. These thrifts had every incentive to make overly risky loans, frequently to affiliated persons, without receiving any adequate collateral or other assurances of repayment. Even the most long-shot gambles can make sense if someone else—in this case the government insurance fund and taxpayers—picks up the tab if you lose.

When the search for scapegoats began, the new breed of thrift owners with their expensive tastes and fancy lifestyles made attractive targets. Jurors were bound to be unsympathetic to multimillionaire S&L tycoons who used their thrifts as private piggy banks but then left taxpayers holding the bag when the institutions failed. It was also no problem showing that many thrifts made risky loans and engaged in other questionable business practices that did not meet the standards of customary banking practice. But these practices were a symptom, not the cause, of the industry's problems. After all, the whole thrift industry was insolvent before this new breed even appeared. In fact, the industry's insolvency was the reason the government encouraged individuals and entities with no experience or interest in running a traditional thrift to acquire failing thrifts to save the government from having to close them down. When the industry's problems didn't disappear, the government then turned around and blamed the new breed of thrift owners—who only entered the industry at the government's behest—for the savings and loan crisis.

The government's attack on accountants and lawyers was even worse. These professionals, the government charged, concealed thrifts' insolvency and prevented government banking regulators from learning of their true financial condition. For shameless revisionist history, this account rivaled the government's blaming Milken for thrifts' losses in high-yield bonds. The government knew the thrift industry was insolvent and chose to hide the problem. And it was the government that invented the idea of using phony accounting gimmicks to allow insolvent savings and loans to report positive net worth. What is it the government didn't know? Blaming accountants and lawyers for the consequences of the government's own policy of forbearance—allowing insolvent thrifts to remain open—was a scandal. But big law and accounting firms had assets that could be expropriated, and this made them irresistible scapegoats. They would end up paying huge sums to avoid having to explain to a jury why it was wrong for the government to hold them responsible for the savings and loan crisis, particularly in light of the government's own policies, which created the crisis in the first place. The government should have been too ashamed to take the money.

Ultimately, the government's scapegoating created the appearance that those responsible for the savings and loan crisis were being held accountable, but this was an illusion. The real problem, ignored by the FIRREA, is the conflict of interest between failing industries, elected officials, and taxpayers. When an industry is in danger, it has every incentive to use the political process to improve its chances of survival. Elected officials who see an opportunity to extract political contributions and other favors often are eager to help. Regulators are also willing participants in assuring survival of the industry because their current positions and future ability to market themselves to the private sector are enhanced in the process. Elected officials and regulators know that there is a good chance the problem will get worse, but they don't care. By the time the industry's problems become too visible to be ignored, they will be long gone and a new generation of elected officials and regulators in place. And for this new generation, the "crisis" presents additional opportunities to search for scapegoats and "rescue" the industry. These efforts are then used

2

to convince taxpayers, who are left to foot the bill, that the government is on their side and something is being done to bring the guilty to justice.

This is a good description of what occurred with the savings and loan industry during the 1980s. And it could happen again. The FIRREA did nothing to solve the basic problem that the thrift industry was obsolete and prone to mass failures when interest rates or economic conditions changed suddenly. In fact, the FIRREA, by unfairly blaming the industry's problems on junk bonds, S&L crooks, and derelict professionals, virtually guarantees that another thrift crisis will occur in the future. The only question is when.

CHAPTER 8

Charles Keating and Lincoln Savings

When Congress in the FIRREA toughened criminal penalties for S&L crooks, the man they most had in mind was Charles Keating. The government blamed Keating for the failure of Lincoln Savings and Loan, which was seized by federal regulators in April 1989 at a claimed cost to taxpayers of $2.5 billion, the costliest savings and loan failure in history. After Lincoln's failure, Keating was prosecuted and convicted in separate state and federal criminal trials and sued by every conceivable state and federal regulatory agency that could possibly have jurisdiction over his actions. Keating is currently in prison, and appealing both of his convictions. Multiple judgments have been entered against him totaling billions of dollars.

Keating came to symbolize everything that went wrong with savings and loans in America. The *Los Angeles Times,* for example, reported that his name will be sealed "in history as the symbol of greed and excess in the savings and loan industry during the high-flying 1980's." *Playboy* described Keating as "a veteran swindler . . . who recognized the Reagan era as Camelot for the rapacious . . . [and] seized his chance when the federal government deregulated the savings and loan industry. He didn't invent the S&L crisis, but he defined it by the magnitude of his scandalous behavior." Others openly compared Keating to Milken and Boesky as the living embodiments of the "decade of greed." Milken and Keating, according to *U.S. News & World Report,* were the "symbols of swindling, greed and materialism in contemporary America." The *Monthly Review* went further: "The Casino Society is the apt term that came to characterize the U.S. economy in the 1980s—the speculation-driven free-for-all symbolized by three of the wealthiest convicted felons in history: Charles Keating of Lincoln Savings and Loan infamy, junk bond king Michael Milken, and arbitrage operator Ivan Boesky."

Keating in many ways was an unlikely candidate for such notoriety. Born in Cincinnati in 1923, he lived the first fifty years of his life unremarkably except for his accomplishments as a champion swimmer. Then in 1976 Keating, at age fifty-three, and others purchased control of American Continental Corporation (ACC), an Arizona-based company specializing in land development and residential-home building. ACC prospered under Keating's leadership, its net worth increasing from about $10 million in 1977 to $80 million by year-end 1984. Emboldened by his initial success, Keating decided to expand his land-development operations, but he needed capital to do so. Acquiring a savings and loan with its captive source of insured deposits seemed like the perfect solution, particularly since the government was virtually begging successful entrepreneurs to enter the moribund thrift industry.

At the same time, Lincoln Savings and Loan, headquartered in Southern California, was searching for solutions to the interest-rate squeeze that had ravaged the industry. Like other traditional home-mortgage-dominated thrifts, Lincoln had been paying increasingly high interest rates to retain short-term deposits but was earning low interest rates on its long-term, fixed-rate home mortgages. Lincoln had been losing money with no obvious solution in sight. When ACC came along and offered $51 million to acquire Lincoln, the deal was too good to turn down. ACC then applied to the California Department of Savings and Loans and to the FHLBB for approval to acquire Lincoln. After a four-month review of ACC's application, both agencies approved the acquisition on February 21, 1984.

Keating then immediately implemented a major shake-up of Lincoln. Existing employees were replaced and facilities upgraded. Lincoln also discontinued making home mortgages and shifted instead to other, nontraditional investments, including high-yield bonds, stocks, ADC real estate loans, and direct investments in commercial and residential real estate. By objective criteria, Lincoln under Keating's control was a spectacular success, at least in the first few years. In January 1987, *Forbes* ranked Lincoln the second-most profitable thrift in the country.

Thrift regulators, however, did not share this rosy view of Lincoln. Almost from the beginning, Keating and the regulators clashed about virtually every aspect of Lincoln's operations. The dispute became so bitter that some regulators favored seizing Lincoln as early as 1986. Keating reacted just as adamantly, claiming that the FHLBB and its then-chairman, Edwin Gray, had a vendetta against him because of Lincoln's nontraditional activities and Keating's vigorous opposition to Gray's various proposals to reregulate the industry. So long as Lincoln appeared to be such a success, Keating's vendetta claim had the ring of truth. He even persuaded five United States senators to whom he had made campaign contributions—later to be known as the "Keating Five"—to intervene with regulators on Lincoln's behalf. Keating continued the fight against federal and state thrift regulators nonstop until Lincoln was seized in April 1989 immediately after ACC, Lincoln's parent corporation, declared bankruptcy.

The failure of ACC and Lincoln affected more than the government insurance fund. Beginning in late 1986, ACC began selling subordinated debentures to the public in Lincoln Savings and Loan branch locations. The sales in Lincoln branches continued until February 1989, with more than $200 million of ACC junior debt securities sold in total. Many of the purchasers were elderly and unsophisticated; some invested their life savings. When ACC declared bankruptcy, these subordinated debentures, which were an uninsured obligation of ACC and not a government-insured obligation of Lincoln, became worthless. For the first time, the savings and loan crisis had real, identifiable victims, not just faceless taxpayers. The poignancy of these victims' hardships—the press reported that one elderly purchaser was so despondent over his losses he committed suicide—outraged the public.

When the bondholders called ACC headquarters after the bankruptcy asking for advice, Keating instructed his representatives to direct the callers to the FHLBB in Washington. Keating told everyone who would listen that the demise of ACC and Lincoln was solely attributable to the government's misguided and vindictive regulatory policies. If the regulators had only left Lincoln alone, Keating said, it would have thrived. And since Lincoln was ACC's primary asset, ACC would have thrived as well and been in a position to make good on its obligation to the bondholders. If the bondholders were upset, in other words, they should blame the government.

The regulators, of course, said the exact opposite. Keating, they said, ran ACC and Lincoln into the ground, costing taxpayers $2.5 billion and the bondholders their money. Their only mistake was allowing Lincoln to remain open as long as it did, and even this, the regulators claimed, could be blamed on Keating and his allies—his hired lawyers and accountants and the Keating Five— who held the regulators at bay.

Keating and the regulators were both wrong. ACC and Lincoln failed because of the collapse of the Arizona real estate economy in the late 1980s. Faced with plummeting real estate prices and skyrocketing foreclosures, vacancy rates, and bankruptcies, Arizona thrifts could not survive. In fact, every major Arizona thrift in existence in 1985 subsequently failed or was acquired. None survived the economic collapse as an independent entity.

The Fate of Major Arizona Thrifts in Existence in 1985

NAME IN 1985	CITY	Disposition
Capital Savings & Loan Assoc.	Phoenix	Acquired 6/87
First Commercial Savings & Loan Assoc.	Phoenix	Acquired 1/88
First Federal Savings Bank of AZ (Merabank)	Phoenix	Failed 1/31/90
Great American First Savings Bank, FSB	Tucson	Failed 5/94
Home Federal Savings & Loan Assoc.	Tucson	Failed 3/20/86
Pima Savings & Loan Assoc.	Tucson	Failed 3/2/90
Security Savings & Loan Assoc.	Scottsdale	Failed 2/17/89
Sentinel Savings & Loan Assoc.	Phoenix	Failed 2/2/90
Southwest Savings & Loan Assoc.	Phoenix	Failed 2/17/89
Sun State Savings & Loan Assoc.	Phoenix	Failed 6/14/89
Tucson Savings & Loan Assoc.	Tucson	Acquired 11/87

The Fate of Major Arizona Thrifts in Existence in 1985 (cont'd)

Name in 1985	City	Disposition
Union Savings & Loan Assoc.	Phoenix	Acquired 5/88
Universal Savings & Loan Assoc.	Kingman (Scottsdale)	Failed 5/25/88
Western Savings & Loan Assoc.	Phoenix	Failed 6/14/89

Lincoln was a California thrift, but most of its assets were in real estate in Arizona, where ACC was located. It too could not survive when the bottom fell out of the Arizona real estate market. As *Barron's* commented in a December 1988 article entitled "Phoenix Descending: Is Boomtown U.S.A. Going Bust?" the same economic collapse that doomed Arizona's thrift industry and its commercial banks also was ruining ACC and Lincoln. "Of late, American Continental's regulatory problems have been the least of its worries. . . . [M]ore than anything else, it's American Continental's massive real-estate exposure in the sliding Phoenix market that, perhaps, is cause for concern." When the Arizona real estate market continued its free fall in 1989, Lincoln's fate was sealed. Highly leveraged savings and loans were simply not structured to survive severe economic downturns, which explains why every major savings and loan in the state failed or was acquired, regardless of its investment practices or whether it was run by a controversial figure like Keating.

Predictably, neither Keating nor the regulators could accept the notion that the other was not to blame for the demise of ACC and Lincoln, and a series of lawsuits ensued. Keating sued the government, claiming the regulators exceeded their authority in seizing Lincoln in April 1989. The regulators in turn sued Keating and others for causing the failure of Lincoln Savings. Congress, not to be outdone, also took an active interest in the subject, holding extensive hearings in the fall of 1989 on Lincoln's demise and the plight of the elderly purchasers of now worthless ACC subordinated debentures.

Keating's lawsuit against the government was the first to be decided. The suit was assigned to Judge Stanley Sporkin, a former director of Enforcement of the Securities and Exchange Commission who in that position was well known as a megalomaniac, a publicity-seeking regulator who expanded his turf at every opportunity with little regard for the effect of his overreacting on the securities markets. Judge Sporkin was probably one of the least likely judges in the country to be sympathetic to Keating's position, but he treated Keating with respect and challenged the government to prove its position. Keating and his lawyers were encouraged, but suing the government was a big mistake, as they soon would learn. In August 1990, Judge Sporkin issued a scathing opinion, finding that Keating had systematically "looted" Lincoln and that the government acted properly in seizing the institution. Judge Sporkin's conclusions were the first of many legal catastrophes Keating was about to experience.

Keating's Criminal Trials

Keating was still protesting his innocence and blaming the government for the demise of ACC and Lincoln when he was indicted by the state of California for securities fraud, arrested, and thrown in jail. Pictures of a chained and handcuffed Keating wearing an orange jumpsuit were broadcast across the country to the delight of an incensed public eager for revenge. Commentators were quick to voice their support. Everyone thought that Charles Keating, the man who made millions by defrauding elderly and defenseless bond purchasers of their life savings, was just getting what he deserved.

The trial began in August 1991. The first two witnesses called by the prosecution, Leon and Esther Bonan, set the tone for the trial. The Bonans, eighty and seventy-seven years old respectively at the time of trial, testified about how they had just sold their town house and wanted to invest the $101,000 they received in an insured certificate of deposit at their bank, Lincoln Savings. "We wanted to make it grow a little to buy a better home," Esther Bonan explained. But as soon as a Lincoln teller saw the $101,000 check, she directed the Bonans to two ACC bond salesmen located in the same branch office. One of the salesmen, Leon Bonan testified, then told them, "I have a better deal for you than a certificate of deposit," an ACC bond that payed a higher interest rate. Esther Bonan then was told that the ACC bonds were insured, and when she asked who insured the bonds, the salesman replied, "We do."

When the prosecutor asked her if she would have purchased had she known she was buying uninsured, high-risk "junk bonds," Esther Bonan gave the obvious answer. "To me, junk is something you throw away, not buy." Leon Bonan answered the same way. "I don't take these chances. . . . I never would have bought."

A parade of bond-purchaser witnesses, all elderly and unsophisticated, followed the Bonans and told the same story.

Ray Fidel and Robin Symes were the other key government witnesses. Fidel and Symes were the two ACC employees in charge of running the bond program. Both were charged and arrested along with Keating but then pled guilty and agreed to cooperate. Both testified at trial that they pled guilty because the bond purchasers were not told of ACC's deteriorating financial condition as it headed toward bankruptcy in 1989. The inescapable inference was that if Fidel and Symes were guilty of defrauding bondholders, then Keating, the man at the top, was guilty as well. That's what the jury decided, convicting Keating on all counts. Judge Lance Ito then gave Keating the maximum sentence he could, ten years in prison. Justice, it seemed, was finally served.

But was it? The record reveals a different story from the one told by the government and accepted by the jury and the press. Keating was indicted for violating California Corporations Code §25401, which provides:

> It is unlawful for any person to offer or sell a security in this state or buy or offer to buy a security in this state by means of any written or oral communication which includes an untrue statement of a material fact or omits to state a material fact necessary in order to make the statements made, in the light of the circumstances under which they were made, not misleading.

During the grand jury proceedings leading up to the indictment, the district attorney argued that Keating—who personally sold no bonds nor made any statements to bond purchasers—could still be criminally convicted because he was the employer—the boss who was ultimately responsible for hiring the bond salesmen who made fraudulent statements. This was true, the district attorney said, even if Keating himself had no direct involvement or knowledge of any fraudulent statements made to bond purchasers. Based on the district attorney's instructions that the boss is a criminal if any of the company's employees commit crimes, the grand jury returned the indictment.

Judge Ito, however, recognized that the district attorney's theory that the boss is automatically a criminal amounted to the proposition "that all Keating had to do was be a corporate officer, and then he would therefore be liable for all the wrongdoing." Because he was troubled by such a sweeping theory of criminal liability, Judge Ito ruled that Keating could only be convicted if he personally violated California Corporations Code §25401. But after hearing the evidence, Judge Ito concluded that Keating could not be convicted under §25401 because he made no false statements to bond purchasers. "I think the evidence is clear," Judge Ito explained, "that Mr. Keating never actually had any face-to-face contact with any of the bond purchasers."

That should have ended the matter. After rejecting the district attorney's "the boss is liable" theory of criminal responsibility and ruling that no evidence existed that Keating himself violated the law under which he was being prosecuted, Judge Ito should have dismissed the indictment. Instead, Judge Ito ruled that Keating could be convicted if he "aided and abetted" a violation of §25401, even though §25401 itself does not criminally prohibit aiding and abetting.

Judge Ito's decision to save the indictment—and not be known as the judge who let the notorious Charles Keating go on what would be publicly perceived as a legal technicality—was wrong. Put simply, aiding and abetting a violation of §25401 was not a crime under California law at the time of Judge Ito's decision. In fact, the whole concept of criminal liability for aiding and abetting a violation of §25401 made no sense. Statute §25401 as then interpreted by the California Supreme Court imposed what is known in law as strict criminal liability—liability without regard to whether the defendant had a guilty state of mind. If a defendant intended to sell a security, and if false statements were made in the sale, the defendant was criminally responsible whether or not he or she intended or knew of the misrepresentation.

Aiding and abetting the commission of a strict liability offense is a contradiction in terms. An aider and abettor, by definition, must assist in the underlying offense. But almost any conduct could be construed as assistance in connection with a strict liability offense involving making false statements, even if made innocently in connection with the sale of securities. Is the financial printer responsible for the sale documents a criminal aider and abettor? How about the lawyers and accountants who work on the sale documents? If knowledge of wrongdoing is irrelevant, then these individuals became potential criminals because they "aided and abetted" the commission of the crime.

Judge Ito recognized this dilemma but wasn't sure how to solve it. "The deeper I get into this," he admitted, "the more perplexed I become." Judge Ito had to improvise, because Keating was being prosecuted for a crime that previously didn't exist. The judge eventually ruled that Keating could be convicted as an aider and abettor only if Keating knew that misrepresentations were being made and intended to facilitate them. When it came time to charge the jury, however, Judge Ito ignored his own prior ruling that Keating could not be convicted for directly violating §25401 because he made no statements to bond purchasers. Judge Ito instructed the jury that Keating could be convicted either for directly violating §25401 or as an aider and abettor. The jury then convicted Keating without specifying which theory it was relying on.

The conviction, no matter how popular with the public, was improper no matter which theory the jury picked. Judge Ito's previous ruling that there was no basis for prosecuting Keating for directly violating §25401 meant that Keating could not be legally convicted on this ground. The aiding and abetting theory of prosecution was also wrong because this "crime" did not previously exist. Rather, Judge Ito created a crime out of thin air tailor-made for Charles Keating, a crime for which nobody in the history of California had ever been prosecuted.

Our Constitution, however, prohibits ex post facto crimes, crimes created after the fact to prosecute particular individuals. This basic safeguard was intended to protect the rights of unpopular individuals—individuals just like Charles Keating—from the arbitrary imposition of power by the government responding to powerful interest groups or mob hysteria. But Judge Ito ignored the constitutional prohibition against ex post facto laws, and the related maxim that criminal statutes must be construed narrowly, in allowing Keating to be tried and convicted. Maybe Judge Ito was himself swept up in the mob hysteria against Keating, the man whom the public believed defrauded elderly investors of their life savings and cost taxpayers over $2 billion when Lincoln failed. Or maybe Judge Ito was concerned, as an ambitious judge, with what the impact on his career would be if he dismissed the indictment. Either way, Judge Ito bungled the trial and ignored the constitutional rights of Charles Keating.

The government's case had other problems. Bond purchasers testified that they were confused by ACC personnel selling uninsured ACC bonds in Lincoln branches, since Lincoln was a government-insured savings and loan. But the government specifically approved the sale of the uninsured ACC bonds at Lincoln branches, as it did in many other comparable situations. The government had a strong interest in having these sales occur. Lincoln was ACC's primary asset. To finance its operations and meet its senior debt obligations, ACC had to either withdraw assets from Lincoln by having Lincoln pay dividends or make other forms of payments, or raise additional capital itself. Having ACC withdraw assets reduced Lincoln's capital position and therefore placed additional strains on the government's insurance fund. The sale of the ACC-subordinated debentures in Lincoln branches, by contrast, allowed ACC to raise additional capital, which the government could require be contributed to Lincoln, strengthening its financial position. And if ACC defaulted on its obligations, bond purchasers had no claims on the government's insurance fund. That's why the government approved, even encouraged, these sales of uninsured ACC bonds in Lincoln branches. But the prosecutors in the Keating trial, of course, had no interest in blaming the government for any confusion this arrangement produced.

Another problem for the government's case was the language of the bond prospectuses. The securities laws require that every potential bond purchaser be given a prospectus before investing, and the ACC bond salespeople were instructed to comply with this requirement. The front page of each prospectus made clear, in capital letters and boldface type, that the bonds were not federally insured:

THE DEBENTURES BEING OFFERED ARE THE SOLE OBLI-GATION OF THE COMPANY AND ARE NOT BEING OFFERED AS SAVINGS ACCOUNTS OR DEPOSITS AND ARE NOT INSURED BY THE FEDERAL SAVINGS AND LOAN INSURANCE CORPORATION.

The cover page of each prospectus also warned, in boldface type, that no salespeople were authorized to make any oral representations that were in addition to, or in conflict with, the information contained in the prospectus:

No dealer, salesman or any other person has been authorized to give any information or to make any representations in connection with this offering other than those contained in this Prospectus and any Prospectus Supplement, and if given or made, such information or representations must not be relied upon as having been authorized by the Company.

This disclaimer is standard because no company that sells securities can control what every individual who sells the securities says to potential purchasers. The disclaimer also prevents investors who lose money after knowingly making a risky investment from claiming later that they were told orally that the securities were safer than what was disclosed in the prospectus. The disclaimer, in short, is used to insulate the company from liability for oral statements by salespeople, real or manufactured, at variance with the prospectus. In the Keating trial the testimony of the bond purchasers who were misled into believing the ACC bonds were insured, when the prospectus clearly and unambiguously disclosed that they were not, was precisely this type of claim. Yet Keating was still criminally prosecuted and convicted, notwithstanding the clear language of the prospectus. And no evidence was presented at trial that Keating instructed anyone to tell the bond salesmen to mislead purchasers into believing the bonds were insured, or that he was even aware oral representations were being made at variance to the prospectuses.

When the prosecution finished its case, Stephen Neal, Keating's lawyer, announced that the defense rested. Neither Keating nor any other defense witnesses were called to testify. Neal decided instead to argue to the jury that the government had not proved its case beyond a reasonable doubt. When Keating was convicted after two weeks of jury deliberations, Neal's decision was immediately second-guessed. Critics speculated that Keating, a man who had received so much negative publicity even during the trial, had no chance of acquittal if he was unwilling to take the witness stand and tell his side of the story. Even though the jury was instructed that Keating was presumed innocent and had a constitutional right not to testify, this, the critics charged, was a fiction. The reality was that in the emotionally charged atmosphere of the trial, Keating was presumed guilty. It's not clear that Keating could have done anything to overcome the presumption of guilt, but to have any chance he had to take the risk of testifying and putting on a defense. With the benefit of hindsight, it's difficult to dispute this assessment. He could hardly have done any worse.

Neal certainly had a hard decision to make. The government's case made clear that ACC salespeople operating in Lincoln branches sold risky uninsured ACC-subordinated debentures to at least some people who had no business buying them. Whether the purchasers were in fact misled about the existence of government insurance is almost irrelevant. Elderly and unsophisticated investors should not have been encouraged to invest a large percentage of their life savings in junior ACC debt securities even if the purchasers were never told that the bonds were insured. In a civil suit for damages, these bond purchasers would clearly have a claim for fraud against ACC and Keating for selling unsuitable securities. In this type of civil suit for damages, the law is much less concerned with whether the head of the enterprise had any actual knowledge of the wrongdoing. The government's original criminal-responsibility theory presented to the grand jury—the boss is responsible for the acts of his employees—works fine in a civil case where one of the main goals is to compensate victims.

But a criminal case is different. For the jury to convict Keating even under Judge Ito's made-up crime, prosecutors still had to prove beyond a reasonable doubt that Keating knew and intended that false statements be used to sell the ACC-subordinated debentures. The government didn't come close to meeting this standard, and Neal concluded the best chance for an acquittal was not to take the risk of putting Keating on the stand. If Keating testified and then was cross-examined, jurors might have been offended by his extreme statements about how the regulators should be blamed for everything or his use of private jets for trips to Europe on company accounts while the bondholders were losing everything they had. If Keating had testified and then was convicted, the same critics who second-guessed the decision not to put on a defense would have questioned why Neal didn't know enough to quit while he was ahead.

The jury in the California case returned its verdict against Keating in early December 1991. Not content with the state conviction of Keating, now sixty-eight, the federal government immediately indicted him later that month. The new seventy-seven-count indictment filed in California accused Keating of multiple acts of racketeering, and securities, banking, bankruptcy, mail, and wire fraud. The government was still not satisfied. The next month, in January 1992, Keating was indicted again in Arizona. The cases were consolidated, and after a two-month trial before judge Mariana Pfaelzer in Los Angeles, Keating was convicted again and sentenced to serve twelve and a half years in prison.

Alice Hill and David Sklansky, the two U.S. attorneys who prosecuted the federal case, avoided the infirmities of the state court trial. Keating was charged with his personal involvement in real crimes that did not have to be invented so that he could be prosecuted.

The government's case focused on Keating's involvement in a series of allegedly sham real estate transactions designed to allow ACC and Lincoln to report phony profits. Back in 1986, ACC and Lincoln entered into a "tax-sharing agreement" that required Lincoln to pay ACC the tax it would have owed had Lincoln been a stand-alone entity. But in fact ACC and Lincoln owed no taxes on a consolidated basis because ACC had millions of dollars in unused tax-loss carryforwards. So the more profits Lincoln reported, the more it paid to ACC, which in turn kept the money, since no taxes were actually owed. Keating, the government charged, caused Lincoln to report bogus profits so that money could be siphoned from Lincoln to ACC under this tax-sharing agreement. Ultimately, Lincoln paid ACC $94 million under the agreement, which ACC used, the government said, to pay Keating's multimillion-dollar salary, maintain an expensive fleet of private aircraft and other extravagant perks, and keep many of Keating's unqualified relatives on the payroll. Every dollar wrongfully taken from Lincoln was a dollar the government, in reality taxpayers, had to pay when Lincoln went under and the government had to make good on its insurance obligation.

Judy Wischer, a longtime Keating confidante and former high-level ACC employee, was the government's key witness at trial on the sham real estate transactions. Wischer was indicted along with Keating in both the state and federal cases but escaped trial by pleading guilty and agreeing to cooperate. Testifying in detail about various real estate deals over several days, Wischer described how the sham real estate transaction scheme operated. Keating, Wischer explained, typically obtained the participation of a straw buyer who would nominally purchase property from Lincoln but who in fact was assured by Keating that the property would be repurchased in the future. The straw buyers also frequently had none of their own funds invested because Lincoln lent them the down payment in a connected, but nominally separate, transaction.

The scheme's goal was to allow Lincoln to retain ownership of property and simultaneously make it look like Lincoln sold the property at a profit. Wischer also explained how ACC's auditor, Arthur Young, was misled into approving the reporting profits from these sham transactions with straw buyers since they weren't told about Keating's secret oral agreements to repurchase the property or that nominally separate transactions with the same straw buyer were all part of a single transaction. Wischer's testimony was corroborated by other former ACC/Lincoln employees, several of the straw buyers, and by Nancy Matusiak, one of the accountants at Arthur Young.

The sham real estate transactions, the tax-sharing scheme, and the collapsing Arizona real estate market were all related under the government's view of the case. As economic conditions worsened, Lincoln was under increasing pressure to maintain adequate capital levels, making it more difficult for Lincoln to pay dividends to ACC without incurring the wrath of regulators. But by creating phony profits from the sham real estate transactions, Keating could use the tax-sharing agreement to do an end run around the dividend restrictions. This enabled Lincoln to upstream funds to a cash-starved ACC, which otherwise would have been impossible. At the same time, the secret oral agreements allowing Keating to maintain control of the properties were a way for Keating to buy time in the hope the Arizona economy would turn around. Unfortunately, it never did.

The bond sales were also part of the federal trial, but this time the government relied on a different theory. The ACC prospectuses given to investors contained ACC's financial statements, which, under the government's theory, were false because they reported the phony profits from the sham real estate transactions. But this mattered only to a purchaser who was sophisticated enough to read the financial statements in the prospectus. False financial statements made no difference to the elderly and unsophisticated bond-purchaser witnesses in the state trial, all of whom testified that they didn't read or understand the prospectuses. Prosecutors solved this problem in the federal trial by calling different bond-purchaser witnesses, sophisticated investors who testified that they relied on the false financial statements.

Fidel and Symes testified again and supported this new version of the government's case.

The government's allegations of the sham real estate transactions were similar to the Wall Street prosecutions for stock parking. In both situations, the government relied on claimed oral agreements that supposedly demonstrated that assets transferred in apparent sales were in fact retained by the nominal seller. But there was a difference—the existence of victims. Unlike the stock-parking cases, where there were no victims, Keating's scheme, if the government's story was believed, hurt taxpayers by looting Lincoln of its assets and bondholders who paid too much for their securities. Another difference was the number of corroborating witnesses. The volume of proof against Keating, witnesses who testified about the alleged oral agreements, far exceeded what the government came up with in any of the stock-parking prosecutions.

Stephen Neal, again representing Keating in the federal trial, forcefully attacked the credibility of the government's witnesses who described the claimed secret oral agreements. Wischer, other ex-ACC employees, and the straw buyers all were testifying as cooperating witnesses with strong incentives to help the government to avoid going to jail themselves. Neal, who like the government shifted tactics from the state trial, also put Keating on the witness stand to deny that he ever entered into sham real estate transactions. And Neal extracted a major concession from Matusiak, the Arthur Young auditor, who was the only witness who testified about the effect of the claimed secret oral agreements on ACC and Lincoln's reported profitability. After testifying that she had no personal knowledge that any of the claimed secret oral agreements were ever made, Matusiak admitted that she could not say whether the agreements, even assuming they occurred, would change the proper accounting treatment for the transactions:

Q. Once again if those facts were true, you would have taken additional analysis and done additional audit work in connection with the transactions, correct?

A. If comments had been told to us about promises to purchase back property or promises of profits on the resale of properties which were previously sold, having been told to us, yes, we would have done more audit work on those transactions but I cannot say what the conclusions would be until I learned more about the particulars and fully analyzed those transactions.

Q. Which you already said you haven't done and nobody has asked you to do.

A. That's correct.

Q. As you sit there, again you don't know whether the result of that would have changed the gain recognition on any of these transactions that we are talking about, correct?

A. That's correct.

Matusiak admitted, in other words, that even if everything the government's witnesses said about the secret oral agreements were true, ACC and Lincoln still might have been able to report the same profits. And if this was true, there were no false financial statements, no defrauded bond purchasers, and no looting of Lincoln through the tax-sharing agreement.

Neal made all these points, but the jury convicted Keating anyway. Jurors hear conflicting evidence in most cases, and it's their job to decide whom to believe. That Keating lost makes him no different from countless other criminal defendants who were tried and convicted after jurors disbelieved their stories. The jury concluded that the financial statements would have been different and that Keating was a crook, and there was abundant evidence to support the verdict.

But there are some nagging doubts about Keating's guilt, even after he was convicted by a jury for the second time. The most pressing doubt arises from the simple fact that there were two trials. While the double jeopardy clause permits successive state and federal trials, multiple criminal trials give the government a very potent weapon. The government can try a defendant once, learn from its mistakes, and do a better job the second time after the defense is forced to reveal its strategy in the first trial. This is exactly what happened in Keating's case. The government tried a much better case on much stronger evidence the second time around. One of the reasons Michael Milken pled guilty was to avoid this risk of multiple criminal trials. In fact, Milken's guilty plea, as repugnant as it was, likely saved him from going through the same ordeal as Keating.

In Keating's case, the prejudice from being tried twice was particularly acute. Judge Pfaelzer ruled in the second trial that

Keating's conviction in the first trial was inadmissible. But after the second conviction, the defense obtained sworn affidavits from several jurors documenting that they learned of Keating's earlier conviction before deliberations began. Jurors' knowledge of the result in the first trial, when the judge had ruled it inadmissible as evidence, clearly taints the verdict in the second trial. And the taint is even stronger because of the legal problems and defects in the first trial.

Prosecutors' conduct in the second trial was also a cause for concern. A key component of the government's strategy in the second trial was demonstrating that Keating misled Arthur Young, ACC's auditor. Prosecutors took this position to negate Keating's defense that he relied on his lawyers and accountants to decide how the real estate transactions should be treated in ACC's financial statements. From what prosecutors said in the second trial, the jurors were led to believe that the auditors at Arthur Young were innocent, hardworking professionals, duped by the wily and unscrupulous Keating. What the jurors were not told was that in other cases the government sued Arthur Young for being a willing participant in reporting the phony profits from the sham real estate transactions. Arthur Young wound up paying the government $400 million, in significant part to settle these allegations. Who knows what the jury would have done had they been told about the government's inconsistent positions about Arthur Young's role?

A final issue concerned the government's use of immunity to distort the integrity of the fact-finding process. Judy Wischer and many of the government's witnesses in the federal trial testified under cooperation agreements with the government. But two key witnesses who could have contradicted Wischer's testimony refused to come forward because the government wouldn't immunize them from prosecution. The double whammy here for the defense is obvious. Friendly government witnesses have every reason to stretch the truth beyond recognition to avoid prosecution or jail time while those who can contradict them are deterred from testifying. Refusing to grant immunity is proper, of course, if the potential witnesses are genuinely the targets of a bona fide criminal investigation. But the risk also exists that prosecutors will use a claimed investigation as a pretext to prevent witnesses who might help the defense from testifying. The usual procedure when there is a serious question about whether the government's use of immunity in a criminal case is distorting the integrity of the fact-finding process is to hold a hearing, but Judge Pfaelzer refused to do so in Keating's case.

Whether any of these problems with Keating's two criminal trials are sufficient to overturn either conviction remains to be seen. Both convictions are on appeal, and no matter how the appellate courts rule, further appeals to the United States Supreme Court are likely. It will be many years before Keating's ultimate fate is known. Whether or not his convictions are overturned, Keating seems destined to go down in history as the most notorious of all the "S&L crooks" during the "decade of greed."

The Government's Humiliation of Kaye, Scholer

When Judge Stanley Sporkin issued his opinion blasting Keating and upholding the government's seizure of Lincoln Savings, he also attacked Keating's lawyers and accountants with characteristic bombast:

> It is abundantly clear that ACC's officials abused their positions with respect to Lincoln. Bluntly speaking, their actions amounted to a looting of Lincoln. This was not done crudely. Indeed, it was done with a great deal of sophistication. The transactions were all made to have an aura of legality about them. . . . Keating testified that he was so bent on doing the "right thing" that he surrounded himself with literally scores of accountants and lawyers to make sure all the transactions were legal. . . . Where were these professionals . . . when these clearly improper transactions were being consummated? What is difficult to understand is that with all the professional talent involved (both accounting and legal), why at least one professional would not have blown the whistle to stop the overreaching that took place in this case.

Encouraged by Judge Sporkin's attack on Lincoln's lawyers and accountants, the government also blamed several of Lincoln's outside professionals for the thrift's collapse. Eventually, several of Lincoln's prominent law and accounting firms, including Kaye, Scholer; Fierman, Hays & Handler; Sidley & Austin; Jones, Day, Reavis & Pogue; Troutman Sanders; Ernst & Young; and Arthur Anderson & Company, all reached multimillion-dollar settlements with the government to avoid going to trial.

The best-known, and most controversial, of these cases was the Office of Thrift Supervision's suit against Kaye, Scholer. This case, better than any other, demonstrates how far the government was willing to go in its search for scapegoats. Who better to blame for the savings and loan crisis than wealthy Wall Street lawyers—a class of people easy to arouße public sentiment against, particularly when they received millions of dollars in fees representing "S&L crooks" like Keating.

On March 1, 1992, the OTS filed a $275 million suit against Kaye, Scholer, Peter Fishbein, the firm's senior partner and lead lawyer for Lincoln Savings, and two other partners. The same day the OTS issued a temporary cease and desist order freezing the assets of the firm and the three partners. The freeze, which required the firm to escrow a significant percentage of its earnings and to notify the OTS in writing five days before making any expenditures greater than $50,000, restricted the ability of the firm, its partners, and their families to dispose of their assets. The asset freeze was effective immediately upon service, without any notice or hearing before an impartial judge. Six days later, Kaye, Scholer settled the OTS charges for $41 million.

The asset freeze was unnecessary and a gross abuse of governmental power. Congress in the FIRREA gave the OTS power to issue asset freezes in the guise of temporary cease and desist orders whenever regulators determined that improper conduct was likely to dissipate a thrift's assets and threaten the insurance fund before legal proceedings could be completed. But in the Kaye, Scholer case, thrift assets were not a concern since Lincoln was seized in April 1989, three years before the freeze. The OTS imposed the freeze anyway, stating that Kaye, Scholer was "likely to dissipate its assets and thereby prejudice the OTS's ability to recover restitution."

This justification for the freeze was obviously pretextual. Kaye, Scholer has been in existence for more than seventy years and is one of the country's most established law firms. The notion that the firm's partners would withdraw funds and flee the country to avoid a judgment was ludicrous. Moreover, the firm had insurance that covered the years in question. Although the OTS claimed that Kaye, Scholer might amend its insurance policy to impair the collectibility of any judgment, this claim also made no sense. The OTS never explained why Kaye, Scholer's partners would prefer to be exposed personally rather than be covered by insurance, nor how a policy for past years where coverage was fixed could be altered after the fact.

The asset freeze was an outrage because it had nothing to do with preventing dissipation of assets. Rather, the freeze was intended to panic Kaye, Scholer's partners, clients, and lenders, conjuring up images of how Princeton/Newport went bankrupt when its assets were frozen long before there was a trial on the underlying charges. The freeze had its desired effect, and Kaye, Scholer capitulated within a week. The government had "won" another case, but only by denying Kaye, Scholer an opportunity to defend itself.

The government would have had problems in a fair fight. Kaye, Scholer was hired when Keating and the San Francisco FHLBB were already embroiled in a bitter dispute in connection with the 1986 regulatory examination of Lincoln Savings. The examination dragged on interminably until early 1987 when the regulators finally issued their report, sharply criticizing Lincoln's real estate investments, high-yield bond purchases, and compliance with applicable regulations. The San Francisco regulators also recommended that Lincoln be seized because of its unsafe banking practices.

Kaye, Scholer responded to the 1986 examination report as Lincoln's lawyer and disputed every one of the regulators' major criticisms. The FHLBB in Washington, now headed by a new chairman, M. Danny Wall, ultimately rejected the San Francisco regulators' recommendation that Lincoln be seized. Significantly, the San Francisco regulators, as critical as they were, did not conclude that Lincoln was insolvent. Nineteen eighty-seven was, after all, the year that *Forbes* ranked Lincoln the second-most profitable thrift in the country. Since Lincoln was not insolvent, the FHLBB in Washington concluded that seizure of the institution would not survive a court challenge. None of this had anything to do with Kaye, Scholer.

After 1987 the Arizona economy worsened and Lincoln began experiencing greater difficulties. Kaye, Scholer continued to represent Lincoln in its ongoing regulatory disputes, but neither the firm nor the government could stop the slide of Arizona real estate values. And Lincoln was weakened further by the bogus tax-sharing agreement that resulted in nearly $100 million of badly needed capital being upstreamed to ACC, its parent corporation. Regulators ultimately concluded that Lincoln's financial condition was hopeless and seized the institution in April 1989.

The OTS's notice of charges against Kaye, Scholer challenged the firm's legal advice to Lincoln as well as its representations made to the FHLBB on Lincoln's behalf. But nowhere in the OTS's eighty-two-page complaint is there any explanation of how anything Kaye, Scholer supposedly did wrong had any effect on regulatory policy toward Lincoln. In fact, there is a serious question whether Kaye, Scholer did anything other than vigorously represent its client, which it had every right, indeed obligation, to do. Anticipating this argument, the OTS, as the government did so often in challenging practices of the 1980s, changed the rules in the middle of the game.

In its best-known allegation, for example, the OTS accused Kaye, Scholer of failing to come forward with the "real reason" Arthur Anderson & Company resigned as Lincoln's independent auditor in late 1986. In October 1986, ACC filed a Form 8(k) with the Securities and Exchange Commission, as required by law, explaining why Arthur Anderson resigned as independent auditor. The form reported that the resignation "was not the result of any concern by [Arthur Anderson] with [Lincoln's] operations . . . or asset/liability management." Rather, the reason was Lincoln's aggressive business practices and confrontational approach with the government, particularly "in view of the very litigious environment controlled to a large degree by regulators." Kaye, Scholer, which did not prepare this Form 8(k), submitted the document to the FHLBB.

According to the OTS, Kaye, Scholer "knew" that the stated reasons for the auditor's resignation were false because it was aware of an earlier statement made by an Arthur Anderson partner expressing concern that Lincoln's investments were too risky. But this statement didn't contradict the stated reason for the resignation in the Form 8(k), which was approved by Arthur Anderson's management, which filed its own statement to the SEC. It also didn't contain any information the regulators didn't already know given their view of Lincoln's business practices. Moreover, the notion that a law firm has an obligation to provide negative information about its own client to a government agency transforms the firm from an agent for its client to an agent for the government. This is a radically different conception of a lawyer's role than that previously recognized.

The OTS argued, however, that a heightened standard of responsibility was appropriate because Kaye, Scholer "interposed" itself between Lincoln and the agency by directing that all FHLBB requests for information be routed through the firm. Because of this "interposition" making the firm the "sole source of facts made available by the client to the regulators," the OTS claimed, Kaye, Scholer became part of Lincoln, and not just its lawyer. But this claim was nonsensical because there is nothing unusual about a law firm acting as a clearinghouse for information in an adversary proceeding. And, in any event, the "interposition" theory in Kaye, Scholer's case was false. There were countless meetings between Lincoln and the regulators without any lawyers from Kaye, Scholer present.

The OTS also attempted to justify its novel theory that Kaye, Scholer owed special disclosure obligations to the government by arguing that financial institutions and their advisors have an obligation to protect the federal deposit insurance fund. In the words of Harris Weinstein, then the OTS's general counsel, directors of federally insured financial institutions:

> . . . are not legally free to view themselves as having duties only to common shareholders. So truncated a view would result in a complete disregard of the duty owed to the true party in interest. The reason is that the directors owe a fiduciary duty to the federal government, whose interest in the institution exceeds that of any other person, and who insures the deposits, holds the unlimited equity risk, and is the primary creditor in insolvency.

Lawyers for federally insured deposit institutions like Kaye, Scholer, according to the OTS, have the same obligation.

But this claimed additional obligation to protect the federal deposit insurance fund had never before been recognized, and it was wrong for the OTS to seek to punish Kaye, Scholer, and freeze its assets, for violating a duty that did not exist. And if the duty did exist, the primary violator would be the government itself, both the Congress and state and federal regulators. It was the government, after all, that made the disastrous decision to cover up the insolvency of the savings and loan industry and encourage thrifts, no matter how weak financially, to engage in risky activities with no market discipline. Under these circumstances, it was hypocrisy and scapegoating to the extreme for the OTS to blame Kaye, Scholer for not "protecting" the federal deposit insurance fund.

The OTS's other highly publicized allegation was that Kaye, Scholer committed malpractice when it advised Lincoln that $750

million of its direct real estate investments were legally grandfa-
thered under an FHLBB rule while knowing, the OTS charged,
that the key documents had been backdated. The rule in question
provided that thrifts that held more than 10 percent of their assets
in direct investments after January 30, 1985, were prohibited
from making any further such investments without FHLBB
approval. The rule also contained a grandfather clause, however,
permitting further direct investments where there were definite
plans in existence before December 10, 1984. Kaye, Scholer contended that its advice was proper because the relevant legal question was the date when there was a definite plan to undertake the
investments, not the date when the plans were documented, and
that Lincoln had such a plan prior to the relevant date. The sinister-sounding "backdating" of key documents was in reality nothing more than formalizing in writing the approval of direct investments that had actually occurred earlier.

The OTS's backdating allegation was apparently premised on the
assumption that had Kaye, Scholer advised Keating, contrary to its
belief, that the direct investments were improper, Keating would
have heeded the advice and used the $750 million to make "safe"
home mortgages or for some other lawful use. This assumption is
questionable, at the very least, given the government's view that
Keating was a master criminal bent on doing what he wanted no
matter what the law required. The more plausible assumption under
this view would be that Keating would have made the investments
anyway or that the money would have been lost in some other way.
This seems likely even if Keating invested the money lawfully, given
what happened to Arizona real estate values. Every major thrift in
Arizona failed or was acquired for a reason.

The OTS's hodgepodge of other allegations accuse Kaye,
Scholer of various misrepresentations and omissions in communications with regulators. In reality, the OTS accused Kaye, Scholer
of disagreeing with the government's characterization of Lincoln's
practices. The government, for example, repeatedly challenged
Lincoln's underwriting practices when making risky real estate
investments. Kaye, Scholer, in its response to the 1986 FHLBB
examination report, disagreed, maintaining that "[w]hat is
unusual about Lincoln's underwriting is its particular emphasis
on, and the thoroughness of, its underwriting of the collateral."
The OTS charged that Kaye, Scholer "knew" that this statement
was false, but an alternative interpretation is that the firm, on

behalf of its client, simply disagreed with the government's position. The quality of underwriting is necessarily a subjective judgment, and skill at assessing underlying real estate values is not the same thing as keeping extensive files. In any event, given the government's view of Lincoln's lack of sound underwriting, it's hard to see how Kaye, Scholer's contrary opinion misled anyone.

Kaye, Scholer had nothing to do with the FHLBB's decision in 1987 not to follow the recommendation of its San Francisco office to seize Lincoln. The FHLBB at that time was following the official government policy of forbearance, allowing even insolvent institutions to remain open. There was simply no way the FHLBB was going to close Lincoln when it was rated the second most profitable thrift in the country.

Ultimately, Kaye, Scholer and Peter Fishbein obtained some vindication when several task forces investigated the OTS's allegations and concluded they were baseless. But there was a serious ethical violation in the Kaye, Scholer case. The Code of Professional Responsibility provides that "a government lawyer . . . should not use his or her position or the economic power of the government to harass parties or to bring about unjust settlements or results." The OTS's unilateral and unjustified imposition of the asset freeze, which coerced Kaye, Scholer into settling the government's groundless charges, was a clear violation of this ethical principle. It's unfortunate the government was never held accountable.

The Keating Five

During his acrimonious battles with bank regulators over the length of the 1986 examination and the proposed direct-investment rule, Keating lobbied five United States senators—John Glenn, John McCain, Dennis DeConcini, Don Riegle, and Alan Cranston—to meet with Ed Gray, then chairman of the FHLBB, to work things out. McCain was a Republican, the others were Democrats. McCain and DeConcini were from Arizona, Glenn from Ohio, Cranston from California, Riegle from Michigan. All five senators received extensive campaign and PAC contributions from Keating and ACC: Glenn $234,000; McCain $112,600; DeConcini $81,100; Riegle $78,250; and Cranston $49,900. ACC also contributed $935,000 to various organizations associated with Cranston. Keating's business ties to Arizona, California, and Ohio explain his connection to the senators from those states. ACC also owned property in Michigan, and Senator Riegle was also a member of the Senate Banking Committee.

After Lincoln was seized in April 1989, Gray and others charged that Keating used improper political influence to impede the regulatory process. When asked directly whether he received special treatment from the senators in exchange for the contributions, Keating responded with characteristic bluntness: "I certainly hope so." Keating's comment was met with outrage. How could five United States senators allow themselves to be bought by the satan of the savings and loan industry, a man who was so openly purchasing special favors?

In October 1989, Common Cause, a nonprofit public interest lobbying group, filed a complaint with the Senate Select Committee on Ethics, demanding an investigation of Keating's attempts to influence senators with financial contributions. In December 1990, the Ethics Committee appointed Robert Bennett as special counsel and began an investigation into the relationships between Keating, the five senators, and regulatory policy toward Lincoln. Bennett submitted his report containing his findings and recommendations in early September 1990, although the committee delayed hearings until November, after the midterm elections.

The committee's most difficult task was reconciling the public's perception of corrupt political influence with the simple reality that Congress had no rules preventing senators or other elected officials from intervening with regulators on behalf of constituents or contributors. Senator Herb Kohl put the point succinctly when he asked, "What are we supposed to say to our campaign contributors? Once you give me money, I can never do anything for you anymore?" The *New York Times*, in an article entitled "The Confusing Case of the Keating 5," expressed this difficulty of determining what standard the senators should be judged against:

> It would be much simpler if the Senators under scrutiny in the "Keating Five" case had been caught taking cash-stuffed brown paper bags from lobbyists, or putting call girls on their office payrolls.
>
> Those are the easy questions, and they have happened before. But there is no legal precedent for the case of the Senators accused of using their political influence to help a political contributor,

Charles H. Keating Jr., fend off Federal regulators as his savings and loan neared collapse.

When the Ethics Committee began televised hearings in November, however, it was obvious that the absence of standards or precedent to judge the senators by was less important than public outrage about the savings and loan crisis. Senator Howell Heflin set the tone for the hearings when he began by telling the five senators that they had already been convicted in the court of public opinion: "I need not tell you . . . many of our fellow citizens apparently believe that your services were bought by Charles Keating, that you were bribed, that you sold your office, that you traded your honor and your good names and other benefits. Many of these same people believe that your actions . . . were solely responsible for S&L failures of scandalous proportions."

The hearings themselves focused on two meetings the senators had with banking regulators on April 2 and April 9, 1987. Ed Gray and Bill Black, general counsel of the FHLBB's San Francisco office, were the two most damaging witnesses against the senators. Gray, whose reputation had been badly tarnished by revelations that he accepted improper gifts from thrift lobbyists and whose tenure as chairman ended soon after the April meetings, cast himself as a crusading regulator fighting improper political influence. Gray repeatedly insisted that campaign contributions by powerful thrift interests were no different from bribery. "It's a case of too much money chasing too many politicians."

Gray also charged that the Senate had ignored its duty to protect the public welfare. "I have always assumed that we send our Senators to Washington because we think they will have the sense to know when narrow constituent demands must take a back seat to the safety of their constituents as a whole." He then criticized the Keating Five, particularly Senator DeConcini, who, Gray claimed, improperly pressured regulators to drop the direct-investment rule in exchange for a promise from Keating to make more home mortgages. The April meetings initiated by the senators, Gray said, "were designed not just to change particular decisions by the Bank Board but to render us unable to carry out our central responsibilities." Black provided details of the April 9 meeting, and testified that he believed the senators held up Lincoln's closing and were responsible for increasing taxpayers' losses.

Each senator testified in his own defense, emphasizing that he broke no Senate rules and the propriety of his conduct. Senator DeConcini, for example, said that he intervened with regulators to save the jobs of ACC's two thousand Arizona employees, not to help Keating. "I resent the fact that I have to tell this committee and the American people that I intervened for 2,000 Arizonans and not for Charles Keating." Senator Cranston went even further, stressing that fund-raising and providing services to constituents were inextricably linked. "I say that it's absurd to suggest that fund-raising and substantive issues are separated in Senate offices by some kind of wall."

Senator Inouye, the only senator to testify in defense of the embattled Keating Five, stated that he believed the senators were guilty only of fighting for a constituent with "vigor and assertiveness." What the Keating Five did, in other words, was what senators do routinely: "The political realities of life dictate that whatever we do should please our constituents." If Lincoln hadn't failed, Inouye said, "these men would be heroes to their constituents. . . . Today, they are attacked because the endeavor failed."

Robert Bennett, the committee's special counsel, emphatically rejected this "everybody does it defense," stressing that courts don't accept it when made by "some of the more unfortunate in our society." If that's true, Bennett continued, "Why should it be a defense for the most fortunate . . . the most privileged in our society." Bennett's response to the senators sounded good to the public, but it missed the point. The issue wasn't that what the senators did was appropriate because everybody violated the rules, but rather that nobody could say what the rules were so it was impossible to tell if violations occurred. This problem of never defining the standards that the senators were being judged against permeated the entire hearings process.

The committee's muddled findings, released in late February 1991, reflected the same confusion. The committee began its report by emphasizing that no senator violated any law or Senate rule, and that "the Senate has no specific written standards embodied in the Senate rules respecting contact or intervention with Federal executive or independent regulatory agency officials." Nevertheless, the committee concluded that there was "substantial credible evidence" that Senator Cranston, the most aggressive fund-raiser of the five, "may have engaged . . . in an impermissible pattern of conduct in which fund raising and official activities were substantially linked." In support of this finding, the committee listed numerous instances where Cranston received contributions from Keating that were close in time to actions taken by Cranston on Keating's behalf.

The committee recommended that Cranston, now seventy-seven years old and suffering from prostate cancer, be reprimanded by the full Senate. Cranston accepted the reprimand to avoid a censure vote but defended his actions and raised the specter of hypocrisy in a speech to a packed Senate chamber:

> There is no precedent and there is no rule establishing that it is unethical for a Senator to engage in legitimate constituent service on behalf of a constituent, because it was close in time to a lawful contribution to the Senator's campaign or to a charity that the Senator supports. How many of you, after really thinking about it, could rise and declare you have never, ever helped—or agreed to help—a contributor close in time to the solicitation of receipts of a contribution? I do not believe any of you could say never.

The other Keating Five members got off easier. The Ethics Committee concluded that the conduct of Senators DeConcini and Riegle "gave the appearance of being improper and was certainly attended with insensitivity and poor judgment." In both cases, however, the committee recommended that the Senate take no further action. Senators McCain and Glenn were exonerated completely, the committee finding that they engaged in no improper conduct. The committee's findings were met with ridicule. As the *Washington Post* commented in an editorial:

> 1: Lamentably there are no written rules regarding "contact or intervention" by senators with executive branch or independent regulatory agency officials, yet
>
> 2: One of the five accused, Sen. Alan Cranston, nonetheless managed to break the rules by engaging on behalf of lapsed savings and loan operator Charles Keating in an "impermissible pattern of conduct in which fund-raising and official activities were substantially linked," while
>
> 3: At least two other senators, Dennis DeConcini and Donald Riegle, whose similar conduct gave the acknowledged "appearance of being improper and was certainly attended with insensitivity and poor judgment," somehow did not break the rules.

Many in the press speculated that Cranston was scapegoated because of his age, poor health, and political expendability. "He was an easy sacrifice," the *New York Times* reported, "because he wasn't going to run for election again." The *Times* concluded that the whole proceedings were a "farce."

Cranston was easy to single out because of his self-righteous positions. Throughout his career, Cranston campaigned as "an enemy of special interests" and had always been an outspoken proponent of campaign-finance reform. Yet, as the whole Keating Five episode demonstrated, nobody was more skilled at raising money from "special interests" nor more willing to give them special access in exchange for contributions. Cranston raised more money from Keating than the other Keating senators combined, and he showed his appreciation. For example, the Ethics Committee reported one incident where Senator Cranston solicited and received $250,000 from Keating for two voter-registration groups. When the contribution was delivered, Senator Cranston called Keating, who asked the senator if he would contact M. Danny Wall, then the new chairman of the FHLBB. Senator Cranston agreed to do so and made the call six days later.

But the other Senators who received slaps on the wrist from the Ethics Committee or were exonerated completely also received money from Keating and either contacted or attended meetings with regulators on Keating's behalf. The only difference between Cranston and the others, apart from Cranston's expendability, was one of degree. Cranston raised more money and had more contacts with regulators than the others, but they all engaged in the same practices. And Cranston, like Keating, was also more candid, acknowledging that, of course, major contributors expected and received special access in return. After all, why else do big donors give the money in the first place?

Regrettably, the Ethics Committee hearings, probably due to the public furor about the Keating Five, focused almost exclusively on this irrelevant issue of whether the senators contacted regulators or attended meetings on Keating's behalf because of Keating's campaign contributions. Of course they did. The important question, all but ignored in the controversy, is what the senators actually did. Did any senator threaten or intimidate any regulator into not taking any action? Did any senator use his influence to interfere with or block any pending regulatory initiative? From the record developed by the Ethics Committee, the answer to these questions appears to be a resounding no.

The two April 1987 meetings that the committee focused on were a complete nonevent. On April 2, 1987, four of the five senators met with Ed Gray to discuss the regulatory status of Lincoln. Gray later claimed that Senator DeConcini suggested a deal in which the direct-investment rule would be withdrawn in exchange for Lincoln making more home mortgages. The four senators present disputed Gray's account, but in any event, even under Gray's version the proposed deal went nowhere. The proposed rule wasn't withdrawn, although many economists believed it should have been.

Gray testified that he considered the April 2 meeting improper, but he never reported it to anyone at the time. In fact, Gray proposed another meeting between the senators and regulators from the San Francisco FHLBB, which occurred on April 9 in Senator DeConcini's office. Bill Black, one of the Keating Five's principal accusers, took notes on what occurred at the meeting, which have also been disputed by the others present. Nevertheless, Black's account, which is far less favorable to the senators than their own accounts of what occurred, is instructive of how careful the senators were to avoid any impropriety.

According to Black's notes, which have now been published, the meeting, which lasted about two hours, began with the regulators present introducing themselves and some pleasantries. Senator DeConcini then told the regulators that the senators wanted the meeting because "potential actions of yours could injure a constituent." Lincoln, Senator DeConcini continued, was "a viable organization" that "wanted to reach a compromise" in its continuing disputes with the bank board. Senator McCain then also questioned the regulators' approach to Lincoln, but also made clear that he wasn't asking that ACC be given any "special favors": "One of our jobs as elected officials is to help constituents in a proper fashion. ACC is a big employer and important to the local economy. I wouldn't want any special favors for them. . . . I don't want any part of our conversation to be improper. We asked Chairman Gray about that, and he said it wasn't improper to discuss Lincoln."

Senator Glenn next complained about the "unusually adversary" regulatory approach toward Lincoln and the length of the 1986 bank-board examination: "To be blunt, you should charge them or get off their backs. If things are bad there, get to them. . . . Why has the exam dragged on and on?"

Next it was Senator Riegle's turn; he expressed concern about "the struggle between Keating and Gray" and told the regulators that he was "glad to have this opportunity to hear your side of the story." Senator Glenn then made the same point: "I'm not trying to get anyone off. If there is wrongdoing, I'm on your side. But I don't want any unfairness against a viable entity." Senator Cranston was present only briefly at the meeting and said nothing other than that he "shares the concerns of the other senators."

The regulators in turn launched into a detailed discussion of Lincoln's lack of underwriting, its problem loans, and its violations of law. "Have you done anything about these violations of law?" Senator Glenn then asked.

Michael Patriarca, head of the San Francisco FHLBB, responded: "We're sending a criminal referral to the Department of Justice. Not maybe, we're sending one."

"The criminality surprises me," Senator DeConcini reacted. "We're not interested in discussing those issues. Our premise was that we had a viable institution concerned that it was being over-regulated."

Senator Riegle then asked, "Is this institution so far gone that it can't be salvaged?"

"I don't know," Patriarca responded, "but I can guarantee you that if an institution continues such behavior it will eventually go bankrupt."

"Well, I guess that's pretty definitive," Senator Riegle responded.

At that point, Senator DeConcini had to leave and the meeting ended.

The public perception of the Keating Five, as Senator Heflin stated at the beginning of the Ethics Committee hearings, was that the senators were "bribed" and "sold their office" in exchange for campaign contributions. But the record, even accepting Black's disputed version of the April 9 meeting at face value, reveals the exact opposite. The senators began with concerns about a constituent, expressed their concerns about regulatory unfairness, but also stressed that they were not asking for any "special favors." When the regulators disclosed the criminal referral, the senators backed off immediately and asked only whether Lincoln would be taken over. The senators made no attempt to influence any specific regulatory decision. All they did was seek information and, at the beginning of the meeting, volunteer some very general concerns that Lincoln not be treated unfairly.

In fact, Black's version of the April 9 meeting comes closer to being a model of how democracy is supposed to work than proving wrongdoing by any member of the Keating Five. Elected officials should investigate charges of regulatory unfairness; as Senator McCain said, that's their job. And regulators should not be allowed to operate autonomously in a vacuum. They should receive input and be accountable. And if regulators delay or change their approach because of what they learn, that's good too. It's no accident that the First Amendment of the Constitution guarantees the right of every citizen to petition the government for redress of grievances. And elected officials like the Keating Five also have the right, indeed the obligation, to seek information and communicate their views about regulatory decisions.

Of course, the Keating Five did not wind up being commended for their role in exemplifying the democratic process. On the contrary, they were vilified. The Ethics Committee's investigation and reprimand ended the political career of Alan Cranston. Senators Riegle and DeConcini, who were criticized by the committee with no formal action taken, also paid the price. In what was generally regarded as continued fallout from the Ethics Committee's investigation, both decided not to run for re-election. Of the original Keating Five, only Senators Glenn and McCain are still in office, and their reputations have been tarnished as well. The Keating Five should be included in the long list of scapegoats who have paid a big price after being unfairly blamed for the savings and loan crisis.

CHAPTER 9

More S&L Scapegoats

Michael Milken and Charles Keating were the best known of the S&L scapegoats, but they were far from alone. Whenever a major savings and loan failed, the government brought a wave of lawsuits and frequently initiated criminal prosecutions as well. Most of the time the government won, but not always. The government's cases against four of the best known S&L figures—Don Dixon, Neil Bush, David Paul, and Tom Spiegel—are profiled in this chapter.

Their stories reveal much about the sorry history of the savings and loan crisis. In each case, their thrifts enjoyed spectacular success and explosive growth during much of the 1980s only to be followed by collapse. The early growth and success was accomplished by abandoning the traditional mission of savings and loans to protect small savers and provide home mortgages for ordinary Americans. Instead, these thrifts engaged in aggressive real estate and/or high-yield bond investing funded by government-insured brokered deposits. This, of course, was a complete perversion of the rationale for having thrifts in the first place, but it is exactly what the government encouraged thrifts to do. During the growth and success phase, thrifts that followed this course were hailed as saviors of the industry.

But when collapse occurred, either because of plummeting real estate values or the government's own actions in wrecking the high-yield bond market, the government pretended that it never encouraged thrifts to take radical measures to save the industry from insolvency. Instead, the government turned on prominent thrift officials with a vengeance, unfairly blaming them for costing taxpayers billions of dollars. Even when wrongdoing occurred, as it surely did in many cases, the amounts involved were trivial relative to what thrift officials were being blamed for. The government engaged in this blatant scapegoating to hide its own responsibility for the thrift crisis.

Donald Dixon

The Vernon Savings and Loan was founded in 1960 by R. B. Tanner, a former bank examiner. At the beginning of 1981, Vernon Savings had $82 million in assets and only $90,000 in delinquent loans. High inflation and the subsequent federal deregulation of interest rates, however, combined to undermine the profitability of the thrift's mortgage portfolio. "We had a lot of loans that were earning about six percent," Tanner later said, "but we were paying twelve, fourteen percent for our money. That's where the pressure came." In June 1981, Vernon Savings and Loan posted the first loss in its history. The thrift's financial condition had gone from solid to desperate overnight, and there was no solution in sight.

Donald Dixon was a condominium builder whose company, Dondi Construction, was well known for its Spanish-style houses with signature red tile roofs. Like Keating, Dixon saw purchasing a savings and loan as a great opportunity because of regulatory developments at the federal and state level allowing thrifts to make direct real estate investments with federally insured deposits. Dixon was particularly interested in Vernon Savings because he grew up in Vernon (population 13,000), where his father was editor of the local newspaper and a commentator on the local radio station. Vernon was also attractive because Tanner was willing to sell it for next to nothing. Dixon acquired Vernon for $1.1 million in cash (which he borrowed) and a note for $4.7 million to be paid off over the next seven years at the far-below-market interest rate of 8 percent. Dixon accomplished his goal of acquiring a sure-bet source of financing for his various real estate projects without having to put up any of his own money.

Dixon immediately began implementing his plan to convert Vernon into a "developers bank" focusing on rapid growth through aggressive real estate lending. The regulators initially hailed Dixon as a hero, exactly the type of entrepreneur the thrift industry needed to grow out of its problems. Woody Lemons, the former chairman of Vernon Savings, later recalled that Dixon:

> ... went over to the Federal Home Loan Bank of Little Rock and told them exactly what he was going to do. After the meeting, they said we need more men like you. Things couldn't have gone on like they were, because we were paying fifteen percent for our money and our loan portfolio was yielding only about ten percent. He told them we were going to make construction loans, land loans, and take profit participations in projects. ... That worked for a while and everything we touched turned to gold. The regulators held us up as a model.

In mid-1983, regulators also approved the restructuring of Dixon's financial interests, which resulted in Dondi Group being placed under the control of Vernon Savings. Although Don Dixon was not the chairman of Vernon Savings, he controlled the S&L through Dondi Financial Corporation, a holding company in which Dixon owned 70 percent of the stock.

Vernon Savings began to aggressively engage in profit-participation real estate deals, often providing 100 percent financing and then some (a legal transaction under the new regulatory rules for S&L's). Developers flocked to Vernon Savings because it was willing to finance risky deals and developers would still receive a 2 to 4 percent up-front developer's fee out of the loan proceeds even if the deal subsequently fell through. Vernon Savings also profited handsomely from these deals by charging interest rates and loan-origination and renewal fees that were often twice as high as the rest of the industry charged. All of this was completely legal and disclosed to the regulators.

In order to raise deposits to finance this increased lending, Vernon Savings dealt with deposit brokers. The S&L offered high interest rates to attract $100,000 brokered deposits from around the country. By 1984, more than 40 percent of Vernon's deposits came from brokers, and deposit growth soared to more than $400 million by year-end 1983 from $82 million in 1981. By 1987, Vernon Savings had $1.7 billion in deposits, an increase of more than 2,000 percent in just five years.

During the period of Vernon Savings and Loan's explosive growth, Dixon received $4.5 million in bonuses in addition to a $272,500 annual salary paid to him through Dondi Financial

Corporation. However, direct compensation was only the tip of the iceberg. On December 31, 1984, Vernon Savings bought a $2 million beach house in Del Mar, California, and spent an additional $200,000 on furnishings. Dixon and his wife moved into it six months later and lived rent-free for a year. During one eighteen-month period Dixon billed Vernon for $561,874 in personal living expenses, including $36,780 for flowers, $37,339 for phone calls, $4,420 for pool service, $386 for pet services, and $44,095 for out-of-pocket incidentals. The S&L invested heavily in Western art, to the tune of $5.5 million, which was mainly kept in Dixon's homes. Vernon Savings also paid for a $2.6 million yacht named "High Spirits" and purchased a Rolls-Royce and Ferrari dealership to indulge Dixon's interest in fine automobiles. Finally, Vernon Savings owned five airplanes to fly executives and their spouses on trips.

Dixon's expenditures were a favorite topic of journalists who wrote about Vernon Savings and the savings and loan crisis. As the *New Republic* recounted:

> At a 1988 bankruptcy hearing Dixon pleaded that he should be able to keep his personal Vernon-financed car because it had four doors and served as "the family Ferrari." But the peak of Dixonian indulgence was something Don's wife, Dana, called "Gastronomique Fantastique," a two-week tour the Dixons and their friends took in October 1983 of the best restaurants of France, paid for by Vernon Savings and Loan. In a document found by regulators, Dana assiduously recorded the details of every meal. They dined at seven restaurants rated three stars by the Guide Michelin, supping on pressed duck, truffle soup, and minced kidneys. "It was truly a dream trip," she wrote, "hardly to be imagined by most, and barely to be believed even by those of us who experienced it first hand . . . a flying house party . . . of pure unadulterated pleasure."

A *New York Times* article reported a similarly sarcastic description of another trip by the Dixons:

> In the spring of 1985, Mr. Dixon took along Roman Catholic Bishop Leo T. Maher of San Diego on another European jaunt. They traveled on a company-owned Falcon 50 and rested in the finest hotels. The highlight was when Bishop Maher arranged a visit with Pope John Paul II. Mrs. Dixon didn't know what to say. Mr. Dixon always felt you could never go wrong with a nice present. He handed the Pope a $40,000 oil painting, "Night Sentry" by Olaf Wieghorst, plucked from Vernon's huge collection of Western art.

Mr. Dixon's expenditures would soon symbolize the culpability of directors in the savings and loan crises. Where had all the money gone if not into the pockets of people like Don Dixon?

But the real problem for Vernon was not Dixon's extravagant lifestyle but deteriorating economic conditions in Texas during the 1980s, which forced Dixon to engage in increasingly shaky transactions to keep his empire afloat. In one transaction, Dixon learned that real estate owned by one of Vernon's subsidiaries was worth $20 million less than the company's books reflected. Vernon Savings then lent major borrowers and Dixon's friends $98 million in forty-seven nominally separate transactions to purchase the real estate with the assurance that the real estate would be resold later when the Texas economy recovered. Vernon Savings ended up recording a $13 million profit on the deal, but court records later revealed that the borrowers never paid any interest or principal on the loans, which all defaulted.

Regulators later claimed that they had no knowledge of Vernon's business practices, but the record demonstrates the opposite. In 1983, state banking examiners noted that more than 80 percent of Vernon's assets were concentrated in interim construction and land-development loans. In 95 percent of the deals, Vernon had financed the cost of the land, the closing costs, and interest charges—creating the kind of economics that made the thrift precariously dependent on continually rising land values. In the same year, federal examiners reported significant regulatory violations: unsafe and unsound banking practices; lending deficiencies; inadequate books and records; incomplete financial statements on borrowers; violations of loans-to-one-borrower regulations; and conflicts of interest. The only action taken against Vernon Savings, however, was to make the board members sign a "supervisory agreement" promising to develop a new business plan.

In 1985, an examination by the state concluded that Vernon's troubled loans equaled 7.8 percent of its assets. At the time, Vernon's reports to the federal government put the percentage at 1.6 percent. A month later, a federal examination concluded that Vernon Savings was fraught with conflicts of interest, unsecured loans, and sham transactions. Still, the thrift was allowed to stay open and keep taking in federally insured deposits.

In truth, Dixon and the regulators were playing the same game. Both were betting on a turnaround in the Texas economy, which would in turn lead to higher real estate values. For Dixon, an economic rebound would have allowed him to hold on to Vernon and preserve his lavish lifestyle. For the regulators, a turnaround would have avoided having to make good on the government's insurance obligation and the embarrassment of previously having welcomed Dixon as the savior of the thrift industry. But no turnaround occurred; if anything, economic conditions in Texas worsened and real estate values continued their free fall.

Eventually, Dixon resigned under pressure from Vernon's board of directors in the summer of 1985. In September 1986, the state regulators seized control and made a bad situation worse. Rather than closing the thrift, the regulators kept it open under government control. Loans started lapsing into default rapidly as borrowers encountered due dates and could not get their loans extended by the state authorities in charge. Vernon's income from loans fell off dramatically. By late 1986, federal regulators were pushing for a complete federal takeover of the S&L. Dixon attempted to get Speaker of the House Jim Wright to exert pressure on Edwin Gray, then chairman of the Federal Home Loan Bank Board, to give Dixon time to find new investors to inject capital into Vernon Savings. Although Wright did call Gray and ask him to look into the situation (Dixon had been a major campaign contributor, and his yacht had been used frequently for Democratic Congressional Campaign Committee fund-raisers in 1985 and 1986), Vernon was too far gone for Wright's intervention to do any good.

In March 1987, the Federal Home Loan Bank Board convened to decide what the federal government should do about Vernon Savings. It was estimated that 96 percent of the thrift's loans were in default. Rather than shut down the S&L, take over its assets, and pay off depositors, the FHLBB, repeating the earlier decision by state regulators, voted to allow Vernon to remain open under the control of new managers appointed by the government under a program for troubled thrifts known as the Management Consignment Program. The Bank Board even agreed to advance funds to Vernon in order to cover its mounting cash needs, thereby throwing good money after bad. The thrift's new managers were also authorized to raise cash by getting fresh deposits from the marketplace, which they did by bidding up interest rates.

Vernon Federal, as it was now called, would continue to lose money under federal control while the regulators' attempt to save the thrift by bidding up interest rates only made it harder for the rest of the industry to attract funds. The irony here was obvious. The regulators condemned Dixon and many others for their reckless and irresponsible banking practices, including financing aggressive growth strategies in a declining market by paying above-market rates of interest to attract deposits. But when the regulators seized control, they did exactly the same thing.

In November 1987, the federal government implemented its final plan for Vernon Federal, splitting the thrift into two organizations. Montfort Savings was created to manage Vernon's deposits and, incredibly, was given $200 million in cash and issued a $1.1 billion interest-paying note by the FSLIC. In theory, Montfort would be able to pay off its depositors slowly, saving the government from paying Vernon's depositors all of their money ($1.3 billion) up front. The second organization existed only on paper and was called Old Vernon. It consisted entirely of Vernon's troubled assets, which would be sold to raise money to settle some of the five hundred lawsuits that had been filed against the thrift by creditors and others. The idea was to have the new managers of Montfort Savings collect interest on the note, pay depositors just enough to prevent a run, and improve the portfolio of the thrift to a point where it could be sold. Instead, the reorganization was a bust, with Montfort losing an additional $20 million in the first nine months of 1988—mostly because the interest paid by the FSLIC on its note was far below the interest Montfort officials had to pay to keep depositors from taking their money elsewhere.

The government's continued losses on Vernon Savings heightened the pressure to find scapegoats for the debacle. A special Justice Department bank-fraud task force had been set up in Dallas in 1986, and it began its investigation of Vernon Savings in the summer of 1987, immediately focusing on Dixon as the primary target. The government built its case methodically over a three-year period. By the time Dixon was indicted on June 13, 1990, the government had convicted two Vernon executives at trial and made plea agreements with five others and two associates. Until the trial of Dixon, the main catch for the task force had been Woody Lemons, the former chairman of Vernon Savings, who was sentenced to thirty years for fraud related to his personal use of thrift loans made to a third party.

Dixon was charged with thirty-eight counts of conspiracy and bank fraud for allegedly bankrolling his flamboyant lifestyle with

Vernon Savings and Loan's funds. The money, prosecutors said, paid for political contributions, rent for his home in California, and the hiring of prostitutes to entertain politicians and thrift regulators at parties. The indictment was also noteworthy for what it omitted. The government made no attempt in its formal allegations to blame Dixon for Vernon's failure or in any way to explain the claimed taxpayer losses of $1.3 billion. Dixon's lawyer, William Ravkind, made clear this point would be central in Dixon's upcoming trial. "They can't find that there is any money missing. I hope to make the jury mad because [prosecutors] didn't find out what brought down the institution." Dixon echoed the same theme when he told reporters at a court appearance that he was a scapegoat for failed regulatory policies:

> So far the government has been successful in hiding behind the so-called crooks. We are the easy target. All the stories you've heard about the millions of dollars the savings and loan crooks took—it's totally dead wrong. The true villains are the politicians, the regulators. The whole system of deregulation was improperly handled.

Prosecutors, on the other hand, were mainly concerned with making what little they had on Dixon stick, so that there would be someone to blame. As one prominent criminal lawyer in Dallas told *American Lawyer*: "They can't prove what they really think these guys did, so they are putting a bunch of minor things in an indictment that they can prove, and they're counting on the judge to sentence according to what else is out there."

The trial began at the end of October 1991 and was presided over by United States District Judge A. Joe Fish. Witnesses testified that Dixon convinced Jack Atkinson, a Vernon borrower and real estate developer, to pay the rent on his California home with advances on construction loans. Karen Wilkening of San Diego, known as the "Rolodex Madam," testified that some of her high-priced call girls were hired to work Vernon parties at a cost of more than $15,000. Other witnesses testified that Dixon encouraged Vernon employees to make political contributions and seek reimbursement from the thrift for expenses.

The defense made a halfhearted attempt to blunt some of the more lurid testimony about hookers and orgies, with Dixon himself taking the stand to testify that he hired women as hostesses, not prostitutes. "I knew they were hired from an escort service," Dixon testified, "but I had no idea what services they would perform."

Dixon also admitted to hiring topless dancers from the Million Dollar Saloon in Dallas but claimed the purpose was only to provide entertainment at a meeting of Vernon's board of directors. But the defense's principal focus was to put Dixon's extravagant expenditures in context. Dixon, the defense claimed, was simply doing everything he could to save a savings and loan threatened by the sudden downturn in the Texas economy. Dixon used the California house that he had Vernon purchase and furnish to cultivate potential real estate developer clients. Similarly, the use of "hostesses" from escort services and the campaign contributions were just attempts to garner as much support as possible from powerful people who could help in difficult economic times. Even the seemingly impossible-to-justify "Gastronomique Fantastique," the Dixon's two-week eating extravaganza in France, was really field research on potential exclusive restaurant investments. Dixon, the defense tried to convince the jury, was an uncouth and unsavory individual who used poor judgment, but everything he did was to save Vernon Savings.

Dixon was convicted of twenty-three of the thirty-eight charges, including those related to the leasing of the house and three charges of using Vernon funds to hire prostitutes. He was acquitted, however, of allegations that he used thrift money to reimburse employees for political contributions. Nonetheless, Dixon faced up to 120 years in jail and a $5.7 million fine.

In a cover story interview with *USA Today* prior to his sentencing, Dixon continued to maintain his innocence. "You can certainly fault my judgment and activities from a moral and ethical point of view. A lot of my activities, actions, and decisions, in hindsight, were very inappropriate. But I don't feel I'm guilty of any crimes."

But the government saw things differently. "Don Dixon was the highest of the high fliers among the savings and loan crooks," declared United States attorney general Richard Thornburgh. "His excessive life-style and illegal management practices stood as a symbol of the wrongdoing of our national thrift industry." Some in the press resisted this transparent scapegoating. In a scathing article following Dixon's conviction but prior to sentencing, the *New York Times* concluded that "[r]ather than bring charges against Mr. Dixon for the ruinous loans that helped topple Vernon, the prosecutors tackled the sorts of crime that juries find easier to comprehend." Still, the *Times* predicted that Dixon "is expected to be dealt the lengthiest jail sentence of any savings defendant." The *Times* turned out to be completely wrong, precisely because the government could not attack Vernon's risky loan policies without putting its own behavior on trial.

On April 2, 1991, to the shock of government prosecutors and the press, Judge Fish sentenced Dixon to five years in prison and a $611,000 fine. In explaining his sentence, Judge Fish emphasized the need to protect Dixon from the prevailing "lynch mob mentality" and expressed disbelief that after a lengthy examination of Vernon Savings the government had only managed to indict Dixon on limited fraud charges:

> There was no showing by the evidence at trial that criminal conduct by Mr. Dixon and the relatively small dollar amounts involved there caused the failure of Vernon with whatever ultimate loss to these government agencies or taxpayers. Those are apples and oranges as far as I am concerned, and so I do not think that it is fair to say that we should attribute the reported cost of the failure of Vernon, whatever the $1 billion-plus sum is, to any criminal conduct by Mr. Dixon.

Judge Fish also read from a letter he received urging a light sentence from someone concerned about the government's responsibility for the thrift crisis. "I think politically Washington would like to see an example made of the top man in the failed S&L's. It might take some of the spotlight off the job or lack of job that the regulators were doing or the timing of some of the bills that Congress passed that really facilitated this whole S&L fiasco."

Some of the harshest reactions to Dixon's sentence came, not surprisingly, from current and former regulators. Edwin Gray, the former head of the Federal Home Loan Bank Board, criticized the sentence as too lenient, saying, "If not Don Dixon, then who? And why not Don Dixon?" And Timothy Ryan, the Office of Thrift Supervision director, opined, "It is a small price to pay given the damage Mr. Dixon did to the thrift industry. Substantial sentences are required to provide punishment commensurate with the losses to taxpayers and to deter similar conduct in the future."

Most major newspapers were no more sympathetic. An editorial in the *Miami Herald* concluded that "poetic justice it wasn't" and focused on Dixon's lavish expenditures. The *Washington Post* concluded that "[t]he fact that Mr. Dixon's sentence was such a small fraction of the penalty that might have been given, and that it varies so widely from that meted out to others convicted of similar crimes, is an illustration of the injustice of sentence disparity that recent reforms seek to address . . . one judge's leniency should not discourage the government from proceeding against every last one of the savings and loan crooks and seeking the stiff penalties they deserve." The press much preferred the thirty-year sentence meted out to Woody Lemons, Vernon's former chairman, a longer sentence than that given to most murderers, for allegedly diverting $200,000 from a $3.5 million loan for his personal use.

It was left to the *Wall Street Journal* to provide some perspective on the case. Based on Judge Fish's calculations, the paper argued that a mere .05 percent of Vernon's collapse had been attributed to Dixon. "The Don Dixon case proves it's possible to be both sinner and scapegoat. Yes, he broke laws, but his guilt cannot explain the collapse of the thrift. The 99.95% explanation of the Vernon collapse instead was Mr. Dixon's perfectly legal activity of perfectly outrageous high-risk lending." The *Wall Street Journal* concluded that "[o]ne problem with yelling 'fraud' is that politicians get off the hook. . . . The Dixon case shows that no amount of criminal prosecutions can protect us from what is legal."

In February 1992, a new eight-count indictment was levied against Dixon, accusing him of conspiracy, bank fraud, misapplication of funds, and false bookkeeping entries for the purchase of two corporate jets. Dixon pled guilty to the charges and received a second five-year sentence, which U.S. district judge Robert Maloney directed would begin after Dixon became eligible for parole on the first conviction. In December 1993, however, Judge Fish reduced the original sentence, ruling that it had ended at the time of the second indictment. Although Judge Fish did not decide on the issue, he noted that questions had been raised about the possibility that the second indictment was obtained because of prosecutors' outrage over the original sentence. Finally, in July 1994, due to Dixon's ill health and his cooperation with prosecutors on other cases, Judge Maloney reduced Dixon's sentence to make him eligible for parole.

Neil Bush

Neil and Sharon Bush arrived in Denver in 1980, soon after the city had become a hub for energy companies scrambling to

expand drilling in the Rockies. The real estate market was booming, and young professionals, attracted by job opportunities,
flocked to Denver. Neil Bush spent his first three years in the city
pursuing oil and natural-gas leases for Amoco Production
Company, while his wife taught in the public school system. The
Bushes quickly became integrated into Denver society. Sharon
volunteered to help at Children's Hospital, Denver's most chic
charity, and sold cookies through Cookie Express, a minibusiness
she started with the daughter of Denver oil tycoon Marvin Davis.
For his part, Neil played squash at the Denver Club and became a
fixture at local Republican dinners where he was in demand
because his father, George Bush, in 1980 had been elected vice-
president of the United States.

In 1983, Bush founded JNB Exploration with partners James
Judd and Evans Nash. The new company, which was dedicated to
oil exploration in Wyoming's Powder River Basin, received financial backing from two individuals who would later be involved in
Bush's troubles with savings and loan regulators, Bill L. Walters
and Kenneth Good. In 1984 Good lent Bush $100,000 to invest in
a high-risk commodities pool. Good agreed that the loan would
not have to be paid back if the investment was unsuccessful. Bush
lost the money and Good forgave the loan. Bush later acknowledged that the deal was "fishy," although Good argued that it was
a regular practice of his for favored business associates. Bush did
not declare the loan as income until 1990, following an investigation into his dealings with Walters and Good.

Silverado Savings & Loan, like many of the high-flying thrifts of
the 1980s, arose from humble origins. Established in 1956 by a
Denver builder, Franklin Burns, Silverado was originally called
Mile High Savings and Loan and was based in Littleton, Colorado.
When the small thrift ran into trouble during the inflationary climate of the mid-1970s, it was taken over by Denver businessman
James Metz. In 1979, Metz hired Michael Wise, the former director of Columbia Savings in Emporia, Kansas, to run Mile High.
Wise, who was anxious to transform Mile High's conservative
image, moved the thrift to Denver in 1980, renamed it Silverado,
and later absorbed two smaller thrifts.

Denver's energy boom provided Wise with plenty of opportunities for big returns on risky projects. Silverado quickly abandoned
its former status as a small home-mortgage lender and became
instead a major investment firm with ambitious real estate and

commercial building ventures. To finance these ventures, Wise aggressively advertised high interest rates, which brought in brokered deposits from around the country. Between 1980 and 1987, Silverado's assets grew from less than $100 million to $2.4 billion. Silverado's growth was paralleled by Wise's rise in the regulatory ranks. Wise served two terms on the board of the Federal Home Loan Bank of Topeka, which regulated thrifts in the region, and also became chairman of the regulatory policy committee of the U.S. League of Savings and Loan Institutions.

Wise, who knew of Neil Bush's close ties to Walters and Good, met Bush at a party in the summer of 1985. Silverado had underwritten Good's financial ventures with more than $35 million in loans. Wise was also involved in a number of deals with Walters, who was a major stockholder in Silverado. Soon after the party, Wise offered Bush a seat on the S&L's board of directors. Bush accepted the position, even though he knew nothing about banking and had no relevant experience other than his family name and his connections to Walters and Good. In a 1990 *Time* interview, Bush conceded, "I would be naive if I were to sit here and deny that the Bush name didn't have something to do with it. . . . Maybe the advantage of being part of the Vice President's family at the time was that I was accepted more quickly in terms of age and years in this community than others of my peer group."

By the time Bush joined Silverado, the Denver economy had begun to go bust in response to collapsing crude-oil prices. Bankruptcies and office-space vacancies rose dramatically. Real estate values plummeted, just as they did in Arizona and Texas. Silverado, which had a portfolio of high-risk real estate and energy investments, was now in trouble, but the regulators did nothing.

As early as 1982, Silverado received consistently poor reviews from middle-level bank examiners at the Home Loan Bank Board in Topeka. An October 1982 evaluation noted "significant underwriting deficiencies" and "weak appraisals . . . Silverado appeared to acquire appropriate loan documentation after loans had been originated." By 1985, when Bush joined the board, the examiners were severely alarmed. A November evaluation assigned Silverado a rating of 4 on a scale of 1 to 5, 5 being the worst: "Appraisal deficiencies continue. Concentration of high-risk loans equal to 66 percent of total assets. Substandard assets equal 22 percent of assets."

Regulators did not take any action, however, because the government encouraged thrifts on the brink of insolvency to embark on a strategy of rapid growth just as Silverado had done. David Paul (no relation to CenTrust's CEO), Colorado's chief thrift regulator, justified regulatory inaction on the following basis: "Frankly, we were at the time more worried about their conservative brethren who were resistant to change. Silverado certainly had its problems. However, Silverado management had an answer for every question." Before all the revisionist history began, in other words, the regulators were more concerned with traditional thrifts that refused to alter their business practices than with aggressive thrifts like Silverado. The government got exactly what it wanted.

Silverado's growth strategy failed, however, when the Colorado economy continued to worsen. Still the regulators took no action. Michael Wise, with his position on the board of the Federal Home Loan Bank in Topeka, enjoyed a close relationship with Kermit Mowbray, president of the board and chief regulator for the region. Mowbray's continued support of Silverado allowed the thrift to stave off closure while losses mounted. In March 1987, Mowbray even rejected a request from thrift auditors that Silverado be slapped with a mild order to "cease and desist" all "unsafe and unsound" practices. Mowbray's position, consistent with the government's policy of forbearance toward troubled thrifts, was that Colorado's adverse economic conditions were "short-term" and that the "Federal Home Loan Bank is not going to appraise institutions out of existence."

Mowbray, like the thrift regulators in Texas, was hoping for an economic turnaround, but none occurred. Eventually, in August 1988 the regulators gave Silverado an ultimatum to raise additional capital or be taken over. Neil Bush then resigned from the Silverado board, citing concerns about his father's presidential candidacy and a desire to avoid any appearance of affecting the regulatory process. On November 9, 1988, one day after George Bush was elected president of the United States, Mowbray formally recommended that Silverado be placed in receivership.

Silverado's demise triggered the usual flurry of lawsuits. The Federal Deposit Insurance Corporation sued Neil Bush and eleven other Silverado officials for "gross negligence" in running the thrift. The Office of Thrift Supervision also sued Bush for engaging in various alleged conflict-of-interest transactions with

Walters and Good while a director of Silverado. The House Banking Committee also held hearings on Silverado, which focused in significant part on Neil Bush.

The most damaging allegation against Bush focused on his receipt of the $100,000 interest-free "loan" from Good for commodities speculation that Bush had no obligation to repay because he lost the money. Bush never disclosed the existence of this payment from Good even when the Silverado board took action, at Bush's suggestion, in which Bush and Good had a financial interest. For example, Bush wrote a letter to Michael Wise on November 5, 1986, urging Silverado to issue a $900,000 line of credit to one of Good's companies, Good International, which was trying to enter the oil and gas business in Argentina. Bush did not disclose that Good International had been created for the express purpose of funding exploration efforts in Argentina by JNB, Bush's company, in addition to failing to mention the earlier payment received from Good. Bush also failed to disclose his increasing ties to Good, including Good's willingness to inject substantial capital into JNB to keep it from failing, when the Silverado board voted to restructure Good's outstanding obligations to the thrift. Similarly, Bush as a Silverado director voted to approve over $100 million in loans to Walters even though Walters was an investor in JNB and Bush had received a $1.75 million loan from a bank that Walters controlled.

Bush denied these conflict-of-interest allegations vigorously in the House hearings and the OTS proceeding. His receipt of the $100,000 interest-free loan from Good didn't have to be disclosed, Bush insisted, because he received it in 1984 before becoming a Silverado director in 1985. Silverado's transactions with Good also created no conflict of interest for himself, Bush said, because he abstained from all board votes involving Good. Bush acknowledged in the House hearings, however, that his receipt of the $100,000 loan from Good, which he never repaid and never disclosed, "sounds a little fishy":

MR. NEAL OF NORTH CAROLINA: May I ask you to do this also, because there is one other allegation that is presented here that maybe you could respond to, and that is that Mr. Good, who has been mentioned here earlier, loaned you $100,000 which you have not repaid, and that you approved loans to Mr. Good.

MR. BUSH: The loan was forgiven. You have to understand Mr. Good. This was in 1984, and Mr. Good was doing very well. He was worth tens of millions of dollars, and he enjoyed having people that he worked with participate in ventures with him, so what he did was loan me $100,000 which he maintained 100 percent control over, full discretion over, invested in a very high-risk pool, a commodities deal, I believe, and he meant to have that loan repaid out of the success of his investment.

I know it sounds a little fishy, but I have heard this happened before, the loan was never meant to be repaid in the case there was no success. There was no success, so the loan was forgiven.

I also never voted on any Ken Good transaction, so I am not sure where you are leading with that.

MR. NEAL OF NORTH CAROLINA: When was the loan forgiven?

MR. BUSH: It was cancelled in 1990, but it was never intended to be paid back except only from the success of the investment. So, as a practical matter, it was forgiven the day the investment was unsuccessful.

MR. NEAL OF NORTH CAROLINA: There is a question about disclosures. Was it disclosed?

MR. BUSH: The forgiveness was disclosed in 1990, sure. It is disclosed in the . . .

MR. NEAL OF NORTH CAROLINA: Was the loan disclosed originally?

MR. BUSH: To the board. No, I am not sure that it was. I don't think it was.

Bush also defended his dealings with Walters. In Bush's view, he had no obligation to abstain from voting on Walters's deals since Walters was only a "passive investor in JNB." Besides, Bush stressed, the Silverado board knew all about Walters and Good and his dealings with them. That's why, after all, he was asked to be a Silverado director in the first place.

Predictably, others had a different view. House Democrats led by Representative Patricia Schroeder demanded that Attorney General Thornburgh appoint a special prosecutor to investigate possible criminal wrongdoing by Bush, a request Thornburgh refused. Then in December 1990, the administrative-law judge hearing the OTS suit issued a lengthy opinion finding that Bush's justifications for his actions while a Silverado director revealed "either an unwillingness or an inability to understand the underlying purposes of conflict of interest policy." The judge recommended that the OTS issue a cease and desist order against Bush, which OTS director Tim Ryan approved and entered in April 1991.

Bush's lawyer, James Nesland, denounced the OTS ruling as "ridiculous" and vowed to appeal. But the plan changed when on May 30, 1991, Bush and the other defendants in the FDIC civil suit settled for $49.5 million, with Bush reportedly paying a relatively nominal $50,000. Following the settlement, Nesland announced that Bush no longer intended to appeal the government's cease and desist order: "At some point in time you have to just put this behind you. The agencies have enormous staying power compared with a private person. You can't just spend the better part of your life jousting with the government over a matter of principle."

Bush himself, however, continued to protest his innocence, claiming that Silverado was the victim of an economic downturn. "When real estate values go from X to one-third X, the success of the institution is impaired. Not for any wrongdoing, not because the board of directors didn't act properly, but because of circumstances." Bush was partially right. Silverado's failure was unquestionably caused by adverse developments in the Colorado economy, and the regulatory policy of forbearance exacerbated the problem. And, even though Bush's disclosure and voting practices fell far short of what the law requires when a director is financially interested in a transaction, there was no evidence that what he did made any difference. Wise and the other Silverado directors wanted to do business with Walters and Good because they were prominent real estate developers and entrepreneurs. No Silverado director ever said the board was fooled by what Bush did into approving a transaction that otherwise would have been rejected.

But the $100,000 interest-free loan Bush received from Good to speculate in commodities, which Bush never repaid and didn't declare as income until six years later when the government was actively investigating his affairs, is much harder to defend. The payment has the appearance of a bribe paid to the politically well-connected Bush that Bush failed to report for income-tax purposes. Considering the lynch-mob atmosphere of the times, Bush should consider himself lucky he wasn't indicted and prosecuted for tax fraud. What Bush did in not reporting the payment was, after all, real tax fraud unlike, for example, the phony "aiding and abetting a false tax return" felony count that Michael Milken pled guilty to. But Bush had the right family name, and Attorney General Thornburgh, who was so quick to condemn Milken, Dixon, and others, made sure no criminal charges were brought against him.

Bush's claim that he and the other Silverado directors were just scapegoats was also more than a little ironic. The Bush administration, beginning with the passage of the FIRREA in August 1989, engaged in unprecedented scapegoating and finger-pointing for the savings and loan crisis. The government's bogus suits with Bush administration approval against Milken and various professionals blaming them for the thrift crisis were in the same mode. Maybe some of the allegations against Neil Bush were unfounded, but it seems only fair that the Bush family get a dose of its own medicine, particularly since Neil Bush was more deserving of blame than many other victims of the government's witch-hunt.

David Paul

David Paul's purchase of Miami's Dade Savings & Loan Association, a deeply insolvent traditional thrift with a negative net worth of over $500 million, was mired in controversy from the beginning. Paul first borrowed $12 million in 1981 to buy control of Westport Corporation, an ailing real estate investment trust. In October 1982, Paul then applied to acquire Dade, which was losing $4 million a month, in exchange for Westport stock that Paul claimed was worth $25.7 million.

As desperate as the regulators were to unload Dade and avoid recognizing the $500 million loss, they almost rejected Paul's application because he was offering so little. As it was, regulators took more than a year to examine the offer, questioning the market value of some of Westport's real estate assets and the health of a Chicago condominium project. To allay regulators' concerns, Paul pledged the assets of the newly formed David Paul Properties, claimed to be worth an additional $7.2 million. Paul's application to acquire Dade was then approved, with the deal closing in late 1983. Less than a month later, Westport revised its prior financial statements to boost the loss on the Chicago condo project from $600,000 to $4.6 million. But the deal was done, and Paul now owned Dade, now renamed to CenTrust, no matter what Westport and David Paul Properties were really worth.

Paul and the regulators, as was standard practice at the time, agreed to use accounting gimmickry to disguise CenTrust's negative $526 million net worth. The $526 million was to be treated as an asset, regulatory "goodwill," for accounting purposes and had to be amortized over twenty-five years. CenTrust was still $526 million in the hole, of course, but the accounting gimmickry gave Paul time to turn the institution around. The rational course for anyone in Paul's position, the course encouraged by the government's regulatory policies, was to adopt a high-risk, rapid-growth investment strategy. If the strategy was successful, Paul, as CenTrust's largest shareholder, would be the biggest winner. And if the strategy flopped, taxpayers would be the losers.

Paul began implementing CenTrust's new aggressive business strategy immediately after gaining control. Dade's management had previously approved the construction of a multimillion-dollar office building in downtown Miami. Paul decided to go ahead with construction, expanding plans for the luxurious interior design of the building and raising the cost to more than $140 million. The CenTrust Tower was opened in December 1985 and became one of the country's most recognized buildings when it was featured in the opening montage of the highly rated television series "Miami Vice."

Paul also decided to invest heavily in high-yield bonds and mortgage-backed securities, financing these investments with brokered deposits and numerous public securities sales. He brought in a skilled professional staff to manage CenTrust's investments, installed the most advanced computer systems, and assembled a blue-chip board of directors. Paul bragged that CenTrust was the most sophisticated risk-management institution in the country, and the early results seemed to prove the point. CenTrust's assets grew from less than $2 billion to close to $10 billion, with more than $1 billion invested in high-yield bonds. Its reported net income was among the highest in the country for any thrift, and its investment performance was spectacular. CenTrust's early success seemed to completely vindicate the regulators' controversial earlier decision to allow Paul to acquire and operate a deeply insolvent thrift while putting up so little in return.

But there was another side to the story. From the beginning, Paul was responsible for an extravagant waste of CenTrust's assets that made Don Dixon look like a cheapskate by comparison. At Paul's direction, for example, CenTrust paid $29 million for Old Masters paintings. One painting alone cost $13.2 million, and it hung in David Paul's personal residence until the regulators complained and it was moved for the first time to the CenTrust Tower. CenTrust also paid $1.5 million to redecorate the corporate jet, $280,000 for Oriental rugs, $119,000 for rare books, and $300,000 for china, crystal, silver, and linen. Paul's office and conference room had gold ceilings, and even his private bathroom sinks and plumbing pipes were gold-plated.

Paul also entertained lavishly at CenTrust's expense. On one notorious occasion, CenTrust paid $122,000 for a great chef's dinner at Paul's home, where six famous European chefs were flown in to cook delicacies for Paul and his guests, who included celebrities and politicians. Paul even directed CenTrust to pay almost $500,000 for a security system and guards for his home and more than $100,000 for fresh flowers, much of which also went to his home.

Obviously, these extravagant expenditures offended regulators who also challenged Paul's investment practices, particularly CenTrust's heavy concentration in high-yield bonds. Intense acrimony developed between Paul and the regional FHLBB in Atlanta, but the Washington regulators were more influenced by CenTrust's reported profitability, just as they were in the analogous situation with Lincoln Savings. The FHLBB was reluctant to take any drastic steps against Paul because CenTrust, like Lincoln, appeared to be among the nation's most profitable thrifts and Paul, for all his wasteful spending, was the man responsible.

But the regulators' approach changed when CenTrust began losing money in late 1988. When Milken was indicted in early 1989 and the FIRREA became law that summer, CenTrust's demise was all but assured. Paul attempted to forestall the inevitable by agreeing to scale down CenTrust's high-yield bond portfolio, cut the amount of brokered deposits, and sell most of the institution's branches to Great Western Bank, a huge California thrift. He even acquiesced in state regulators' demand that CenTrust sell its collection of Old Masters paintings even though a substantial loss was expected.

But it was too little too late. In December 1989, the Office of Thrift Supervision issued a cease and desist order against CenTrust to "curb a serious dissipation of assets." Less than two weeks later, state regulators began efforts to oust Paul, alleging that his extravagant spending had squandered $45 million in federally insured funds. By January 1990, Paul's use of CenTrust funds for personal consumption was being investigated by multiple government agencies. Paul responded to the investigations by denying that he did anything illegal. "I don't think I misappropriated any funds for personal use. I'm not sure everything done here is perfect, but there's a big difference between an error in judgment and doing something illegal." And then Paul made the worst prediction he would ever make: "I don't expect any criminal charges."

On February 2, 1990, the federal government seized CenTrust and Paul was removed as chairman. The CenTrust Tower was soon patriotically bathed in red, white, and blue lights to signify the government's new ownership. In June 1990, Great Western's purchase of CenTrust's branch offices and accompanying assets was finally approved.

Prior to his ouster, Paul was a well-known civic leader in Miami and CenTrust was a major contributor to the arts, local charities, and politicians. In November 1988, Paul was elected to membership in the Non-Group, Miami's unofficial leadership council. After CenTrust's collapse, one Non-Group member admitted: "In hindsight, it was a misjudgment, but David Paul is a spectacular guy. He's a super salesman, a gambler. And Miami is a place where people are awed by money as a status symbol of achievement." The *Miami Herald,* in a front-page article on Paul's rise and fall, offered a harsher assessment:

> Paul's official CenTrust biography said he had a Ph.D. from Harvard and an MBA from Columbia University. He did not. He said the Citicorp and American Express buildings in New York were among "his most successful real estate projects." They were not. He had told the *Herald* that his mother was Catholic. She was Jewish.

Paul, in short, was a liar, a con man who had spent lavishly on himself and defrauded taxpayers in the process.

The press also began exploring CenTrust's connections to Drexel Burnham and BCCI, whose spectacular collapse led to the criminal indictments of Robert Altman and Washington legend Clark Clifford. Drexel was CenTrust's investment banker, raising $150 million for CenTrust by selling high-yield bonds. At the same time, Drexel as bond broker sold CenTrust $1 billion worth of high-yield bonds from other issuers. Finally, Drexel also borrowed $15 million from CenTrust in an unsecured loan. The *New York Times,* commenting on Drexel's multiple roles as capital raiser, bond broker, and borrower, editorialized that CenTrust was an integral part of the "web of transactions" with Drexel that resulted in S&L's being used as a dumping ground for overpriced junk bonds. Other stories focused on stock transactions between Drexel, CenTrust, and Lincoln Savings, speculating that Drexel offered Paul inside deals as an inducement to buy its worthless junk bonds. The press never considered that these "worthless junk bonds" performed quite well until the government wrecked the high-yield bond market.

CenTrust's dealings with BCCI also involved Drexel. Ghaith Pharaon, an Arab businessman who acted as a front for BCCI's holdings in American banks, owned a large block of CenTrust stock. After BCCI's collapse, the government charged that Pharaon persuaded top aides to then-FHLBB chairman M. Danny Wall to approve the $150 million CenTrust bond issue underwritten by Drexel. The offering infused capital into CenTrust to meet regulatory capital requirements and therefore protected the value of Pharaon's investment. Paul and Pharaon, the government claimed, entered into a stock-parking agreement to stimulate interest in the offering under which Pharaon would buy $25 million of the bonds and then resell them to CenTrust with a guarantee against loss.

On October 22, 1990, the OTS filed suit against Paul seeking to recover $30.8 million for fraudulent expenditures for his personal benefit consisting of a $15 million legal defense fund, a $4.9 million pension fund, $4 million in losses on the sale of the Old Masters paintings, $35,000 for the twenty-four-karat gold-leaf ceilings for Paul's private office and conference room, and many other alleged abuses. Using the same asset-freeze power it used against Kaye, Scholer, the OTS also secured a temporary restraining order prohibiting Paul from transferring or spending more than $5,000 of his personal assets without specific approval. Paul was also forced to turn over the $15 million legal defense fund to the government, reducing the disputed amount to $15.8 million.

By February 1991, Paul was being sued by numerous regulatory agencies. The government also sought to put Paul in jail in February for contempt after he violated the temporary restraining order by transferring $200,000 to Israel to invest in a housing project. In August 1991, the OTS proposed that a $3,172,500 civil penalty be levied against Paul for violations of the temporary restraining order. At a hearing on the proposed penalty before an administrative law judge, Paul stormed out after denouncing the proceeding. Appearing without a lawyer, which he claimed he couldn't afford, Paul told the judge that "if this unauthorized exercise in power is allowed to continue as it has, with even the so-called administrative law judges not willing to hold the advocates which practice before you in check, this country risks self-destruction." Outside court, Paul told reporters: "This is outrageous. This is a charade. This is a media event. That's what it is. Why should I give it credibility." The judge, unimpressed, recommended that Paul pay a fine of $2.2 million for violating the temporary restraining order.

On February 28, 1992, Paul was indicted on twenty-two counts of securities fraud arising from his alleged stock-parking agreement with Ghaith Pharaon involving the $25 million of CenTrust debt securities, secret stock transactions with American Continental Corporation in two securities at escalating prices using Drexel as the intermediary, and CenTrust's fraudulent credit reviews of its high-yield bonds. At the time of the indictment, Paul was already in jail for contempt after refusing to turn over documents to the grand jury. Even though Paul soon agreed to release the documents after he lost his appeal on the contempt ruling, he still couldn't get out of jail. Bail had been set at $750,000 after the indictment, and the OTS restraining order prohibited Paul from making any asset transfers.

Eventually, bail was restructured and Paul was indicted again. The new one-hundred-count indictment incorporated the old charges and also accused Paul of using $3.2 million of CenTrust funds for his personal use, most of it for renovations of his personal island estate, and of not paying taxes on the amounts received. The new indictment also charged Paul with obstruction of justice and perjury for instructing an interior decorator at this home to tell banking regulators she did no work for Paul personally and telling federal regulators he had no assets overseas after transferring the $200,000 to Israel. Judge Donald Graham decided to hold two trials on the indictment, the first on the bank fraud and related charges and a second on the securities fraud counts.

The bank-fraud trial began in October 1993 with Paul being represented by Stephen Neal, the same lawyer who defended Keating. The government never tried to prove in the trial that the $3.2 million of CenTrust funds that Paul was accused to have taken for personal use was in any way responsible for causing CenTrust's failure, only that he was a crook. "This trial is about theft. It's about deception. It's about the abuse of trust," assistant U.S. attorney Allan Sullivan told the jury in his opening statement, then proceeded to show them color photographs of Paul's $7 million yacht, the "Grand Chu," and a diagram of his $9 million island estate that was renovated with CenTrust funds. Conceding that some invoices for work done on Paul's property may have "slipped through the cracks" and been paid out of CenTrust funds, Neal argued that Paul did not knowingly defraud the bank.

The government, however, had an avalanche of evidence to back up its accusations. The bulk of the testimony came from contractors who worked on Paul's house and former CenTrust officers who described how Paul schemed to disguise his personal expenditures as CenTrust expenses by padding bills for work performed on the CenTrust Tower. The former mayor of Miami Beach, Alex Daoud, who had earlier pled guilty to accepting bribes, also testified how he accepted a $35,000 bribe from Paul, paid for by CenTrust, to get approval for a second boat dock at Paul's home. Even Paul's former lawyer testified, explaining how Paul attempted to circumvent the OTS's restraining order by transferring the $200,000 to Israel.

Paul testified in his own defense. Choking back tears, he described how he relied on his employees to tell him what expenses to reimburse the bank. "I presumed I was being billed for them," he said of his personal expenses. "And I paid for them." The $35,000 payment to Daoud was just a contribution in the ordinary course because Daoud was doing such a "good job" and helping CenTrust raise deposits. And as for the $200,000 sent to Israel, Paul testified that he had been told the OTS asset freeze was unconstitutional and that he had "forgotten" about the transfer when questioned by the government.

Prosecutors on cross-examination pointed out the many inconsistencies in Paul's testimony and highlighted his lifetime pattern of lying about his background and credentials. After only a few hours of deliberations, the jury convicted Paul on sixty-eight felony counts.

In February 1994, Paul decided to avoid a second trial on the securities-related offenses, and the possibility of being sentenced as a multiple offender if he were convicted again, by pleading guilty to twenty-nine counts of fraud and racketeering. But Paul was still unrepentant. "I'd like to get the whole story out someday," Paul said. "It's just a nightmare that the government can do this to someone." In late November 1994, Judge Graham sentenced Paul to serve eleven years in prison.

The remaining question is whether Paul is a petty crook who, like Leona Helmsley, misused his position over relatively trivial sums given his wealth, or whether he was responsible for CenTrust's failure, which, the government claims, cost taxpayers close to $2 billion, the second costliest failure after Lincoln. The government has avoided answering this question directly, blaming Paul in public statements for the claimed $2 billion loss while trying him for misappropriating $3.2 million. Who was responsible for the rest of the claimed losses?

At Paul's sentencing hearing, the prosecutors tried to blame him for a big chunk of the loss, arguing that he was responsible for the government's claimed $400 million loss when it liquidated CenTrust's high-yield bond portfolio. But the defense effectively countered that the government itself was responsible for this loss by selling at the bottom of the market after driving Drexel and Milken out of business and enacting the FIRREA. Ultimately, Judge Graham concluded that Paul could not be held responsible for any losses attributable to the high-yield bond portfolio.

The government, not David Paul, destroyed CenTrust. If the government hadn't wrecked the high-yield bond market, CenTrust would be alive and well today with its bond portfolio the envy of the financial world. David Paul should still have been ousted, prosecuted, and convicted for embezzling money. But his ouster in this hypothetical world wouldn't have doomed the institution. He would simply have been replaced by someone else. Unfortunately, Paul's conviction and the surrounding hysteria about S&L crooks have obscured responsibility for who was really responsible for destroying CenTrust and creating the S&L crisis in the first place.

Thomas Spiegel

Columbia Savings & Loan, like CenTrust, was ruined by the government's misguided attack on the high-yield bond market. But this didn't stop the government from indicting and prosecuting

Tom Spiegel, Columbia's CEO, whose generous compensation ($9 million in 1985), aggressive purchases of high-yield bonds, and close ties to Michael Milken had long made him anathema to regulators. The government's strategy in going after Spiegel was the same as with Dixon and Paul—blame Spiegel for Columbia's failure and the resulting claimed cost to taxpayers of $1.2 billion while formally accusing him of personal excesses involving relatively trivial sums that bore no relationship to the causes of failure or the costs involved.

Spiegel had a long track record of success in investments. During his first year of law school at Loyola University in Los Angeles, he made so much money in the stock market—about $100,000—that he dropped out to become a stockbroker. Spiegel then worked for various investment firms in New York (including Drexel) for several years before venturing into real estate in the midseventies, marketing condominiums in Iran for Starrett Corporation. He became involved in Columbia after his father, a prominent real estate developer in the San Fernando Valley, purchased a stake in the thrift and became its chairman. Spiegel took over as president and CEO of Columbia in 1977, and the Spiegel family eventually controlled 60 percent of Columbia's voting stock.

As a state-chartered thrift, Columbia took full advantage of the deregulation of the industry by the California legislature in 1982. Spiegel became one of the first proponents of using high-yield bonds and brokered deposits to accelerate the growth and profits of a thrift. From 1981 to 1987, Columbia's assets grew from $373 million to $9.6 billion. About 65 percent of Columbia's deposits were in the form of brokered deposits. In 1980, Spiegel met Michael Milken at a dinner party, and six months later Columbia bought its first high-yield bond. By 1987, one-third of Columbia's assets were in high-yield bonds, and Drexel owned a 5 percent stake in the thrift.

The government began its assault on Spiegel in July 1990 with the now familiar tactic of an OTS suit and the accompanying asset freeze. To even hire a lawyer to defend himself, Spiegel, once the highest-paid thrift executive in the country, now needed government approval. Spiegel responded by throwing down the gauntlet: "The OTS and its predecessors have been abysmal failures, and now—in panic and purely for political reasons—OTS is seeking scapegoats to divert public attention away from its gross incompetence." Spiegel, again following the Paul pattern, was then sued by the FDIC and RTC and ultimately indicted on June 24, 1992. Spiegel's lawyers denounced the indictment, much as Spiegel himself had done in response to the OTS charges, and made clear they intended to put the government on trial for its role in destroying Columbia by creating havoc with the high-yield bond market:

> . . . in order to cover up the gross incompetence of the S&L regulators. Those regulators, vested with outrageous powers from a panicked Congress, itself seeking to divert public attention from its major role in the S&L fiasco and the temporary destruction of the high-yield bond market in 1989 and 1990, have hounded him daily, restricted his ability to conduct business and have even barred him from paying normal legal fees to defend himself.

The charges against Spiegel covered four categories: improperly causing Columbia to purchase a condominium known as Vintage Cottage in Palm Springs, California, by falsely stating it was needed for business use; defrauding Columbia by purchasing the Storer warrants from Milken through the MacPherson limited partnership without disclosing the purchase to Columbia; misapplying Columbia's funds by causing Columbia to purchase forty-seven guns and several thousand dollars of ammunition for his personal use; and knowingly accepting false financial statements from Howard Schneider to cause Columbia to make a $10 million loan to Gregg Motors, a luxury car dealer owned by Schneider, so that Spiegel could use the cars.

The trial began in October 1994. Prosecutors should have known this trial was going to be different when Judge Robert Takasugi ruled that they could not use the term "junk bonds" when describing Columbia's investments because of its negative implications and possible prejudicial impact on jurors. Prosecutors were also hurt when Judge Takasugi ruled that the defense could introduce evidence of Columbia's spectacular performance until the government's ill-advised crackdown on high-yield bonds. That's exactly what the defense did, telling the jurors in opening statements that the government was to blame for Columbia's collapse. And, the defense said, further setting the tone for the trial, the biggest victims of Columbia's demise were Tom Spiegel, whose stock declined in value by more than $140 million, and his family, including Abe Spiegel, his father and a Holocaust survivor, who lost $300 million.

The government's case went downhill from there. Two weeks into trial, the government got into trouble by failing to turn over required material to the defense, which cast doubt on the testimony of the key cooperating government witness in the Gregg Motors deal, Howard Schneider. As a result, the government was forced to dismiss the Gregg Motors charges from the case. The dismissal badly hurt the government's case because the Gregg Motors charges were viewed as the most serious and involved the largest amount of money lost. Then the government suffered another major setback when Judge Takasugi, after hearing the evidence, dismissed a second set of counts involving Spiegel's use of the Vintage Cottage condominium. Noting that Spiegel was a workaholic, the judge ruled that prosecutors failed to prove that Spiegel had not used the condominium "for business-related purposes 95% to 100% of the time" and that "it's rather curious that we did not have one witness testify that Mr. Spiegel even dipped his toe in the pool."

The trial did offer some unusual testimony about Spiegel's bizarre fascination with guns. Witness after witness described how Columbia, for Spiegel's benefit, bought dozens of weapons including hunting rifles, assault weapons, commemorative pistol sets, and handguns. But the defense argued that these purchases were attributable to Spiegel's paranoid concern about security and that all the purchases were openly disclosed in Columbia's books and records for everyone, including regulators, to observe. Spiegel may have been a nut whose concern about security went beyond what could be reasonably justified, in other words, but he made no attempt to mislead anyone. Spiegel's behavior was odd, but it was nothing like Paul telling contractors who worked on his house to disguise what they did by submitting inflated invoices for work on the CenTrust Tower. Judge Takasugi dismissed the gun charges as well before the case went to the jury.

The fraud charges concerning the Storer warrants also went nowhere. The government's theory, as it was in the Milken Fatico hearing and the Ostrander trial, was that the warrants were a bribe to individuals to induce them to purchase the unattractive Storer preferred on behalf of their institutions. This wasn't a very convincing claim in Spiegel's case, however, because Columbia made $78 million in profits by buying the Storer preferred that the government claimed nobody would buy. Moreover, when Spiegel was told by Ken Heitz, Columbia's general counsel, that he should have followed formal procedures when purchasing the warrants for his own account, Spiegel turned over the $7 million in profits he made on the transaction. Heitz testified that Spiegel did so reluctantly, but the fact remained that Spiegel gave up the money.

But the defense did more than respond to the government's allegations. As promised in opening statements, the defense also put the government on trial. Witnesses described how Tom Spiegel devoted his life to Columbia and built it up to be the most profitable thrift in the United States until the government targeted it for destruction. The defense even found a government memorandum discussing the "vendetta" against Tom Spiegel because he made so much money. During one memorable exchange, Ken Heitz, testifying for the government, described a letter he wrote blaming Columbia's demise on the Resolution Trust Corporation, one of the government agencies created by the FIRREA to administer failing thrifts. When Heitz was asked by the prosecutor John Walsh to explain the RTC for the jury, Heitz responded that it was "probably the worst government agency ever created." Prosecutor Walsh then agreed, no doubt trying to ingratiate himself with the jury: "The government would stipulate to that."

Brad Brian, Spiegel's defense lawyer, reminded the jury of this exchange and the government's admission of its vendetta against Spiegel during his impassioned closing argument. The RTC, Brian argued, not Spiegel, should have been on trial. "This agency put Columbia out of business. It cost a thousand people their jobs. It cost Tom Spiegel $144 million dollars. It cost the taxpayers a couple of billion dollars. It was one of the worst financial disasters of the 1990's." When Brian finished, the jury acquitted Spiegel on all counts after deliberating just a few hours.

Immediately after the verdict, the *Wall Street Journal* ran an editorial on December 14, 1994, applauding the verdict and speculating about what would have happened if Michael Milken, like Spiegel, had fought until the end:

> The purest court trial of the marathon case U.S. v. the 1980's ended in two hours Monday in a Los Angeles courtroom. The verdict: Thomas Spiegel, chief executive of defunct Columbia Savings and Loan, was found not guilty.
>
> Mr. Spiegel was a guy who made and spent millions from Michael Milken's junk bonds, which are widely supposed to have caused the downfall of his and other thrifts and cost the taxpayers billions. . . .

If there was a case that anybody stuck Columbia and conse-
quently the taxpayers in fraudulent securities, it was never made in
this federal court. . . .

What has to be wondered, again, is how Mike Milken himself
would have fared if he, the ultimate financial symbol of the '80s,
had fought his tormentors to the mat as Mr. Spiegel did. Instead,
the Drexel mastermind chose like most others caught up in this
prosecutorial whirlwind to settle in order to salvage part of his life
and wealth.

Spiegel's acquittal did prove that being wealthy and called
greedy by the government doesn't automatically guarantee a conviction. Many pundits had assumed the opposite when Milken
was indicted. And wouldn't Milken have been able to use the
same strategy of putting the government on trial for destroying
Drexel? Maybe, as the *Journal* suggested, Milken made the wrong
decision after all.

But ultimately, the two situations were very different. For one
thing, times had changed. The high-yield bond market had
rebounded by 1994, and the government's handling of the savings and loan crisis had begun to attract criticism. The level of the
government's commitment in securing a conviction or guilty plea
was also different. While prosecutors prosecuted Spiegel vigorously, it was not the same maniacal life-or-death struggle that
Milken encountered. For example, the government never
indicted Spiegel's elderly father, the chairman of the bank, to use
him as a bargaining chip in plea-bargain discussions as it did with
Milken's brother Lowell. Nor did prosecutors coerce other senior
Columbia officials to make deals and cooperate as they did with
Drexel officials.

Milken was the biggest fish, and convicting him was essential
for the government to justify its prosecutorial efforts and attack
against the "decade of greed." The government would do anything to win, and everyone knew it. The stakes were not nearly
so high with Spiegel, who was more of an afterthought, almost a
footnote. By convicting Milken, Keating, Paul, and so many others, the government could claim success regardless of what happened to Spiegel.

Spiegel also got lucky when his case got assigned to Judge
Takasugi, who, unlike Milton Pollack and so many of the other
judges, had no other agenda than giving the defendant a fair trial.
There is no assurance that Judge Wood, who sentenced Milken to

ten years even after the government's case was exposed to be a fraud in the Fatico hearing, would have done the same.

Finally, Spiegel's "victory" must be put in context. True, he is not a convicted felon like Milken, and he won't spend time in prison. These are benefits of incalculable value. But he has been stripped of most of his wealth, and his career is in a shambles. No one knows whether he will be able to pick up the pieces and start all over again. Also, Spiegel's legal problems aren't over. He still faces the OTS suit seeking $40 million in damages, and his assets are still frozen, even though he was acquitted. Whether Spiegel can avoid complete financial and professional ruin after his "victory" remains to be seen.

CHAPTER 10

More Victims: Fred Carr and Executive Life

The story of Fred Carr and Executive Life has striking similarities to and is inextricably linked with the story of Michael Milken. Like Milken, Carr had an unpretentious childhood in Los Angeles where his father, a Romanian immigrant, owned a grocery and liquor store. Born Seymour Fred Cohen, Carr changed his name before college to avoid anti-Semitism, just as the Milken family name had been changed from Milkewitz. And Carr, like Milken, was interested in finance, which he studied in college. Although Carr never finished college because he was drafted into the army, he, like Milken, decided to pursue an investment career.

Carr joined Bache & Company as a trainee. There he developed an interest in small companies that had the potential for growth, now known as "emerging growth" companies. By the age of thirty-five, Carr had made and saved enough money to purchase an ownership interest in Shareholders Management Company, a holding company that controlled a number of mutual funds. By the late 1960s, Carr himself was personally managing the small fund known as the Enterprise Fund.

Like Milken, Carr had stunning success. Under Carr's management, Enterprise Fund earned stellar returns by investing in emerging growth companies like Kentucky Fried Chicken, Tonka Toys, Kelly Services, Commerce Clearing House, and Jostens. Enterprise Fund ranked number one in performance in both 1967 and 1968 with returns of 117 percent and 44 percent, respectively. Assets under management soared from $29 million when Carr took control to a peak of $950 million. The May 3, 1969, issue of *Business Week* observed, "The dazzling success of Enterprise Fund has earned Fred Carr a reputation as perhaps the best fund manager around."

Carr's success was short-lived however, as he abruptly left Enterprise and the mutual fund business in November 1969 after a control dispute with his partners. The Enterprise Fund crashed in the period surrounding his departure, a victim of the stock market downturn that began in 1969. For his role in building the Enterprise Fund and then leaving just before it crashed, Carr was labeled a "gunslinger," a reputation that would follow him the rest of his career. For the next five years, Carr dabbled in various ventures waiting to make his next big move. The insurance industry had always attracted him, and in 1974 he got the chance to begin a career in that business.

That year, Fred Carr became president and chief executive officer of First Executive Corporation, a holding company that controlled two insurance companies, Executive Life of California and its subsidiary, Executive Life of New York. At that time, the company was in desperate shape. First Executive held about $77 million in assets, making it the 355th-largest U.S. life insurance company. Of the $77 million, $22 million was in the form of policy loans, which were unlikely to be repaid. The investment portfolio showed losses of $20 million, and the company was in default on a $14.6 million loan that had been used to purchase the New York subsidiary. Earnings were a negative $1 million, and bankruptcy was a serious risk.

By the 1980s Carr had transformed Executive Life, turning it into one of the country's most successful and profitable life insurance companies. He did this by developing innovative new products, cutting costs, and cutting prices, all to the benefit of consumers. Executive Life's success also had a major effect on the life insurance industry as a whole, which itself was transformed during the 1980s. But Carr's success and controversial business practices—particularly his major investments in high-yield bonds and close connections to Drexel Burnham and Michael Milken—also made him a favorite target of competitors and regulators. Carr fought hard, but ultimately he too could not survive the government's vendetta against Drexel, Milken, and the high-yield bond market.

First Executive Transforms the Life Insurance Industry

In 1977 the Federal Trade Commission finally published its long-awaited and highly publicized Task Force Insurance Report on the state of the insurance industry. The report was a scathing exposé, which concluded that the rate of return on the savings component of whole-life policies was near zero. While the FTC did not specifically recommend that consumers should not buy whole-life policies but instead should "buy term and invest the difference," the message of the report was clear. Life insurance was a rip-off, and consumers needed to beware.

For the industry as a whole, the FTC report could not have come at a worse time. Rising interest rates in the late 1970s and early 1980s made the negligible rate of return that consumers earned on the savings component of their life insurance policies increasingly unattractive. Also, most existing whole-life policies had given policyholders the option of borrowing against their policies at the low rates prevailing at the time of issuance. When interest rates skyrocketed, policyholders exercised this option, borrowing from insurance companies at single-digit rates and investing the proceeds at double-digit market rates. At the same time, new sales of whole-life policies were scarce, because established insurance companies with their portfolios of long-term low-yielding assets found it difficult to offer market rates on the savings components of the policies. In certain respects, the problems facing life insurance companies were quite similar to those being simultaneously experienced by the savings and loan industry.

For new entrants like Carr, however, the problems of established life insurance companies only presented opportunity. Carr recognized that insurance companies had a big advantage over other financial-services firms because they sold a product in which amounts invested could accumulate tax-free. He also understood that the insurance industry was mired in inefficiency and bureaucracy. Distribution costs were prohibitively high, and investment practices were primitive. Since First Executive was not saddled with a large book of existing insurance policies or a portfolio of low-yielding long-term investments, Carr was free to innovate in response to changed market conditions.

He responded aggressively. Carr, as the *Wall Street Journal* later reported, was "the first insurance executive to see that he must sell policies that hold their own with other investments." Surging inflation in the late 1970s pushed increasing numbers of people into the 70 percent marginal federal tax bracket, creating a demand for tax-sheltered investments. Recognizing this demand, First Executive initially emphasized single-premium deferred-annuity contracts, a type of tax-advantaged savings account. Deferred annuities were a simple but attractive savings vehicle for high-marginal-rate investors trying to cope with unprecedented inflation. Earnings on the premiums accumulated tax-free, so the higher a person's marginal tax rate, the more attractive deferred annuities became.

Carr knew that the better an insurance company's investment performance, the better the deal it could offer consumers on its annuities. Carr decided to maximize investment returns by investing heavily in high-yield bonds, which he did with success. Since First Executive's portfolio was earning high returns, Carr was able to offer consumers the best product. And consumers bought it. Sales surged from $11.6 million in 1976 to $90.7 million in 1979. The next year, they hit $468.1 million. In 1981, annuity sales crossed the $1 billion mark, reaching $1.1 billion.

First Executive's annuity sales continued to grow rapidly through the first three quarters of 1982 but fell sharply in the fourth quarter. Falling interest rates and inflation, tax-law changes, and the bankruptcy of Baldwin United, another major annuity provider, combined to lessen the attractiveness of tax-deferred annuity products. But the adverse effect on First Executive was minimal as Carr shifted focus to the company's new interest-rate-sensitive life insurance products. First Executive's "Irreplaceable Life" series of whole-life insurance products, first introduced in 1979, again became the standard of the industry. The series consisted of whole-life policies that offered lower premiums and higher cash-accumulation yields than traditional whole-life policies. The return the company was earning on its high-yield bonds was one reason Executive Life was able to offer consumers a superior product.

But investing in high-yield bonds was not the only reason First Executive was successful. Carr also streamlined distribution, relying more on independent than in-house agents, and giving them a share of profits on policies that remained in force. This profit-sharing arrangement discouraged agents from seeking new commissions by persuading policyholders to switch insurers. Carr also worked out special compensation arrangements with the most successful independent agents who concentrated on selling policies to the most desirable customers—wealthy individuals who were likely to maintain their investments. By lowering the costs of distribution, Carr was able to pass on some of the savings to consumers.

Another reason the Irreplaceable Life series was so successful was the design of the policies themselves. Traditional policies typically allocated expenses across the board to all policies no matter how long they remained in effect. Executive Life instead allocated expenses in the form of a heavy surrender charge, applied only to those policies that lapsed during the first twenty years. These insurance contracts contained two schedules, an accumulation account and a cash surrender value, both of which were clearly reported to consumers on an annual basis. The accumulation account was the premium plus a stated interest rate minus a charge for mortality risk. The cash surrender value was the accumulated amount less a penalty for early surrender. The policies took the mystery out of life insurance. Now everyone knew exactly what they were getting.

First Executive also designed innovative insurance products for high-risk individuals. Other insurance companies charged high-risk individuals higher rates. First Executive did the same, but with a twist. High-risk individuals paid premiums for a longer time, but if they lived a certain number of years, the company returned the extra premiums by an offsetting increase in the cash values of the policies. Once again the idea was simple, but an advance over the existing alternatives.

Executive Life's innovations had a major effect on the staid insurance industry, which had long been resistant to new products and price competition. But Carr forced the industry to change, and he made plenty of enemies in the process. When Executive Life's interest-rate-sensitive products, policy design, and distribution efficiencies proved too attractive to consumers, the established companies were forced to lower prices and follow suit, even if grudgingly. What competitors lost, however, consumers gained, as *Dun's Business Month* reported at the time:

The natural result of competition and all the new products was a drop in prices. The average price of life insurance dropped 32% during the 1970's, according to the American Council of Life Insurance. Ten years ago, a 40 year old male paid about $460 to buy $100,000 of term insurance. Today, he could pay just $160. Today, there is real competition in the industry. With it has come an increased emphasis on cutting expense, chiefly by finding a cheaper distribution system, and on increasing income, by concentrating on investment prowess.

Executive Life, of course, also benefited from the changed industry conditions. The company experienced phenomenal success and growth during the first half of the 1980s, peaking in 1986. That year First Executive had revenues of $3.6 billion and earnings of $157 million on assets of $14.3 billion. The comparable numbers for 1979 were $140 million, $5 million, and $303 million. This growth and success were fueled in significant part by Executive Life's investment performance, which consistently ranked at or near the top of the industry. Executive Life's high-yield-bond investments, which comprised an increasing percentage of its total assets, performed particularly well. By June 1986, the *Wall Street Journal* reported that "First Executive and its Chairman, Fred Carr, seem to have gotten respect" in the marketplace, even if they were still "outsiders" in the "staid" life insurance business.

In the summer of 1986, Standard & Poor's gave Executive Life its highest rating for claims-paying ability, AAA. At the time, Standard & Poor's gave this rating to fewer than thirty insurance companies, and these tended to be the most established, conservatively run companies. Many, particularly Carr's many enemies and those companies with lower ratings, questioned how the maverick Executive Life, with its heavy investments in high-yield bonds, could possibly merit a AAA rating. But Standard & Poor's held its ground for reasons given by Larry Hayes, its senior vice-president, as reported in the *Bond Buyer*:

> Mr. Hayes said many of Executive Life's assets, unlike those of other life insurance companies, are heavily invested in junk bonds. He added, however, that the diversification of its portfolio is "appropriate" and "prudent," which reduces the risk to "a more conservative level." A greater part of Executive Life's portfolio is invested in fixed-income instruments that more closely match its liabilities, he noted, unlike other insurers who have large holdings in other areas such as real estate.

Balancing its portfolio, Mr. Hayes said, is Executive Life's very conservative balance sheet. Its ratio of total liabilities to statutory capital, he said, is about 10 to 1, or half that of other life insurance companies, whose average liabilities-to-capital ratio is 20 to 1.

First Executive's success enabled it to expand into new areas. For example, the company developed a line of annuity products for the booming private pension-plan industry. One type of annuity was designed to fund the normal retirement benefits of active participants in ongoing qualified defined-benefit pension plans. Another and more controversial product was targeted to fund benefits for participants in defined-benefit plans that had been terminated. When private pension plans during the 1980s contained more assets than were needed to fund promised payments, corporate sponsors had the option of terminating the plan and capturing the surplus. Such terminations, which frequently occurred after hostile takeovers, required the terminating sponsor to purchase an annuity to guarantee that plan participants would receive their promised benefits. Executive Life, due to its superior investment performance, aggressive pricing, and operating efficiency, was typically able to provide these annuities at the lowest cost.

Critics complained that there was something sinister about Executive Life bidding on these annuity contracts because it frequently purchased the Drexel-underwritten high-yield bonds that helped finance the hostile takeover that made the termination possible in the first place. But so long as Executive Life was willing to offer the annuities at the lowest cost, and agencies like Standard & Poor's vouched for its safety with a AAA rating, the critics didn't have much ammunition.

Standard & Poor's AAA rating also enabled Executive Life to offer another controversial product, guaranteed investment contracts ("GIC's"), to municipal-security issuers. After the Tax Reform Act of 1986 restricted the use of tax-exempt bonds, municipalities and other public bodies scrambled for ways to raise funds. Municipal GIC's were one solution to the problem and were particularly attractive to public entities with low or no credit ratings. If these entities tried to issue bonds on their own after the Tax Reform Act of 1986, the yields demanded by investors would have been prohibitive. But if the entities committed to use the funds raised to purchase GIC's from the AAA-rated Executive Life or invest the proceeds in other AAA investments, the bonds could be issued at attractive yields. When the funds were used to purchase GIC's, Executive Life paid the public entities a lower rate than it was earning on its high-yield bond investments, but a higher rate than the public entities promised to their bondholders.

The GIC's initially were a tremendous success, with Executive Life selling almost $2 billion worth in the last few months of 1986 alone. Once again, however, Carr's critics came out of the woodwork, claiming that the GIC's were inappropriate uses for public funds, which were supposed to be used for public purposes such as financing housing or waterworks. The municipal GIC market soon disappeared.

But the critics still weren't satisfied. The more successful Executive Life became, the more it came under attack. The giant Eastern insurers that dominated the industry, like Prudential and Metropolitan Life, constantly questioned Executive Life's practices and its financial stability. Relationships with regulators grew increasingly acrimonious. As early as the late 1970s, the company became embroiled in a dispute with California insurance regulators over the accuracy of promotional materials for its whole-life insurance products. In 1984, the New York Insurance Department fined Executive Life of New York $100,000 for failure to file required financial records. And the press began to question the propriety of the interrelationships between Carr, Milken, and other participants in the world of high-yield bonds and hostile takeovers.

Carr was Milken's biggest and best customer. First Executive routinely bought Drexel-underwritten issues, accumulating the single largest portfolio of high-yield bonds. And when First Executive needed to raise capital, it also turned to Drexel for help. Many of First Executive's large investors, it turned out, were entities controlled by such regular Drexel customers as Saul Steinberg, Victor Posner, and Tom Spiegel. *Barron's* compared this set of interrelationships to the hub-and-spoke system used by airlines, with Milken at the center:

> Milken has adopted something akin to the airlines' hub-and-spoke pattern as the structure of his junk bond empire. From his Beverly Hills offices, Milken's hub, the spokes fan out, connecting such names as Carr, financier Victor Posner, Saul Steinberg of Reliance Group, and Thomas Spiegel of Columbia Savings & Loan. The members of a rather loose circle of investors tend to buy each other's junk bonds, many of which are underwritten by Milken's

firm, which also acts as market maker for a goodly number of their speculative securities.

An article in *Forbes* described the relationships similarly:

You take in my washing and I'll take yours, and we'll all wind up richer. . . . Thus does Drexel-raised money frequently flow back and forth among Drexel clients. Thus does Drexel maintain its firm hold on the high-yield bond market. There is nothing illegal about this. It is simply a case of one hand washing the other—to the mutual profit of customers and broker.

Later litigants in civil suits, including the United States government, would characterize the relationship between Milken, Carr, Spiegel, and others as a "daisy chain"—a network run by Milken where each of the participants invested in high-yield bonds issued by the other participants with the quid pro quo understanding that the favor would be returned. The crux of the "daisy chain" allegation—a variant of the Ponzi scheme claims that were also made— was that participants in the chain knew that high-yield bonds were bad investments but didn't care so long as prices were artificially controlled by the Milken empire. When prices later collapsed, proponents could then claim this was the inevitable consequence of the daisy chain participants' own actions in artificially propping up prices.

The daisy chain variant of the high-yield bond market as a Ponzi scheme claim was ludicrous. There is nothing suspicious about sophisticated institutional investors being involved in one another's deals. Nor is there any reason to believe that anybody purchased any bond for any reason other than their belief that the investment was attractive. After all, Drexel and Milken developed the high-yield bond market and were involved in most of the big deals. Anyone interested in investing in high-yield bonds would inevitably be attracted to Drexel deals. And the superior performance of high-yield bonds, particularly Drexel deals, during much of the 1980s would only encourage investors to keep coming back. It wasn't until later, when the government began its assault on Drexel, Milken, and the high-yield bond market, that investing in high-yield bonds became a problem.

And there were other contradictions. Under the daisy chain theory, Executive Life, which was one of the largest purchasers of high-yield bonds from Drexel, should also have been one of the largest issuers. But it wasn't. In fact, Standard & Poor's described the absence of debt on Executive Life's balance sheet as one of its desirable characteristics. When First Executive needed capital, it sold preferred stock in public offerings, not high-yield debt.

Moreover, the daisy chain theory cannot explain why major investors like Carr and others continued to purchase and hold high-yield bonds. If they knew that the bonds were bad investments and market collapse was inevitable, as the daisy chain proponents insisted they did, they would have done everything possible to sell their bonds at the artificially high prices before the truth became known. Instead, Carr accumulated a high-yield bond portfolio worth $11 billion in 1989. This behavior would be irrational if Carr knew prices were too high. Why would Carr knowingly inflict losses on himself and his firm? Carr's behavior is far more consistent with a belief that high-yield bonds were good investments, which they were until the government wrecked the market.

And the spectacular rebound of the market in recent years also cannot be reconciled with the daisy chain theory. The fundamentals of high-yield bonds, not the machinations of Milken, Carr, and others, explain their success as investments.

From Boesky Day to Collapse

The November 14, 1986, announcement of Boesky's deal with the government and the speculation that Drexel and Milken were targets had a major effect on First Executive. As the *Wall Street Journal* reported on November 19, 1986:

> Uncertainty about securities regulators' probe of Drexel Burnham Lambert's junk bond operations—and about the health of the junk bond market—have quickly spilled over onto Los Angeles–based First Executive.
>
> Short-sellers and nervous stockholders continued to pummel the shares of the insurance concern, whose chairman, Fred Carr, is a longstanding junk bond customer of Michael Milken, head of Drexel's junk bond operation in Beverly Hills. First Executive has a large portfolio of speculative-grade securities issued by debt-heavy companies. It also holds more than $100 million of $660 million in debentures issued last March by Ivan Boesky's major arbitrage fund.

Investors' concern wasn't just about the quality of First Executive's high-yield bonds and its Boesky investment. As the *Journal* noted, investors also worried "about Mr. Carr's ties with Drexel and the takeover game."

After Boesky day, First Executive's relationships with insurance regulators, never good to begin with, got much worse. Insurance companies, like banks and savings and loans, are required to meet reserve or minimum-capital requirements. Regulators always required First Executive to post greater reserves than the typical insurance company because it promised such a high return on its annuity products. Additional reserves were also required because regulators treated high-yield bonds differently from other risky assets and First Executive had such a large high-yield bond portfolio. But First Executive, like other insurance companies, could hold less reserves if it entered into contracts with reinsurance companies. By spreading the risks involved with reinsurers, insurance companies could avoid having to post the full reserves themselves.

The trouble was that First Executive did not deal with the typical reinsurance company. Back in 1980, Carr created First Stratford Life, a reinsurance company owned 50 percent by First Executive and 50 percent by Michael Milken and other investors. First Stratford conducted business out of First Executive's Los Angeles offices, and the vast majority of contracts it reinsured were originated by Executive Life. Moreover, First Stratford, like First Executive, invested heavily in high-yield bonds. Thus, while First Stratford had additional capital that could be used in the event First Executive was unable to make good on its obligations, it was unclear whether this would still be true if there were a decline in the high-yield bond market. The whole idea of requiring lower reserves when reinsurance contracts were in place was called into question when the reinsurer was a company like First Stratford. Other reinsurance companies used by Executive Life and First Stratford, unknown offshore companies with suspect balance sheets, also provided little comfort.

In March 1987, New York insurance regulators fined Executive Life of New York $250,000, the largest fine they had ever levied, because of improper reductions of reserves relating to the reinsurance contracts. First Executive was also required to inject $151.5 million of capital into its New York subsidiary to make up the difference. California regulators immediately announced that they would also require Executive Life of California to increase its capital. Also in 1987, New York passed a new regulation, clearly aimed at Executive Life, which restricted insurers from investing more than 20 percent of their assets in high-yield bonds. Executive Life of New York had about 50 percent of its assets invested in high-yield bonds at the time.

First Executive's increasing problems with regulators resulted from the regulators' increasingly hostile stance toward high-yield bonds and the government's intensifying insider-trading investigation after Boesky day. While the additional safety provided by First Executive's reinsurance contracts with First Stratford could legitimately be questioned, it was also true that regulators had known about First Stratford for a long time, and that other insurers had similar arrangements. What changed, as was obvious from the New York regulation limiting high-yield bond investments by insurers, was that everyone connected to Drexel was now under siege.

Carr responded to the new attacks in 1987 by announcing a shift to a slow-growth strategy. First Executive would discontinue its controversial municipal GIC's and pension annuities, deemphasize high-yield bonds, and raise additional capital by selling its New York subsidiary. With the additional capital, Executive Life of California could reduce its reliance on reinsurance contracts. The sale would also enable Carr to avoid any further contact with New York regulators, with whom relationships, according to one analyst, fell "just short of hand-to-hand combat." As the *Wall Street Journal* reported in March 1988, the slow-growth strategy meant that First Executive was no longer the fast-growing, entrepreneurial company it once was:

> The once-astounding growth of First Executive Corp. has slowed to a crawl, mostly because of tougher regulation by state insurance commissioners.
>
> In its annual report to the Securities and Exchange Commission, the aggressive life insurance holding company provided its most detailed explanation for last year's drop in premium revenue and indicated its responses to regulatory changes will slow further growth. However, it held out the hope that profit margins may increase. . . .
>
> First Executive said it is de-emphasizing the sale of certain types of single-premium insurance policies and annuities that put a strain on its capital as figured under accounting rules set by insurance regulators. The single-premium products once had been a mainstay of First Executive's business.

In addition, First Executive said it will consider redesigning some of its products, reducing the interest rates it guarantees to pay, or relying less on investments in high-yield, low-rated "junk bonds." Much of First Executive's success in the past stemmed from the higher rates it offered to pay policyholders, fueled by its investments in junk bonds.

Last year, First Executive's annuity sales fell 42% to $997.6 million. Life insurance sales increased 20% to $850.7 million, but single-premium life insurance sales, which had been 55% of the total in 1986, fell to 44% in 1987. First Executive's total assets, which had grown 65% in 1986, grew only 14% last year to $16.4 billion.

First Executive's turn for the worse was so pronounced that the company, which had long invested in the high-yield bonds used to finance hostile takeovers, itself became a rumored takeover target. I.C.H. Corp. (an insurance holding company), Travis Reed (a large investor), and Rosewood Financial Partners (an affiliate of Rosewood Corporation, which was owned by the Caroline Hunt Trust Estate) were all rumored acquirers.

Unfortunately, Carr's slow-growth strategy did not stop regulatory pressures from increasing. In November 1988, Rudy Giuliani and the SEC began to investigate First Executive's involvement with Drexel and Milken. After Drexel pled guilty in December 1988 and Milken was indicted in March 1989, these investigations intensified. Various congressional committees also launched their own investigations. In February 1990, the Senate Labor Committee began hearings focused on what were called First Executive's "junk pensions." A month later in March, the SEC started yet another investigation into First Executive's financial reporting practices.

Despite this, Carr did what he could to downsize and survive in the changed environment. New high-yield bond investments were all but discontinued, and in May 1989, First Executive finally reached an agreement to sell Executive Life of New York. But these steps were too little and too late. Once the high-yield bond market crashed after the passage of the FIRREA in the summer of 1989, First Executive, which still held a huge portfolio of high-yield bonds, had no viable options.

Nervous policyholders began surrendering their policies back to the company for their cash value. Paying the surrender charges, many policyholders reasoned, was better than being left with nothing if First Executive went under. The company paid out over $1 billion in 1989 for policy surrenders, a big increase over prior years. The proposed sale of Executive Life of New York was another casualty of the collapse of the high-yield bond market. The deal fell apart in December 1989.

Year-end 1989 also brought more regulatory problems related to First Executive's huge high-yield bond portfolio. The controversy centered on the packaging of high-yield bonds into collateralized bond obligations (CBO's) to reduce First Executive's stated holdings of high-yield bonds, thereby also reducing its required reserves. The CBO's were created when First Executive transferred $756 million of high-yield bonds and some cash to six newly formed companies and received in exchange $771 million in securities issued by the six companies. The securities received were in tiers, with the top tier being the safest and offering the lowest interest rate because it had first call on the assets in the high-yield bond pool. The bottom two tiers had more junior claims and offered higher interest rates. The CBO's were designed to be easier to sell than the underlying high-yield bonds because they were more liquid and allowed investors to select among different categories of risk. But the insurance regulators concluded that the CBO's, which were backed by the same high-yield bonds, were a sham designed to improperly lower required reserves, and ordered First Executive to post additional reserves of $110 million.

In early January 1990, Alan Snyder replaced Carr as president and chief operating officer of First Executive, but Carr remained as the company's chairman and chief executive officer. And on January 22, 1990, First Executive shocked the financial world by announcing that it expected to take a $515 million charge for 1989 because of losses on its high-yield bonds and that the company would report a "substantial loss" for the year. The announcement triggered an SEC investigation and guaranteed massive lawsuits. After the January 22 announcement, the company's stock price fell to $3 per share, a tiny fraction of what it had been just six months earlier.

And there were other consequences. All the rating agencies immediately downgraded their assessments of First Executive's claims-paying ability. Standard & Poor's lowered its rating from AAA to A, and the other major agencies, Moody's and A.M. Best, followed suit. A wave of further downgrades followed as First Executive's financial condition worsened during 1990. Sales of new policies became almost nonexistent. By early February 1990, within ten days of the January 22 announcement, the California Department of Insurance installed two full-time examiners at Executive Life of California to monitor every aspect of the insurer's operations. But the biggest problem was policy surrenders. Cash-withdrawal demands skyrocketed in the first few months of 1990; by mid-February, First Executive was receiving 25,000 phone calls per week inquiring about surrenders. For the year 1990, the company paid out a staggering $3.5 billion in policy surrenders.

Meanwhile, First Executive was becoming a hot political issue, particularly in California, the home of Lincoln Savings. First Executive's problems in 1990 coincided with the arrest and indictment of Charles Keating for defrauding elderly California bondholders in Lincoln branches and the announcements of Drexel's bankruptcy and Milken's guilty plea. For John Van de Kamp, California's Democratic attorney general and an aspiring candidate for higher office, the comparisons were irresistible:

> I fear that other kinds of supposedly safe financial institutions may also be at risk in this go-go era of junk bond financing. . . . I am concerned that the Executive Life situation could point to another sleeping danger for tens of thousands of California consumers. . . . I am convinced that there is as much potential for abuse and consumer damage as anything we've found at Lincoln.

Other national politicians, particularly Ohio senator Howard Metzenbaum, also began to regularly attack Executive Life and call for more and more new investigations.

Executive Life was now caught in the ultimate negative spiral. The more the press, politicians, and regulators harped on how horrible Executive Life was and the potential for consumer abuse, the more nervous policyholders and investors became. This in turn only gave First Executive's critics more ammunition to sharpen their attacks on the ailing insurer. A fatal run on the insurance company seemed like a distinct possibility.

First Executive survived the rash of negative publicity and policy surrenders in 1990, but barely. Stiff policy-surrender charges provided the company with some revenue and deterred other policyholders from cashing in. And the company had billions of dollars in cash and short-term liquid investments in addition to its high-yield bond holdings, which it used to meet withdrawal obligations. By the end of 1990, the company's prospects were even improving. Surrenders were declining, and the high-yield bond market was finally beginning to level off after its collapse. Maybe all was not lost.

Still the company badly needed a new owner and a fresh infusion of capital. An insurance company that is unable to sell new policies and is forced to rely on surrender charges for revenue cannot survive indefinitely. Earlier in 1990, longtime investor Rosewood Financial announced an acquisition offer, but it was rejected and expired soon after. By the end of 1990, another possible deal materialized, this time with Carr's approval. Hartford Insurance Company would buy about half of the company's insurance policies, and Leon Black, a former senior Drexel official, and Altus Financial, a subsidiary of the French bank Credit Lyonnais, would buy a large chunk of the high-yield bond portfolio.

But the deal stalled when John Garamendi, the newly elected California insurance commissioner who had just taken office on January 7, 1991, refused to sign off. Garamendi hoped to curry political favor by maintaining the regulatory attack on First Executive. When the company's new auditor, Price Waterhouse, contacted Garamendi's office to determine whether the commissioner was planning to seize Executive Life, the regulators wouldn't respond. Price Waterhouse then was forced to withhold its opinion on the company's financial statements because of concern about its ability to remain in business. As a result, Carr had to announce that he now expected a fresh wave of surrender demands that would be difficult to meet. When the company reported its fourth-quarter results for 1990 coupled with the judgment of its own auditor questioning its ability to survive, seizure became inevitable.

On April 11, 1991, just three days later, the California Insurance Department seized Executive Life of California. Garamendi milked the seizure for all it was worth. The real villain, Garamendi told the press, was "an ethic of greed" during the 1980s that encouraged the company to amass such a huge portfolio of high-yield bonds. Garamendi also blamed his regulator predecessors for failing to prevent the problem: "Inadequate oversight permitted an orgy of paper profits. . . . Many got rich on leveraged buyouts financed by junk bonds . . . [but now] the junk bond chickens are coming home to roost." The *Los Angeles Times* agreed, also blaming Executive Life's failure on the "decade of greed":

The ultimate cost of the Executive Life debacle is yet to be known. Salvaging the house-of-cards empire built on junk bonds will be a challenge to state regulators. The painful effects of the free-wheeling 1980s that spawned junk bonds unfortunately will continue to haunt this generation of taxpayers, as well as generations to come.

On April 16, 1991, the New York Insurance Department seized Executive Life of New York. In May 1991, First Executive declared bankruptcy.

First Executive's collapse led to the predictable wave of lawsuits and finger-pointing. The company and its accountants were sued for failing to disclose the company's problems in a timely manner. The municipal GIC holders and Garamendi waged a lengthy court dispute over whether the GIC's constituted "insurance." This dispute affected how much the GIC investors would receive, since Garamendi was arguing that the GIC's were not insurance and thus the GIC investors were not entitled to receive the same treatment as policy and annuity holders.

The Department of Labor filed a series of lawsuits against companies that purchased First Executive annuities after terminating their pension plans. Garamendi, not to be outdone, filed a civil suit against Carr, Milken, First Executive's accountants, and the rating agencies for their role in the company's demise. Carr, the accountants, and the rating agencies were all charged with responsibility for the supposedly incorrect public perception that First Executive had been in sound financial condition. As for Milken, Garamendi charged him with sucking First Executive into his "vast intertwined junk bond financial network." Apparently, high-yield bonds were now a type of addictive narcotic, and Milken was the drug dealer preying on innocent and unsophisticated victims like First Executive.

Even the regulators got a share of the blame. Howard Metzenbaum declared that regulators "failed to exercise responsible regulatory control to protect the policyholders and the public by allowing the company to experience spectacular growth even though the company's financial position endangered existing policyholders." Garamendi also continued to blame his Republican predecessors for lax regulation of Executive Life. Everyone seemed to agree something should have been done earlier. Even Richard Fogel from the General Accounting Office, the same Richard Fogel who had defended high-yield bond investments by savings and loans in March 1989, jumped on the bandwagon. State insurance regulators were at fault, Fogel told a Senate subcommittee in February 1992, for not preventing the two Executive Life insurers from pursuing "a reckless strategy of high growth and investment in high-risk assets . . . most notably junk bonds."

Of course these self-serving Monday-morning criticisms, so in sync with the "decade of greed" attacks on the 1980s, were completely off the mark. In truth, Carr built First Executive from nothing into a financial powerhouse through competitive pricing and innovative investing, product design, and distribution systems. First Executive fully deserved its Standard & Poor's AAA rating. While First Executive had a higher percentage of its assets in high-yield bonds, it held fewer types of other risky assets, particularly real estate, than other insurers. First Executive also had no debt and a far greater equity cushion as a percentage of total assets than the typical insurer. At the time the rating was assigned, no one expected the government's misguided assault on the high-yield bond market. And even with the government-caused collapse in the high-yield bond market after the FIRREA was enacted in August 1989, First Executive's problems were no greater than those of many large insurers. In fact, commercial real estate assets held by other large insurers declined in value by a greater percentage than high-yield bonds. But regulators and the press didn't target insurers who invested in risky real estate assets, preferring instead to attack First Executive because of Carr's connections to Drexel and Milken. By their efforts, they guaranteed the firm's destruction.

Garamendi Creates More Victims

When it became clear the California Insurance Department would not approve a private sale of Executive Life, Leon Black, the former Drexel honcho, began negotiating with Garamendi directly on behalf of his French clients. At the same time, Black continued talking to Carr. In early April 1991, just before the seizure, Black's high-yield bond fund, Apollo Investments, purchased a small block of First Executive's high-yield bonds, which the firm was more than willing to sell because it was then desperate for cash. But Black, with his intimate knowledge of the Drexel-underwritten high-yield bonds in Executive Life's portfolio from his Drexel days, wanted more. And Garamendi, who wanted to run for governor as the man who purged the insurance industry of evil junk bonds, was more than willing to oblige.

In August 1991, Garamendi accepted a $2.7 billion bid by Black's French client, Altus Finance, for Executive Life's high-yield bond portfolio. Altus's joint venture partner, Mutuelle Assurance Artisanale de France (MAAF), agreed as part of the bid also to provide $300 million in new capital for a successor insurance company to Executive Life. Credit Lyonnais, the huge French bank and Altus's parent, guaranteed the financial performance of both Altus and MAAF. The plan provided Executive Life of California policyholders with about 81¢ on the dollar. No provision was made for the muni-GIC holders, who were left out of the plan altogether. The bid was contingent on a subsequent auction process to give other parties a chance to bid.

But the auction was structured in a way that made it hard for others to bid. First, all buyers were required to bid for the entire $6 billion high-yield bond portfolio as a single block. No partial bids were allowed. This all-or-nothing requirement itself excluded most potential purchasers. Also, all bidders had to agree to take over Executive Life's insurance operations if they wanted to purchase the bond portfolio. This also limited the set of potential buyers because there is no reason why an investor in high-yield bonds would necessarily also want to run an insurance company. In fact, domestic banks are prohibited by regulation from owning an insurance company, so they were eliminated from the bidding altogether. Other insurance companies were also knocked out by Garamendi's requirement that the successor to Executive Life's insurance operations not retain any high-yield bonds. In effect, the bidding was limited to joint ventures that had the ability to bid in excess of $3 billion and that included both a purchaser for the bond portfolio and an insurance company willing to take over Executive Life's insurance business. And even for this limited class of potential purchasers, Altus had an enormous advantage because of its earlier extended negotiations and study of the high-yield bond portfolio. By contrast, all other bidders were required to analyze the portfolio, obtain financing, and submit bids within sixty days.

Still, several other bidders did come forward, recognizing that Executive Life's bond portfolio had increased in value significantly because of the emerging recovery of the high-yield bond market. This competition forced Altus to raise its bid by $500 million to

$3.2 billion. On November 14, 1991, Garamendi accepted the revised offer.

The deal ran into immediate problems. The auction procedures were roundly criticized as inadequate. Garamendi's rush to claim political credit for chasing "the junk bondsters from the insurance temple," critics claimed, made him neglect maximizing the sale proceeds from the bond portfolio for policyholders. If Garamendi had only acted more deliberately, he could have gotten more than $3.2 billion for the $6 billion bond portfolio. And the continued recovery of the high-yield bond market made Garamendi's haste look even worse. Garamendi's regulatory judgments were also called into question. The California courts rejected Garamendi's contention that the muni-GIC's were not insurance, which had been a key premise of the Altus bid. Now the muni-GIC holders, who had been excluded from the Altus bid, would have to be covered, meaning insurance policyholders would receive less. Garamendi was attacked for harming the very people he claimed he was trying to help.

But nothing that Garamendi did produced as much criticism as his hypocrisy in giving a sweetheart deal to Leon Black, who under Garamendi's view of the world was one of the people responsible for bringing down Executive Life in the first place. The press, which largely agreed with Garamendi's assessment that Drexel and Milken should be blamed for Executive Life's collapse, just couldn't understand what Garamendi was doing. *Barron's* made the point directly:

> Garamendi has made no bones about bringing to account the malefactors who helped lay Executive Life low. And certainly high on his list ought to be the Milken crew at Drexel Burnham. For Executive Life's junk bond portfolio was their favorite hazardous-waste dump site. In fact, Drexel underwritings were the main culprit in the demise of the insurance company. And yet the fingerprints of Drexel alumni are all over the proposed sales pact.
>
> Start with Altus. Its primary U.S. adviser and co-venturer is none other than Lion Advisers, the boutique of former Drexel merger and acquisition honcho Leon Black.
>
> No one has a more intimate knowledge of Executive Life's junk holdings than Black, for it bristles with bombed-out Drexel deals, some of which he worked on personally. . . .
>
> The more things change, the more they remain the same. For there's a measure of irony in the fact that Drexel insiders are poised to profit remediating the site they helped mess up. Put another way, they may be able to buy low what they sold high.

Others were equally scathing. *Institutional Investor* in a January 1992 article entitled "Deal of the Year" described how the purchase was a "coup for Black," who was now well on his way to becoming "a powerful phoenix rising from Drexel's ashes." Similarly, *Forbes* in March 1992 quoted sources describing the deal as "the steal of the century" and concluded that as a result Leon Black might well reach "billionaire status." In a follow-up story in March 1994 entitled "Smart Buyer, Dumb Seller," *Forbes* described how the episode illustrates "what happens when politicians with scant understandings of how markets work match wits with financiers who do." The moral of the story, *Forbes* concluded, was "quite clear": "a) When politicians try to fix things, they more often than not make them worse, and b) Their bumbling actions often create financial opportunities that are hidden from most people but are there for people who know the ropes."

There was some justice. Garamendi tried to capitalize on his misguided attack on Executive Life by running for governor in California in 1994. His platform stressed that he was the champion of "the little guy" who fought the insurance companies, whom he called "greedy pigs at the trough." "My predecessors kissed the insurance industry's butt here for 100 years, and consumers got screwed for it," Garamendi said. "I've kicked butt instead of kissed it." California voters apparently had a different view as Garamendi was soundly defeated in the Democratic primary by state treasurer Kathleen Brown, who herself was beaten badly by governor Pete Wilson.

As for Garamendi, *Forbes* reported that he made personal pleas to California insurance companies, the "greedy pigs at the trough," to buy tickets at a $5,000-a-head fund-raiser in Washington, D.C., to help him retire his $1.4 million campaign debt. Few of the "greedy pigs" were interested in helping out. What Garamendi should have done, *Forbes* suggested, is "put the arm on" the one person he really helped—Leon Black.

More ironically, Garamendi, the persistent critic of the go-go 1980s, may have launched a new takeover wave but of a different type. Black's control over Executive Life's huge high-yield bond portfolio gives him tremendous leverage if the issuers of those companies restructure their debt obligations, either voluntarily or in bankruptcy. Black has already earned hundreds of millions in fees from managing these restructuring transactions, and in many his debt stake may be converted into equity giving him control.

Other "vulture funds" are pursuing the same strategy of purchasing distressed high-yield bonds but without the benefit of a sweetheart deal with Garamendi. In subsequent years, Garamendi may be remembered as the man who was most responsible for triggering the new takeover wave of the 1990s. This legacy, so contrary to what Garamendi thought he was accomplishing, may be the one positive development from the sorry history of how the regulators destroyed First Executive.

CHAPTER 11

Assessment

The 1980s were a period of tremendous wealth creation and innovation in financial markets. This financial revolution occurred because of the entrepreneurial efforts and creativity of those who capitalized on the opportunities created by market shocks such as unprecedented high interest rates, the computer age, and the emerging global economy. Michael Milken and the high-yield bond department of Drexel Burnham embodied this new breed of entrepreneur, as did the emerging class of takeover and restructuring specialists. Society, investors, workers, and consumers all benefited from the changes they brought.

But the 1980s, like all periods of rapid change and innovation, also produced dislocation and backlash. Old-line Wall Street investment banking firms that watched on the sidelines while the upstart Drexel went from near bankruptcy to become the most profitable investment banking firm in the country deeply resented Drexel and Milken's meteoric rise. Entrenched corporate management of the Fortune 500, who were forced to streamline their operations and be more accountable or be replaced altogether, were also opponents of change.

The same market forces and technological advances that revolutionized Wall Street had other profound effects. The savings and loan industry, for example, a staple of government housing policy since the 1930s, became insolvent and obsolete. The life insurance industry also experienced dramatic changes as survival depended on adapting to meet consumer needs in the new economic environment.

When the losers in the marketplace went to the government for help, the government should have refused and allowed the financial revolution to run its course. Some more corporate executives may have lost their jobs or some perks, and the savings and loan industry, in its modern form itself a creature of government regulation, may have disappeared, but the country and the economy would have been much stronger. Instead, the government, led by prosecutors like Rudy Giuliani, formed an alliance with the losers in the financial revolution to attack the winners. Freely using the rhetoric of greed to enlist popular support, the government waged its campaign against the winners by expanding the scope of the criminal law beyond recognition and trampling civil liberties in the process.

The government's efforts were a disaster. Drexel Burnham, Columbia Savings, and Executive Life, three of the most profitable and innovative companies of the 1980s, were prosecuted or regulated out of existence. The government also created the savings and loan crisis of the late 1980s, wreaked havoc with the high-yield bond market, and worsened the recession of 1990. Many innocent people had their reputations and livelihoods destroyed, and some even lost their liberty. Michael Milken, who should be viewed as the ultimate personification of the American dream, is instead today a convicted felon.

There is more than enough blame to go around for the government's scandalous behavior during this period in our history. Prosecutors and regulators acting like prosecutors completely forgot that their paramount responsibility is to do justice, not to win at any cost. It was wrong to criminalize routine trading practices and prosecute individuals for conduct such as "stock parking" that nobody ever had reason to believe constituted a crime. And it was wrong to prosecute individuals using novel theories of "insider trading" when the government to this day cannot define the elements of this offense. Many of the government's prosecutions can also be faulted because the underlying conduct was so trivial— allegedly causing a stock price to move by $$^1/8$$ when such small price changes occur routinely or making a phone call and finding out that "your bunny has a good nose."

Prosecutors also abused their positions by overrewarding witnesses to cooperate while trying to destroy those who refused. If someone was willing to cooperate, prosecutors would do just about anything. The government was so excited about Ivan

Boesky's guilty plea that he was allowed to plead to one felony, pick his sentencing judge, and engage in massive insider selling (i.e., commit further crimes with government approval) before his deal was announced. Martin Siegel was treated as a hero for his false allegations, which led to the disgraceful handcuff arrests of Robert Freeman, Timothy Tabor, and Robert Wigton. Even the deliberate use of discredited testimony at trial, as occurred in the Sherwin, Wallach, and Spiegel trials, was not a problem so long as it helped the government win.

By the same token, no treatment was too harsh for those who stood in the government's way. Prosecutors treated Lisa Jones, a trading assistant who was little more than a clerk, like Al Capone because she refused to implicate her superiors at Drexel. And prosecutors had no reluctance using RICO to put Princeton/Newport out of existence long before trial because its officials refused to cooperate. Kaye, Scholer received the same treatment by the OTS for having the temerity to defend Charles Keating and Lincoln Savings, and was only saved from demise when it agreed to pay $41 million in extortion money.

Congress also deserves its share of blame. The ITSA and the ITSFEA, which both increased the penalties, civil and criminal, for "insider trading" without defining the offense, were terrible pieces of legislation. By creating the false impression that financial markets and takeovers were corrupt, the main effect of these laws was to give comfort to the losers in the restructuring revolution and the "decade of greed" rich-haters. Congress's role in creating the savings and loan crisis also cannot be overemphasized. Rather than allow the thrift industry to fail when it was obviously insolvent and no longer served any function, Congress decided to hide the problem and hope it would go away. When its policies failed and made the problem worse, the government launched a search for scapegoats. High-yield bonds and S&L "crooks" were the primary targets, but both pale in importance relative to Congress's own misguided regulatory policies. In fact, high-yield bonds were a major source of profitability for thrifts and other major investors such as Executive Life until Congress enacted the counterproductive FIRREA. Its search for scapegoats even caused Congress to turn on its own members, as it did in the farcical Ethics Committee investigation of the Keating Five.

The performance of the press was another disappointment. In

too many instances the press became a tool of the government's prosecutorial efforts and propaganda campaign, and some journalists who parroted the government's line about widespread abuses in financial markets were themselves guilty of conflicts of interest. James Stewart became famous, for example, by becoming the government's favorite mouthpiece in the press. Stewart capitalized by writing a series of front-page stories for the *Wall Street Journal* based on "sources close to the government's investigation" and then expanding these stories into a book. Nowhere did Stewart disclose that, when he was supposedly acting as an objective reporter, he was in truth inciting public opinion to stimulate sales of the big-money book that he was simultaneously writing.

Other reporters who in theory act as watchdogs for the public were either asleep or didn't understand what was going on. Why the press (with a few notable exceptions such as Gordon Crovitz and the other editorial-page writers of the *Wall Street Journal*) stood silent during the prosecutorial excesses of Rudy Giuliani is unfathomable. Even when the excesses were the most obvious—the government's police-state tactics with Wigton, Freeman, or Tabor, or when the government's case against Milken was exposed as a fraud in the Fatico hearing—the press was largely silent. But this same press that gave the government a free pass had no problem popularizing the ridiculous claim that "stock parking" threatened "public confidence" in securities markets and was the white-collar equivalent of murder.

The legal system also performed poorly. Some judges like Judge Milton Pollack were so progovernment as to make a mockery of the basic principle that every litigant is entitled to a fair and impartial judge. Others, like Judge Lance Ito, were unwilling to buck public opinion to protect the constitutional rights of defendants like Charles Keating. Judge Kimba Wood did not have the courage to take the government to task when the case against Michael Milken was exposed as a fraud in the Fatico hearing she ordered. Instead, she gave Milken ten years, only to reduce it later using the pretense of his "substantial cooperation." And even when judges tried to do the right thing—like when Judge Robert Stanton protected the speedy-trial rights of the Giuliani Three after their handcuff arrests or when Judge Joe Fish refused to sentence Don Dixon for the failure of Vernon Savings or when

Judge Robert Takasugi ensured that Tom Spiegel received a fair trial—it wasn't enough to protect defendants from prosecutorial abuse.

Sometimes the system worked, but at tremendous cost. John Mulheren ultimately prevailed, but only after spending time in prison and losing his company. James Sherwin also avoided conviction, but only after three grueling criminal trials and several appeals over a $1/8 change in stock price. His career and reputation ruined, Sherwin left the country to start a new life in Europe. The Princeton/Newport defendants, too, beat the odds and got most of their convictions reversed, but they couldn't beat the RICO monster. They lost everything before they could even defend themselves. And Tom Spiegel also "won," but lost his institution, his fortune, and his reputation in the process.

Plaintiffs' lawyers were another villain in the story. The Cravath law firm's multibillion-dollar lawsuit blaming Milken for the savings and loan crisis and claiming that the entire high-yield bond market was the product of manipulation and fraud was a joke. The suit, brought by a law firm that itself prospered from its involvement in the financial innovations of the 1980s, was more fraudulent than anything about the high-yield bond market. The same is true about the absurd Cravath lawsuit blaming Milken for the fall of Drexel. The private class-action securities bar worked in close tandem with Cravath and government prosecutors, filing a torrent of piggy-back frivolous lawsuits intended to shake down as much money as possible from the targets of the government's witch-hunt.

When the cases ended, the government prosecutors and regulators who were most responsible for the abuse left the government in droves for higher paying positions in the defense bar. They and their new employers no doubt hope that they will be able to peddle their skills as former insiders to the targets of the next generation of prosecutors and regulators. Most of these former government officials had no problem making the transition from denouncing "greed" in financial markets to focusing instead on how much money they could now make.

What should we as a society learn from the 1980s? The main lesson is the need to be vigilant to guard against the arbitrary exercise of power by the government against those who are unpopular because they threaten the economic establishment. We need to be particularly suspicious about the rhetoric of greed.

Powerful interest groups and their allies in the government use the rhetoric of greed to discredit and delegitimize the success of others. The more successful the effort, the easier it is for the government to regulate the group out of business or, in the extreme case as occurred in the 1980s, put them in jail. Rudy Giuliani's win-at-any-cost mentality, and his police-state tactics, were as far removed from the pursuit of justice as is imaginable. Regrettably, Giuliani's election as mayor of New York will only encourage others to try and follow in his footsteps.

Steps must be taken to limit prosecutorial discretion and abuses. Repealing the government's ability to seize assets under RICO would be a good start. In fact, repealing RICO altogether, at least for nonviolent financial "crimes," would be a major step in the right direction. So too would limiting the power of federal regulatory agencies, particularly the OTS, to coerce settlements by freezing assets making it impossible for targets to defend themselves, so preventing repeats of the Kaye, Scholer episode.

When prosecutors overreach, the courts must act as safeguards. Criminal prosecutions should occur only when the legislature has clearly defined in advance the conduct proscribed. Only then can there be confidence that defendants had notice that their conduct was criminal. The criminal law is not the place to trap the unwary by changing the rules in the middle of the game. If courts had applied these principles consistently, many of the 1980s prosecutions would never have occurred. In fact, Michael Milken, Drexel Burnham, John Mulheren, James Sherwin, Paul Bilzerian, Robert Freeman, and the Princeton/Newport defendants, among many others, would never have been prosecuted had these simple principles been followed.

We should also learn from the 1980s that government intervention in the economy frequently has unanticipated and perverse consequences. One such consequence is the incentive and ability to engage in criminal conduct that would otherwise not exist. Before Congress enacted the Williams Act, requiring disclosure of ownership levels and mandatory waiting periods, acquirers could operate quickly and secretly. Information flow could be better controlled, and there was no need for an industry of takeover arbitrageurs to speculate on takeover outcomes. But after Congress intervened to help besieged corporate management fight off takeover bids, the resulting delay and uncertainty fostered a new marketplace for information that did not previously exist. In a very real sense, Congress was responsible for creating the conditions that produced real criminals like Ivan Boesky, Dennis Levine, and Martin Siegel.

Similarly, the government's misguided efforts to salvage the insolvent savings and loan industry created an environment conducive to criminal behavior. Deposit insurance weakens market discipline and thus increases the discretion of thrift operators to use thrift assets in improper ways. The temptation is greatest when thrifts at or near insolvency are allowed to remain open, as occurred routinely in the 1980s. The problem was also exacerbated when Congress lured a new class of owners with no previous thrift experience into the industry in the early 1980s. This new class of owners—men like Charles Keating, Don Dixon, and David Paul—viewed savings and loans as a captive source of financing for their investment activities. These men, operating in an environment without market discipline, also turned out to be unable to resist using their thrifts as captive sources of financing for their extravagant lifestyles. If Congress had allowed the insolvent thrift industry to fail, Keating, Dixon, and Paul would never have become household names.

Interest groups in the future who cannot compete in the marketplace will continue to seek help from the government. If the 1980s have taught us anything, it is that such pleas for governmental intervention should be viewed with the greatest suspicion. The so-called Wall Street and savings and loan scandals of the 1980s wouldn't have occurred if the government hadn't intervened. This important point should not be forgotten as America approaches the twenty-first century.

Endnotes

Preface

Page xii The many books written by journalists about the scandals on Wall Street include: Douglas Frantz, *Levine & Co.: Wall Street's Insider Trading Scandal* (New York: Henry Holt, 1987); Connie Bruck, *The Predators' Ball: The Junk Bond Raiders and the Man Who Staked Them* (New York: Simon & Schuster, 1988); James B. Stewart, *Den of Thieves* (New York: Simon & Schuster, 1991); David A. Vise and Steve Coll, *Eagle on the Street* (New York: Macmillan, 1991); Benjamin J. Stein, *A License to Steal: The Untold Story of Michael Milken and the Conspiracy to Bilk the Nation* (New York: Simon & Schuster, 1992). The two books of higher quality are Jesse Kornbluth, *Highly Confident: The Crime and Punishment of Michael Milken* (New York: William Morrow, 1992); and Fenton Bailey, *Fall from Grace: The Untold Story of Michael Milken* (New York: Carol Publishing Group, 1991). Excellent colums about the period have been written by a few journalists—particularly Gordon Crovitz, George Gilder, and Paul Craig Roberts.

Journalists also have written a number of books on the savings and loan scandals. Examples include: Stephen Pizzo, Mary Fricker, and Paul Muolo, *Inside Job: The Looting of America's Savings and Loans* (New York: McGraw-Hill, 1989); Martin Mayer, *The Greatest-Ever Bank Robbery: The Collapse of the Savings and Loan Industry* (New York: Charles Scribner's Sons, 1990); James O'Shea, *The Daisy Chain: The Tale of Big Bad Don Dixon and the Looting of a Texas S&L* (New York: Simon & Schuster, 1991); Michael Binstein and Charles Bowden, *Trust Me: Charles Keating and the Missing Billions* (New York: Random House, 1993); Kathleen Day, *S&L Hell: The People and the Politics behind the $1 Trillion Savings and Loan Scandal* (New York: Norton, 1993).

Introduction

Page 1 The number of books on the subject of greed published in the last few years is incredible. A partial list includes: J. Arthur Baird,

The Greed Syndrome: An Ethical Sickness in American Capitalism (Akron: Hampshire Books, 1989); Laurence Shames, *The Hunger for More: Searching for Values in an Age of Greed* (New York: Random House, 1989); Barbara Ehrenreich, *Worst Years of Our Lives: Irreverant Notes from a Decade of Greed* (New York: HarperCollins Publishers, 1991); J. Edmund Clarke, *Adam Smith Meets "Greedy Gus": A Review of the "Wealth of Nations" Then & Now* (New York: Vantage, 1992); M. Hirsch Goldberg, *The Greed Factor: The Incredible Things Money Does to People & People Do with Money* (New York: William Morrow, 1994).

"Greed" has been detected at financial institutions: Ken Auletta, *Greed & Glory on Wall Street: The Fall of the House of Lehman* (New York, G K Hall, 1987); William E. Fitzgerald, *Arena of Greed: The Great Chicago Commodity Market Scam* (Elk Grove Village, IL: DeVin Publishers, 1990); R. T. Naylor, *Bankers, Bagmen & Bandits: Business & Politics in the Age of Greed* (Concord, MA: Paul & Co., 1990); James Sterngold, *Burning Down the House: How Greed, Deceit & Bitter Revenge Destroyed E. F. Hutton* (New York: Summit Books, 1990). And "greed" is found in law firms: Kim Eisler, *Shark Tank: Greed, Politics & the Collapse of Finley Kumble, America's Second-Largest Law Firm* (New York: St. Martin's Press, 1990); Stephen and Frances Magee, *A Plague of Lawyers: Greed & the American Legal System* (New York: Warner Books, 1994).

Corporations are riddled with "greed": Hope Lampert, *True Greed: What Really Happened in the Battle for RJR Nabisco* (New York: Simon & Schuster, 1990); Christopher Byron, *Skin Tight: The Bizarre Story of "Guess" vs. "Jordache"—Glamour, Greed & Dirty Tricks in the Fashion Industry* (New York: Simon & Schuster Trade, 1992); Kunen, *Reckless Disregard: Corporate Greed, Government Indifference & the Kentucky School Bus Crash* (New York: Simon & Schuster Trade, 1994); Janie Roberts, *Glitter & Greed: Inside the Secret World of the Diamond Cartel* (Bethesda: National Press Books, 1994). And unions are riddled with greed, too: Allen Friedman and Ted Schwarz, *Power & Greed: Inside the Teamsters Empire of Corruption* (New York: Watts, 1989).

There is "greed" in the mental health care system: Joseph Sharkey, *Bedlam: Greed, Profiteering & Fraud in a Mental Health System Gone Crazy* (New York: Shapolsky Publishers, 1994). "Greed" has been exposed in sports: V. Simson, *Dishonored Games: Corruption, Money & Greed at the Olympics* (New York: Shapolsky Publishers, 1992); John Arezzi, *Pro Wrestling Confidential: Sex, Greed, Death & Drugs In & Out of the Ring* (New York: Shapolsky Publishers, 1994). And, shockingly, "greed" has even been unmasked in politics: Joseph Stedino and Dary Matera, *What's in It for Me?: How an Ex-Wiseguy Exposed the Greed, Jealousy & Lust that Drive Arizona Politics* (New York: HarperCollins Publishers, 1992).

The titles of these books serve as a good illustration of how "greed" has been recklessly wielded like a club. However, it is possible to find a few discussions of greed that are quite enlightening. A good example is

Robert Bartley, *The Seven Fat Years—And How to Do It Again* (Seattle: Free Press, 1992). In chapter 15, entitled "Greed and Envy," Bartley provides a historical perspective on the attack on American entrepreneurs for being "greedy." He also notes the selective use of the word *greedy* in recent times to describe those entangled in the "insider trading" scandals but not the politicians who played a role in the savings and loan scandal.

A few magazines published articles exposing the hypocrisy of those who accuse others of being "greedy." Two examples are: David Brooks, "Greedy Like Me," *National Review,* March 4, 1988; and Daniel Seligman, "Good Greed," *Fortune,* November 29, 1993. Seligman discusses the dictionary definition of *greed,* while Brooks shows how the word's definition has changed since the 1950s.

Michael Novak has published several interesting articles that provide a more theological perspective on greed and show that America's greed-bashing bears more than a faint resemblance to what has historically gone on in Communist countries. See "'Politics of Resentment' Is Sign of Desperate Left; Democrats' Attempt to Foster Feelings of Envy Are Mean and Self-Destructive," *Los Angeles Times,* January 13, 1988; "Greed Does Not Explain It," *Forbes,* April 3, 1989; "Eastern Europe's Moral Pollution," *Forbes,* June 25, 1990.

Nobel Prize–winning economist Harry Markowitz and George Gilder assess greed from an economic perspective. See Gilder, "The Enigma of Entrepreneurial Wealth," *Inc.,* October 1992; Markowitz, "Markets and Morality," *Journal of Portfolio Management,* Winter 1992.

Pages 3–4   For a fuller description of charitable contributions during the 1980s compared with earlier periods, see: Robert Reich, "The Great Divide: Is the Traditional American Community with Its Sense of Responsibility for the Common Good Disappearing?" *Orlando Sentinel Tribune,* April 21, 1991; Richard McKenzie, "Was It a Decade of Greed?" *Public Interest,* vol. 106 (Winter 1992); Thomas Sowell, "Was Adam Smith a Closet Socialist?" *Forbes,* December 20, 1993.

Both McKenzie and Sowell view the rise in charitable giving in the 1980s as a refutation of the charge that the 1980s were a "decade of greed." Reich counters that, as a percentage of income, the very wealthy were less charitable than the very poor. Moreover, Reich argues that the contributions of the wealthy did not go to help the poor but rather went to places like art museums, opera houses, theaters, orchestras, ballet companies, private hospitals, and elite universities. In other words, the rich were the beneficiaries of their own donations. Interestingly, Reich offers no statistics to support this claim.

Chapter 1: The Restructuring of Corporate America

Page 11   The relationship between the critique of the 1980s and the critique of the robber barons during the second industrial revolution is developed in Michael Jensen, "The Modern Industrial Revolution, Exit, and the Failure of Internal Control Systems," *Journal of Finance,* vol. 48,

1993. The same article quantifies the gains from restructuring transactions.

The robber barons also are discussed in Robert Bartley, *The Seven Fat Years—And How to Do It Again* (Seattle: Free Press, 1992). Bartley points out that the Morgans and the Vanderbilts accused upstart rivals like Sam Insull and Jay Gould of "consummate greed." And Bartley adds, "The Morgans and the Vanderbilts have seldom understood with whom they were making common cause, that they too would go down as robber barons and moneychangers."

Pages 17–18 The reversal of corporate diversification in the 1980s is examined in Sanjai Bhagat, Andrei Shleifer, and Robert W. Vishny, "Hostile Takeovers in the 1980's: The Return to Corporate Specialization," *Brookings Papers on Economic Activity,* 1990; Amar Bhide, "Reversing Corporate Diversification," *Journal of Applied Corporate Finance,* vol. 3, Summer 1990.

There are many economic studies of the impact of corporate restructurings on various aspects of firm-operating performance. The impact on productivity is investigated in Frank Lichtenberg and Donald Siegel, "Productivity and Changes in Ownership of Manufacturing Plants," *Brookings Papers on Economic Activity,*1987; George Baker and Karen Wruck, "Organizational Changes and Value Creation in Leveraged Buyouts: The Case of the O. M. Scott & Sons Company," *Journal of Financial Economics,* 1989; Clive Bull, "Management Performance in Leveraged Buyouts: An Empirical Analysis," appears in Yakov Amihud, ed., *Leveraged Management Buyouts: Causes and Consequences* (Burr Ridge, IL: Irwin Professional Publishing, 1989); Steven Kaplan, "The Effects of Management Buyouts on Operating Performance and Value," *Journal of Financial Economics,* 1989; Glenn Yago, Frank Lichtenberg, and Donald Siegel, "Leveraged Buyouts and Industrial Competitiveness: The Effects of LBOs on Productivity, Employment, and Research and Development," unpublished manuscript, July 12, 1989; Frank Lichtenberg and Donald Siegel, "The Effects of Leveraged Buyouts on Productivity and Related Aspects of Firm Behavior," *Journal of Financial Economics,* 1990; Abbie J. Smith, "Corporate Ownership Structure and Performance: The Case of Management Buyouts," *Journal of Financial Economics,* 1990; Paul M. Healy, Krishna G. Palepu, and Richard S. Ruback, "Does Corporate Performance Improve After Mergers?," *Journal of Financial Economics,* 1992. A good review of the economic evidence is Krishna G. Palepu, "Consequences of Leveraged Buyouts," *Journal of Financial Economics,* 1990. These studies provide overwhelming evidence that, on average, productivity and other performance measures improve substantially following corporate restructurings.

A frequently heard claim is that corporate restructurings lead firms to make cutbacks in research and development. This hypothesis has been explored in John Pound, Kenneth Lehn, and Gregg Jarrell, "Are Takeovers Hostile to Economic Performance?" *Regulation,* September/October 1986; Bronwyn H. Hall, "The Effect of Takeover Activity on Corporate Research and Development," appears in Alan J. Auerbach, ed., *Corporate Takeovers: Causes and Consequences* (Chicago: University of Chicago Press, 1988); Glenn Yago, Frank Lichtenberg, and Donald Siegel, *Leveraged Buyouts and Industrial Competitiveness*. The general conclusion to be drawn from these studies is that R&D that is productive is not cut back following a corporate restructuring, but R&D that is perceived to be wasteful by the market is. A firm does not become a takeover target simply because it spends a great deal on R&D.

The impact of corporate restructurings on labor is studied in Brown and Medoff, *The Impact of Firm Acquisitions on Labor,* in Alan J. Auerbach, *Corporate Takeovers*; Andrei Shleifer and Lawrence H. Summers, "Breach of Trust in Hostile Takeovers," in Alan J. Auerbach, *Corporate Takeovers*; Amar Bhide, "The Causes and Consequences of Hostile Takeovers," *Journal of Applied Corporate Finance,* Summer 1989; Mark L. Mitchell and Harold J. Mulherin, "The Stock Price Response to Pension Plan Terminations and the Relation of Termination with Corporate Takeovers," *Financial Management,* Autumn 1989; Glenn Yago, Frank Lichtenberg, and Donald Siegel, "Leveraged Buyouts and Industrial Competitiveness"; Glenn Yago and Gelvin Stevenson, "Employment Impacts of Mergers and Acquisitions," *Journal of Applied Corporate Finance,* Summer 1989; Jeffrey Pontiff, Andrei Shleifer, and Michael S. Weisbach, "Reversions of Excess Pension Assets after Takeovers," *Rand Journal of Economics,* Winter 1990; Joshua G. Rosett, "Do Union Wealth Concessions Explain Takeover Premiums?" *Journal of Financial Economics,* 1990; David A. Cather, Elizabeth S. Cooperman, and Glenn A. Wolfe, "Excess Pension Asset Reversions and Corporate Acquisition Activity," *Journal of Business Research,* December 1991; Richard A. Ippolito and William H. James, "LBOs, Reversions and Implicit Contracts," *Journal of Finance,* March 1992. These studies suggest that even if corporate restructurings are associated with employment cutbacks, wage concessions, and overfunded pension-plan terminations, these factors account for only a small fraction of the premium typically paid to target shareholders.

The extent to which corporate restructurings are motivated by the tax laws is discussed in Alan J. Auerbach and David Reishus, "The Effects of Taxation on the Merger Decision," in Alan J. Auerbach, *Corporate Takeovers;* Carla Hayn, "Tax Attributes as Determinants of Shareholder Gains in Corporate Acquisitions," *Journal of Financial Economics,* 1989; Michael C. Jensen, Steven Kaplan, and Laura Stiglin, "Effects of LBOs on Tax Revenues of the U.S. Treasury," *Tax Notes,* February 6, 1989; Steven Kaplan, "Management Buyouts: Evidence on Taxes as a Source of Value," *Journal of Finance,* July 1989; Myron S. Scholes and Mark A. Wolfson, "The Effects of Changes in Tax Laws on Corporate Reorganization Activity," *Journal of Business,* 1990. These studies find that, while some tax savings are associated with corporate restructurings, the magnitude of the savings is generally small relative to the premium typically paid to target shareholders. Moreover, when all the tax implications of leveraged buyouts are considered, the net effect on the tax revenues of the U.S. Treasury is actually positive.

Pages 18–19 The RJR Nabisco transaction is analyzed in Gerard A. Cahill and Camille P. Castorina, "Did the Treasury Win or Lose in the RJR Buyout?," *Mergers & Acquisitions*, March/April 1990; Nancy J. Mohan and Carl R. Chen, "A Review of the RJR-Nabisco Buyout," *Journal of Applied Corporate Finance*, Summer 1990; Michael C. Jensen, "Corporate Control and the Politics of Finance," *Journal of Applied Corporate Finance*, vol. 4, Summer 1991; Allen Michel and Israel Shaked, "RJR Nabisco: A Case Study of a Complex Leveraged Buyout," *Financial Analysts Journal*, September/October 1991. The evidence indicates that RJR Nabisco was a particularly attractive leveraged buyout candidate and that the LBO has been quite successful.

Pages 19–22 The Goodyear, Allegis, and other restructuring transactions are discussed in David J. Denis and Diane K. Denis, "Leveraged Recaps and the Curbing of Corporate Overinvestment," *Journal of Applied Corporate Finance*, vol. 6, 1993. The Unocal transaction and the role of restructuring transactions in the energy industry are discussed in Michael C. Jensen, "The Takeover Controversy: Analysis and Evidence," *Midland Journal of Corporate Finance*, vol. 4, 1986. The evidence on restructuring transactions in general is collected in Frank H. Easterbrook and Daniel R. Fischel, *The Economic Structure of Corporate Law* (Cambridge: Harvard University Press, 1991).

Pages 24–25 The growth and success of Drexel is described in Samuel L. Hayes, "The Transformation of Investment Banking," *Harvard Business Review*, January/February 1979; "Drexel Burnham Lambert Expects Record Profit in 2nd Quarter," *Wall Street Journal*, June 19, 1980; "Drexel Burnham Finds Its Niche," *Pensions & Investment Age*, September 13, 1982; "Drexel's Rise Among Underwriters Stems from Its Focus on 'Junk Bonds,'" *Wall Street Journal*, July 11, 1984; "The Firm That Fed on Wall Street's Scraps," *Fortune*, September 3, 1984; "Drexel Continues to Gain Force, Stature in Underwriter Rankings," *Pensions & Investment Age*, February 4, 1985; "How Drexel's *Wunderkind* Bankrolls the Raiders," *Business Week*, March 4, 1985; "How Linton Made Drexel the Hottest Name on the Street," *Business Week*, April 1, 1985; "At Drexel, A New Chief's New Problems," *New York Times*, May 26, 1985; "Fast Growing Drexel Irritates Many Rivals with Tough Tactics," *Wall Street Journal*, June 13, 1986; "Milken the Magnificent," *Institutional Investor*, August 1986; "Drexel Was Most Profitable Firm on Street in 1986," *Wall Street Journal*, May 8, 1987.

Pages 29–30 The table is from Ben S. Bernanke and John Y. Campbell, "Is There a Corporate Debt Crisis?," *Brookings Papers on Economic Activity*, 1988; Ben S. Bernanke, John Y. Campbell, and Toni M. Whited, "U.S. Corporate Leverage: Developments in 1987 and 1988," *Brookings Papers on Economic Activity*, 1990.

Other studies that have analyzed the change in leverage of corporate

America during the 1980s include Robert A. Taggart, Jr., "Corporate Financing: Too Much Debt?," *Financial Analysts Journal,* May/June 1986; Henry Kaufman, "Debt: The Threat to Economic and Financial Stability," *Economic Review,* Federal Reserve Bank of Kansas City, December 1986; Stephen S. Roach, "Living with Corporate Debt," *Journal of Applied Corporate Finance,* vol. 2, Spring 1989; Mark B. Baribeau, "Leverage Risk in the Nonfinancial Corporate Sector," *Business Economics,* July 1989; Richard W. Kopcke, "The Roles of Debt and Equity in Financial Corporate Investments," *New England Economic Review,* July/August 1989; Richard A. Clark and Emil M. Sunley, "Corporate Debt: What Are the Issues and What Are the Choices?" *National Tax Journal,* September 1989; Robert A. Taggart, Jr., "Corporate Leverage and the Restructuring Movement of the 1980s," *Business Economics,* April 1990; Frederick T. Furlong, "Tax Incentives for Corporate Leverage in the 1980s," *Economic Review,* Federal Reserve Bank of San Francisco, Fall 1990; Karl A. Scheld, David R. Allardice, and Carolyn McMullen, "Debt in the 1990s," *Chicago Fed Letter,* Federal Reserve Bank of Chicago, May 1993; Paula R. Worthington, "Recent Trends in Corporate Leverage," *Economic Perspectives,* Federal Reserve Bank of Chicago, May/June 1993.

These studies employ a wide range of leverage measures, including book-value debt-asset and debt-equity ratios and the fraction of cash flow devoted to interest payments. In general, use of the market value of equity and assets leads to leverage ratios that refute the hypothesis that corporate leverage increased significantly in the 1980s. If leverage is measured as the fraction of cash flow devoted to interest payments, the statistics may or may not show an increase in leverage in the 1980s. Different studies reach different conclusions depending on how the measure is calculated.

International comparisons of leverage ratios are presented in Norman Toy, Arthur Stonehill, Lee Remmens, Richard Wright, and Theo Beekhuisen, "A Comparative International Study of Growth, Profitability, and Risk as Determinants of Corporate Debt Ratios in the Manufacturing Sector," *Journal of Financial and Quantitative Analysis,* 1974; Masahiko Aoki, "Aspects of the Japanese Firm," Masahiko Aoki, ed., *The Economic Analysis of the Japanese Firm* (New York: Elsevier Science Publishers, 1984); David Flath, "Debt and Taxes: Japan Compared with the U.S.," *International Journal of Industrial Organization,* 1984; Ravi Sarathy and Sangit Chatterjee, "The Divergence of Japanese and U.S. Corporate Financial Structure," *Journal of International Business Studies,* Winter 1984; Sadahiko Suzuki and Richard W. Wright, "Financial Structure and Bankruptcy Risk in Japanese Companies," *Journal of International Business Studies,* Spring 1985; John D. Paulus, "Corporate Restructuring, 'Junk,' and Leverage: Too Much or Too Little?," *Economic Perspectives,* Morgan Stanley, March 12, 1986; Kopcke, "Roles of Debt and Equity"; Stephen D. Prowse, "Institutional Investment Patterns and Corporate Financial Behavior in the United States and Japan," *Journal of Financial Economics,*

1990; Mark J. Roe, "Some Differences in Corporate Structure in Germany, Japan, and the United States," *Yale Law Journal,* June 1993.

A significant finding of these studies is that Japanese corporations tend to be much more leveraged than their American counterparts. This finding persists even after various adjustments are made to the Japanese figures to correct for differing accounting practices.

Robert Bartley reports that, based on International Monetary Fund data, the ratio of debt-to-assets in production industries in 1988 was 45.3% in the U.S., 55.7% in Germany, and 69.6% in Japan. See Robert Bartley, *Seven Fat Years.* Bartley observes that this empirical fact did not stop the CEO's of many large companies from claiming that high leverage would harm the international competitiveness of American corporations.

Page 32 The relationship between firm performance and the likelihood of being the target of a takeover bid is discussed in Michael C. Jensen, "The Takeover Controversy: Analysis and Evidence," *Midland Journal of Corporate Finance,* vol. 4, 1986.

Pages 32–33 The leading study on the market's reaction to research and development expenditures is John J. McConnell and Chris J. Muscarella, "Corporate Capital Expenditure Decisions and the Market Value of the Firm," *Journal of Financial Economics,* vol. 14, 1985. They find, "For a sample of industrial firms (that are likely to have positive net present value investment opportunities) announcements of increases in planned capital expenditures are associated with statistically significant increases in the market value of common stock and announcements of decreases in planned capital expenditures are associated with statistically significant decreases in the market value of common stock."

Page 33 For data on job creation during the 1980s, see U.S. Department of Commerce, *Statistical Abstract of the United States* (various years). For information on job creation at high-yield bond issuers, see Glenn Yago, *Junk Bonds: How High Yield Securities Restructured America* (New York: Oxford University Press, 1991). The figure on job loss at Fortune 100 firms comes from Michael C. Jensen, "The Modern Industrial Revolution, Exit, and the Failure of Internal Control Systems," *Journal of Finance,* vol. 48, July 1993.

Pages 33–34 The Campeau-Federated transaction and the effect of the eventual bankruptcy are analyzed in Steven N. Kaplan, "Campeau's Acquisition of Federated," *Journal of Financial Economics,* vol. 25, 1989; Steven N. Kaplan, "Campeau's Acquisition of Federated: Post-Bankruptcy Results," *Journal of Financial Economics,* vol. 35, 1994.

Chapter 2: The War Against Insider Trading

Pages 43–44 On the frequency and profitability of insider trading even today, see H. Nejat Seyhun, "The Effectiveness of the Insider-Trading Sanctions," *Journal of Law & Economics,* vol. 35, 1992. Seyhun finds that the volume and profitability of trading by corporate insiders continues to increase even as penalties have escalated. See also Dennis W. Carlton and Daniel R. Fischel, "The Regulation of Insider Trading," *Stanford Law Review*, vol. 35 1983.

Page 47   The factors influencing whether the target's management will resist an acquisition attempt are studied in Ralph A. Walkling and Michael S. Long, "Agency Theory, Managerial Welfare, and Takeover Bid Resistance," *Rand Journal of Economics*, vol. 1, 1984.

Stock-price run-ups preceding takeover announcements are documented in many studies that were published prior to the 1980s takeover wave. Such studies include: Gershon Mandelker, "Risk and Return: The Case of Merging Firms," *Journal of Financial Economics*, 1974; Peter Dodd and Richard Ruback, "Tender Offers and Stockholder Returns: An Empirical Analysis," *Journal of Financial Economics*, 1977; Donald R. Kummer and J. Ronald Hoffmeister, "Valuation Consequences of Cash Tender Offers," *Journal of Finance*, May 1978; Terence C. Langetieg, "An Application of a Three-Factor Performance Index to Measure Stockholder Gains from Merger," *Journal of Financial Economics*, 1978; Peter Dodd, "Merger Proposals, Management Discretion and Stockholder Wealth," *Journal of Financial Economics*, 1980; Pieter T. Elgers and John J. Clark, "Merger Types and Shareholder Returns: Additional Evidence," *Financial Management*, Summer 1980; Arthur J. Keown and John M. Pinkerton, "Merger Announcements and Insider Trading Activity: An Empirical Investigation," *Journal of Finance*, September 1981. The evidence presented in these articles clearly demonstrates that price run-ups preceding takeover announcements are not a phenomena unique to the 1980s.

Studies published during the 1980s takeover wave and thereafter include: K. Paul Asquith and E. Han Kim, "The Impact of Merger Bids on the Participating Firms' Security Holders," *Journal of Finance*, December 1982; K. Paul Asquith, "Merger Bids, Uncertainty, and Stockholder Returns," *Journal of Financial Economics*, 1983; Michael Bradley, Anand Desai, and E. Han Kim, "The Rationale Behind Interfirm Tender Offers: Information or Synergy?," *Journal of Financial Economics*, 1983; Paul H. Malatesta, "The Wealth Effect of Merger Activity and the Objective Functions of Merging Firms," *Journal of Financial Economics*, 1983; Frank H. Easterbrook and Gregg A. Jarrell, "Do Targets Gain from Defeating Tender Offers?," *New York University Law Review*, May 1984; Debra K. Dennis and John J. McConnell, "Corporate Mergers and Security Returns," *Journal of Financial Economics*, 1986; Michael Bradley, Anand Desai, and E. Han Kim, "Synergistic Gains from Corporate Acquisitions and Their Division Between the Stockholders of Target and Acquiring Firms," *Journal of Financial Economics*, 1988; Jeffrey M. Netter, Annette B. Poulsen, and Philip L. Hersch, "Insider Trading: The Law, The Theory, The Evidence," *Contemporary Policy Issues*, July 1988; Richard S. Ruback, "Do Target Shareholders Lose in Unsuccessful Control Contests?" in Alan J. Auerbach, ed., *Corporate Takeovers: Causes and Consequences* (Chicago: University of Chicago Press, 1988); Gregg A. Jarrell and Annette B.

Poulsen, "Stock Trading Before the Announcement of Tender Offers: Insider Trading or Market Anticipation?" *Journal of Law, Economics, and Organization,* Fall 1989; In-Mu Haw, Victor S. Pastena, and Steven B. Lilien, "Market Manifestation of Nonpublic Information Prior to Mergers: The Effect of Ownership Structure," *Accounting Review,* April 1990. These studies, not surprisingly, find that a target's stock price begins to rise prior to the actual takeover announcement.

A study that looks at the stock-price reaction to published takeover rumors is John Pound and Richard J. Zeckhauser, "Clearly Heard on the Street: The Effect of Takeover Rumors on Stock Prices," *Journal of Business,* July 1990. The stock-price reaction to 13(d) filings is examined in Gerald P. Madden, "Potential Corporate Takeovers and Market Efficiency: A Note," *Journal of Finance,* vol. 36, December 1981; Clifford G. Holderness and Dennis P. Sheehan, "Raiders or Saviors? The Evidence on Six Controversial Investors," *Journal of Financial Economics,* vol. 14, 1985; Wayne H. Mikkelson and Richard S. Ruback, "An Empirical Analysis of the Interfirm Equity Investment Process," *Journal of Financial Economics,* vol. 14, 1985. Both published takeover rumors and 13(d) filings are studied in In-Mu Haw, Victor S. Pastena, and Steven B. Lilien, "Market Manifestation of Nonpublic Information." These studies demonstrate that a target's stock price reacts positively to both takeover rumors and 13(d) filings. Moreover, the stock-price reaction to a 13(d) filing is particularly large if the filer is a "corporate raider."

The determinants of tender-offer premiums are analyzed in Ralph A. Walkling and Robert O. Edmister, "Determinants of Tender Offer Premiums," *Financial Analysts Journal,* January/February 1985; Nikhil P. Varaiya, "Determinants of Premiums in Acquisition Transactions," *Managerial and Decision Economics,* vol. 8, 1987.

The factors influencing whether an acquisition attempt will succeed are discussed in J. Ronald Hoffmeister and Edward A. Dyl, "Predicting Outcomes of Cash Tender Offers," *Financial Management,* vol. 10, Winter 1981; Ralph A. Walkling, "Predicting Tender Offer Success: A Logistic Analysis," *Journal of Financial and Quantitative Analysis,* vol. 20, December 1985; Wayne H. Mikkelson and M. Megan Partch, "Managers' Voting Rights and Corporate Control," *Journal of Financial Economics,* vol. 25, 1989.

Pages 55 The relationship between insider trading and stock-price run-ups preceding takeover announcements is discussed in Arthur J. Keown and John M. Pinkerton, "Merger Announcements and Insider Trading Activity: An Empirical Investigation," *Journal of Finance,* vol. 36, September 1981; Jeffrey M. Netter, Annette B. Poulsen, and Philip L. Hersch, "Insider Trading: The Law, the Theory, the Evidence," *Contemporary Policy Issues,* July 1988; Gregg A. Jarrell and Annette B. Poulsen, "Stock Trading Before the Announcement of Tender Offers: Insider Trading or Market Anticipation?" *Journal of Law, Economics, and Organization,* vol. 5, Fall 1989; Lisa K. Meulbroek, "An Empirical

Analysis of Illegal Insider Trading," *Journal of Finance*, vol. 47, December 1992.

Page 62   Stock-price reactions to takeover rumors appearing in the "Heard on the Street" column are documented in John Pound and Richard J. Zeckhauser, "Clearly Heard on the Street: The Effect of Takeover Rumors on Stock Prices," *Journal of Business*, July 1990.

Chapter 3: The Criminalization of Regulatory Offenses

Page 71   The stock-price reactions to 13(d) filings by six corporate "raiders" (i.e., Charles Bluhdorn, Carl Icahn, Irwin Jacobs, Carl Lindner, David Murdock, and Victor Posner) are analyzed in Clifford G. Holderness and Dennis P. Sheehan, "Raiders or Saviors? The Evidence on Six Controversial Investors," *Journal of Financial Economics*, vol. 14, 1985. Stock-price reactions to 13(d) filings in general are discussed in Wayne H. Mikkelson and Richard S. Ruback, "An Empirical Analysis of the Interfirm Equity Investment Process," *Journal of Financial Economics*, vol. 14, 1985. Stock prices are found to react positively to 13(d) filings, particularly those filed by "corporate raiders."

Page 79   For information on how stock prices react to standstill-agreement announcements, see Larry Dann and Harry DeAngelo, "Standstill Agreements, Privately Negotiated Stock Repurchases, and the Market for Corporate Control," *Journal of Financial Economics*, vol. 11, 1983. They find that, on average, a firm's stock price declines in response to an announcement of a standstill agreement.

Page 80   In 1985, Clifford G. Holderness and Dennis P. Sheehan, both of the University of Rochester, published a study of whether stockholders in companies in which Victor Posner acquired at least a 5 percent stake during the period 1977–1982 were benefited or harmed by Posner's actions. They find that the stock-price reaction to the first public announcement of Posner's stake averaged 3.3 percent and over the period from ten days before through the public announcement date the stock price rose an average of 7 percent. Both increases are statistically significant.

Holderness and Sheehan conduct a similar analysis for five other corporate "raiders": Charles Bluhdorn, Carl Icahn, Irwin Jacobs, Carl Lindner, and David Murdock. However, they observe, "While all six have been viewed as corporate raiders, the most notorious raiding reputation undoubtedly belongs to Victor Posner." An article in the November 19, 1979, issue of *Barron's* said that Posner has "all the talent of an accomplished raider: boldness, ferocity, tenacity and greed. He may not be a promising candidate for charitable work, but for the provision of loot his credentials are excellent."

For the six corporate raiders taken together, the average stock-price reaction to the public announcement that one had acquired at least a 5 percent stake was a statistically significant 1.8 percent, versus a statistically insignificant 0.4 percent for public announcements of similar stakes acquired by a random sample of investors. Over the eleven days up to and including the public-announcement day, the average price increase in the firms being "raided" was 5.9 percent, versus 3.4 percent in the control sample. Both increases are statistically significant.

Based on these results, Holderness and Sheehan report that "the empirical evidence shows that announcements of initial stock purchases by these six investors were on average associated with statistically significant increases in the wealth of target firms' stockholders" and "on average these increases, at least for the announcement day, exceeded the increases associated with initial stock purchases by random (typically less controversial) investors." Moreover, the "activities of the six in target firms after they file an initial 13(d) also provide no support for the raiding hypothesis," since even "when the controversial investors' shares were ultimately repurchased by the target firm (so-called 'greenmail'), target firms' stockholders on average experienced statistically significant wealth increases when the investor's entire tenure from the initial stock purchase through the repurchase as a stockholder is examined." Holderness and Sheehan conclude their study with a question: "Given that the six investors are on average associated with increases in the wealth of other stockholders, how did they ever obtain the label of corporate raider, and why has that label persisted?"

For further information, see Clifford G. Holderness and Dennis P. Sheehan, "Raiders or Saviors? The Evidence on Six Controversial Investors," *Journal of Financial Economics*, vol. 14, 1985.

Page 84 For information on the economic theory of stock-price manipulation, see Jean-Luc Vila, "Simple Games of Market Manipulation," *Economics Letters*, vol. 29, 1989; Franklin Allen and Douglas Gale, "Stock-Price Manipulation," *Review of Financial Studies*, vol. 5, 1992; Robert A. Jarrow, "Market Manipulation, Bubbles, Corners, and Short Squeezes," *Journal of Financial and Quantitative Analysis*, vol. 27, September 1992. These articles demonstrate that under certain conditions, at least in theory, it may be possible to manipulate a stock's price simply by buying and selling. Apparently, a necessary condition for such a manipulation to be theoretically possible is for some sort of "feedback" effect to be at work whereby past purchases by the "manipulator" lead to current purchases by other investors. However, it should be emphasized that these studies are strictly theoretical and do not subject their theories to empirical tests.

For a law and economics perspective on stock-price manipulation, see Daniel R. Fischel and David J. Ross, "Should the Law Prohibit Manipulation in Financial Markets," *Harvard Law Review*, vol. 105, 1991.

Pages 85–90 Mulheren's behavior before and after his trial and sentencing is described in Connie Bruck, "The World of Business: No One Like Me," *New Yorker*, vol. 66–67, March 11, 1991.

Chapter 5: The End of Drexel

Page 130 Drexel's revenues in 1987 are found in "Drexel, Despite Inquiries, Surges Back," *Wall Street Journal,* May 9, 1988; "Drexel 6-Month Net Neared Total for All of 1987," *Wall Street Journal,* October 20, 1988.

Page 142 Drexel's performance in 1988 comes from "Drexel 6-Month Net Neared Total for All of 1987," *Wall Street Journal,* October 20, 1988; "Drexel Burnham Retains Its Junk Bond Crown," *Wall Street Journal,* January 3, 1989.

Page 144 For data on the performance of the high-yield bond market in 1989, see Edward I. Altman, "How 1989 Changed the Hierarchy of Fixed Income Security Performance," *Financial Analysts Journal,* May/June 1990; Marshall E. Blume, Donald B. Keim, and Sandeep A. Patel, "Returns and Volatility of Low-Grade Bonds: 1977–1989," *Journal of Finance,* vol. 46, March 1991; Bradford Cornell and Kevin Green, "The Investment Performance of Low-Grade Bond Funds," *Journal of Finance,* vol. 46, March 1991; Bradford Cornell, "Liquidity and the Pricing of Low-Grade Bonds," *Financial Analysts Journal,* January/February 1992.

Pages 144–46 For information on events occurring in the junk-bond market during 1989, see "Junk Managers Brace for Redemptions; Market Stabilizing," *Dow Jones News Wire,* April 14, 1989; "Junk Bonds Face the Big Unknown," *Fortune,* May 22, 1989; "Investors Grab Junk Bonds Despite a Recent Poor Record," *Wall Street Journal,* June 12, 1989; "Focus on Risk of Junk Bond Funds Shifts to the Question of Liquidity," *Wall Street Journal,* July 20, 1989; "Junk Bond Market Bracing for Loss of Its S&L Clients," *Wall Street Journal,* July 27, 1989; "The Bills Are Coming Due," *Business Week,* September 11, 1989; "Some Junk Fund Investors Bail Out, but Managers Doubt Rout," *Dow Jones News Wire,* September 15, 1989; "Mounting Losses Are Watershed Event for Era of Junk Bonds," *Wall Street Journal,* September 18, 1989; "Don't Put Away the Smelling Salts Yet," *Business Week,* October 2, 1989; "Junkyard," *Barron's,* October 9, 1989; "The Junk Market's Black Hole," *Business Week,* November 27, 1989; "A Tumultuous Year for 'Junk Bonds,'" *New York Times,* January 2, 1990; "Poor Results in '89 May Show Profit Erosion for Junk Bonds," *Wall Street Journal,* January 2, 1990.

Pages 146–47 Data regarding Drexel's performance in 1989 are contained in "S&P Downgrades Drexel Burnham Commercial Paper to A-3," *Dow Jones News Wire,* November 29, 1989; "A Tumultuous Year for 'Junk Bonds,'" *New York Times,* January 2, 1990; Dan G. Stone, *April Fools: An Insider's Account of the Rise and Collapse of Drexel Burnham* (New York: Warner Books, 1991).

Page 152 The data on the performance of high-yield bonds come from Edward I. Altman, "Setting the Record Straight on Junk Bonds: A Review of the Research on Default Rates and Returns," *Journal of Applied Corporate Finance,* Summer 1990.

Page 153 For a discussion of Drexel's share of defaults vs. other firms, see Harlan D. Platt, "Underwriter Effects and the Riskiness of Original-Issue High-Yield Bonds," *Journal of Applied Corporate Finance*, Spring 1993.

Studies that look at different time periods are discussed in "Underwriters Find Junk Bond Pitfalls: Defaults Mar Record at Some Brokerages," *Wall Street Journal*, September 29, 1986; Paul Asquith, David W. Mullins, and Eric D. Wolff, "Original Issue High Yield Bonds: Aging Analyses of Defaults, Exchanges, and Calls," *Journal of Finance*, vol. 44, September 1989; "Milken Sales Pitch on High-Yield Bonds Is Contradicted by Data," *Wall Street Journal*, November 20, 1990; Stein, "Good Junk and Bad Junk: Here's How to Tell One from the Other," *Barron's*, January 25, 1993. Of these four studies, the first two present results where Drexel performs well relative to its rivals, while the opposite conclusion is reached by the last two studies.

Page 154 The data on the recent performance of the high-yield bond market come from Martin S. Fridson, "The State of the High Yield Bond Market: Overshooting or Return to Normalcy?," *Journal of Applied Corporate Finance*, vol. 7, Spring 1994.

Page 155 For data on the number of new jobs created during the 1980s, see U.S. Department of Commerce, *Statistical Abstract of the United States* (various years); Yago, *Junk Bonds: How High Yield Securities Restructured America* (New York: Oxford University Press, 1991).

For data on the fall in the amount of new capital raised, see Martin S. Fridson, "State of the High Yield Bond Market."

Chapter 7: Michael Milken and the Savings and Loan Crisis

Page 190 For a discussion of the number of S&L failures and the cost of the crisis, see Andrew S. Carron, *The Plight of the Thrift Institutions* (Washington, D.C.: The Brookings Institute, 1982); R. Dan Brumbaugh, Jr., *Thrifts Under Siege: Restoring Order to American Banking* (1988); James R. Barth, Philip F. Bartholomew, and Carol J. Labich, "Moral Hazard and the Thrift Crisis: An Analysis of 1988 Resolutions," in *Banking System Risk: Charting a New Course*, Federal Reserve Bank of Chicago, 1989; R. Dan Brumbaugh, Jr., Andrew S. Carron, and Robert E. Litan, "Cleaning Up the Depository Institutions Mess," *Brookings Papers on Economic Activity*, 1989; "Troubled Financial Institutions: Solutions to the Thrift Industry Problem," U.S. General Accounting Office, February 1989; James R. Barth, Philip F. Bartholomew, and Michael Bradley, "Determinants of Thrift Institution Resolution Costs," *Journal of Finance*, vol. 45, July 1990; James R. Barth and R. Dan Brumbaugh, Jr., "The Tough Road from FIRREA to Deposit Insurance Reform," *Stanford Law & Policy Review*, vol. 2, Spring 1990; G. Christian Hill, "A Never Ending Story: An Introduction to the S&L Symposium," *Stanford Law & Policy Review*, vol. 2, Spring 1990; Robert E. Litan, "Getting Out of the Thrift

Crisis, Now!" *Brookings Review*, Winter 1990/91; "The Cost of Forbearance During the Thrift Crisis," Congressional Budget Office, staff memorandum, June 1991; Lawrence J. White, *The S&L Debacle: Public Policy Lessons for Bank and Thrift Regulation* (New York: Oxford University Press, 1991); "The Economic Effects of the Savings & Loan Crisis," Congressional Budget Office, January 1992; "Resolving the Thrift Crisis," Congressional Budget Office, April 1993.

Estimates of S&L bailout costs have varied tremendously over time and across studies. Much of the variation in the estimates over time reflects the growing awareness of the industry's problems. The variation in the estimates across studies often arises because of differing assumptions about the number of insolvent thrifts and the quality of their assets. However, in some instances, the disparate estimates across studies result from very different methodologies. For example, while many studies report bailout costs in present-value terms and generally report figures of $200 billion or less, a few studies include future interest payments into the cost figure and thus estimate the cost of the S&L bailout to be in the range of $500 billion to $1 trillion.

Sometimes two estimates will seem to be very far apart but upon closer examination be found to be perfectly consistent. For example, estimates vary with respect to the time frame over which the costs are calculated. Some are purely retrospective (i.e., how much has it cost so far?); others are purely prospective (i.e., how much will it cost in the future?). Moreover, some estimates refer to "loss funds" (i.e., the hole between the institution's deposits and the value of its assets), while others include additional costs such as administrative costs and interest expense. Some estimates are present values, others are not. Some are simply the undiscounted sum of prior budget allocations plus the current budget request for resolving all insolvent thrifts. Some calculate bailout costs in nominal dollars, while others use constant dollars. Some assume that all insolvent thrifts are resolved immediately, while others assume that there is at least some delay.

To illustrate how S&L bailout-cost estimates can be so different, consider two estimates published in the Spring 1990 issue of *Stanford Law & Policy Review*. G. Christian Hill reports that, as of May 1990, the estimated cost of the thrift rescue over the period 1989–1999 is $456.3 billion and consists of the following components: zero-coupons to repay non-Treasury debt ($11.0 billion), interest on non-Treasury debt ($92.7 billion), old case expense ($68.0 billion), new case expense ($124.0 billion), Savings Association Insurance Fund ($8.8 billion), administrative costs ($19.0 billion), interest on working capital debt ($28.0 billion), lost tax revenues from FSLIC deals ($9.0 billion), and Treasury interest ($95.8 billion). In addition to the $456.3 billion cost estimate for the period 1989–1999, it is estimated that interest expense on non-Treasury and Treasury debt over the period 2000–2029 will be $274.8 billion and $638.8 billion, respectively. Therefore, the total cost of the thrift rescue over the period 1989–2029 is estimated to be $1.37 trillion.

In contrast, James Barth and R. Dan Brumbaugh, Jr., note that 519 thrifts with assets totaling $292 billion were currently insolvent. They observe that average loss rates in 1987 and 1988 were 35¢ and 31¢ per dollar of assets, respectively. The fifty most recent closures by the RTC had loss rates averaging 46¢ per dollar of assets. These three loss rates yield estimates of the cost of resolving the 519 insolvent thrifts of $102 billion, $91 billion, and $134 billion, respectively. Barth and Brumbaugh conclude that "a reasonable estimate is that the closure cost today is at least $100 billion, especially when one considers the large number of candidates for closure among the tangible solvent but financially weak institutions."

Page 192 Data on the decline of thrifts as home mortgage originators and holders appear in Kent W. Colton, "The Report of the President's Commission on Housing: The Nation's System of Housing Finance," *AREUEA Journal*, vol. 11, 1983; "The Federal Home Loan Banks in the Housing Finance System," Congressional Budget Office, July 1993; U.S. Department of Commerce, *Statistical Abstract of the United States* (various issues).

In 1975, savings and loans originated 62.6 percent of conventional long-term mortgages on one- to four-family homes, and another 5.9 percent was originated by savings banks. By 1980, their respective shares of the mortgage-origination market had fallen to 54.7 and 4.9 percent. In 1989, the figures were 38.2 and 6.6 percent. The role of home-mortgage originator was increasingly being filled by commercial banks as their share rose from 18.5 percent in 1975 to 20.8 percent in 1980 and 35.0 percent in 1989.

The thrifts' decline with respect to their role as holders of home mortgages was even more dramatic. Savings institutions (which include both S&L's and mutual savings banks) held 56.8 percent of the home mortgages outstanding in 1975. Five years later their share was down to 50.5 percent, and by 1989 it was down to 27.5 percent. Over the same period, the share of home mortgages held by mortgage pools or trusts soared from 5.8 to 37.8 percent.

Page 193 Thrift losses in the early 1980s and the insolvency of the thrift industry are discussed in Carron, *Plight of the Thrift Institutions*; Edward J. Kane, *The Gathering Crisis in Federal Deposit Insurance* (Cambridge: MIT Press, 1985) and *The S&L Insurance Mess: How Did It Happen?* (Washington, D.C.: Urban Institute Press, 1989); Brumbaugh, *Thrifts Under Siege*; James R. Barth, *The Great Savings and Loan Debacle* (1991); White, *The S&L Debacle*.

Page 196 Texas and other energy-producing states were the hardest hit. Oil prices had been steadily declining in the early 1980s. From $38 a barrel in January 1981, the posted price of West Texas Intermediate Crude was $10 lower in February 1985. Then, in the three months at the beginning of 1986, it fell nearly another $10, to $18.75. Prices hit a low for the 1980s of $12.25 a barrel in August 1986.

Natural gas prices at the wellhead followed. After the annual average increased from $1.59 per thousand cubic feet in 1980, to $2.65 in 1984, it dropped to $1.94 two years later. In 1987 the price bottomed at $1.66. See "Energy Statistics Sourcebook," *Oil and Gas Journal*. The decline in commercial real estate values is described in White, *The S&L Debacle*, pp. 110–11.

Page 198 The table comes from Yago, *Regulating Into Decline: FIRREA and the Unmasking of a Financial Institution* (unpublished paper, 1994).

Page 206 The data on Columbia, and the effect of the decline in the high-yield bond market on Columbia, come from Yago, *Regulating Into Decline*.

Pages 209–10 Bert Ely, an S&L consultant, performed a study in which he calculated a breakdown of the S&L bailout cost by where the money went. He estimated that the present-value bailout cost as of mid-1990 was $147 billion and consisted of the following components: interest on pre-1983 losses ($43 billion), real estate losses ($28 billion), pre-1983 losses ($25 billion), excess operating costs at insolvent S&L's ($14 billion), excess interest paid at insolvent S&L's ($14 billion), deteriorated franchise costs ($7 billion), fraud ($5 billion), excess cost of 1988 deals ($5 billion), losses on junk bonds ($3 billion), and losses on other non–real estate investments ($3 billion). Consequently, Ely's numbers imply that fraud and losses on high-yield bonds are responsible for only 3.4 and 2.0 percent, respectively, of the cost of the S&L bailout.

For further information on the Ely study, see "Fraud Is Called Small Factor in S&L Cost: Consultant's Study Cites Real Estate Values, High Rates," *Wall Street Journal*, July 20, 1990; "S&Ls: Where Did All Those Billions Go?" *Fortune*, September. 10, 1990.

Page 210 In 1993 the General Accounting Office (GAO) produced two separate reports for the Senate Judiciary Committee on bank and thrift criminal fraud, which offer the most current overall numbers on the criminal proceedings and civil liability suits brought by the federal government against insiders and borrowers of savings and loans. The first report, dated January 8, 1993, and titled "Bank and Thrift Criminal Fraud: The Federal Commitment Could Be Broadened," offers an overview of the government's efforts at prosecuting criminal financial-institution fraud and is based on numbers provided by the Justice Department, FBI, and U.S. Attorney. The second report, dated August 10, 1993, and titled "Thrift Failures: Federal Enforcement Actions Against Fraud and Wrongdoing in RTC Thrifts," focuses on thrifts taken over by the Resolution Trust Corp. and includes a discussion of civil actions initiated by the government.

Chapter 8: Charles Keating and Lincoln Savings

Page 215 Data on the growth of American Continental Corp. come from the Center for Research in Securities Prices.

Pages 217–18 The acquisition and failure data on Arizona thrifts in existence in 1985 come from the Office of Thrift Supervision.

Pages 236–37 First, the American Bar Association appointed a special task force to investigate the OTS charges. Then the New York State courts established a committee to conduct its own investigation. Both concluded that the charges against Kaye, Scholer were baseless.

Chapter 9: More S&L Scapegoats

Page 247 The terms of the sale of Vernon Savings to Don Dixon appear in James O'Shea, *The Daisy Chain: The Tale of Big Bad Don Dixon and the Looting of a Texas S&L* (New York: Simon & Schuster, 1991).

Page 248 The figures on deposit growth come from James O'Shea, "New Entrepreneurs Build Massive S&L Losses," *Chicago Tribune,* September 26, 1988.

Pages 248–49 The figures on Don Dixon's lifestyle come from James K. Glassman, "The Great Banks Robbery: Deconstructing the S&L Crisis," *New Republic,* Oct. 8, 1990; N. R. Kleinfield, "He Had Money, Women, a S&L. Now Don Dixon Has Jail," *New York Times,* March 17, 1991.

Page 250 The transaction is detailed in James O'Shea, "New Entrepreneurs."

Page 257 Neil Bush's failure to declare the loan as income until 1990 is reported in "Inside the Silverado Scandal," *U.S. News & World Report,* Aug. 13, 1990.

Page 260 Neil Bush's conflicts of interest are examined in Steven K. Wilmsen, *Silverado* (Bethesda: National Press, 1991).

Page 262 The terms of the settlement appear in "FDIC to Get $49.5 Million from Silverado Settlement," *New York Times,* May 31, 1991.

Pages 263–64 David Paul's purchase of Dade Savings is detailed in "Even for a Go-Go Banker, There Are Certain No-Nos," *Business Week,* May 22, 1989; "The CenTrust Failure: A Chronology," *Miami Herald,* June 30, 1990.

Pages 264–65 The figures on David Paul's lifestyle come from "Office of Thrift Supervision Press Conference," Federal News Service, October 22, 1990.

Pages 266–67 CenTrust's links to Drexel and BCCI are investigated in "The S&L-Junk Bond Link," *Washington Post,* February 18, 1990; "Looking for New S&L Culprits," *Newsweek,* November 26, 1990; "CenTrust's Deep Entanglement with BCCI," *National Mortgage News,* September 23, 1991.

Page 267 The figures on Paul's allegedly fraudulent expenditures come from "$31 Million Sought from Centrust's Ex-Chief," *Los Angeles Times*, October 23, 1990; "Thrift Head Told to Pay $30 Million," *Washington Post*, October 23, 1990.

Page 271 The 1981 figure for assets comes from "Columbia S&L Thrives on Taking Risks," *Los Angeles Times*, October 20, 1985. The 1987 figures for assets and brokered deposits come from "The Thrift That Junk Bonds Built," *Business Week*, June 29, 1987.

Chapter 10: More Victims: Fred Carr and Executive Life

Page 278 The financial condition of First Executive when Carr became president and CEO is described in Gary Schulte, *The Fall of First Executive: The House that Fred Carr Built* (New York: HarperCollins Publishers, 1991); Vic Modugno, *Broken Promises: The Inside Story of the Failure of Executive Life* (Torrance: Pacific Insurance Press, 1992). Both Schulte and Modugno are former Executive Life employees who joined the company in 1986. The two books also describe the company's innovative products and distribution system.

Page 279 In 1985, expenses were 15 percent of premiums at Executive Life, versus 20 percent at Prudential and 33 percent at John Hancock Life. See "Carr Suffers Slings, Arrows of First Executive's Fortune," *Wall Street Journal*, March 13, 1987.

Page 280 For information on First Executive's annuity business, see "Fred Carr's Second Hurrah: He's Built First Executive More Quietly than Enterprise Fund," *Financial World*, March 15, 1983; "First Executive's Prospects Are Dealt Blow as Hutton Drops Its Single-Premium Annuity," *Wall Street Journal*, August 3, 1984; Schulte, *Fall of First Executive*; Modugno, *Broken Promises*.

Page 282 The financial performance figures for First Executive come from Modugno, *Broken Promises*.

Page 284 For information on First Executive's early regulatory problems, see "First Executive Unit Fined for Not Providing Records to Regulators," *Wall Street Journal*, April 17, 1984; Schulte, *Fall of First Executive*; Modugno, *Broken Promises*.

For the California Insurance Department's history of Executive Life of California's regulatory problems, see Garamendi, "Statement before the Subcommittee on Oversight and Investigations," Committee on Energy and Commerce, U.S. House of Representatives, September 9, 1992.

For the New York Insurance Department's history of Executive Life of New York's regulatory problems, see Curiale, "Statement before the Subcommittee on Oversight and Investigations," Committee on Energy and Commerce, U.S. House of Representatives, September 9, 1992.

Pages 284–85 The interrelationships between Milken, Carr, and other Drexel clients are examined in "Taking in Each Other's Laundry; Combine Some of America's Biggest Dealmakers with Drexel Burnham Lambert, and You Have a Money Machine That Is the Envy of the

Investment Business," *Forbes,* November 19, 1984; "All for One, and . . . " *Barron's,* October 12, 1987; Connie Bruck, *The Predators' Ball: The Junk-Bond Raiders and the Man Who Staked Them* (New York: Simon & Schuster, 1988); "Peril to Pensions: Junk Bond Woes Put Retirement Benefits in Danger for Many," *Wall Street Journal,* February 12, 1990; Stein, "Sunk by Junk: First Executive's Woes Put Policyholders at Risk," *Barron's,* April 1, 1991.

Page 286 The value of First Executive's high-yield bond portfolio in 1989 comes from Harry DeAngelo, Linda DeAngelo, and Stuart Gilson, "The Collapse of First Executive Corporation: Junk Bonds, Adverse Publicity, and the 'Run on the Bank' Phenomenon," *Journal of Financial Economics,* vol. 36, 1994. The figure combines the high-yield bond holdings of the California and New York units of Executive Life.

Pages 287–88 For information on First Executive's regulatory problems regarding reinsurance contracts, see "First Executive Gives $151.5 Million to Unit That Admitted State Violations," *Wall Street Journal,* March 5, 1987; "First Executive Unit Isn't Complying on Reinsurance Order, California Says," *Wall Street Journal,* March 10, 1987; "Three First Executive Aides Agree to Quit New York Unit Jobs under State Pressure," *Wall Street Journal,* May 13, 1987; "Liabilities Dangereuses," *Forbes,* September 18, 1989.

For details on a controversy regarding promissory notes included in Executive Life of California's 1987 financial statement, see "Belth Says Executive Life 'Insolvent' at End of 1987," *National Underwriter* (Life, Health/Financial Services Edition), October 17, 1988.

An article that investigates the financial performance of First Stratford is Nick Gilbert, "Fred and Mike: A Dynamic Duo's Disappointing Performance," *Barron's,* October 12, 1987. Given the press's generally sinister portrayal of First Stratford, Gilbert is surprised to find that the reinsurance company's financial performance has been quite unspectacular.

Page 290 The impact of First Executive's $515 billion writedown announcement is analyzed in George Fenn and Rebel Cole, "Announcements of Asset-Quality Problems and Contagion Effects in the Life Insurance Industry," *Journal of Financial Economics,* vol. 35, 1994. They argue that the critical factor accounting for the plunge in First Executive's stock price following the writedown announcement is the anticipated response of policyholders. The expectation was that policyholders would reevaluate their policies' risks and returns and many would decide to surrender them. Moreover, this expectation applied to other life insurance companies with above-average holdings of junk bonds. Such companies saw their stock prices decline by an average of 3.7 percent in response to First Executive's writedown announcement.

First Executive's regulatory problems regarding CBO's are discussed in "First Executive's Alchemy Refines $700 Million of Junk," *Wall Street Journal,* December 6, 1989; "First Executive's Junk-Bond Action Prompts Inquiry," *Wall Street Journal,* December 26, 1989.

For information on the surge in policy surrenders following the $515 million writedown announcement, see "First Executive Cash Outflow Is $1.33 Billion," *Wall Street Journal*, May 16, 1990; "No More Horsing Around; Fred Carr Presses Effort to Make Equine Melodies, but Gets Only Neigh-Sayers," *Newsday*, May 20, 1990; "Fewer First Executive Policies Redeemed in 2nd Quarter but Woes Seen Remaining," *Wall Street Journal*, August 16, 1990; "First Executive Net Fell 55% in 3rd Quarter," *Wall Street Journal*, November 15, 1990.

Page 291–92 The differential press coverage received by First Executive relative to that received by life insurers with troubled real estate assets is documented in DeAngelo, DeAngelo, and Gilson, "Collapse of First Executive." They point out that the decline in the market value of real estate holdings from July 1989 to year-end 1990 was two and one-half times as great as the decline in the market value of junk bonds over the same period. Yet, during the two-year period 1989–1990, "the number of adverse feature articles about FE [First Executive] far exceeds the *total* on the top ten life insurers, although these firms had statutory capital near ELIC's [Executive Life Insurance Company's] and real estate exposure approaching ELIC's junk bond exposure."

Why did First Executive receive so much adverse publicity relative to its competitors if they too had troubled assets? The authors note that "an institution's exposure to negative publicity can depend on the 'political correctness' of its investment policy and the general perception of such investments," and First Executive's "investment policy helped make it a target in the political climate of the late 1980's, in which relationships with Drexel were viewed with suspicion and hostility." They believe that the negative media coverage undercut public confidence in the safety of the company's products and contributed to its collapse.

Index